Lecture Notes in Computer Science 14678

Founding Editors

Gerhard Goos
Juris Hartmanis

Editorial Board Members

The series Lecture Notes in Computer Science (LNCS), including its subseries Lecture Notes in Artificial Intelligence (LNAI) and Lecture Notes in Bioinformatics (LNBI), has established itself as a medium for the publication of new developments in computer science and information technology research, teaching, and education.

LNCS enjoys close cooperation with the computer science R & D community, the series counts many renowned academics among its volume editors and paper authors, and collaborates with prestigious societies. Its mission is to serve this international community by providing an invaluable service, mainly focused on the publication of conference and workshop proceedings and postproceedings. LNCS commenced publication in 1973.

Valentina Castiglioni · Adrian Francalanza
Editors

Formal Techniques for Distributed Objects, Components, and Systems

44th IFIP WG 6.1 International Conference, FORTE 2024
Held as Part of the 19th International Federated Conference
on Distributed Computing Techniques, DisCoTec 2024
Groningen, The Netherlands, June 17–21, 2024
Proceedings

Editors
Valentina Castiglioni 🄳
Eindhoven University of Technology
Eindhoven, The Netherlands

Adrian Francalanza 🄳
University of Malta
Msida, Malta

ISSN 0302-9743   ISSN 1611-3349 (electronic)
Lecture Notes in Computer Science
ISBN 978-3-031-62644-9   ISBN 978-3-031-62645-6 (eBook)
https://doi.org/10.1007/978-3-031-62645-6

This Springer imprint is published by the registered company Springer Nature Switzerland AG
The registered company address is: Gewerbestrasse 11, 6330 Cham, Switzerland

If disposing of this product, please recycle the paper.

Foreword

The 19th International Federated Conference on Distributed Computing Techniques (DisCoTec) took place in Groningen, The Netherlands, during June 17–21, 2024. It was organized by the Bernoulli Institute of Mathematics, Computer Science, and Artificial Intelligence at the University of Groningen, The Netherlands.

The DisCoTec series is one of the major events sponsored by the International Federation for Information Processing (IFIP). It comprises three main conferences:

- COORDINATION, the IFIP WG6.1 26th International Conference on Coordination Models and Languages – Program Chairs: Ilaria Castellani (Inria Sophia Antipolis, France) and Francesco Tiezzi (University of Florence, Italy).
- DAIS, the IFIP WG6.1 24th International Conference on Distributed Applications and Interoperable Systems – Program Chairs: Rolando Martins (University of Porto, Portugal) and Mennan Selimi (South East European University, North Macedonia).
- FORTE, the IFIP WG6.1 44th International Conference on Formal Techniques for Distributed Objects, Components and Systems – Program Chairs: Valentina Castiglioni (Eindhoven University of Technology, The Netherlands) and Adrian Francalanza (University of Malta, Malta).

Together, these conferences cover a broad spectrum of distributed computing subjects—from theoretical foundations and formal description techniques, testing and verification methods, to language design and system implementation approaches.

Following recent developments in the research community, all conferences included an Artifact Evaluation track, whose goal is to improve and reward research reproducibility and to increase visibility of the efforts of tool developers. Each conference implemented this track independently, in close coordination with Roberto Casadei (University of Bologna, Italy) who served as Artifact Evaluation chair.

In addition to the individual sessions of each conference, the event included several plenary sessions that gathered attendants from the three conferences. In coordination with the General Chair, the three DisCoTec conferences selected the plenary keynote speakers. The three keynote speakers and the title of their talks is listed below:

- Prof. Laura Kovács (Vienna University of Technology, Austria) – *Automated Reasoning in BlockChain Security*
- Prof. Paulo Veríssimo (KAUST, CEMSE, RC3 - Resilient Computing and Cybersecurity Center, Saudi Arabia) – *Platform Resilience? Beware of Threats from the "basement"*
- Prof. Marieke Huisman (University of Twente, The Netherlands) – *VerCors: Inclusive Software Verification*

As traditional in DisCoTec, the program included an additional joint session with the best papers from each conference. The best papers were:

- *A Probabilistic Choreography Language for PRISM*, by Marco Carbone and Adele Veschetti;
- *Compact Storage of Data Streams in Mobile Devices*, by Rémy Raes, Olivier Ruas, Adrien Luxey-Bitri, and Romain Rouvoy;
- *Weak Simplicial Bisimilarity for Polyhedral Models and SLCSη*, by Nick Bezhanishvili, Vincenzo Ciancia, David Gabelaia, Mamuka Jibladze, Diego Latella, Mieke Massink, and Erik De Vink.

The federated event was further enriched with the following three satellite events:

- DiDiT: The 1st International Workshop on Distributed Digital Twins, organized by Victoria Degeler (University of Amsterdam, The Netherlands), Dilek Dustegor (University of Groningen, The Netherlands), Heerko Groefsema (University of Groningen, The Netherlands), and Elena Lazovik (TNO, The Netherlands).
- ICE: 17th Interaction and Concurrency Experience, organized by Clément Aubert (Augusta University, USA), Cinzia Di Giusto (Université Côte d'Azur, France), Simon Fowler (University of Glasgow, UK), and Violet Ka I Pun (Western Norway University of Applied Sciences, Norway).
- PLNL: The Fourth Workshop on Programming Languages in The Netherlands, organized by Daniel Frumin (University of Groningen, The Netherlands) and Wouter Swierstra (Utrecht University, The Netherlands) on behalf of VERSEN, the Dutch National Association for Software Engineering.

I would like to thank the Program Committee chairs of the different events for their cooperation during the preparation of the federated event, the Artifact Evaluation chair for his dedicated coordination work, and the Steering Committee of DisCoTec and their conferences for their guidance and support. Moreover, I am grateful to the keynote speakers and all conference attendees for joining us in Groningen.

The organization of DisCoTec 2024 was only possible thanks to the hard work and dedication of the Organizing Committee, including Bas van den Heuvel (publicity chair), Daniel Frumin and Claudio Antares Mezzina (workshop co-chairs), Magda Piekorz and Ineke Schelhaas (logistics and finances), as well as all the colleagues and students who volunteered their time to help.

Finally, I would like to thank IFIP WG6.1 for sponsoring this event, Springer's Lecture Notes in Computer Science team for their support and sponsorship, EasyChair for providing the reviewing infrastructure, the Dutch Research Council (NWO) for financial support (file number 21382), and the Faculty of Science and Engineering of the University of Groningen for providing meeting rooms and administrative support.

June 2024   Jorge A. Pérez

Preface

This volume contains the papers presented at the 44th IFIP WG 6.1 International Conference on Formal Techniques for Distributed Objects, Components, and Systems (FORTE 2024), held as one of three main conferences of the 19th International Federated Conference on Distributed Computing Techniques (DisCoTec 2024), during June 17–21, 2024. The conference was hosted by the Bernoulli Institute of Mathematics, Computer Science, and Artificial Intelligence at the University of Groningen, The Netherlands.

FORTE is a well-established forum for fundamental research on theory, models, tools, and applications for distributed systems, with special interest in

- Language concepts for concurrency and distribution, supported by rigorous semantics, well-supported pragmatics, and/or expressive illustrative use-cases.
- Analysis techniques, methodologies, and/or algorithms, using testing and/or verification, to validate (aspects of) the soundness of various types of concurrent and distributed systems, including communication and network protocols, service-oriented systems, adaptive distributed systems, cyber-physical systems, and sensor networks.
- Principles for qualitative and quantitative security analysis of distributed systems.
- Applications of formal methods and techniques for studying the quality, reliability, availability, and safety of concrete distributed systems.
- Emerging challenges and hot topics in distributed systems (broadly construed), such as software-defined networks, distributed ledgers, smart contracts, and blockchain technologies, etc.

The Program Committee received a total of 33 submissions, written by authors from 15 different countries. Of these, 13 papers were selected for inclusion in the scientific program. Each submission was single-blind reviewed by at least three Program Committee members with the help of 13 external reviewers in selected cases. The selection of accepted submissions was based on electronic discussions via the EasyChair conference management system. In addition, 2 papers have complementary·artefacts that were carefully tested by the Artefact Evaluation Committee members. These papers are marked with the awarded badges for the artefacts in the proceedings.

As Program Committee, we actively contributed to the selection of the keynote speakers for DisCoTec 2024:

- Prof. Laura Kovács (Vienna University of Technology, Austria) – *Automated Reasoning in BlockChain Security*.
- Prof. Paulo Veríssimo (KAUST, CEMSE, RC3 - Resilient Computing and Cybersecurity Center, Saudi Arabia) – *Platform Resilience? Beware of Threats from the "basement"*.
- Prof. Marieke Huisman (University of Twente, The Netherlands) – *VerCors: Inclusive Software Verification*.

We are most grateful to Laura Kovács for accepting our invitation to be the FORTE-related keynote speaker. This volume contains the abstract of her talk entitled "*Automated Reasoning in BlockChain Security*".

We wish to thank all the authors of submitted papers, all the members of the Program Committee for their thorough evaluations of the submissions, and the external reviewers who assisted the evaluation process. We would also like to thank the Artefact Evaluation Chairs, Duncan P. Attard and Emanuele D'Osualdo, who, together with the members of the Artefact Evaluation Committee, helped us to enrich the program of FORTE with the selection of the artefacts. We are also indebted to the Steering Committee of FORTE for their advice and suggestions. Last but not least, we thank the DisCoTec general chair, Jorge Pérez, and his organization team for their hard, effective work in providing an excellent environment for FORTE 2024 and all other conferences and workshops.

April 2024   Valentina Castiglioni
                                                                        Adrian Francalanza

Organization

Program Committee

Duncan P. Attard	University of Glasgow, UK
Giovanni Bernardi	Université Paris Cité, France
Petra van den Bos	University of Twente, The Netherlands
Valentina Castiglioni (Co-chair)	Eindhoven University of Technology, The Netherlands
Silvia Crafa	University of Padova, Italy
Carla Ferreira	Universidade Nova de Lisboa, Portugal
Simon Fowler	University of Glasgow, UK
Adrian Francalanza (Co-chair)	University of Malta, Malta
Cinzia di Giusto	Université Côte d'Azure, CNRS, I3S, France
Daniele Gorla	University of Rome La Sapienza, Italy
Ross Horne	University of Strathclyde, UK
Andreas Katis	KBR Inc. at NASA Ames Research Center, USA
Wen Kokke	University of Strathclyde, UK
Vasileios Koutavas	Trinity College Dublin, Ireland
Peter Olveczky	University of Oslo, Norway
Ana-Maria Oprescu	University of Amsterdam, The Netherlands
Kirstin Perters	University of Augsburg, Germany
Emanuele D'Osualdo	Max Planck Institute for Software Systems, Germany
Anna Philippou	University of Cyprus, Cyprus
Michela Quadrini	University of Camerino, Italy
Anne Remke	WWU Munster, Germany
Larisa Safina	Inria – Lille Nord Europe, France
Alceste Scalas	Technical University of Denmark, Denmark
Simone Tini	University of Insubria, Italy
Dmitriy Traytel	University of Copenhagen, Denmark
Jana Wagemaker	Reykjavik University, Iceland

Artefact Evaluation Committee

Duncan P. Attard (Co-chair)	University of Glasgow, UK
Lennard Gäher	Max Planck Institute for Software Systems, Germany

Bas van den Heuvel	Karlsruhe University of Applied Sciences and University of Freiburg, Germany
Emanuele D'Osualdo (Co-chair)	Max Planck Institute for Software Systems, Germany
Dominika Regéciová	Brno University of Technology, Czech Republic
Felix Stutz	University of Luxembourg, Luxembourg
Gerard Tabone	University of Malta, Malta

Additional Reviewers

Eugene Asarin
Georgiana Caltais
Kaustuv Chaudhuri
Lorenzo Gheri
Roman Kniazev
Dimitrios Kouzapas
Michael Köhler-Bußmeier

Milan Lopuhaä-Zwakenberg
Claudio Antares Mezzina
Ivano Salvo
Bernardo Toninho
Evangelia Vanezi
Martin Vassor

Automated Reasoning in BlockChain Security
(Keynote Talk)

Laura Kovács 🆔

Vienna University of Technology, Austria

We describe a game-theoretic framework for the security analysis of blockchain protocols. We apply automated reasoning techniques to determine whether a game-theoretic protocol model is game-theoretically secure, that is, Byzantine fault tolerant and incentive compatible. Doing so, we reduce security analysis to satisfiability checking in first-order real arithmetic. Our approach is implemented in the CheckMate verifier and successfully applied to decentralized protocols, board games, and game-theoretic examples.

Contents

Short Papers

Full Papers

A Multi-agent Model for Opinion Evolution in Social Networks Under Cognitive Biases

Mário S. Alvim[1], Artur Gaspar da Silva[1(⊠)], Sophia Knight[2], and Frank Valencia[3,4]

[1] Department of Computer Science, UFMG, Belo Horizonte, Brazil
artur.gaspar@dcc.ufmg.br
[2] Department of Computer Science, University of Minnesota Duluth, Duluth, USA
[3] CNRS-LIX, École Polytechnique de Paris, Palaiseau, France
[4] Pontificia Universidad Javeriana Cali, Cali, Colombia

Abstract. We generalize the DeGroot model for opinion dynamics to better capture realistic social scenarios. We introduce a model where each agent has their own individual *cognitive biases*. Society is represented as a directed graph whose edges indicate how much agents influence one another. Biases are represented as the functions in the square region $[-1, 1]^2$ and categorized into four sub-regions based on the potential reactions they may elicit in an agent during instances of *opinion disagreement*. Under the assumption that each bias of every agent is a *continuous* function within the region of receptive but resistant reactions (**R**), we show that the society converges to a consensus if the graph is strongly connected. Under the same assumption, we also establish that the entire society converges to a unanimous opinion if and only if the *source components* of the graph-namely, strongly connected components with no external influence-converge to that opinion. We illustrate that convergence is not guaranteed for strongly connected graphs when biases are either discontinuous functions in **R** or not included in **R**. We showcase our model through a series of examples and simulations, offering insights into how opinions form in social networks under cognitive biases.

Keywords: Cognitive bias · Multi-Agent Systems · Social Networks

1 Introduction

In recent years, the significance and influence of social networks have experienced a remarkable surge, capturing widespread attention and shaping users' opinions in substantial ways.

M.S. Alvim and A. Gaspar da Silva— were partially supported by CNPq, CAPES, and FAPEMIG. Frank Valencia's contribution to this work is partially supported by the SGR project PROMUEVA (BPIN 2021000100160) supervised by Minciencias.

V. Castiglioni and A. Francalanza (Eds.): FORTE 2024, LNCS 14678, pp. 3–19, 2024.
https://doi.org/10.1007/978-3-031-62645-6_1

The *dynamics of opinion/belief formation* in social networks involves individuals expressing their opinions, being exposed to the opinions of others, and adapting or reinforcing their own views based on these interactions. Modeling these dynamics allows us to gain insights into how opinions form, spread, and evolve within social networks.

The DeGroot multi-agent model [8] is one of most prominent formalisms for opinion formation dynamics in social networks. Society is represented as a directed graph whose edges indicate how much individuals (called *agents*) influence one another. Each agent has an opinion represented as a value in $[0, 1]$ indicating the strength of their agreement with an underlying proposition (e.g., "*vaccines are safe*"). They repeatedly update their opinions with the weighted average of their opinion differences (level of *disagreement*) with those who influence them. The DeGroot model is valued for its tractability, derived from its connection with matrix powers and Markov chains, and it remains a significant focus of study providing a comprehensive understanding of opinion evolution [9].

Nevertheless, the DeGroot model has an important caveat: It assumes *homogeneity* and *linearity* of opinion update. In social scenarios, however, two agents may update their opinions differently depending on their individual *cognitive biases* on disagreement-i.e., how they interpret and react towards the level of disagreements with others. This results in more complex updates that may involve non-linear even non-monotonic functions. For example, an individual under *confirmation (cognitive) bias* [5] may ignore the opinion of those whose level of disagreement with them is over a certain threshold. In fact, much of the unpredictability in opinion formation is due to users' *biases* in their belief updates, where users sometimes tend to reinforce their original beliefs, instead of questioning and updating their opinions upon encountering new information. Indeed, rather than perfect rational agents, users are often subject to cognitive biases.

In earlier work [1,2], we introduced a DeGroot-like model with a *non-linear* update mechanism tailored for a specific type of confirmation bias. The model was shown to be tractable and it provides insights into the effect of this cognitive bias in opinion dynamics. Nevertheless, it also assumes homogeneity of opinion update, and choosing a particular function to represent the bias, although natural, may seem somewhat ad-hoc.

To address the above-mentioned caveat, in this paper we introduce a generalization of the DeGroot model that allows for *heterogeneous* and *non-linear* opinion updates. Each agent has their own individual cognitive biases on levels of disagreement. These biases are represented as arbitrary functions in the square region $[-1, 1]^2$. The model then unifies disparate belief update styles with bias into a single framework which takes *disagreement* between agents as the central parameter. Indeed, standard cognitive biases of great importance in social networks such as backfire effect [11], authority bias [12], and confirmation bias [5], among others, can be represented in the framework.

We classify the biases in $[-1, 1]^2$ into four sub-regions $(\mathbf{M}, \mathbf{R}, \mathbf{B}, \mathbf{I})$ based on the cognitive reactions they may cause in an agent during instances of *opinion disagreement*. For example, agents that are malleable, easily swayed, exhibit fanaticism or prompt to follow authoritative figures can be modelled with biases in **M**. Agents that are receptive to other opinions, but unlike malleable ones, can exhibit some skepticism to fully accepting them can be modelled with biases in the region **R**. Individuals that become more extreme when confronted with opposing opinions can be modelled by biases in **B**. Finally insular agents can be modelled with the bias in **I**.

Consensus is a central property for opinion formation dynamics. Indeed the inability to converge to consensus is often a sign of a polarized society. In this paper we use the above-mentioned region classification to provide the following insightful theoretical results for consensus.

- Assuming that each bias of every agent is a *continuous* function in **R**, the society converges to a consensus if that society is strongly connected. This implies that a strongly connected society can converge to a consensus if its members are receptive but resistant to the opinions of others.
- Under the same assumption, we also establish that the entire society converges to a unanimous opinion if and only if the *source components* of the graph, i.e., strongly connected components with no external influence, converge to that opinion. This implies that upon agreeing on an opinion, closed and potentially influential groups, can make all individuals converge to that opinion in a society whose members are receptive but resistant.
- We show that convergence is not guaranteed for strongly connected graphs when biases are either discontinuous functions in **R** or not included in **R**.

We also demonstrate our model with examples and computer simulations that provide insights into opinion formation under cognitive biases. The open code for these simulations can be found at https://github.com/bolaabcd/polarization2.

2   An Opinion Model with Cognitive Biases

The DeGroot model [8] is a well-known model for social learning. In this formalism each individual (*agent*) repeatedly updates their current opinion by averaging the opinion values of those who influence them. But one of its limitation is that the model does not provide a mechanism for capturing the *cognitive biases* under which each individual may interpret and react to the opinion of others.

In this section we introduce a generalization of the DeGroot model with a mechanism to express arbitrary cognitive bias based on opinion disagreement.

2.1   Influence Graph

In social learning models, a *community/society* is typically represented as a directed weighted graph with edges between individuals (agents) representing the direction and strength of the influence that one carries over the other. This graph is referred to as the *Influence Graph*.

Definition 1 (Influence Graph). *An (n-agent) influence graph is a directed weighted graph $G = (A, E, I)$ with $A = \{1, \ldots, n\}$ the vertices, $E \subseteq A \times A$ the edges, and $I : A \times A \to [0, 1]$ a weight function s.t. $I(i, j) = 0$ iff $(i, j) \notin E$.*

The vertices in A represent n agents of a given community or network. The set of edges $E \subseteq A \times A$ represents the (direct) influence relation between these agents; i.e., $(i,j) \in E$ means that agent i influences agent j. The value $I(i,j)$, for simplicity written $I_{i,j}$, denotes the strength of the influence: 0 means no influence and a higher value means stronger influence. We use A_i to denote the set $\{j \mid (j,i) \in E\}$ of agents that have a direct influence over agent i.

Remark 1. In contrast to [1], we do not require agents to have nonzero self-influence. Furthermore, since we do not require the sum of influences over a given agent to be 1 (unlike [8]), we will use the following notation for *proportional influence* of j over i: $\overline{I_{j,i}} = \frac{I_{j,i}}{\sum_{k \in A_i} I_{k,i}}$ if $(j,i) \in E$, else $\overline{I_{j,i}} = 0$.

2.2 General Opinion Update

Similar to the DeGroot-like models in [9], we model the evolution of agents' opinions about some underlying *statement* or *proposition*. For example, such a proposition could be "*vaccines are unsafe*," "*human activity has little impact on climate change*,", "*AI poses a threat to humanity*", or "*Reviewer 2 is wonderful*".

The *state of opinion* (or *belief state*) of all the agents is represented as a vector in $[0,1]^{|A|}$. If B is a state of opinion, $B_i \in [0,1]$ denotes the *opinion* (*belief*, or *agreement*) value of agent $i \in A$ regarding the underlying proposition. If $B_i = 0$, agent i completely disagrees with the underlying proposition; if $B_i = 1$, agent i completely agrees with the underlying proposition. Furthermore, the higher the value of B_i, the stronger the agreement with such a proposition.

At each time unit $t \in \mathbb{N}$, every agent $i \in A$ updates their opinion. We shall use B^t to denote the state of opinion at time $t \in \mathbb{N}$. We can now define a general DeGroot-like opinion model as follows.

Definition 2 (Opinion Model). *An* Opinion Model *is a tuple* (G, B^0, μ_G) *where G is an n-agent influence graph, B^0 is the initial state of opinion, and* $\mu_G : [0,1]^n \to [0,1]^n$ *is a state-transition function, called* update function. *For every $t \in \mathbb{N}$, the state of opinion at time $t+1$ is given by $B^{t+1} = \mu_G(B^t)$.*

The update functions can be used to express any deterministic and discrete transition from one opinion state to the next, possibly taking into account the influence graph. This work singles out and characterizes a meaningful family of update functions extending the basic DeGroot model with cognitive biases that are based on opinion *disagreement*. Intuitively, these update functions specify the reaction of an agent to the opinion disagreements with each of their influencers. To build some intuition, we first recall the update function of the DeGroot model.

Below we omit the index from the update function μ_G if no confusion arises.

2.3 DeGroot Update

The standard DeGroot model [8] is obtained by the following update function:

$$\mu(B)_i = \sum_{j \in A_i} \overline{I_{j,i}} B_j \tag{1}$$

for every $i \in A$. Thus, in the DeGroot model each agent updates their opinion by taking the weighted average of the opinions of those who influence them. We can rewrite Eq. 1 as follows:

$$\mu(B)_i = B_i + \sum_{j \in A_i} \overline{I_{j,i}}(B_j - B_i).$$ (2)

Notice that DeGroot update is *linear* in the agents' opinions and can be expressed in terms of *disagreement*: The opinion of every agent i is updated taking into account the weighted average of their *opinion disagreement* or *opinion difference* with those who influence them.

Intuitively, if j influences i, then i's opinion would tend to move closer to j's. The *disagreement term* $(B_j - B_i) \in [-1, 1]$ in Eq. 2 realizes this intuition. If $(B_j - B_i)$ is a negative term in the sum, the disagreement can be thought of as contributing with a magnitude of $|B_j - B_i|$ (multiplied by $\overline{I_{j,i}}$) to *decreasing* i's belief in the underlying proposition. Similarly, if $(B_j - B_i)$ is positive, the disagreement contributes with the same magnitude but to *increasing* i's belief.

2.4   Disagreement-Bias Update

Now we generalize DeGroot updates by defining a class of update functions that also allows for *non-linear* updates, and for each agent to react differently to opinion disagreement with distinct agents. We capture this reaction by means of bias functions $\beta_{i,j} : [-1, 1] \to [-1, 1]$, where $(j, i) \in E$, on opinion disagreement stating how the bias of i towards the opinion of j, $\beta_{i,j}$, affects i's new opinion.

In the following definition we use the clamp function for the interval $[0, 1]$ which is defined as $[r]_0^1 = \min(\max(r, 0), 1)$ for any $r \in \mathbb{R}$.

Definition 3 (Bias Update). *Let* (G, B^0, μ_G) *be an opinion model with* $G = (A, E, I)$. *The function* μ_G *is a* (disagreement) *bias update if for every* $i \in A$,

$$\mu_G(B)_i = \left[B_i + \sum_{j \in A_i} \overline{I_{j,i}} \beta_{i,j}(B_j - B_i) \right]_0^1$$ (3)

where each $\beta_{i,j}$ *with* $(j, i) \in E$, *called the* (disagreement) *bias from i towards j, is an endo-function[1] on $[-1, 1]$. The model (G, B^0, μ_G) is a* (disagreement) *bias opinion model if μ_G is a disagreement bias update function.*

The clamp function $[\cdot]_0^1$ guarantees that the right-hand side of Eq. 3 yields a valid belief value (a value in $[0, 1]$). Intuitively, the function $\beta_{i,j}$ represents the direction and magnitude of how agent i reacts to their disagreement $B_j - B_i$ with agent j. If $\beta_{i,j}(B_j - B_i)$ is a negative term in the sum of Eq. 3, then the bias of

---

[1] The biases we wish to capture can be seen as distortions of disagreements, themselves disagreements. It seems then natural to choose $[-1, 1]$ as the domain and co-domain of the bias function.

agent i towards j contributes with a magnitude of $|\beta_{i,j}(B_j - B_i)|$ (multiplied by $\overline{I_{j,i}}$) to *decreasing* i's belief in the underlying proposition. Conversely, if $\beta_{i,j}(B_j - B_i)$ is positive, it contributes to *increasing* i's belief with the same magnitude.

Below we identify some particular examples of the cognitive biases that can be captured with disagreement-bias opinion models.

Example 1 (Some Cognitive Biases). Clearly, the classical DeGroot update function Eq. 2 can be recovered from Eq. 3 by letting every bias $\beta_{i,j}$ be the identity on disagreement: i.e., $\beta_{i,j} = \mathtt{degroot}$ where $\mathtt{degroot}(x) = x$.

Confirmation Bias. We now illustrate some form of *confirmation bias* [5] where agents are more *receptive* to opinions that are closer to theirs. An example of confirmation bias can be obtained by letting $\beta_{i,j} = \mathtt{conf}(x) = x(1 + \delta - |x|)/(1 + \delta)$ for a very small non-negative constant δ.[2] In the following plots and simulations we fix $\delta = 1 \times 10^{-4}$. This bias causes i to pay less attention to the opinion of j as their opinion distance $|x| = |B_j - B_i|$ tends to 1.

Backfire Effect. Let us now consider another important cognitive bias called backfire effect [11]. Under this effect an agent strengthens their position of disagreement with another agent if their opinions are significantly distant. A form of backfire effect can be obtained by letting $\beta_{i,j} = \mathtt{backf}$ where $\mathtt{backf}(x) = -x^3$. Notice that unlike the DeGroot update, this bias contributes to changing i's opinion with a *magnitude* of $|\mathtt{backf}(B_j - B_i)|$ (multiplied by $\overline{I_{j,i}}$) *but in the opposite direction* of the opinion of j. This potentially makes the new opinion of agent i *more* distant from that of j.

Authority Bias. Another common cognitive bias in social networks is the authority bias [12] under which individuals tend to blindly follow authoritative or influential figures often to the extreme. Let $\beta_{i,j} = \mathtt{fan}$ be the *sign* function, i.e., $\mathtt{fan}(x) = x/|x|$ if $x \neq 0$, otherwise $\mathtt{fan}(x) = 0$. This bias illustrates a case of die-hard *fanaticism* of i towards j. Intuitively, when confronted with any disagreement $x = B_j - B_i \neq 0$, this bias contributes to changing i's opinion with the *highest magnitude*, i.e., $|\beta_{i,j}(x)| = 1$, in the *direction* of the opinion of j.

Finally we illustrate a bias that, unlike the previous, causes agents to ignore opinions of others. We call it the *insular* bias $\beta_{i,j} = \mathtt{ins}$ and it is defined as the zero function $\mathtt{ins} : x \mapsto 0$.   □

The particular bias function examples of Ex. 1 are depicted in the *square region* $[-1, 1]^2$ in Fig. 1. The functions may seem somewhat ad hoc but in Sect. 3 we identify a broad *family* of *bias functions* in the region $[-1, 1]^2$ that guarantees a property of central interest in multi-agent opinion evolution; namely, whether all the agents will converge to the same opinion, i.e. *convergence to consensus*.

Remark 2. We conclude this section by noting that unlike the DeGroot model, in Eq. 3 we allow agents to react with a distinct bias function to each of their influencers. This broadens the range of captured opinion dynamics and we illustrate this in the next section with an example exhibiting agents with different bias functions including those in Ex. 1. This, however, comes at a price; the update

---

[2] The confirmation bias function from [1] uses $\delta = 0$.

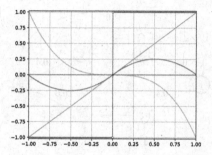

Fig. 1. Bias functions from Ex. 1 in the region $[-1,1]^2$: `degroot` (in green), `conf` (in blue), `backf` (in yellow), `fan` (in red), `ins` (in orange). (Color figure online)

function can be non-linear in the agents' opinions (see e.g., functions `backf` and `conf`). Thus, the analysis of opinion convergence using Markov chain theory for linear-system evolution as done for the DeGroot model is no longer applicable. In Sect. 3 we study opinion convergence using methods from real analysis.

2.5 Vaccine Example

Let us suppose that the proposition of interest is *"vaccines are unsafe"* and $G = (A, E, I)$ is as in Fig. 2. Suppose that initially the agents $1, 2, 3$ are *anti-vaxers* with opinion values $1.0, 0.9, 0.8$ about the proposition. In contrast, agents $4, 5, 6$ are initially *pro-vaxers*, with opinion values $0.2, 0.1, 0.0$ about the proposition. Thus, the initial state of opinion is $B^0 = (1.0, 0.9, 0.8, 0.2, 0.1, 0.0)$.

Notice that although agent 1 is the most extreme anti-vaxer, agent 6, the most extreme vaxer, has the highest possible influence over them. As we shall illustrate below, depending on the bias of 1 towards 6, this may have a strong impact on the evolution of the opinion of agent 1.

We now consider the evolution of their opinion under different update functions obtained by combining biases from Ex. 1. In Fig. 3 we show the evolution of opinions of vaxxers and anti-vaxxers using combinations of the bias functions from Fig. 1. Consider Fig. 3a. Agent 2 reaches the extreme opinion value 1.0 rather quickly because of their die-hard fanaticism towards the opinion of 1 (i.e., $\beta_{2,1} = $ `fan`). As the influence of 6 on agent 1 backfires ($\beta_{1,6} = $ `back`), agent 1 stays with belief value 1.0. Eventually, all the other biases contribute to changing the belief value of the influenced agents towards 1.0. Indeed, the agents converge to a consensus that vaccines are unsafe.

In Fig. 3b, the influence of 3 on agent 5 backfires, since $\beta_{5,3} = $ `backf`. This makes their disagreement increase, moving agent 5's opinion closer to 0. On the other hand, the opinion of agent 6 is influenced at the same time by the belief values of 5 and 4 as in the DeGroot model ($\beta_{6,5} = \beta_{6,4} = $ `degroot`) so her opinion stays between theirs.

Notice that in Fig. 3c agent 5 reacts to 3 with die-hard fanaticism ($\beta_{5,3} = $ `fan`) while 3's belief value does not converge to 0.0 or 1.0. Thus we obtain the looping

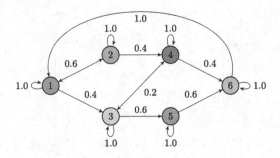

Fig. 2. Influence graph for vaccine example. The weight on edge (i, j) is the value $I_{i,j}$.

behaviour of agent 5. The fanaticism of agent 5 propagates also to agent 6 since he is influenced by agent 5 by `degroot` bias.

Finally, notice the behaviours in Fig. 3 when all the agents have the same bias. In particular, Fig. 3g suggests convergence to consensus when all the agents are under confirmation bias. In fact convergence to consensus is indeed guaranteed for this example as we shall later see in this paper. Also, Fig. 3f is an example of why the clamp function might be necessary to guarantee that the belief values are always in $[0, 1]$.

The above illustrates that different types of biases can have strong impact on opinion evolution for a given influence graph. In the next section, we will identify meaningful families of bias as functions in the region $[-1, 1]^2$.

3   Bias Region and Consensus

Consensus is a property of central interest in social learning models. Indeed, failure to converge to a consensus is often an indicator of polarization in a society.

Definition 4 (Consensus). *Let* (G, B^0, μ_G) *be an opinion model with* $G = (A, E, I)$. *We say that the subset of agents* $A' \subseteq A$ *converges to an opinion value* $v \in [0, 1]$ *iff for every* $i \in A'$, $\lim_{t \to \infty} B_i^t = v$. *We say* $A' \subseteq A$ *converges to consensus iff* A' *converges to an opinion value* v *for some* v.

In this section we identify a broad and meaningful region of $[-1, 1]^2$ where all the *continuous* disagreement bias functions guarantee that agents converge to consensus under certain topological conditions on the influence graph.

3.1   Bias Regions

In what follows we say that a bias $\beta_{i,j}$ is in a region $R \subseteq [-1, 1]^2$ if its function graph is included in R, i.e., if $\{(x, \beta_{i,j}(x)) \mid x \in [-1, 1]\} \subseteq R$. We now identify regions of $[-1, 1]^2$ that capture several notions of cognitive bias.

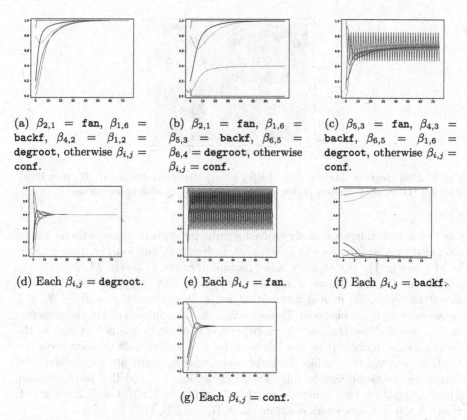

(a) $\beta_{2,1}$ = fan, $\beta_{1,6}$ = backf, $\beta_{4,2}$ = $\beta_{1,2}$ = degroot, otherwise $\beta_{i,j}$ = conf.

(b) $\beta_{2,1}$ = fan, $\beta_{1,6}$ = $\beta_{5,3}$ = backf, $\beta_{6,5}$ = $\beta_{6,4}$ = degroot, otherwise $\beta_{i,j}$ = conf.

(c) $\beta_{5,3}$ = fan, $\beta_{4,3}$ = backf, $\beta_{6,5}$ = $\beta_{1,6}$ = degroot, otherwise $\beta_{i,j}$ = conf.

(d) Each $\beta_{i,j}$ = degroot.

(e) Each $\beta_{i,j}$ = fan.

(f) Each $\beta_{i,j}$ = backf.

(g) Each $\beta_{i,j}$ = conf.

Fig. 3. Simulations for G in Fig. 2 with $B^0 = (1.0, 0.9, 0.8, 0.2, 0.1, 0.0)$ using different biases. Each plot represents the evolution in time of the opinion of the agent in Fig. 2 with the same color.

Definition 5 (Bias Regions). *Let* **S** *be the square region* $[-1,1]^2$. *Let the (sub)regions* **M, R, B, I** $\subseteq$ **S**, *named* Malleability, Receptive-Resistant, Backfire *and* Insular, *be defined as follows:*

$$\mathbf{M} = \{(x,y) \in \mathbf{S} \mid (x < 0 \text{ and } y \le x) \text{ or } (x > 0 \text{ and } y \ge x) \text{ or } x = 0\}$$
$$\mathbf{R} = \{(x,y) \in \mathbf{S} \mid (x < 0 \text{ and } x < y < 0) \text{ or } (x > 0 \text{ and } 0 < y < x) \text{ or } x = y = 0\}$$
$$\mathbf{B} = \{(x,y) \in \mathbf{S} \mid (x < 0 \text{ and } 0 < y) \text{ or } (x > 0 \text{ and } y < 0) \text{ or } x = y = 0\}$$
$$\mathbf{I} = \{(x,y) \in \mathbf{S} \mid y = 0\}.$$

The regions are depicted in Fig. 4. Notice that if a point (x,y) of a bias $\beta_{i,j}$ is in the *Malleability* region **M** (i.e., $y = \beta_{i,j}(x)$ and $(x,y) \in \mathbf{M}$) it means that for a disagreement $x = B_j - B_i$ between j and i, the bias will contribute with a magnitude $|y| \ge |x|$ (multiplied by $\overline{I_{j,i}}$) to changing the opinion of i in the direction of j's opinion. Since $|y| \ge |x|$, depending on the value of $\overline{I_{j,i}}$, the opinion of i may move to match j's opinion or even further (which can make i's new opinion even more extreme than that of j). Individuals that blindly follow authorita-

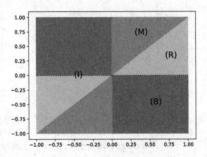

Fig. 4. Bias Regions: Malleability (**M**, in blue), Receptive-Resistant (**R**, in yellow), Backfire (**B**, in red), Insular (**I**, the dotted line $y = 0$). (Color figure online)

tive or influential figures, easily swayed agents, fanaticism, among others, can be modelled by bias functions in this region. Indeed the function `fan` from Ex. 1 is in **M** (see Fig. 1). The identity bias function `degroot` is also in **M**.

Like in the case above, if a point (x, y) of a bias $\beta_{i,j}$ is in the *Receptive-Resistant* region **R**, it also means that for a disagreement $x = B_j - B_i \neq 0$ between j and i, the bias contributes to changing the opinion of i in the direction of j's opinion. Nevertheless, the magnitude of contribution is not as high as the previous case, namely it is $|y|$ with $|x| > |y| > 0$. Individuals that are receptive to other opinions but, unlike malleable ones, may demonstrate some resistance, reluctance, or skepticism to fully accept them, can be modelled in this region. The confirmation bias function $\texttt{conf}(x) = x(1 + \delta - |x|)/(1 + \delta)$ from Ex. 1, where $\delta > 0$ is a very small constant, is in **R** (see Fig. 1).

In fact, it is worth noticing that for any constant $\delta > 0$, the resulting bias function $\beta_{i,j}(x) = x(1 + \delta - |x|)/(1 + \delta)$ is in **R**. In the limit, however, we have $\lim_{\delta \to \infty} x(1 + \delta - |x|)/(1 + \delta) = x = \texttt{degroot}(x)$ which is not in **R** but in **M**. Therefore, δ could be viewed as a *parameter of receptiveness*; the higher the value of δ, the more receptive and less resistant agent i is toward j's opinion. In the limit, agent i is not resistant and behaves as a malleable agent towards j.

Contrary to the previous two cases, if a point (x, y) of a bias $\beta_{i,j}$ is in the *Back-Fire* region **B**, it means that for a disagreement $x = B_j - B_i \neq 0$ between j and i, the bias contributes to changing the opinion of i *but in the opposite direction* of j's opinion. This bias can then cause the disagreement between i and j to grow. Individuals that become more extreme when confronted with a different opinion can be modelled by bias functions in this region. Indeed, the function `backf` from Ex. 1 is in **B** (see Fig. 1).

Finally, if a point (x, y) of a bias $\beta_{i,j}$ is in the Insular region **I**, it means that $y = 0$, thus for a disagreement $x = B_j - B_i \neq 0$ between j and i, the bias causes i to completely ignore the opinion of j. Individuals that are stubborn or closed-minded can be modelled with the function in this region. In fact, the function `ins` from Ex. 1 is the only function in **I** (see Fig. 1).

We conclude this section with a proposition stating that we can dispense with the clamp function whenever all the bias functions are in the **R** region.

Proposition 1 (Update with Bias in R). *Given a Bias Opinion Model* (G, B^0, μ_G) *with* $G = (A, E, I)$, *if for all* $(a, b) \in E$ *we have* $\beta_{b,a} \in \mathbf{R}$, *then for all* $B \in [0, 1]^{|A|}$ *and* $i \in A$: $\mu_G(B)_i = B_i + \sum_{j \in A_i} \overline{I_{j,i}} \beta_{i,j}(B_j - B_i)$.

The proof of this proposition can be found in the technical report [4].

3.2 Consensus Under Receptiveness in Strongly Connected Graphs

Our first main result states the convergence to consensus for strongly connected societies when all bias functions are continuous and in the Receptive-Resistant Region defined in 3.1. We need some standard notions from graph theory.

Recall that a *path* from i to j in $G = (A, E, I)$ is a sequence $i_0 i_1 \ldots i_m$ such that $i = i_0$, $j = i_m$ and $(i_0, i_1), (i_1, i_2), \ldots (i_{m-1}, i_m)$ are edges in E. The graph G is *strongly connected* iff there is path from any agent to any other. We can now state our first consensus result.

Theorem 1 (Consensus I). *Let* (G, B^0, μ) *be a bias opinion model with a strongly connected graph* $G = (A, E, I)$. *Suppose that for every* $(j, i) \in E$, $\beta_{i,j}$ *is a continuous function in* $\mathbf{R}$. *Then the set of agents* A *converges to consensus.*

Hence, the continuous bias functions in $\mathbf{R}$ guarantee consensus in strongly connected graphs, regardless of initial beliefs. Intuitively, the theorem says that a strongly connected community/society will converge towards consensus if its members are receptive but resistant to the opinions of others.

Notice that the Vaccine Example in Sect. 2.5 with all agents under confirmation bias satisfy the conditions of Th. 1, so their convergence to consensus is guaranteed. In fact, the opinion difference between any two agents grows smaller rather rapidly (Fig. 3g illustrates this). In contrast, Fig. 5 illustrates an example, with a different bias also in $\mathbf{R}$, where the opinion difference grows smaller much slowly. But since such an example also satisfies the conditions of Th. 1, convergence to consensus is guaranteed.

Before outlining the proof of this theorem, we elaborate on its conditions.

Discontinuous Bias. Requiring continuity for the bias functions in Th. 1 seems reasonable; small changes in an opinion disagreement value $x = B_j - B_i$ should result in small changes in i's biased reaction to x. Nevertheless, if we relaxed the continuity requirement, we would have the following counter-example.

Consider a strongly connected graph with two agents with $I_{1,2} = I_{2,1} = 1$, agent 1 influences agent 2 with the bias functions $\beta_{1,2} = \beta_{2,1} = f$, satisfying $f(x) = \frac{x}{8}$ if $x \in [-\frac{1}{2}, \frac{1}{2}]$, $f(x) = \frac{x-0.5}{8}$ if $x \in (\frac{1}{2}, 1]$ and $f(x) = \frac{x+0.5}{8}$ if $x \in [-1, -\frac{1}{2})$. If one agent starts with belief value 1.0 and the other 0.0, then they will not converge to consensus (their belief values will approach $\frac{3}{4}$ and $\frac{1}{4}$, but will never reach those values). Figure 6 illustrates this example.

Bias Outside $\mathbf{R}$. Notice that Th. 1 requires bias functions to be in the responsive-resistant region $\mathbf{R}$. We consider counter-examples where we allow bias functions outside this region in Th. 1. If we allowed continuous bias functions outside

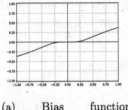

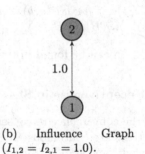

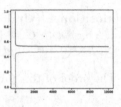

(a)   Bias   function
$\beta_{1,2}(x)$ $=$ $\beta_{2,1}(x)$ $=$
$\begin{cases} 0 & \text{if } x = 0 \\ \frac{x}{|x|} \cdot e^{-\frac{1}{|x|}} & \text{if } x \neq 0 \end{cases}$

(b)   Influence   Graph
$(I_{1,2} = I_{2,1} = 1.0)$.

(c) Each plot represents the evolution in time of the opinion of the agent in Fig. 5b with the same color.

Fig. 5. Simulations with $B^0 = (0.0, 1.0)$ using a bias function in region **R**, with very slow convergence.

R with points in the backfire region **B**, then the scenario in Fig. 3f provides a counter-example to consensus. If we allow continuous bias functions outside **R** with points in region **M**, then the scenario in Fig. 7 is a counter-example to consensus: notice how the absolute value of their disagreement begins at 0.001 and increases until it reaches 1. Finally, it is clear that if we allowed the only function in **I**, the insular bias, with the graph in Fig. 5b and initial beliefs $B^0 = (0, 1)$, consensus will never be reached since the agents will ignore each other.

3.3   Proof Outline of Th. 1

In this Section we outline the proof of Th. 1. In the process we single out the central properties of the behaviour of agents that are receptive and yet resistant

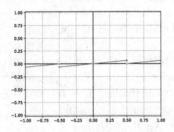

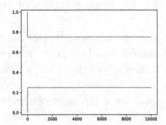

(a)   Bias   function
$\beta_{1,2}(x)$ $=$ $\beta_{2,1}(x)$ $=$
$\begin{cases} \frac{x+0.5}{8} & \text{if } -1 \leq x < -\frac{1}{2} \\ \frac{x}{8} & \text{if } -\frac{1}{2} \leq x \leq \frac{1}{2} \\ \frac{x-0.5}{8} & \text{if } \frac{1}{2} < x \leq 1 \end{cases}$

(b) Each plot represents the evolution in time of the opinion of the agent in Fig. 5b with the same color.

Fig. 6. Counter-example to consensus for two agents with non-continuous bias functions in **R**, for G in Fig. 5b and $B^0 = (1.0, 0.0)$.

to disagreement. The complete proof can can be found in the technical report [4].

Let (G, B^0, μ) be as in the statement of Th. 1. Suppose $B = \mu^t(B^0)$ is the state of opinion at some time $t \geq 0$ where consensus has not yet been reached: i.e., assume $\min(B) \neq \max(B)$ where $\min(B)$ and $\max(B)$ are the minimum and maximum opinion values in B. By assumption, all the biases $\beta_{i,j}$ are in **R**. Thus $\beta_{i,j}(x) = y$, where $x = B_j - B_i$, contributes to update the opinion of i in the direction of the opinion of j but with a magnitude $|y| > 0$ strictly smaller than $|x|$ if $|x| > 0$ (or equal to 0 if $|x| = 0$). Using this and Prop. 1^3, we show the new (updated) opinion of each i, $\mu(B)_i$, is bounded as follows:

Lemma 1 (Update Bounds). *For each $i \in A$, $\min(B) \leq \mu(B)_i \leq \max(B)$.*

We use the above lemma to prove that the bounded sequences of minimum and maximum opinion values at each time, $\{\min(B^t)\}_{t\geq 0}$ and $\{\max(B^t)\}_{t\geq 0}$, are monotonically non-decreasing and monotonically non-increasing. Thus by the Monotone convergence theorem [13], they both converge. Therefore, by the Squeeze theorem [13], to prove Th. 1, it suffices to show that $\{\min(B^t)\}_{t\geq 0}$ and $\{\max(B^t)\}_{t\geq 0}$ converge to the same value.

We first prove the following lemma which intuitively states that the number of extreme agents decrease with time.

Lemma 2 (Extreme Agents Reduction). *Suppose that $\min(B) \neq \max(B)$ and let $M = \max(B)$. If G has a path $i_1 \ldots i_n$ such that $B_{i_n} = M$ and $B_{i_1} < M$, then $|\{j \in A : B_j \geq M\}| > |\{j \in A : \mu(B)_j \geq M\}|$. A symmetric property applies to the minimum.*

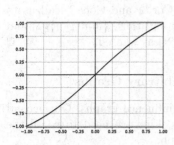

(a) Bias function $\beta_{1,2}(x) = \beta_{2,1}(x) = \frac{\arctan x}{\arctan 1}$

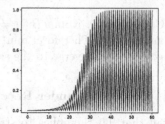

(b) Each plot represents the evolution in time of the opinion of the agent in Fig. 5b with the same color.

Fig. 7. Counter-example for consensus when all bias function are continuous but allowed to have points in **M**, with initial belief vector $B^0 = (0.0, 0.001)$ and influence graph 5b.

---

^{3} This follows from the known property that weighted averages of any set of values are always between the minimum and the maximum of those values.

To see the lemma's intuition, notice that since G is strongly connected and $\min(B) < \max(B)$, G indeed has a path $i_1 \ldots i_n$ such that $B_{i_n} = M = \max(B)$ and $B_{i_1} < M$. In the path some agent i_k whose belief value is equal to M will be influenced by some agent with smaller belief value. Thus, since the bias functions are in $\mathbf{R}$, the opinion of i_k will change in the direction of the smaller value, and thus will strictly decrease. Also, no agent that had a smaller belief value will reach the current maximum, as the bias functions are in the region $\mathbf{R}$.

Thus, because of Lem. 2 and G being strongly connected, we conclude that the maximum (minimum) belief value will eventually decrease (increase). I.e.,

Corollary 1. *Suppose that* $\min(B) \neq \max(B)$. *Then there exist* $s, t > 0$ *such that* $\max(\mu^s(B)) < \max(B)$ *and* $\min(\mu^t(B)) > \min(B)$.

We now apply Bolzano-Weierstrass theorem [13][4] to find a sub-sequence $\{B^t\}_{t \in \Delta}$ of $\{B^t\}_{t \in \mathbb{N}}$ that converges to some B^∞. Notice that $\{\max(B^t)\}_{t \in \Delta}$ converges to $\max(B^\infty)$ and it is a sub-sequence of the convergent sequence $\{\max(B^t)\}_{t \in \mathbb{N}}$, so $\{\max(B^t)\}_{t \in \mathbb{N}}$ should also converge to $\max(B^\infty)$. Since each bias function $\beta_{i,j}$ is continuous, the update function μ is continuous. Therefore, $\{\mu(B^t)\}_{t \in \Delta}$ converges to $\mu(B^\infty)$, and thus $\{\max(\mu(B^t))\}_{t \in \Delta}$ converges to $\max(\mu(B^\infty))$. But since the sequence $\{\max(\mu(B^t))\}_{t \in \Delta} = \{\max(B^{t+1})\}_{t \in \Delta}$ is a sub-sequence of the convergent sequence $\{\max(B^t)\}_{t \in \mathbb{N}}$, both must converge to the same value, hence $\max(B^\infty) = \max(\mu(B^\infty))$. Similarly, we can show that $\min(B^\infty) = \min(\mu(B^\infty))$. It can thus be shown that if we repeatedly apply μ to B^∞, the maximum should not change, and the same applies to the minimum. More precisely, we conclude the following.

Corollary 2. $\max(B^\infty) = \max(\mu^t(B^\infty))$ *and* $\min(B^\infty) = \min(\mu^t(B^\infty))$ *for each* $t \geq 0$.

Consequently, if $\min(B^\infty) \neq \max(B^\infty)$ then Cor. 1 and Cor. 2 lead us to a contradiction. Therefore, $\min(B^\infty) = \max(B^\infty)$ and thus, $\{\min(B^t)\}_{t \geq 0}$ and $\{\max(B^t)\}_{t \geq 0}$ converge to the same value $\max(B^\infty)$ as wanted. $\qquad\square$

3.4 Consensus Under Receptiveness in Arbitrary Graphs

Recall that Th. 1 applies to strongly connected influence graphs. Our second main result applies to arbitrary influence graphs. First we need to recall the notion of strongly-connected components of a graph.

A *strongly-connected component* of G is a *maximal subset* $S \subseteq A$ such that for each two $i, j \in S$, there is path from i to j. A strongly-connected component S is said to be a *source component* iff there is no edge $(i, j) \in E$ such that $i \in A \setminus S$ and $j \in S$. We use $\mathcal{S}(G)$ to denote the set of source components of G.

---

[4] Every infinite bounded sequence in $\mathbb{R}^n$ has a convergent sub-sequence.

Intuitively, a source component of a graph can be thought of as a closed group that is not externally influenced but may influence individuals outside the group. The following theorem gives a characterization of consensus with biases in **R** for arbitrary graphs in terms of source components.

Theorem 2 (Consensus II). *Let (G, B^0, μ) be a bias opinion model with $G = (A, E, I)$. Suppose that for every $(j, i) \in E$, $\beta_{i,j}$ is a continuous function in **R**. Then the set of agents A converges to consensus iff there exists $v \in [0, 1]$ such that every source component $S \in \mathcal{S}(G)$ converges to opinion v.*

The above theorem, whose proof can be found in the technical report [4], provides the following intuitive yet insightful remark. Namely, upon agreeing on an opinion, the closed and potentially influential groups, can make all individuals converge to that opinion in a society whose members are receptive but resistant.

4   Concluding Remarks and Related Work

We introduced a generalization of the DeGroot Model where agents interact under different biases. We identified the notion of bias on disagreement and made it the focus our model. This allowed us to identify families of biases that capture a broader range of social dynamics. We also provided theoretical results characterizing the notion of consensus for a broad family of cognitive biases.

The relevance of biased reasoning in human interactions has been studied extensively in [3, 12, 14, 15], and others.

There is a great deal of work on formal models for belief change in social networks; we focus on the work on *biased* belief update, which is the focus of this paper. Some models were previously proposed to generalize the DeGroot model and introduce bias, for instance [6, 7, 17] analyse the effects of incorporating a bias factor for each agent to represent biased assimilation: how much of the external opinions the agent will take into consideration. [16] extends the model [7] to include the effect of backfire-effect as well. The main difference of these models to our model is that biases are not incorporated in those models in terms of the disagreement level between agents, but either as an exponential factor that reduces the impact of the opinion of neighbours or by dynamically changing the weights of the DeGroot model. Thus, our model brings a new point of view to how distinct types of biases can be represented and identified.

In [10], it is proved that "constricting" update functions, roughly, functions where the extreme agents move closer to each other, lead to convergence in strongly connected social networks. This is similar to our theorem, indeed, the functions in our **R** region are easily shown to be constricting. However, their social network model is more abstract than ours and further from real social networks, and they do not directly analyse biases as a function of disagreement.

References

1. Alvim, M.S., Amorim, B., Knight, S., Quintero, S., Valencia, F.: A multi-agent model for polarization under confirmation bias in social networks. In: Peters, K., Willemse, T.A.C. (eds.) Formal Techniques for Distributed Objects, Components, and Systems: 41st IFIP WG 6.1 International Conference, FORTE 2021, Held as Part of the 16th International Federated Conference on Distributed Computing Techniques, DisCoTec 2021, Valletta, Malta, June 14–18, 2021, Proceedings, pp. 22–41. Springer International Publishing, Cham (2021). https://doi.org/10.1007/978-3-030-78089-0_2

2. Alvim, M.S., Amorim, B., Knight, S., Quintero, S., Valencia, F.: A formal model for polarization under confirmation bias in social networks. Logical Methods Comput. Sci. **19** (2023). https://hal.science/hal-03872692

3. Alvim, M.S., Knight, S., Valencia, F.: Toward a formal model for group polarization in social networks. In: Alvim, M.S., Chatzikokolakis, K., Olarte, C., Valencia, F. (eds.) The Art of Modelling Computational Systems: A Journey from Logic and Concurrency to Security and Privacy: Essays Dedicated to Catuscia Palamidessi on the Occasion of Her 60th Birthday, pp. 419–441. Springer International Publishing, Cham (2019). https://doi.org/10.1007/978-3-030-31175-9_24

4. Alvim, M.S., da Silva, A.G., Knight, S., Valencia, F.: A multi-agent model for opinion evolution under cognitive biases. CoRR **abs/2402.17615** (2024). https://doi.org/10.48550/ARXIV.2402.17615

5. Aronson, E., Wilson, T., Akert, R.: Social Psychology. Upper Saddle River, NJ : Prentice Hall, 7 edn. (2010)

6. Chen, Z., Qin, J., Li, B., Qi, H., Buchhorn, P., Shi, G.: Dynamics of opinions with social biases. Automatica **106**, 374–383 (2019). https://doi.org/10.1016/j.automatica.2019.04.035, https://www.sciencedirect.com/science/article/pii/S0005109819301955

7. Dandekar, P., Goel, A., Lee, D.: Biased assimilation, homophily and the dynamics of polarization. Proc. Nat. Acad. Sci. United States Am. **110** (03 2013). https://doi.org/10.1073/pnas.1217220110

8. DeGroot, M.H.: Reaching a consensus. J. American Stat. Assoc.**69**(345), 118–121 (1974)

9. Golub, B., Sadler, E.: Learning in social networks. Available at SSRN 2919146 (2017)

10. Mueller-Frank, M.: Reaching Consensus in Social Networks. IESE Research Papers D/1116, IESE Business School (Feb 2015)

11. Nyhan, B., Reifler, J.: When corrections fail: the persistence of political misperceptions. Political Behav. **32**(2), 303–330 (2010). https://doi.org/10.1007/s11109-010-9112-2

12. Ramos, V.J.: Analyzing the role of cognitive biases in the decision-making process. Advances in Psychology, Mental Health, and Behavioral Studies (2018). https://api.semanticscholar.org/CorpusID:150306265

13. Sohrab, H.H.: Basic Real Analysis. Birkhauser Basel, 2nd ed edn. (2014)

14. Tappin, B.M., Gadsby, S.: Biased belief in the Bayesian brain: a deeper look at the evidence. Conscious. Cogn. **68**, 107–114 (2019). https://doi.org/10.1016/j.concog.2019.01.006, https://www.sciencedirect.com/science/article/pii/S1053810018305075

15. Williams, D.: Hierarchical Bayesian models of delusion. Conscious. Cogn. **61**, 129–147 (2018). https://doi.org/10.1016/j.concog.2018.03.003, https://www.sciencedirect.com/science/article/pii/S1053810017306219

16. X, C., P, T., J, L., T, D.B.: Opinion dynamics with backfire effect and biased assimilation. PLoS ONE **16**(9) (2021). https://doi.org/10.1371/journal.pone.0256922, https://journals.plos.org/plosone/article?id=10.1371/journal.pone.0256922
17. Xia, W., Ye, M., Liu, J., Cao, M., Sun, X.M.: Analysis of a nonlinear opinion dynamics model with biased assimilation. Automatica **120**, 109113 (2020). https://doi.org/10.1016/j.automatica.2020.109113,   https://www.sciencedirect.com/science/article/pii/S0005109820303113

Weak Simplicial Bisimilarity
for Polyhedral Models and SLCS$_\eta$

Nick Bezhanishvili[1] , Vincenzo Ciancia[2] , David Gabelaia[3] ,
Mamuka Jibladze[3] , Diego Latella[2] , Mieke Massink[2( )] ,
and Erik P. de Vink[4]

[1] Institute for Logic, Language and Computation, University of Amsterdam,
Amsterdam, The Netherlands
n.bezhanishvili@uva.nl
[2] Istituto di Scienza e Tecnologie dell'Informazione "A. Faedo", Consiglio Nazionale
delle Ricerche, Pisa, Italy
{Vincenzo.Ciancia,Diego.Latella,Mieke.Massink}@cnr.it
[3] Andrea Razmadze Mathematical Institute, I. Javakhishvili Tbilisi State University,
Tbilisi, Georgia
[4] Eindhoven University of Technology, Eindhoven, The Netherlands
evink@win.tue.nl

Abstract. In the context of spatial logics and spatial model checking for
polyhedral models — mathematical basis for visualisations in continuous
space — we propose a weakening of simplicial bisimilarity. We additionally propose a corresponding weak notion of ±-bisimilarity on cell-poset
models, discrete representation of polyhedral models. We show that two
points are weakly simplicial bisimilar iff their representations are weakly
±-bisimilar. The advantage of this weaker notion is that it leads to a
stronger reduction of models than its counterpart that was introduced in
our previous work. This is important, since real-world polyhedral models, such as those found in domains exploiting mesh processing, typically
consist of large numbers of cells. We also propose SLCS$_\eta$, a weaker version of the *Spatial Logic for Closure Spaces* (SLCS) on polyhedral models,
and we show that the proposed bisimilarities enjoy the Hennessy-Milner
property: two points are weakly simplicial bisimilar iff they are logically
equivalent for SLCS$_\eta$. Similarly, two cells are weakly ±-bisimilar iff they
are logically equivalent in the poset-model interpretation of SLCS$_\eta$. This
work is performed in the context of the geometric spatial model checker
PolyLogicA and the polyhedral semantics of SLCS.

Keywords: Bisimulation relations · Spatial bisimilarity · Spatial
logics · Logical equivalence · Spatial model checking · Polyhedral
models

The authors are listed in alphabetical order, as they equally contributed to the work
presented in this paper.

V. Castiglioni and A. Francalanza (Eds.): FORTE 2024, LNCS 14678, pp. 20–38, 2024.
https://doi.org/10.1007/978-3-031-62645-6_2

1   Introduction and Related Work

The notion of bisimulation is central in the theory of models for (concurrent) system behaviour, for characterising those systems which "behave the same". Properties of such behaviours are typically captured by formulas of appropriate logics, such as modal logics and variations/extensions thereof (e.g. temporal, deterministic-/stochastic-time temporal, probabilistic). A key notion, in this context, is the Hennessy-Milner property (HMP), that allows for logical characterisations of bisimilarity. Given a model $\mathcal{M}$, a bisimulation equivalence E over $\mathcal{M}$, and a logic $\mathcal{L}$ intepreted on $\mathcal{M}$, we say that E and $\mathcal{L}$ enjoy the HMP if the following holds: any two states in $\mathcal{M}$ are equivalent according to E iff they satisfy the same formulas of $\mathcal{L}$. Besides the intrinsic theoretical value of the HMP, the latter is also of fundamental importance as mathematical foundation for safe model reduction procedures since it ensures that any formula $\mathcal{L}$ is satisfied by a state s in $\mathcal{M}$ iff it is satisfied by the equivalence class $[s]_E$ of s, that is itself a state in the *minimal* model $\mathcal{M}_{/E}$ — there are nowadays standard procedures for the effective and efficient computation of $\mathcal{M}_{/E}$, for finite models $\mathcal{M}$. Model reduction is, in turn, extremely important for efficient model analysis via, for example, automatic model-checking of logic formulas.

Model-checking techniques have been developed for the analysis of models of *space* as well, with properties expressed in *spatial logics*, i.e. modal logics interpreted over such models, following the tradition going back to McKinsey and Tarski in 1940s [22] (see also [4] for an overview), where *topological models* are considered as models for space. In [13,14] the *Spatial Logic for Closure Spaces* (SLCS) has been proposed together with a model-checking algorithm for finite spaces and its implementation. Closure spaces are a generalisation of topological spaces that allow for a uniform treatment of continuous spaces and discrete spaces, such as general graphs. SLCS is interpreted on models whose carriers are closure spaces. Spatio-temporal versions of the logic and the model-checker have been presented in [11,17]. A version of the model-checker optimised for (2D and 3D) digital images — that can be seen as *adjacency spaces*, a subclass of closure spaces — has been proposed in [3] with SLCS enriched with a *distance* operator. Tools for spatial and spatio-temporal model-checking have been successfully used in several applications [1,2,10,15,16,23] showing that the notions and techniques developed in the area of concurrency theory and formal methods can be extremely helpful in developing a foundational basis for the automatic analysis of spatial models in real applications.

As a natural step forward, and following classical developments in modal logic, in [8,18] several notions of bisimulation for finite closure spaces have been studied. These cover a spectrum from CM-bisimilarity, an equivalence based on *proximity* — similar to and inspired by topo-bisimilarity for topological models [4] — to its specialisation for quasi-discrete closure models, CMC-bisimilarity, to CoPa-bisimilarity, an equivalence based on *conditional reachability*. Each of these bisimilarities has been equipped with its logical characterisation. In [12] an encoding from finite closure models to finite labelled transition systems (LTSs) has been defined and proven correct in the sense that two points in the space are

CoPa-bisimilar iff their corresponding states in the LTS are branching bisimilar. This makes it possible to perform minimisation of the spatial model w.r.t. CoPa-bisimilarity via minimisation of its LTS w.r.t. branching bisimulation. Very efficient tools are available for LTS minimisation w.r.t. branching equivalence [19].

The spatial model-checking techniques mentioned above have been extended to *polyhedral models* [5, 21], that we address in the present paper. *Polyhedra* are sets of points in $\mathbb{R}^n$ generated by *simplicial complexes*, i.e. certain finite collections of *simplexes*, where a simplex is the *convex hull* of a set of affinely independent points in $\mathbb{R}^n$. Given a set PL of *proposition letters*, a *polyhedral model* is obtained from a polyhedron in the usual way, i.e. by assigning a set of points to each proposition letter $p \in$ PL, namely those that "satisfy" p. Polyhedral models in $\mathbb{R}^3$ can be used for (approximately) representing objects in continuous 3D space. This is widely used in many 3D visual computing techniques, where an object is divided into suitable areas of different size. Such ways of division of an object are known as *mesh techniques* and include triangular surface meshes or tetrahedral volume meshes (see for example [20] and the example in Fig. 5a).

In [5] a version of SLCS, referred to as SLCS$_\gamma$ in this paper, has been proposed for expressing spatial properties of points laying in polyhedral models, and in particular *conditional reachability* properties. Many other interesting properties, such as "being surrounded by" can be expressed using reachability (see [5]). Intuitively, a point x in a polyhedral model satisfies the conditional reachability formula $\gamma(\Phi_1, \Phi_2)$ if there is a topological path starting from x, ending in a point y satisfying Φ_2, and such that all the intermediate points of the path between x and y satisfy Φ_1, but note that neither x nor y is required to satisfy Φ_1. A notion of bisimilarity between points has also been introduced in [5], namely *simplicial bisimilarity*, and it has been proven that the latter enjoys the HMP w.r.t. SLCS$_\gamma$. In addition, a representation $\mathbb{F}$ of polyhedral models as finite posets has been built and it has been shown that a point x in a polyhedral model $\mathcal{P}$ satisfies a SLCS$_\gamma$ formula Φ in $\mathcal{P}$ iff its representation $\mathbb{F}(x)$ in the poset model $\mathbb{F}(\mathcal{P})$ representing $\mathcal{P}$ satisfies Φ in $\mathbb{F}(\mathcal{P})$. An SLCS$_\gamma$ model-checking algorithm has been developed for finite poset models that has been implemented in the tool PolyLogicA thus achieving model-checking of continuous space that can be represented by polyhedral models (see [5] for details).

In [9] we addressed the issue of minimisation for polyhedral models and, more specifically, their poset representations. In particular, we defined $\pm$-bisimilarity, a notion based on $\pm$-paths, a subclass of undirected paths over poset models suitable for representing, in such models, topological paths over polyhedral models. We proved that $\pm$-bisimilarity enjoys the HMP w.r.t. SLCS$_\gamma$ interpreted on finite poset models and we showed that it can be used for poset model minimisation: for instance, the minimal model of the poset model of Fig. 1c has only 10 elements.

In this paper we present SLCS$_\eta$, another variant of SLCS for polyhedral models where the γ modality has been replaced by η so that a point x satisfies $\eta(\Phi_1, \Phi_2)$ if there is a topological path starting from x, ending in a point y satisfying Φ_2, and such that all the intermediate points of the path between x and y, *and including x itself*, satisfy Φ_1 (y is not required to satisfy Φ_1). Thus γ and η behave differently *only* in η requiring that x itself satisfies Φ_1.

The result is that SLCS$_\eta$ is weaker than SLCS$_\gamma$ in the sense that it distinguishes less points than SLCS$_\gamma$. Furthermore, SLCS$_\gamma$ can express proximity, here intended as topological closure — that boils down to the standard *possibly* modality $\Diamond$ in the poset model interpretation — whereas SLCS$_\eta$ cannot. Nevertheless, many interesting reachability properties can be expressed in SLCS$_\eta$ and, perhaps most importantly, the latter characterises bisimilarities (in the polyhedral model and the associated poset model) that are coarser than simplicial bisimilarity and $\pm$-bisimilarity, respectively. This allows for a substantial model reduction. For instance, the minimal model, w.r.t. the new equivalence, of the poset of Fig. 1c, shown in Fig. 4, has only 4 states now. This greater reduction in model size is one of the main motivations for the study of SLCS$_\eta$ presented in this paper.

In the remainder of this paper, we provide necessary background information in Sect. 2. Section 3 introduces SLCS$_\eta$ and addresses its relationship with SLCS$_\gamma$. It is also shown that SLCS$_\eta$ is preserved and reflected by the mapping $\mathbb{F}$ form polyhedral models to finite poset models. Weak simplicial bisimilarity and weak $\pm$-bisimilarity are defined in Sect. 4 where it is also shown that they enjoy the HMP w.r.t. the intepretation of SLCS$_\eta$ on polyhedral models and on finite poset models, respectively. A larger example is given in Sect. 5, illustrating the reduction potential of weak $\pm$-bisimulation. Finally, conclusions and a discussion on future work are reported in Sect. 6.

The proofs for all the results presented in Sects. 2, 3 and 4, that are not shown in this paper, as well as all background information, results, and notational details, are provided in [6].

2   Background and Notation

In this section we recall the relevant details of the language SLCS$_\gamma$, its polyhedral and poset models, and the truth-preserving map $\mathbb{F}$ between these models.

For sets X and Y, a function $f : X \to Y$, and subsets $A \subseteq X$ and $B \subseteq Y$ we define $f(A)$ and $f^{-1}(B)$ as $\{f(a) \,|\, a \in A\}$ and $\{a \,|\, f(a) \in B\}$, respectively. The *restriction* of f on A is denoted by $f|A$. The powerset of X is denoted by 2^X. For a relation $R \subseteq X \times X$ we let $R^- = \{(y, x) \,|\, (x, y) \in R\}$ denote its converse and $R^\pm$ denote $R \cup R^-$. In the remainder of the paper we assume that a set PL of *proposition letters* is fixed. The sets of natural numbers and of real numbers are denoted by $\mathbb{N}$ and $\mathbb{R}$, respectively. We use the standard interval notation: for $x, y \in \mathbb{R}$ we let $[x, y]$ be the set $\{r \in \mathbb{R} \,|\, x \leq r \leq y\}$, $[x, y) = \{r \in \mathbb{R} \,|\, x \leq r < y\}$, and so on. Intervals of $\mathbb{R}$ are equipped with the Euclidean topology inherited from $\mathbb{R}$. We use a similar notation for intervals over $\mathbb{N}$: for $n, m \in \mathbb{N}$ $[m; n]$ denotes the set $\{i \in \mathbb{N} \,|\, m \leq i \leq n\}$, $[m; n) = \{i \in \mathbb{N} \,|\, m \leq i < n\}$, and so on.

Below we recall, informally, some basic notions, assuming that the reader is familiar with topological spaces, Kripke models and posets. For all the details concerning basic notions and notation we refer the reader to [5,9].

A *simplex* σ is the convex hull of a set of $d + 1$ affinely independent points in $\mathbb{R}^m$, with $d \leq m$, i.e. $\sigma = \{\lambda_0 \mathbf{v_0} + \ldots + \lambda_d \mathbf{v_d} \,|\, \lambda_0, \ldots, \lambda_d \in [0, 1]$ and $\sum_{i=0}^{d} \lambda_i = 1\}$. For instance, a segment AB together with its end-points A and B is a simplex in $\mathbb{R}^m$, for $m \geq 1$. Note that any subset of the set of points characterising a simplex induces a simplex itself. So, for instance, both A and B are simplexes in turn and AB itself could be part of a larger simplex, e.g., a triangle ABC.

The relative interior $\widetilde{\sigma}$ of a simplex σ is the same as σ "without its borders", i.e. the set $\{\lambda_0 \mathbf{v_0} + \ldots + \lambda_d \mathbf{v_d} \mid \lambda_0, \ldots, \lambda_d \in (0,1]$ and $\sum_{i=0}^{d} \lambda_i = 1\}$. For instance, the open segment $\widetilde{AB}$, without the end-points A and B is the relative interior of segment AB. The relative interior of a simplex is often called a *cell* and is equal to the topological interior taken inside the affine hull of the simplex.[1] There is an obvious partial order between the cells of a simplex: $\widetilde{\sigma_1} \preceq \widetilde{\sigma_2}$ iff $\widetilde{\sigma_1} \subseteq \mathcal{C}_T(\widetilde{\sigma_2})$, where $\mathcal{C}_T$ denotes the classical topological closure operator. So, in the above example, we have $\widetilde{A} \preceq \widetilde{A}, \widetilde{B} \preceq \widetilde{B}, \widetilde{A} \preceq \widetilde{AB}, \widetilde{B} \preceq \widetilde{AB}$, and $\widetilde{AB} \preceq \widetilde{AB}$.

A *simplicial complex* K is a finite collection of simplexes of $\mathbb{R}^m$ such that: (i) if $\sigma \in K$ and $\widetilde{\sigma'} \preceq \widetilde{\sigma}$ then also $\sigma' \in K$; (ii) if $\sigma, \sigma' \in K$ then $\widetilde{\sigma \cap \sigma'} \preceq \widetilde{\sigma} \cap \widetilde{\sigma'}$. Given a simplicial complex K, the *cell poset* of K is the poset $(\widetilde{K}, \preceq)$ where $\widetilde{K}$ is the set $\{\widetilde{\sigma} \mid \sigma \in K \setminus \{\emptyset\}\}$ and the *polyhedron* $|K|$ of K is the set-theoretic union of the simplexes in K. Note that $|K|$ inherits the topological structure of $\mathbb{R}^m$.

A *polyhedral model* is a pair $(|K|, V)$ where $V : \mathrm{PL} \to 2^{|K|}$ maps every proposition letter $p \in \mathrm{PL}$ to the set of points of $|K|$ satisfying p. It is required that, for all $p \in \mathrm{PL}$, $V(p)$ is always a union of cells in $\widetilde{K}$. Similarly, a *poset model* $(W, \preceq, \mathcal{V})$ is a poset equipped with a valuation function $\mathcal{V} : \mathrm{PL} \to 2^W$. Given polyhedral model $\mathcal{P} = (|K|, V)$, we say that $(\widetilde{K}, \preceq, \mathcal{V})$ is the *cell poset model* of $\mathcal{P}$ iff $(\widetilde{K}, \preceq)$ is the cell poset of K and, for all $\widetilde{\sigma} \in \widetilde{K}$, we have: $\widetilde{\sigma} \in \mathcal{V}(p)$ iff $\widetilde{\sigma} \subseteq V(p)$. We let $\mathbb{F}(\mathcal{P})$ denote the cell poset model of $\mathcal{P}$ and, with a little bit of overloading, for all $x \in |K|$, $\mathbb{F}(x)$ denotes the unique cell $\widetilde{\sigma}$ such that $x \in \widetilde{\sigma}$. Note that $\mathbb{F} : |K| \to \widetilde{K}$ is a continuous function [7, Corollary 3.4]. Furthermore, note that poset models are a subclass of Kripke models. In the following, when we say that $\mathcal{F}$ is a cell poset model, we mean that there exists a polyhedral model $\mathcal{P}$ such that $\mathcal{F} = \mathbb{F}(\mathcal{P})$.

Figure 1 shows a polyhedral model. There are three proposition letters, **red**, **green** and **gray**, shown by different colours (1a). The model is "unpacked" into its cells in Fig. 1b. The latter are collected in the cell poset model, whose Hasse diagram is shown in Fig. 1c.

In a topological space (X, τ), a *topological path* from $x \in X$ is a total, continuous function $\pi : [0,1] \to X$ such that $\pi(0) = x$. We call $\pi(0)$ and $\pi(1)$ the *starting* and *ending point* of π, respectively, while $\pi(r)$ is an *intermediate point* of π, for all $r \in (0,1)$. Figure 2a shows a path from a point x in the open segment $\widetilde{AB}$ in the polyhedral model of Fig. 1a.

Topological paths are represented in cell posets by so-called $\pm$-paths, a subclass of undirected paths [5]. For technical reasons[2] in this paper we extend the

---

[1] But note that the relative interior of a simplex composed of just a single point is the point itself and not the empty set.

[2] We are interested in model-checking structures resulting from the minimisation, via bisimilarity, of cell poset models, and such structures are often just (reflexive) Kripke models rather than poset models.

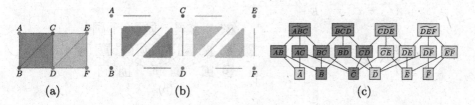

Fig. 1. A polyhedral model $\mathcal{P}$ (1a) with its cells (1b) and the Hasse diagram of the related cell poset (1c).

definition given in [5] to general Kripke frames. Given a Kripke frame (W, R), an *undirected path* of length $\ell \in \mathbb{N}$ from w is a total function $\pi : [0; \ell] \to X$ such that $\pi(0) = x$ and, for all $i \in [0; \ell)$, $R^{\pm}(\pi(i), \pi(i+1))$. The *starting* and *ending* points are $\pi(0)$ and $\pi(\ell)$, respectively, while $\pi(i)$ is an intermediate point for all $i \in (0; \ell)$. The path is a $\pm$-*path* iff $\ell \geq 2$, $R(\pi(0), \pi(1))$ and $R^{-}(\pi(\ell-1), \pi(\ell))$.

The $\pm$-path $(\widetilde{AB}, \widetilde{ABC}, \widetilde{BC}, \widetilde{BCD}, \widetilde{D})^3$, drawn in blue in Fig. 2b, faithfully represents the path from x shown in Fig. 2a. Note that a path π such that, say, $\pi(0) \in \widetilde{CD}$, $\pi(1) = E$ and $\pi((0,1)) \subseteq \widetilde{CDE}$, i.e. a path that "jumps immediately" to $\widetilde{CDE}$ after starting in $\widetilde{CD}$ cannot be represented in the poset by any undirected path π', of some length $\ell \geq 2$ such that $\pi'(0) \succ \pi'(1)$ (or $\pi'(\ell-1) \prec \pi'(\ell)$, for symmetry reasons), while it is correctly represented by the $\pm$-path $(\widetilde{CD}, \widetilde{CDE}, \widetilde{E})$, where $\widetilde{CD} \prec \widetilde{CDE} \succ \widetilde{E}$.

In the context of this paper it is often convenient to use a generalisation of $\pm$-paths, so-called "down paths", $\downarrow$-paths for short: a $\downarrow$-path from w, of length $\ell \geq 1$, is an undirected path π from w of length ℓ such that $R^{-}(\pi(\ell-1), \pi(\ell))$. Clearly, every $\pm$-path is also a $\downarrow$-path. The following lemma ensures that in *reflexive* Kripke frames $\pm$- and $\downarrow$-paths can be safely used interchangeably since for every $\downarrow$-path there is a $\pm$-path with the same starting and ending points and with the same set of intermediate points, occurring in the same order:

Lemma 1. *Given a reflexive Kripke frame (W, R) and a $\downarrow$-path $\pi : [0; \ell] \to W$, there is a $\pm$-path $\pi' : [0; \ell''] \to W$, for some ℓ', and a total, surjective, monotonic, non-decreasing function $f : [0; \ell'] \to [0; \ell]$ with $\pi'(j) = \pi(f(j))$ for all $j \in [0; \ell']$.*

In [5], SLCS$_\gamma$, a version of SLCS for polyhedral models, has been presented that consists of predicate letters, negation, conjunction, and the single modal operator γ, expressing conditional reachability. The satisfaction relation for $\gamma(\Phi_1, \Phi_2)$, for polyhedral model $\mathcal{P} = (|K|, V)$ and $x \in |K|$, as defined in [5], is recalled below:

$$\mathcal{P}, x \models \gamma(\Phi_1, \Phi_2) \Leftrightarrow \text{a topological path } \pi : [0, 1] \to |K| \text{ exists such that } \pi(0) = x,$$
$$\mathcal{P}, \pi(1) \models \Phi_2, \text{and } \mathcal{P}, \pi(r) \models \Phi_1 \text{ for all } r \in (0,1).$$

We also recall the interpretation of SLCS$_\gamma$ on poset models. The satisfaction relation for $\gamma(\Phi_1, \Phi_2)$, for poset model $\mathcal{F} = (W, \preceq, \mathcal{V})$ and $w \in W$, is as follows:

---

[3] For undirected path π of length ℓ we often use the sequence notation $(x_i)_{i=0}^{\ell}$ where $x_i = \pi(i)$ for $i \in [0; \ell]$.

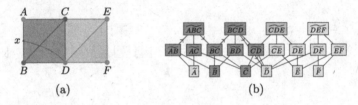

Fig. 2. (2a) A topological path from a point x to vertex D in the polyhedral model $\mathcal{P}$ of Fig. 1a. (2b) The corresponding $\pm$-path (in blue) in the Hasse diagram of the cell poset model $\mathbb{F}(\mathcal{P})$.

$$\mathcal{F}, w \models \gamma(\Phi_1, \Phi_2) \Leftrightarrow \text{a } \pm\text{-path } \pi : [0;\ell] \to W \text{ exists such that } \pi(0) = w,$$
$$\mathcal{F}, \pi(\ell) \models \Phi_2, \text{and } \mathcal{F}, \pi(i) \models \Phi_1 \text{ for all } i \in (0;\ell).$$

In [5] it has also been shown that, for all $x \in |K|$ and SLCS_γ formulas Φ, we have: $\mathcal{P}, x \models \Phi$ iff $\mathbb{F}(\mathcal{P}), \mathbb{F}(x) \models \Phi$. In addition, *simplicial bisimilarity*, a novel notion of bisimilarity for polyhedral models, has been defined that uses a subclass of topological paths and it has been shown to enjoy the classical Hennessy-Milner property: two points $x_1, x_2 \in |K|$ are simplicial bisimilar, written $x_1 \sim^\mathcal{P}_\triangle x_2$, iff they satisfy the same SLCS_γ formulas, i.e. they are equivalent with respect to the logic SLCS_γ, written $x_1 \equiv^\mathcal{P}_\gamma x_2$.

The result has been extended to $\pm$-*bisimilarity* on finite poset models, a notion of bisimilarity based on $\pm$-paths: $w_1, w_2 \in W$ are $\pm$-bisimilar, written $x_1 \sim^\mathcal{F}_\pm x_2$, iff they satisfy the same SLCS_γ formulas, i.e. $x_1 \equiv^\mathcal{F}_\gamma x_2$ (see [9] for details). In summary, we have:

$$x_1 \sim^\mathcal{P}_\triangle x_2 \text{ iff } x_1 \equiv^\mathcal{P}_\gamma x_2 \text{ iff } \mathbb{F}(x_1) \equiv^{\mathbb{F}(\mathcal{P})}_\gamma \mathbb{F}(x_2) \text{ iff } \mathbb{F}(x_1) \sim^{\mathbb{F}(\mathcal{P})}_\pm \mathbb{F}(x_2).$$

We aim to obtain a similar result for a weaker logic introduced in the next section.

We close this section by a small example. With reference to Fig. 1a, we have that no red point, call it x, in the open segment CD is simplicial bisimilar to the red point C. In fact, although both x and C satisfy $\gamma(\mathbf{green}, \mathtt{true})$, we have that C satisfies also $\gamma(\mathbf{gray}, \mathtt{true})$, which is not the case for x. Similarly, with reference to Fig. 1c, cell $\widetilde{C}$ satisfies $\gamma(\mathbf{gray}, \mathtt{true})$, which is not satisfied by $\widetilde{CD}$.

3 SLCS$_\eta$: Weak SLCS on Polyhedral Models

In this section we introduce SLCS_η, a logic for polyhedral models that is weaker than SLCS_γ, yet is still capable of expressing interesting conditional reachability properties. We present also an interpretation of the logic on finite poset models.

Definition 1 (Weak SLCS on polyhedral models - SLCS$_\eta$). *The abstract language of* SLCS_η *is the following:*

$$\Phi ::= p \mid \neg\Phi \mid \Phi_1 \wedge \Phi_2 \mid \eta(\Phi_1, \Phi_2).$$

The satisfaction relation of SLCS$_\eta$ *with respect to a given polyhedral model* $\mathcal{P} = (|K|, V)$, SLCS$_\eta$ *formula* Φ, *and point* $x \in |K|$ *is defined recursively on the structure of* Φ *as follows:*

$\mathcal{P}, x \models p \qquad\qquad \Leftrightarrow x \in V(p);$
$\mathcal{P}, x \models \neg\Phi \qquad\quad \Leftrightarrow \mathcal{P}, x \models \Phi$ *does not hold;*
$\mathcal{P}, x \models \Phi_1 \wedge \Phi_2 \ \Leftrightarrow \mathcal{P}, x \models \Phi_1$ *and* $\mathcal{P}, x \models \Phi_2;$
$\mathcal{P}, x \models \eta(\Phi_1, \Phi_2) \Leftrightarrow$ *a topological path* $\pi : [0,1] \to |K|$ *exists such that* $\pi(0) = x,$
$\qquad\qquad\qquad \mathcal{P}, \pi(1) \models \Phi_2$, *and* $\mathcal{P}, \pi(r) \models \Phi_1$ *for all* $r \in [0,1)$.

As usual, disjunction ($\vee$) is derived as the dual of $\wedge$. Note that the only difference between $\eta(\Phi_1, \Phi_2)$ and $\gamma(\Phi_1, \Phi_2)$ is that the former requires that *also the first element* of a path witnessing the formula satisfies Φ_1, hence the use of the left closed interval $[0, 1)$ here. Although this might seem at first sight only a very minor difference, it has considerable consequences of both theoretical and practical nature, as we will see in what follows.

Definition 2 (SLCS$_\eta$ Logical Equivalence). *Given polyhedral model* $\mathcal{P} = (|K|, V)$ *and* $x_1, x_2 \in |K|$ *we say that* x_1 *and* x_2 *are logically equivalent with respect to* SLCS$_\eta$, *written* $x_1 \equiv_\eta^{\mathcal{P}} x_2$, *iff, for all* SLCS$_\eta$ *formulas* Φ, *the following holds:* $\mathcal{P}, x_1 \models \Phi$ *if and only if* $\mathcal{P}, x_2 \models \Phi$.

In the following, we will refrain from indicating the model $\mathcal{P}$ explicitly as a superscript of $\equiv_\eta^{\mathcal{P}}$ when it is clear from the context. Below, we show that SLCS$_\eta$ can be encoded into SLCS$_\gamma$ so that the former is weaker than the latter.

Definition 3. *We define the following encoding of* SLCS$_\eta$ *into* SLCS$_\gamma$:

$$\begin{aligned} \mathcal{E}(p) &= p & \mathcal{E}(\Phi_1 \wedge \Phi_2) &= \mathcal{E}(\Phi_1) \wedge \mathcal{E}(\Phi_2) \\ \mathcal{E}(\neg\Phi) &= \neg\mathcal{E}(\Phi) & \mathcal{E}(\eta(\Phi_1, \Phi_2)) &= \mathcal{E}(\Phi_1) \wedge \gamma(\mathcal{E}(\Phi_1), \mathcal{E}(\Phi_2)) \end{aligned}$$

The following lemma is easily proven by structural induction:

Lemma 2. *Let* $\mathcal{P} = (|K|, V)$ *be a polyhedral model,* $x \in |K|$ *and* Φ *a* SLCS$_\eta$ *formula. Then* $\mathcal{P}, x \models \Phi$ *iff* $\mathcal{P}, x \models \mathcal{E}(\Phi)$.

A direct consequence of Lemma 2 is that SLCS$_\eta$ is weaker than SLCS$_\gamma$.

Proposition 1. *Let* $\mathcal{P} = (|K|, V)$ *be a polyhedral model. For all* $x_1, x_2 \in |K|$ *the following holds: if* $x_1 \equiv_\gamma x_2$ *then* $x_1 \equiv_\eta x_2$.

Remark 1. The converse of Proposition 1 does *not* hold, as shown by the example polyhedral model $\mathcal{P} = (|K|, V)$ of Fig. 3a. It is easy to see that, for all $x \in \overline{ABC}$, we have $A \not\equiv_\gamma x$ and $A \equiv_\eta x$. Let $x \in \overline{ABC}$. Clearly, $A \not\equiv_\gamma x$ since $\mathcal{P}, A \models \gamma(\mathbf{red}, \mathbf{true})$ whereas $\mathcal{P}, x \not\models \gamma(\mathbf{red}, \mathbf{true})$. It can be easily shown, by induction on the structure of formulas, that $A \equiv_\eta x$ for all $x \in \widetilde{ABC}$. The case for proposition letters, negation and disjunction are straightforward and omitted. Suppose $\mathcal{P}, A \models \eta(\Phi_1, \Phi_2)$. Then there is a topological path $\pi_A : [0,1] \to |K|$ from A such that $\mathcal{P}, \pi_A(1) \models \Phi_2$ and $\mathcal{P}, \pi_A(x) \models \Phi_1$ for all $x \in [0,1)$. Since $\mathcal{P}, A \models \Phi_1$, by the Induction Hypothesis, we have that $\mathcal{P}, p \models \Phi_1$ for all $p \in \widetilde{ABC}$. For each $p \in \widetilde{ABC}$, define $\pi_p : [0,1] \to |K|$ as follows, for arbitrary $v \in (0,1)$:

$$\pi_p(r) = \begin{cases} \frac{r}{v}A + \frac{v-r}{v}p, & \text{if } r \in [0,v), \\[2mm] \pi_A(\frac{r-v}{1-v}), & \text{if } r \in [v,1]. \end{cases}$$

Function π_p is continuous. Furthermore, for all $x \in [0,v)$, we have that $\mathcal{P}, \pi_p(x) \models \Phi_1$, since $\pi_p(x) \in \widetilde{ABC}$. Also, for all $x \in [v,1)$ we have that $\mathcal{P}, \pi_p(x) \models \Phi_1$, since $\pi_p(x) = \pi_A(\frac{x-v}{1-v})$, $0 \leq \frac{x-v}{1-v} < 1$ and for $y \in [0,1)$ we have that $\mathcal{P}, \pi_A(y), \models \Phi_1$. Thus, $\mathcal{P}, \pi_p(x), \models \Phi_1$ for all $x \in [0,1)$. Finally, $\pi_p(1) = \pi_A(1)$ and $\mathcal{P}, \pi_A(1) \models \Phi_2$ by hypothesis. Thus, π_p is a topological path that witnesses $\mathcal{P}, p \models \eta(\Phi_1, \Phi_2)$. The proof of the converse is similar, using instead function $\pi_A : [0,1] \to |K|$ defined as follows, for arbitrary $v \in (0,1)$:

$$\pi_A(r) = \begin{cases} \frac{r}{v}p + \frac{v-r}{v}A, & \text{if } r \in [0,v), \\[2mm] \pi_p(\frac{r-v}{1-v}), & \text{if } r \in [v,1]. \end{cases}$$

*

Remark 2. The example of Fig. 3a is useful also for showing that the classical topological interpretation of the modal logic operator $\Diamond$ cannot be expressed in SLCS_η. We recall that:

$$\mathcal{P}, x \models \Diamond \Phi \Leftrightarrow x \in \mathcal{C}_T(\{x' \in |K| \,|\, \mathcal{P}, x' \models \Phi\}).$$

Clearly, in the model of the figure, we have $\mathcal{P}, A \models \Diamond\mathbf{red}$ while $\mathcal{P}, x \models \Diamond\mathbf{red}$ for no $x \in \widetilde{ABC}$. On the other hand, $A \equiv_\eta x$ holds for all $x \in \widetilde{ABC}$, as we have just seen in Remark 1. So, if $\Diamond$ were expressible in SLCS_η, then A and x should have agreed on $\Diamond\mathbf{red}$ for each $x \in \widetilde{ABC}$. Note that $\Diamond$ *can* be expressed in SLCS_γ as $\gamma(\Phi, \mathbf{true})$, see [5].

Below we re-interpret SLCS_η on finite poset models instead of polyhedral models. The only difference from Definition 1 is, of course, the fact that η-formulas are defined for $\pm$-paths instead of topological ones.

Definition 4 (SLCS_η on finite poset models). *The satisfaction relation of SLCS_η with respect to a given finite poset model $\mathcal{F} = (W, \preceq, \mathcal{V})$, SLCS_η formula Φ, and element $w \in W$ is defined recursively on the structure of Φ:*

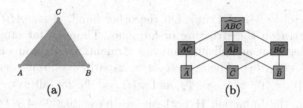

Fig. 3. A polyhedral model (3a) and its cell poset model (3b)

$$
\begin{aligned}
\mathcal{F}, w &\models p &&\Leftrightarrow w \in \mathcal{V}(p);\\
\mathcal{F}, w &\models \neg\Phi &&\Leftrightarrow \mathcal{F}, w \not\models \Phi;\\
\mathcal{F}, w &\models \Phi_1 \wedge \Phi_2 &&\Leftrightarrow \mathcal{F}, w \models \Phi_1 \text{ and } \mathcal{F}, w \models \Phi_2;\\
\mathcal{F}, w &\models \eta(\Phi_1, \Phi_2) &&\Leftrightarrow a \pm\text{-}path\ \pi : [0;\ell] \to W \text{ exists such that } \pi(0) = w,\\
&&&\quad \mathcal{F}, \pi(\ell) \models \Phi_2 \text{ and } \mathcal{F}, \pi(i) \models \Phi_1 \text{ for all } i \in [0;\ell).
\end{aligned}
$$

Definition 5 (Logical Equivalence). *Given a finite poset model* $\mathcal{F} = (W, \preceq, \mathcal{V})$ *and elements* $w_1, w_2 \in W$ *we say that* w_1 *and* w_2 *are logically equivalent with respect to* SLCS$_\eta$, *written* $w_1 \equiv_\eta^{\mathcal{F}} w_2$, *iff, for all* SLCS$_\eta$ *formulas* Φ, *the following holds:* $\mathcal{F}, w_1 \models \Phi$ *if and only if* $\mathcal{F}, w_2 \models \Phi$.

Again, in the following, we will refrain from indicating the model $\mathcal{F}$ explicitly in $\equiv_\eta^{\mathcal{F}}$ when it is clear from the context. It is useful to define a "characteristic" SLCS$_\eta$ formula $\chi(w)$ that is satisfied by all and only those w' with $w' \equiv_\eta w$.

Definition 6. *Given a finite poset model* $(W, \preceq, \mathcal{V})$, $w_1, w_2 \in W$, *define* SLCS$_\eta$ *formula* δ_{w_1,w_2} *as follows: if* $w_1 \equiv_\eta w_2$, *then set* $\delta_{w_1,w_2} = \texttt{true}$, *otherwise pick some* SLCS$_\eta$ *formula* ψ *such that* $\mathcal{F}, w_1 \models \psi$ *and* $\mathcal{F}, w_2 \models \neg\psi$, *and set* $\delta_{w_1,w_2} = \psi$. *For* $w \in W$ *define* $\chi(w) = \bigwedge_{w' \in W} \delta_{w,w'}$.

Proposition 2. *Given a finite poset model* $(W, \preceq, \mathcal{V})$, *for* $w_1, w_2 \in W$, *it holds that* $\mathcal{F}, w_2 \models \chi(w_1)$ *if and only if* $w_1 \equiv_\eta w_2$.

The following lemma is the poset model counterpart of Lemma 2:

Lemma 3. *Let* $\mathcal{F} = (W, \preceq, \mathcal{V})$ *be a finite poset model,* $w \in W$ *and* Φ *a* SLCS$_\eta$ *formula. Then* $\mathcal{F}, w \models \Phi$ *iff* $\mathcal{F}, w \models \mathcal{E}(\Phi)$.

Thus we get, as for the interpretation on polyhedral models, that SLCS$_\eta$ on finite poset models is weaker than SLCS$_\gamma$:

Proposition 3. *Let* $\mathcal{F} = (W, \preceq, \mathcal{V})$ *be a finite poset model. For all* $w_1, w_2 \in W$ *the following holds: if* $w_1 \equiv_\gamma w_2$ *then* $w_1 \equiv_\eta w_2$.

Remark 3. As expected, the converse of Proposition 3 does not hold, as shown by the poset model $\mathcal{F}$ of Fig. 3b. Clearly, $\widetilde{A} \not\equiv_\gamma \widetilde{ABC}$. In fact $\mathcal{F}, \widetilde{A} \models \gamma(\mathbf{red}, \mathbf{true})$

whereas $\mathcal{F}, \widetilde{ABC} \not\models \gamma(\mathbf{red}, \mathbf{true})$. On the other hand, $\widetilde{A} \equiv_\eta \widetilde{ABC}$. We prove this by induction on the structure of formulas. The case for atomic proposition letters, negation and disjunction are straightforward and omitted. Suppose $\mathcal{F}, \widetilde{A} \models \eta(\Phi_1, \Phi_2)$. Then, there is a $\pm$-path π of some length $\ell \geq 2$ such that $\pi(0) = \widetilde{A}$, $\pi(\ell) \models \Phi_2$ and $\pi(i) \models \Phi_1$ for all $i \in [0; \ell)$. Since $\mathcal{F}, \widetilde{A} \models \Phi_1$, by the Induction Hypothesis, we have that $\mathcal{F}, \widetilde{ABC} \models \Phi_1$. Consider then path $\pi' = (\widetilde{ABC}, \widetilde{ABC}, \widetilde{A}) \cdot \pi$. Path π' is a $\pm$-path and it witnesses $\mathcal{F}, \widetilde{ABC} \models \eta(\Phi_1, \Phi_2)$. Suppose now $\mathcal{F}, \widetilde{ABC} \models \eta(\Phi_1, \Phi_2)$ and let π be a $\pm$-path witnessing it. Then, path $(\widetilde{A}, \widetilde{ABC}, \widetilde{ABC}) \cdot \pi$ is a $\pm$-path witnessing $\mathcal{F}, \widetilde{A} \models \eta(\Phi_1, \Phi_2)$. ✲

Remark 4. As for the case of the continuous interpretation of SLCS_η, example of Fig. 3b is useful also for showing that the classical modal logic operator $\Diamond$ cannot be expressed in SLCS_η. We recall that:

$$\mathcal{F}, w \models \Diamond \Phi \Leftrightarrow w' \in W \text{ exists such that } w \preceq w' \text{ and } \mathcal{F}, w' \models \Phi.$$

Clearly, in the model of the figure, we have $\mathcal{F}, \widetilde{A} \models \Diamond\mathbf{red}$ while $\mathcal{F}, \widetilde{ABC} \not\models \Diamond\mathbf{red}$. On the other hand $\widetilde{A} \equiv_\eta \widetilde{ABC}$ holds, as we have just seen in Remark 3. So, if $\Diamond$ were expressible in SLCS_η, then $\widetilde{A}$ and $\widetilde{ABC}$ should have agreed on $\Diamond\mathbf{red}$. Note that $\Diamond$ *can* be expressed in SLCS_γ as $\gamma(\Phi, \mathbf{true})$, see [5]. ✲

The following result is useful for setting a bridge between the continuous and the discrete interpretation of SLCS_η.

Lemma 4. *Given a polyhedral model* $\mathcal{P} = (|K|, V)$, *for all* $x \in |K|$ *and formulas* Φ *of* SLCS_η *the following holds:* $\mathcal{P}, x \models \Phi$ *iff* $\mathbb{F}(\mathcal{P}), \mathbb{F}(x) \models \mathcal{E}(\Phi)$.

As a direct consequence of Lemma 3 and Lemma 4 we get the bridge between the continuous and the discrete interpretation of SLCS_η.

Theorem 1. *Given a polyhedral model* $\mathcal{P} = (|K|, V)$, *for all* $x \in |K|$ *and formulas* Φ *of* SLCS_η *it holds that:* $\mathcal{P}, x \models \Phi$ *iff* $\mathbb{F}(\mathcal{P}), \mathbb{F}(x) \models \Phi$.

This theorem allows one to go back and forth between the polyhedral model and the corresponding poset model without loosing anything expressible in SLCS_η.

4   Weak Simplicial Bisimilarity

In this section, we introduce weak versions of simplicial bisimilarity and $\pm$-bisimilarity and we show that they coincide with logical equivalence induced by SLCS_η in polyhedral and poset models, respectively.

Definition 7 (Weak Simplicial Bisimulation). *Given a polyhedral model* $\mathcal{P} = (|K|, V)$, *a symmetric relation* $B \subseteq |K| \times |K|$ *is a* weak simplicial bisimulation *if, for all* $x_1, x_2 \in |K|$, *whenever* $B(x_1, x_2)$, *it holds that:*

1. $V^{-1}(\{x_1\}) = V^{-1}(\{x_2\})$;
2. for each topological path π_1 from x_1, there is topological path π_2 from x_2 such that $B(\pi_1(1), \pi_2(1))$ and for all $r_2 \in [0,1)$ there is $r_1 \in [0,1)$ such that $B(\pi_1(r_1), \pi_2(r_2))$.

Two points $x_1, x_2 \in |K|$ are weakly simplicial bisimilar, written $x_1 \approx_\triangle^P x_2$, if there is a weak simplicial bisimulation B such that $B(x_1, x_2)$.

For example, the open segments AB, BC, and AC in Fig. 3a are mutually weakly simplicial bisimilar and every point in set $\widehat{ABC} \cup \tilde{A} \cup \tilde{B} \cup \tilde{C}$ is weakly simplicial bisimilar to every other point in the same set.

Definition 8 (Weak $\pm$-bisimulation). *Given a finite poset model $\mathcal{F} = (W, \preceq, \mathcal{V})$, a symmetric binary relation $B \subseteq W \times W$ is a weak $\pm$-bisimulation if, for all $w_1, w_2 \in W$, whenever $B(w_1, w_2)$, it holds that:*

1. $\mathcal{V}^{-1}(\{w_1\}) = \mathcal{V}^{-1}(\{w_2\})$;
2. *for each $u_1, d_1 \in W$ such that $w_1 \preceq^\pm u_1 \succeq d_1$ there is a $\pm$-path $\pi_2 : [0; \ell_2] \rightarrow W$ from w_2 such that $B(d_1, \pi_2(\ell_2))$ and, for all $j \in [0; \ell_2)$, the following holds: $B(w_1, \pi_2(j))$ or $B(u_1, \pi_2(j))$.*

We say that w_1 is weakly $\pm$-bisimilar to w_2, written $w_1 \approx_\pm^\mathcal{F} w_2$ if there is a weak $\pm$-bisimulation B such that $B(w_1, w_2)$. $\bullet$

For example, all red cells in the Hasse diagram of Fig. 3b are weakly $\pm$-bisimilar and all blue cells are weakly $\pm$-bisimilar.

The following lemma shows that, in a polyhedral model $\mathcal{P}$, weak simplicial bisimilarity $\approx_\triangle^P$ (Definition 7) is stronger than $\equiv_\eta$ – logical equivalence w.r.t. SLCS$_\eta$:

Lemma 5. *Given a polyhedral model $\mathcal{P} = (|K|, V)$, for all $x_1, x_2 \in |K|$, the following holds: if $x_1 \approx_\triangle^P x_2$ then $x_1 \equiv_\eta x_2$.*

Proof. By induction on the structure of the formulas. We consider only the case $\eta(\Phi_1, \Phi_2)$. Suppose $x_1 \approx_\triangle x_2$ and $\mathcal{P}, x_1 \models \eta(\Phi_1, \Phi_2)$. Then there is a topological path π_1 from x_1 such that $\mathcal{P}, \pi_1(1) \models \Phi_2$ and $\mathcal{P}, \pi_1(r_1) \models \Phi_1$ for all $r_1 \in [0,1)$. Since $x_1 \approx_\triangle x_2$, then there is a topological path π_2 from x_2 such that $\pi_1(1) \approx_\triangle \pi_2(1)$ and for each $r_2 \in [0,1)$ there is $r_1' \in [0,1)$ such that $\pi_1(r_1') \approx_\triangle \pi_2(r_2)$. By the Induction Hypothesis, we get $\mathcal{P}, \pi_2(1) \models \Phi_2$ and for each $r_2 \in [0,1)$ $\mathcal{P}, \pi_2(r_2) \models \Phi_1$. Thus $\mathcal{P}, x_2 \models \eta(\Phi_1, \Phi_2)$. $\square$

Furthermore, logical equivalence induced by SLCS$_\eta$ is stronger than weak simplicial-bisimilarity, as implied by Lemma 8 below, which uses the following two auxiliary lemmas:

Lemma 6. *Given a finite poset model $\mathcal{F} = (W, \preceq, \mathcal{V})$ and weak $\pm$-bisimulation $B \subseteq W \times W$, for all w_1, w_2 such that $B(w_1, w_2)$, the following holds: for each $\downarrow$-path $\pi_1 : [0; k_1] \rightarrow W$ from w_1 there is a $\downarrow$-path $\pi_2 : [0; k_2] \rightarrow W$ from w_2 such that $B(\pi_1(k_1), \pi_2(k_2))$ and for each $j \in [0; k_2)$ there is $i \in [0; k_1)$ such that $B(\pi_1(i), \pi_2(j))$.*

Lemma 7. *Given a polyhedral model* $\mathcal{P} = (|K|, V)$, *and associated cell poset model* $\mathbb{F}(\mathcal{P}) = (W, \preceq, \mathcal{V})$, *for any* $\downarrow$-*path* $\pi : [0; \ell] \to W$, *there is a topological path* $\pi' : [0, 1] \to |K|$ *such that: (i)* $\mathbb{F}(\pi'(0)) = \pi(0)$, *(ii)* $\mathbb{F}(\pi'(1)) = \pi(\ell)$, *and (iii) for all* $r \in (0, 1)$ *there is* $i < \ell$ *such that* $\mathbb{F}(\pi'(r)) = \pi(i)$.

Lemma 8. *In a given polyhedral model* $(|K|, V)$, $\equiv_\eta$ *is a weak simplicial bisimulation.*

Proof. Let $x_1, x_2 \in |K|$ such that $x_1 \equiv_\eta x_2$. The first condition of Definition 7 is clearly satisfied since $x_1 \equiv_\eta x_2$. Suppose π_1 is a topological path from x_1. $\mathbb{F}(\pi_1([0, 1]))$ is a connected subposet of $\widetilde{K}$. Thus, due to continuity of $\mathbb{F} \circ \pi_1$, a $\downarrow$-path $\hat{\pi}_1 : [0; k_1] \to \widetilde{K}$ from $\mathbb{F}(\pi_1(0))$ to $\mathbb{F}(\pi_1(1))$ exists such that for all $i \in [0; k_1]$ there is $r_1 \in [0, 1)$ with $\hat{\pi}_1(i) = \mathbb{F}(\pi_1(r_1))$. We also know that $\mathbb{F}(x_1) \equiv_\eta \mathbb{F}(x_2)$, as a consequence of Theorem 1, since $x_1 \equiv_\eta x_2$. In addition, due to Lemma 10 below, we also know that $\mathbb{F}(x_1) \approx_\pm \mathbb{F}(x_2)$. By Lemma 6, we get that there is a $\downarrow$-path $\hat{\pi}_2 : [0; k_2] \to \widetilde{K}$ such that $\hat{\pi}_1(k_1) \equiv_\eta \hat{\pi}_2(k_2)$ and for each $j \in [0; k_2]$ there is $i \in [0; k_1]$ such that $\hat{\pi}_1(i) \equiv_\eta \hat{\pi}_2(j)$. By Lemma 7, it follows that there is topological path π_2 from x_2 satisfying the three conditions of the lemma and, again by Theorem 1, we have that $\pi_2(1) \equiv_\eta \pi_1(1)$. In addition, for any $r_2 \in [0, 1)$, since $\mathbb{F}(\pi_2(r_2)) = \hat{\pi}_2(j)$ for $j \in [0; k_2]$ (condition (ii) of Lemma 7) there is $i \in [0; k_1]$ such that $\hat{\pi}_1(i) \equiv_\eta \hat{\pi}_2(j)$. Finally, by construction, there is $r_1 \in [0, 1)$ such that $\mathbb{F}(\pi_1(r_1)) = \hat{\pi}_1(i)$. By Theorem 1, we finally get $\pi_1(r_1) \equiv_\eta \pi_2(r_2)$. $\square$

On the basis of Lemma 5 and Lemma 8, we have that the largest weak simplicial bisimulation exists, it is a weak simplicial bisimilarity, it is an equivalence relation, and it coincides with logical equivalence in the polyhedral model induced by SLCS_η, thus establishing the HMP for $\approx_\triangle^{\mathcal{P}}$ w.r.t. SLCS_η:

Theorem 2. *Given a polyhedral model* $\mathcal{P} = (|K|, V), x_1, x_2 \in |K|$, *the following holds:* $x_1 \equiv_\eta^{\mathcal{P}} x_2$ *iff* $x_1 \approx_\triangle^{\mathcal{P}} w_2$.

Similar results can be obtained for poset models. The following lemma shows that, in every finite poset model $\mathcal{F}$, weak $\pm$-bisimilarity (Definition 8) is stronger than logical equivalence with respect to SLCS_η, i.e. $\approx_\pm^{\mathcal{F}} \subseteq \equiv_\eta^{\mathcal{F}}$:

Lemma 9. *Given a finite poset model* $\mathcal{F} = (W, \preceq, \mathcal{V})$, *for all* $w_1, w_2 \in W$, *if* $w_1 \approx_\pm^{\mathcal{F}} w_2$ *then* $w_1 \equiv_\eta^{\mathcal{F}} w_2$.

Proof. By induction on formulas. We consider only the case $\eta(\Phi_1, \Phi_2)$. Suppose $w_1 \approx_\pm w_2$ and $\mathcal{F}, w_1 \models \eta(\Phi_1, \Phi_2)$. Then, there is (a $\pm$-path and so) a $\downarrow$-path π_1 from w_1 of some length k_1 such that $\mathcal{F}, \pi_1(k_1) \models \Phi_2$ and for all $i \in [0; k_1]$ $\mathcal{F}, \pi_1(i) \models \Phi_1$ holds. By Lemma 6, we know that a $\downarrow$-path π_2 from w_2 exists of some length k_2 such that $\pi_1(k_1) \approx_\pm \pi_2(k_2)$ and for all $j \in [0; k_2]$ there is $i \in [0; k_1]$ such that $\pi_1(i) \approx_\pm \pi_2(j)$. By the Induction Hypothesis, we then get that $\mathcal{F}, \pi_2(k_2) \models \Phi_2$ and for all $j \in [0; k_2]$ we have $\mathcal{F}, \pi_2(j) \models \Phi_1$. This implies that $\mathcal{F}, w_2 \models \eta(\Phi_1, \Phi_2)$.

Furthermore, logical equivalence induced by SLCS_η is stronger than weak $\pm$-bisimilarity, i.e. $\equiv_\eta^{\mathcal{F}} \subseteq \approx_\pm^{\mathcal{F}}$, as implied by the following:

Lemma 10. *In a finite poset model $\mathcal{F} = (W, \preceq, \mathcal{V})$, $\equiv_\eta^{\mathcal{F}}$ is a weak $\pm$-bisimulation.*

Proof. If $w_1 \equiv_\eta w_2$, then the first requirement of Definition 8 is trivially satisfied. We prove that $\equiv_\eta$ satisfies the second requirement of Definition 8. Suppose $w_1 \equiv_\eta w_2$ and let u_1, d_1 as in the above mentioned requirement. This implies that $\mathcal{F}, w_1 \models \eta(\chi(w_1) \vee \chi(u_1), \chi(d_1))$, where, we recall, $\chi(w)$ is the 'characteristic formula' for w as in Definition 6. Since $w_1 \equiv_\eta w_2$, we have that also $\mathcal{F}, w_2 \models \eta(\chi(w_1) \vee \chi(u_1), \chi(d_1))$ holds. This in turn means that a $\downarrow$-path π_2 of some length k_2 from w_2 exists such that $\mathcal{F}, \pi_2(k_2) \models \chi(d_1)$ and for all $j \in [0; k_2)$ we have $\mathcal{F}, \pi_2(j) \models \chi(w_1) \vee \chi(u_1)$, i.e. $\mathcal{F}, \pi_2(j) \models \chi(w_1)$ or $\mathcal{F}, \pi_2(j) \models \chi(u_1)$. Consequently, by Proposition 2, we have: $\pi_2(k_2) \equiv_\eta d_1$ and, for all $j \in [0; k_2)$, $\pi_2(j) \equiv_\eta w_1$ or $\pi_2(j) \equiv_\eta u_1$, so that the second condition of the definition is fulfilled.

On the basis of Lemma 9 and Lemma 10, we have that the largest weak $\pm$-bisimulation exists, it is a weak $\pm$-bisimilarity, it is an equivalence relation, and it coincides with logical equivalence in the finite poset induced by SLCS$_\eta$:

Theorem 3. *For every finite poset model $(W, \preceq, \mathcal{V})$, $w_1, w_2 \in W$, the following holds: $w_1 \equiv_\eta^{\mathcal{F}} w_2$ iff $w_1 \approx_{\pm}^{\mathcal{F}} w_2$.*

By this we have established the HMP for $\approx_{\pm}$ w.r.t. SLCS$_\eta$.

Finally, recalling that, by Theorem 1, given polyhedral model $\mathcal{P} = (|K|, V)$ for all $x \in |K|$ and SLCS$_\eta$ formula Φ, we have that $\mathcal{P}, x \models \Phi$ if and only if $\mathbb{F}(\mathcal{P}), \mathbb{F}(x) \models \Phi$, we get the following final result:

Corollary 1. *For all polyhedral models $\mathcal{P} = (|K|, V)$, $x_1, x_2 \in |K|$:*

$$x_1 \approx_{\triangle}^{\mathcal{P}} x_2 \text{ iff } x_1 \equiv_\eta^{\mathcal{P}} x_2 \text{ iff } \mathbb{F}(x_1) \equiv_\eta^{\mathbb{F}(\mathcal{P})} \mathbb{F}(x_2) \text{ iff } \mathbb{F}(x_1) \approx_{\pm}^{\mathbb{F}(\mathcal{P})} \mathbb{F}(x_2).$$

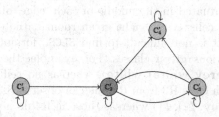

Fig. 4. The minimal model, modulo weak $\pm$-bisimilarity, of the model of Fig. 1.

Saying that SLCS$_\eta$-equivalence in a polyhedral model is the same as weak simplicial bisimilarity, which maps by $\mathbb{F}$ to the weak $\pm$-bisimilarity in the corresponding poset model, where the latter coincides with the SLCS$_\eta$-equivalence.

Figure 4 shows the minimal model $\min(\mathbb{F}(\mathcal{P}))$, modulo $\approx_{\pm}$, of $\mathbb{F}(\mathcal{P})$ (see Fig. 1c). We have the following equivalence classes: $\mathbb{C}'_1 = \{\widetilde{A}\}$, $\mathbb{C}'_2 = \{\widetilde{B}, \widetilde{C}, \widetilde{AB},$ $\widetilde{AC}, \widetilde{BC}, \widetilde{BD}, \widetilde{CD}, \widetilde{ABC}, \widetilde{BCD}\}$, $\mathbb{C}'_3 = \{\widetilde{D}, \widetilde{E}, \widetilde{F}, \widetilde{CE}, \widetilde{DE}, \widetilde{DF}, \widetilde{EF}, \widetilde{DEF}\}$ and, finally, $\mathbb{C}'_4 = \{\widehat{CDE}\}$. Note that the minimal model is not a poset model, but it is a reflexive Kripke model.[4]

5   A Larger Example

As a proof-of-concept and feasibility we show a larger example of a 3D polyhedral structure composed of one white "room" and 26 green "rooms" connected by grey "corridors" as shown in Fig. 5a. In turn, each room is composed of 33 vertices, 122 edges, 150 triangles and 60 tetrahedra, i.e. it is composed of a total of 365 cells. Each corridor is composed of 8 edges, 12 triangles and 5 tetrahedra, i.e. it consists of 25 cells. The corridors are connected to rooms via the four points of the side of a room. In total, the structure consists of 11,205 cells. We have chosen a large, but symmetric structure on purpose. This makes it easy to interpret the various equivalence classes present in the minimal Kripke model of this structure shown in Fig. 5b. Observe that, for this example, the minimal model is also a poset model and, in particular, a cell poset model representing a polyhedron, as shown in Fig. 5c. The latter can be seen as a minimised version of the original polyhedral structure. Note also the considerable reduction that was obtained: from 11,205 cells to just 7 in the minimal model.

In Fig. 5b we have indicated the various equivalence classes with a letter. Those indicated with a "C" correspond to classes of (cells of) corridors, those with an "R" correspond to classes of (cells of) rooms. For reasons of space and clarity, in the following we will not list all the individual cells that are part of a certain class, but instead we will indicate those cells by speaking about certain rooms and corridors, intending the cells that they are composed of.

There is one white class containing all white cells of the white room. Furthermore, there are three green classes corresponding to three types of green rooms, and three grey classes corresponding to three kinds of corridors. The green class R2 is composed of the (cells in) the six green rooms situated in the middle of each side of the cube structure. Those in R3 are the cells in the twelve green rooms situated in the middle of each 'edge' of the cube structure. Those in R4 are the cells in the eight green rooms situated at the corners of the cube structure. It is not difficult to find SLCS_η formulas that distinguish, for instance, the various green classes. For example, the cells in R2 satisfy $\Phi_1 = \eta(\mathbf{green} \vee \eta(\mathbf{grey}, \mathbf{white}), \mathbf{white})$, whereas no cell in R3 or R4 satisfies Φ_1. To distinguish class R3 from R4 one can observe that cells in R3 satisfy $\Phi_2 = \eta(\mathbf{green} \vee \eta(\mathbf{grey}, \Phi_1), \Phi_1)$ whereas those in R4 do not satisfy Φ_2.

In this symmetric case of this synthesised example, it was rather straightforward to find the various equivalence classes. In the general case it is much harder and one would need a suitable minimisation algorithm for SLCS_η. We are currently working on an effective minimisation procedure based on encoding

---

[4] It is worth noting that for model-checking purposes we can safely interpret SLCS_η over (reflexive) Kripke models. The satisfaction relation is defined as in Definition 4 where $\mathcal{F}$ is a Kripke model instead of a poset model (recall that $\pm$-paths are defined on Kripke frames).

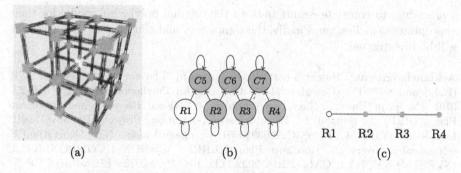

| (a) | (b) | (c) |

Fig. 5. (5a) A simplicial complex of a 3D structure composed of rooms and corridors. (5b) Its minimal Kripke structure. (5c) Its minimal polyhedron.

the cell poset model into a suitable LTS, exploiting behavioural equivalences for LTSs — strong bisimilarity and branching bisimulation equivalence — following an approach similar to that followed in [12] for finite closure spaces. The first results are promising. In fact, the large structure shown in this example can be handled that way and gives results as presented. Details and proofs of correctness of this approach and its potential efficiency gain will be the topic of future work, also for reasons of space limitations.

6   Conclusions

In [5] simplicial bisimilarity was proposed for polyhedral models — i.e. models of continuous space — while ±-bisimilarity, the corresponding equivalence for cell-poset models — discrete representations of polyhedral models — was introduced in [9]. In order to support large model reductions, in this paper the novel notions of weak simplicial bisimilarity and weak ±-bisimilarity have been proposed, and the correspondence between the two has been studied. We have proposed SLCS$_\eta$, a weaker version of the Spatial Logic for Closure Spaces on polyhedral models, and we have shown that simplicial bisimilarity enjoys the Hennessy-Milner property (Theorem 2). We have also proven that the property holds for ±-bisimilarity on poset models and the interpretation of SLCS$_\eta$ on such models (Theorem 3). SLCS$_\eta$ can be used in the geometric spatial model checker `PolyLogicA` for checking spatial reachability properties of polyhedral models. Model checking results can be visualised by projecting them onto the original polyhedral structure in a colour. The results presented in this paper also have a practical value for the domain of visual computing where polyhedral models can be found in the form of surface meshes or tetrahedral volume meshes that are often composed of a huge number of cells.

In future work, in line with our earlier work, we aim to develop an automatic, provably correct minimisation procedure so that model checking could potentially be performed on a much smaller model. We also intend to develop a procedure to translate results back to the original polyhedral model for their appropriate visualisation. Finally, the complexity and efficiency of such methods will be investigated.

Acknowledgments. Research partially supported by Bilateral project between CNR (Italy) and SRNSFG (Georgia) "Model Checking for Polyhedral Logic" (#CNR-22-010); European Union - Next GenerationEU - National Recovery and Resilience Plan (NRRP), Investment 1.5 Ecosystems of Innovation, Project "Tuscany Health Ecosystem" (THE), CUP: B83C22003930001; European Union - Next-GenerationEU - National Recovery and Resilience Plan (NRRP) - MISSION 4 COMPONENT 2, INVESTMENT N. 1.1, CALL PRIN 2022 D.D. 104 02-02-2022 - (Stendhal) CUP N. B53D23012850006; MUR project PRIN 2020TL3X8X "T-LADIES"; CNR project "Formal Methods in Software Engineering 2.0", CUP B53C24000720005; Shota Rustaveli National Science Foundation of Georgia grant #FR-22-6700.

Disclosure of Interests. The authors have no competing interests to declare that are relevant to the content of this article.

References

1. Banci Buonamici, F., Belmonte, G., Ciancia, V., Latella, D., Massink, M.: Spatial logics and model checking for medical imaging. Int. J. Softw. Tools Technol. Transf. **22**(2), 195–217 (2020). https://doi.org/10.1007/s10009-019-00511-9
2. Belmonte, G., Broccia, G., Ciancia, V., Latella, D., Massink, M.: Feasibility of spatial model checking for nevus segmentation. In: Bliudze, S., Gnesi, S., Plat, N., Semini, L. (eds.) 9th IEEE/ACM International Conference on Formal Methods in Software Engineering, FormaliSE@ICSE 2021, Madrid, Spain, 17-21 May 2021, pp. 1–12. IEEE (2021). https://doi.org/10.1109/FormaliSE52586.2021.00007
3. Belmonte, G., Ciancia, V., Latella, D., Massink, M.: VoxLogicA: a spatial model checker for declarative image analysis. In: Vojnar, T., Zhang, L. (eds.) TACAS 2019. LNCS, vol. 11427, pp. 281–298. Springer, Cham (2019). https://doi.org/10.1007/978-3-030-17462-0_16
4. van Benthem, J., Bezhanishvili, G.: Modal logics of space. In: Aiello, M., Pratt-Hartmann, I., Benthem, J.V. (eds.) Handbook of Spatial Logics, pp. 217–298. Springer, Cham (2007). https://doi.org/10.1007/978-1-4020-5587-4_5
5. Bezhanishvili, N., Ciancia, V., Gabelaia, D., Grilletti, G., Latella, D., Massink, M.: Geometric model checking of continuous space. Log. Methods Comput. Sci. **18**(4), 7:1–7:38 (2022). https://lmcs.episciences.org/10348, https://doi.org/10.46298/LMCS-18(4:7)2022. 22 Nov 2022. ISSN: 1860-5974
6. Bezhanishvili, N., et al.: Weak simplicial bisimilarity for polyhedral models and SLCS$_\eta$ — extended version. CoRR **abs/2404.06131** (2024). https://doi.org/10.48550/arXiv.2404.06131
7. Bezhanishvili, N., Marra, V., McNeill, D., Pedrini, A.: Tarski's theorem on intuitionistic logic, for polyhedra. Ann. Pure Appl. Logic **169**(5), 373–391 (2018). https://doi.org/10.1016/j.apal.2017.12.005,https://www.sciencedirect.com/science/article/pii/S016800721730146X

8. Ciancia, V., Latella, D., Massink, M., de Vink, E.P.: Back-and-forth in space: on logics and bisimilarity in closure spaces. In: Jansen, N., Stoelinga, M., van den Bos, P. (eds.) A Journey From Process Algebra via Timed Automata to Model Learning - A Festschrift Dedicated to Frits Vaandrager on the Occasion of His 60th Birthday. LNCS, vol. 13560, pp. 98–115. Springer, Cham (2022). https://doi.org/10.1007/978-3-031-15629-8_6

9. Ciancia, V., Gabelaia, D., Latella, D., Massink, M., de Vink, E.P.: On bisimilarity for polyhedral models and SLCS. In: Huisman, M., Ravara, A. (eds.) Formal Techniques for Distributed Objects, Components, and Systems - 43rd IFIP WG 6.1 International Conference, FORTE 2023, Held as Part of the 18th International Federated Conference on Distributed Computing Techniques, DisCoTec 2023, Lisbon, Portugal, 19-23 June 2023, Proceedings. LNCS, vol. 13910, pp. 132–151. Springer, Cham (2023). https://doi.org/10.1007/978-3-031-35355-0_9

10. Ciancia, V., Gilmore, S., Grilletti, G., Latella, D., Loreti, M., Massink, M.: Spatio-temporal model checking of vehicular movement in public transport systems. Int. J. Softw. Tools Technol. Transf. **20**(3), 289–311 (2018). https://doi.org/10.1007/s10009-018-0483-8

11. Ciancia, V., Grilletti, G., Latella, D., Loreti, M., Massink, M.: An experimental spatio-temporal model checker. In: Bianculli, D., Calinescu, R., Rumpe, B. (eds.) Software Engineering and Formal Methods - SEFM 2015 Collocated Workshops: ATSE, HOFM, MoKMaSD, and VERY*SCART, York, UK, 7–8 September 2015, Revised Selected Papers. LNCS, vol. 9509, pp. 297–311. Springer, Cham (2015). https://doi.org/10.1007/978-3-662-49224-6_24

12. Ciancia, V., Groote, J., Latella, D., Massink, M., de Vink, E.: Minimisation of spatial models using branching bisimilarity. In: Chechik, M., Katoen, J.P., Leucker, M. (eds.) 25th International Symposium, FM 2023, Lübeck, 6–10 March 2023, Proceedings. LNCS, vol. 14000, pp. 263–281. Springer, Cham (2023). https://doi.org/10.1007/978-3-031-27481-7_16

13. Ciancia, V., Latella, D., Loreti, M., Massink, M.: Specifying and verifying properties of space. In: Díaz, J., Lanese, I., Sangiorgi, D. (eds.) Theoretical Computer Science - 8th IFIP TC 1/WG 2.2 International Conference, TCS 2014, Rome, Italy, 1–3 September 2014. Proceedings. LNCS, vol. 8705, pp. 222–235. Springer, Cham (2014). https://doi.org/10.1007/978-3-662-44602-7_18

14. Ciancia, V., Latella, D., Loreti, M., Massink, M.: Model checking spatial logics for closure spaces. Log. Methods Comput. Sci. **12**(4) (2016). https://doi.org/10.2168/LMCS-12(4:2)2016

15. Ciancia, V., Latella, D., Massink, M.: Embedding RCC8D in the collective spatial logic CSLCS. In: Boreale, M., Corradini, F., Loreti, M., Pugliese, R. (eds.) Models, Languages, and Tools for Concurrent and Distributed Programming - Essays Dedicated to Rocco De Nicola on the Occasion of His 65th Birthday. LNCS, vol. 11665, pp. 260–277. Springer, Cham (2019). https://doi.org/10.1007/978-3-030-21485-2_15

16. Ciancia, V., Latella, D., Massink, M., Paškauskas, R.: Exploring spatio-temporal properties of bike-sharing systems. In: 2015 IEEE International Conference on Self-Adaptive and Self-Organizing Systems Workshops, SASO Workshops 2015, Cambridge, MA, USA, 21–25 September 2015, pp. 74–79. IEEE Computer Society (2015). https://doi.org/10.1109/SASOW.2015.17

17. Ciancia, V., Latella, D., Massink, M., Paškauskas, R., Vandin, A.: A tool-chain for statistical spatio-temporal model checking of bike sharing systems. In: Margaria, T., Steffen, B. (eds.) Leveraging Applications of Formal Methods, Verification and

Validation: Foundational Techniques - 7th International Symposium, ISoLA 2016, Imperial, Corfu, Greece, 10–14 October 2016, Proceedings, Part I, LNCS, vol. 9952, pp. 657–673 (2016), https://doi.org/10.1007/978-3-319-47166-2_46

18. Ciancia, V., Latella, D., Massink, M., de Vink, E.P.: On bisimilarity for quasi-discrete closure spaces (2023). https://arxiv.org/abs/2301.11634

19. Groote, J.F., Jansen, D.N., Keiren, J.J.A., Wijs, A.: An $O(m\log n)$ algorithm for computing stuttering equivalence and branching bisimulation. ACM Trans. Comput. Log. **18**(2), 13:1–13:34 (2017). https://doi.org/10.1145/3060140

20. Levine, J.A., Paulsen, R.R., Zhang, Y.: Mesh processing in medical-image analysis - a tutorial. IEEE Comput. Graphics Appl. **32**(5), 22–28 (2012). https://doi.org/10.1109/MCG.2012.91

21. Loreti, M., Quadrini, M.: A spatial logic for simplicial models. Log. Methods Comput. Sci. **19**(3) (2023). https://doi.org/10.46298/LMCS-19(3:8)2023

22. McKinsey, J., Tarski, A.: The algebra of topology. Ann. Math. **45**, 141–191 (1944). https://doi.org/10.2307/1969080

23. Nenzi, L., Bortolussi, L., Ciancia, V., Loreti, M., Massink, M.: Qualitative and quantitative monitoring of spatio-temporal properties with SSTL. Log. Methods Comput. Sci. **14**(4) (2018). https://doi.org/10.23638/LMCS-14(4:2)2018

Noninterference Analysis of Reversible Probabilistic Systems

Andrea Esposito[✉], Alessandro Aldini, and Marco Bernardo

Dipartimento di Scienze Pure e Applicate, Università di Urbino, Urbino, Italy
a.esposito30@campus.uniurb.it

Abstract. Noninterference theory supports the analysis of secure computations in multi-level security systems. In the nondeterministic setting, the approach to noninterefence based on weak bisimilarity has turned out to be inadequate for reversible systems. This drawback can be overcome by employing a more expressive semantics, which has been recently proven to be branching bisimilarity. In this paper we extend the result to reversible systems that feature both nondeterminism and probabilities. We recast noninterference properties by adopting probabilistic variants of weak and branching bisimilarities. Then we investigate a taxonomy of those properties as well as their preservation and compositionality aspects, along with a comparison with the nondeterministic taxonomy. The adequacy of the resulting noninterference theory for reversible systems is illustrated via a probabilistic smart contract example.

1 Introduction

The notion of noninterference was introduced in [22] to reason about the way in which illegitimate information flows can occur in multi-level security systems due to covert channels from high-level agents to low-level ones. Since the first definition, conceived for deterministic systems, a lot of work has been done to extend the approach to a variety of more expressive domains, such as nondeterministic systems, systems in which quantitative aspects – like time and probability – play a central role, and reversible systems; see, e.g., [1,2,5,15,16,24,25,31,39,47].

Noninterference guarantees that low-level agents cannot infer from their observations what high-level ones are doing. Regardless of its specific definition, noninterference is closely tied to the notion of behavioral equivalence [19] because the idea is to compare the system behavior with high-level actions being prevented and the system behavior with the same actions being hidden. A natural framework in which to study system behavior is given by process algebra [32]. In this setting, weak bisimilarity has been employed in [16] both to reason formally about covert channels and illegitimate information flows and to study a classification of noninterference properties for nondeterministic systems.

In [15] we have extended noninterference analysis to reversible systems. Reversibility has started to gain attention in computing since it has been shown that reversible computations may achieve lower levels of energy consumption [6,27]. The applications of reversibility range from biochemical reaction

© IFIP International Federation for Information Processing 2024
Published by Springer Nature Switzerland AG 2024
V. Castiglioni and A. Francalanza (Eds.): FORTE 2024, LNCS 14678, pp. 39–59, 2024.
https://doi.org/10.1007/978-3-031-62645-6_3

modeling [37,38] and parallel discrete-event simulation [34,41] to robotics [30], wireless communications [45], fault-tolerant systems [13,28,46,48], and program debugging [18,29].

As shown in [15], weak bisimilarity is not adequate to study noninterference in a reversible context. A more appropriate semantics turns out to be branching bisimilarity [21] because it coincides with weak back-and-forth bisimilarity [14]. The latter behavioral equivalence requires processes to be able to mimic each other's behavior stepwise not only when performing actions in the standard forward direction, but also when undoing those actions in the backward direction.

In this paper we extend the approach of [15] to a probabilistic setting, so as to address noninterference properties in a framework featuring nondeterministic, probabilistic, and reversible behaviors. The starting point for our study is given by the probabilistic noninterference properties developed in [2] over a probabilistic process calculus based on the generative and reactive models of [20]. In addition to probabilistic choice, in [2] other operators such as parallel composition and hiding are decorated with a probabilistic parameter, so that the selection among all the actions executable by a process is fully probabilistic. Moreover, the considered behavioral equivalence is akin to the weak probabilistic bisimilarity of [4], which is known to coincide with probabilistic branching bisimilarity over fully probabilistic processes.

Here we move to a more expressive model, combining nondeterminism and probabilities, called the strictly alternating model [23]. States are divided into nondeterministic and probabilistic, while transitions are divided into action transitions – each labeled with an action and going from a nondeterministic state to a probabilistic one – and probabilistic transitions – each labeled with a probability and going from a probabilistic state to a nondeterministic one. A more flexible variant, called the non-strictly alternating model [35], allows for action transitions also between two nondeterministic states.

Following [23] we build a process calculus that, unlike the one in [2], does not need probabilistic parameters for operators other than probabilistic choice. As for behavioral equivalences, we introduce a weak probabilistic bisimilarity inspired by the one in [35] and adopt the probabilistic branching bisimilarity developed in [3] for the non-strictly alternating model. By using these two equivalences, we recast the noninterference properties of [15–17] to study their preservation and compositionality aspects, as well as to provide a taxonomy similar to those in [15, 16]. Unlike [2], the resulting noninterference properties do not need additional universal quantifications over probabilistic parameters. Reversibility then comes into play by extending some results of [14] to the strictly alternating model. In particular, a probabilistic variant of weak back-and-forth bisimilarity is shown to coincide with the probabilistic branching bisimilarity of [3].

This paper is organized as follows. In Sect. 2 we recall the strictly alternating model, various notions of bisimilarity for it, and a process calculus based on it. In Sect. 3 we recast in our probabilistic framework a selection of noninterference properties. In Sect. 4 we study their characteristics as well as their taxonomy and relate it to the nondeterministic one of [15]. In Sect. 5 we show that weak probabilistic back-and-forth bisimilarity coincides with probabilistic branching bisimilarity. In Sect. 6 we discuss the example of a lottery implemented through a probabilistic smart contract. Section 7 concludes the paper.

2 Background Definitions and Results

In this section, we recall the strict alternating model of [23] (Sect. 2.1) along with weak probabilistic bisimilarity and probabilistic branching bisimilarity (Sect. 2.2). Then we introduce a probabilistic process language inspired by [23] through which we will express bisimulation-based information-flow security properties accounting for nondeterminism and probabilities (Sect. 2.3).

2.1 Probabilistic Labeled Transition Systems

To represent the behavior of a process featuring nondeterminism and probabilities, we use a probabilistic labeled transition system. This is a variant of a labeled transition system [26] whose transitions are labeled with actions or probabilities. Since we adopt the strictly alternating model of [23], we distinguish between nondeterministic and probabilistic states. The transitions of the former are labeled only with actions, while the transitions of the latter are labeled only with probabilities. Every action transition leads from a nondeterministic state to a probabilistic one, while every probabilistic transition leads from a probabilistic state to a nondeterministic one. In the following, we denote by $\mathcal{S}_n$ (resp. $\mathcal{S}_p$) the set of nondeterministic (resp. probabilistic) states. The action set $\mathcal{A}_\tau$ contains a set $\mathcal{A}$ of visible actions and a single action τ representing unobservable actions.

Definition 1. *A probabilistic labeled transition system (PLTS) is a triple* $(\mathcal{S}, \mathcal{A}_\tau, \longrightarrow)$ *where* $\mathcal{S} = \mathcal{S}_n \cup \mathcal{S}_p$ *with* $\mathcal{S}_n \cap \mathcal{S}_p = \emptyset$ *is an at most countable set of states,* $\mathcal{A}_\tau = \mathcal{A} \cup \{\tau\}$ *is a countable set of actions, and* $\longrightarrow = \longrightarrow_a \cup \longrightarrow_p$ *is the transition relation, where* $\longrightarrow_a \subseteq \mathcal{S}_n \times \mathcal{A}_\tau \times \mathcal{S}_p$ *is the action transition relation whilst* $\longrightarrow_p \subseteq \mathcal{S}_p \times \mathbb{R}_{]0,1]} \times \mathcal{S}_n$ *is the probabilistic transition relation satisfying* $\sum_{(s,p,s') \in \longrightarrow_p} p \in \{0, 1\}$ *for all* $s \in \mathcal{S}_p$. ∎

    An action transition (s, a, s') is written $s \xrightarrow{a}_a s'$ while a probabilistic transition (s, p, s') is written $s \xrightarrow{p}_p s'$, where s is the source state and s' is the target state. We say that s' is reachable from s, written $s' \in reach(s)$, iff $s' = s$ or there exists a sequence of finitely many transitions such that the target state of each of them coincides with the source state of the subsequent one, with the source of the first transition being s and the target of the last one being s'.

2.2 Bisimulation Equivalences

Bisimilarity [32,33] identifies processes that are able to mimic each other's behavior stepwise. In the strictly alternating model, this extends to probabilistic behavior [23]. Let $\mu(s, C) = \sum_{s \xrightarrow{p}_p s', s' \in C} p$ be the cumulative probability with which state s reaches a state in C; note that $\mu(s, C) = 0$ when s is not a probabilistic state or C does not contain any nondeterministic state.

Definition 2. *Let $(\mathcal{S}, \mathcal{A}_\tau, \longrightarrow)$ be a PLTS. We say that $s_1, s_2 \in \mathcal{S}$ are strongly probabilistic bisimilar, written $s_1 \sim_p s_2$, iff $(s_1, s_2) \in \mathcal{B}$ for some strong probabilistic bisimulation $\mathcal{B}$. An equivalence relation $\mathcal{B} \subseteq (\mathcal{S}_n \times \mathcal{S}_n) \cup (\mathcal{S}_p \times \mathcal{S}_p)$ is a strong probabilistic bisimulation iff, whenever $(s_1, s_2) \in \mathcal{B}$, then:*

- *For each $s_1 \xrightarrow{a}_a s_1'$ there exists $s_2 \xrightarrow{a}_a s_2'$ with $(s_1', s_2') \in \mathcal{B}$.*
- *$\mu(s_1, C) = \mu(s_2, C)$ for all equivalence classes $C \in \mathcal{S}_n/\mathcal{B}$.* ■

In [35] a strong probabilistic bisimilarity more liberal than the one in [23] allows a nondeterministic state and a probabilistic state to be identified when the latter concentrates all of its probabilistic mass in reaching the former. Think, e.g., of a probabilistic state whose outgoing transitions all reach the same nondeterministic state. To this purpose the following function is introduced in [35]:

$$
prob(s, s') = \begin{cases} p & \text{if } s \in \mathcal{S}_p \land \sum_{s \xrightarrow{p'}_p s'} p' = p > 0 \\ 1 & \text{if } s \in \mathcal{S}_n \land s' = s \\ 0 & \text{otherwise} \end{cases}
$$

and is then lifted to a set C of states by letting $prob(s, C) = \sum_{s' \in C} prob(s, s')$.

Definition 3. *Let $(\mathcal{S}, \mathcal{A}_\tau, \longrightarrow)$ be a PLTS. We say that $s_1, s_2 \in \mathcal{S}$ are strongly mix-probabilistic bisimilar, written $s_1 \sim_{mp} s_2$, iff $(s_1, s_2) \in \mathcal{B}$ for some strong mix-probabilistic bisimulation $\mathcal{B}$. An equivalence relation $\mathcal{B}$ over $\mathcal{S}$ is a strong mix-probabilistic bisimulation iff, whenever $(s_1, s_2) \in \mathcal{B}$, then:*

- *If $s_1, s_2 \in \mathcal{S}_n$, for each $s_1 \xrightarrow{a}_a s_1'$ there exists $s_2 \xrightarrow{a}_a s_2'$ with $(s_1', s_2') \in \mathcal{B}$.*
- *$prob(s_1, C) = prob(s_2, C)$ for all equivalence classes $C \in \mathcal{S}/\mathcal{B}$.* ■

Weak bisimilarity [32] is additionally capable of abstracting from unobservable actions. In a probabilistic setting, it is also desirable to be able to abstract from probabilistic transitions in certain circumstances. Let $s \Longrightarrow s'$ mean that $s' \in reach(s)$ and, when $s' \neq s$, there exists a finite sequence of transitions from s to s' in which τ-transitions and probabilistic transitions alternate. Moreover $\xrightarrow{\hat{a}}$ stands for $\Longrightarrow$ if $a = \tau$ or $\Longrightarrow \xrightarrow{a}_a \Longrightarrow$ if $a \neq \tau$. The weak probabilistic bisimilarity below is inspired by the one in [35]. The constraint $s_1, s_2 \in \mathcal{S}_n$ is no longer necessary in the first clause due to the use of $\Longrightarrow$.

Definition 4. *Let $(\mathcal{S}, \mathcal{A}_\tau, \longrightarrow)$ be a PLTS. We say that $s_1, s_2 \in \mathcal{S}$ are weakly probabilistic bisimilar, written $s_1 \approx_p s_2$, iff $(s_1, s_2) \in \mathcal{B}$ for some weak probabilistic bisimulation $\mathcal{B}$. An equivalence relation $\mathcal{B}$ over $\mathcal{S}$ is a weak probabilistic bisimulation iff, whenever $(s_1, s_2) \in \mathcal{B}$, then:*

- *For each $s_1 \xrightarrow{a}_a s_1'$ there exists $s_2 \xrightarrow{\hat{a}} s_2'$ with $(s_1', s_2') \in \mathcal{B}$.*
- *$prob(s_1, C) = prob(s_2, C)$ for all equivalence classes $C \in \mathcal{S}/\mathcal{B}$.* ■

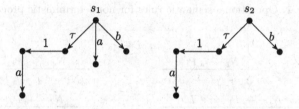

Fig. 1. States s_1 and s_2 are related by $\approx_{\mathrm{p}}$ but distinguished by $\approx_{\mathrm{pb}}$

Branching bisimilarity [21] is finer than weak bisimilarity as it preserves the branching structure of processes even when abstracting from τ-actions – see the condition $(s_1, \bar{s}_2) \in \mathcal{B}$ in the definition below. We adopt the probabilistic branching bisimilarity developed in [3] for the non-strictly alternating model.

Definition 5. *Let $(\mathcal{S}, \mathcal{A}_\tau, \longrightarrow)$ be a PLTS. We say that $s_1, s_2 \in \mathcal{S}$ are probabilistic branching bisimilar, written $s_1 \approx_{\mathrm{pb}} s_2$, iff $(s_1, s_2) \in \mathcal{B}$ for some probabilistic branching bisimulation $\mathcal{B}$. An equivalence relation $\mathcal{B}$ over $\mathcal{S}$ is a probabilistic branching bisimulation iff, whenever $(s_1, s_2) \in \mathcal{B}$, then:*

- *For each $s_1 \xrightarrow{a}_a s_1'$:*
  - *either $a = \tau$ and $(s_1', s_2) \in \mathcal{B}$;*
  - *or there exists $s_2 \Longrightarrow \bar{s}_2 \xrightarrow{a}_a s_2'$ with $(s_1, \bar{s}_2) \in \mathcal{B}$ and $(s_1', s_2') \in \mathcal{B}$.*
- *$prob(s_1, C) = prob(s_2, C)$ for all equivalence classes $C \in \mathcal{S}/\mathcal{B}$.* ∎

An example that highlights the higher distinguishing power of probabilistic branching bisimilarity is given in Fig. 1, where every PLTS is depicted as a directed graph in which vertices represent states and action- or probability-labeled edges represent transitions. The initial states s_1 and s_2 of the two PLTSs are weakly probabilistic bisimilar but not probabilistic branching bisimilar. The only transition that distinguishes s_1 and s_2 is the a-transition of s_1, which can be mimicked by s_2 according to weak probabilistic bisimilarity by performing the τ-transition, the 1-transition, and lastly the a-transition. However, s_2 cannot respond in the same way according to probabilistic branching bisimilarity. The reason is that the state reached after the τ-transition and the 1-transition should be probabilistic branching bisimilar to s_1, which is not the case because of the b-transition departing from s_1.

2.3 A Probabilistic Process Calculus with High and Low Actions

We now introduce a probabilistic process calculus to formalize the security properties of interest. To address two security levels, actions are divided into high and low. We partition the set of visible actions as $\mathcal{A} = \mathcal{A}_\mathcal{H} \cup \mathcal{A}_\mathcal{L}$, with $\mathcal{A}_\mathcal{H} \cap \mathcal{A}_\mathcal{L} = \emptyset$, where $\mathcal{A}_\mathcal{H}$ is the set of high-level actions, ranged over by h, and $\mathcal{A}_\mathcal{L}$ is the set of low-level actions, ranged over by l. We recall that $\mathcal{A}_\tau = \mathcal{A} \cup \{\tau\}$.

The overall set of process terms is denoted by $\mathbb{P} = \mathbb{P}_n \cup \mathbb{P}_p$, ranged over by E. The set $\mathbb{P}_n$ of nondeterministic process terms, ranged over by N, is obtained

Table 1. Operational semantic rules for nondeterministic processes

Prefix	$a \, . \, P \xrightarrow{a}_a P$

Choice	$\dfrac{N_1 \xrightarrow{a}_a P_1}{N_1 + N_2 \xrightarrow{a}_a P_1}$	$\dfrac{N_2 \xrightarrow{a}_a P_2}{N_1 + N_2 \xrightarrow{a}_a P_2}$
Parallel	$\dfrac{N_1 \xrightarrow{a}_a P_1 \quad a \notin L}{N_1 \parallel_L N_2 \xrightarrow{a}_a P_1 \parallel_L [1] N_2}$	$\dfrac{N_2 \xrightarrow{a}_a P_2 \quad a \notin L}{N_1 \parallel_L N_2 \xrightarrow{a}_a [1] N_1 \parallel_L P_2}$
Sync	$\dfrac{N_1 \xrightarrow{a}_a P_1 \quad N_2 \xrightarrow{a}_a P_2 \quad a \in L}{N_1 \parallel_L N_2 \xrightarrow{a}_a P_1 \parallel_L P_2}$	
Restriction	$\dfrac{N \xrightarrow{a}_a P \quad a \notin L}{N \setminus L \xrightarrow{a}_a P \setminus L}$	
Hiding	$\dfrac{N \xrightarrow{a}_a P \quad a \in L}{N / L \xrightarrow{\tau}_a P / L}$	$\dfrac{N \xrightarrow{a}_a P \quad a \notin L}{N / L \xrightarrow{a}_a P / L}$

by considering typical operators from [9,32]. The set $\mathbb{P}_p$ of probabilistic process terms, ranged over by P, is obtained by taking a probabilistic choice operator similar to the one in [23]. In addition to the usual operators for sequential, alternative, and parallel compositions – with the last one taken from [9] so as not to hide the synchronization between high-level actions – we include restriction [32] and hiding [9] as they are necessary to formalize noninterference properties.

The syntax for $\mathbb{P}$ is:

$$N ::= \underline{0} \mid a \, . \, P \mid N + N \mid N \parallel_L N \mid N \setminus L \mid N / L$$
$$P ::= \bigoplus_{i \in I} [p_i] N_i \mid P \parallel_L P \mid P \setminus L \mid P / L$$

where:

- $\underline{0}$ is the terminated process.
- $a \, . \, \_$, for $a \in \mathcal{A}_\tau$, is the action prefix operator describing a process that initially performs action a.
- $\_ + \_$ is the alternative composition operator expressing a nondeterministic choice between two processes based on their initially executable actions.
- $\bigoplus_{i \in I} [p_i] \_$, for I finite and not empty, is the generalized probabilistic composition operator expressing a probabilistic choice among finitely many processes each with probability $p_i \in \mathbb{R}_{]0,1]}$ and such that $\sum_{i \in I} p_i = 1$. We will use $[p_1] N_1 \oplus [p_2] N_2$ as a shorthand for $\bigoplus_{i \in \{1,2\}} [p_i] N_i$ and we will often omit the probability prefix when it is equal to 1.
- $\_ \parallel_L \_$, for $L \subseteq \mathcal{A}$, is the parallel composition operator allowing two processes to proceed independently on any action not in L and forcing them to synchronize on every action in L as well as on probabilistic transitions [23].
- $\_ \setminus L$, for $L \subseteq \mathcal{A}$, is the restriction operator, which prevents the execution of actions belonging to L.
- $\_ / L$, for $L \subseteq \mathcal{A}$, is the hiding operator, which turns all the executed actions belonging to L into the unobservable action τ.

Table 2. Operational semantic rules for probabilistic processes

$$ProbChoice \quad \frac{j \in I}{\bigoplus_{i \in I}[p_i]N_i \xrightarrow{p_j}_{\mathrm{p}} N_j}$$

$$ProbSync \quad \frac{P_1 \xrightarrow{p_1}_{\mathrm{p}} N_1 \quad P_2 \xrightarrow{p_2}_{\mathrm{p}} N_2}{P_1 \,\|_L\, P_2 \xrightarrow{p_1 \cdot p_2}_{\mathrm{p}} N_1 \,\|_L\, N_2}$$

$$ProbRestriction \quad \frac{P \xrightarrow{p}_{\mathrm{p}} N}{P \setminus L \xrightarrow{p}_{\mathrm{p}} N \setminus L}$$

$$ProbHiding \quad \frac{P \xrightarrow{p}_{\mathrm{p}} N}{P / L \xrightarrow{p}_{\mathrm{p}} N / L}$$

The operational semantic rules for the process language are shown in Tables 1 and 2 for nondeterministic and probabilistic processes respectively. Together they produce the PLTS $(\mathbb{P}, \mathcal{A}_\tau, \longrightarrow)$ where $\longrightarrow \;=\; \longrightarrow_{\mathrm{a}} \cup \longrightarrow_{\mathrm{p}}$, $\longrightarrow_{\mathrm{a}} \subseteq \mathbb{P}_{\mathrm{n}} \times \mathcal{A}_\tau \times \mathbb{P}_{\mathrm{p}}$, and $\longrightarrow_{\mathrm{p}} \subseteq \mathbb{P}_{\mathrm{p}} \times \mathbb{R}_{]0,1]} \times \mathbb{P}_{\mathrm{n}}$, to which the bisimulation equivalences defined in Sect. 2.2 are applicable. Note that in the rules *Parallel* the nondeterministic subprocess that does not move has to be prefixed by [1] to make it probabilistic within the overall target process [23].

3 Probabilistic Information-Flow Security Properties

In this section we recast the definitions of noninteference properties of [15–17] – *Nondeterministic Non-Interference* (NNI) and *Non-Deducibility on Composition* (NDC) – by taking as behavioral equivalence each of the two weak bisimilarities of Sect. 2.2. The intuition behind noninterference in a two-level security system is that, if a group of agents at the high security level performs some actions, the effect of those actions should not be seen by any agent at the low security level. To formalize this, the restriction and hiding operators play a central role.

Definition 6. *Let* $E \in \mathbb{P}$ *and* $\approx \; \in \{\approx_{\mathrm{p}}, \approx_{\mathrm{pb}}\}$:

- $E \in \mathrm{BSNNI}_{\approx} \iff E \setminus \mathcal{A}_{\mathcal{H}} \approx E / \mathcal{A}_{\mathcal{H}}.$
- $E \in \mathrm{BNDC}_{\approx} \iff$ *for all* $F \in \mathbb{P}$ *such that every* $F' \in reach(F)$ *can execute only actions in* $\mathcal{A}_{\mathcal{H}}$ *and for all* $L \subseteq \mathcal{A}_{\mathcal{H}}$, $E \setminus \mathcal{A}_{\mathcal{H}} \approx ((E \,\|_L\, F) / L) \setminus \mathcal{A}_{\mathcal{H}}.$
- $E \in \mathrm{SBSNNI}_{\approx} \iff$ *for all* $E' \in reach(E)$, $E' \in \mathrm{BSNNI}_{\approx}.$
- $E \in \mathrm{P\_BNDC}_{\approx} \iff$ *for all* $E' \in reach(E)$, $E' \in \mathrm{BNDC}_{\approx}.$
- $E \in \mathrm{SBNDC}_{\approx} \iff$ *for all* $E' \in reach(E)$ *and for all* E'' *such that* $E' \xrightarrow{a}_{\mathrm{a}} E''$ *for some* $a \in \mathcal{A}_{\mathcal{H}}$, $E' \setminus \mathcal{A}_{\mathcal{H}} \approx E'' \setminus \mathcal{A}_{\mathcal{H}}.$ ∎

Historically, one of the first and most intuitive proposals has been the *Bisimulation-based Strong Nondeterministic Non-Interference* (BSNNI). Basically, it is satisfied by any process E that behaves the same when its high-level actions are prevented (as modeled by $E \setminus \mathcal{A}_\mathcal{H}$) or when they are considered as hidden, unobservable actions (as modeled by $E / \mathcal{A}_\mathcal{H}$). The equivalence between these two low-level views of E states that a low-level agent cannot distinguish the high-level behavior of the system. For instance, in our probabilistic setting, a low-level agent that observes the execution of l in $E = l . \underline{0} + l . ([0.5]h . l_1 . \underline{0} \oplus [0.5]h . l_2 . \underline{0}) + l . ([0.5]l_1 . \underline{0} \oplus [0.5]l_2 . \underline{0})$ cannot infer anything about the execution of h. Indeed, after the execution of l, what the low-level agent observes is either a deadlocked state or the execution of either l_1 or l_2, both with probability 0.5. Formally, $E \setminus \{h\} \approx E / \{h\}$ because $l . \underline{0} + l . \underline{0} + l . ([0.5]l_1 . \underline{0} \oplus [0.5]l_2 . \underline{0}) \approx l . \underline{0} + l . ([0.5]\tau . l_1 . \underline{0} \oplus [0.5]\tau . l_2 . \underline{0}) + l . ([0.5]l_1 . \underline{0} \oplus [0.5]l_2 . \underline{0})$.

BSNNI$_\approx$ is not powerful enough to capture covert channels that derive from the behavior of the high-level agent interacting with the system. For instance, $l . \underline{0} + l . ([0.5]h_1 . l_1 . \underline{0} \oplus [0.5]h_2 . l_2 . \underline{0}) + l . ([0.5]l_1 . \underline{0} \oplus [0.5]l_2 . \underline{0})$ is BSNNI$_\approx$ for the same reason discussed above. However, a high-level agent could decide to enable only h_1, thus turning the low-level view of the system into $l . \underline{0} + l . ([0.5]\tau . l_1 . \underline{0} \oplus [0.5]\underline{0}) + l . ([0.5]l_1 . \underline{0} \oplus [0.5]l_2 . \underline{0})$, which is clearly distinguishable from $l . \underline{0} + l . \underline{0} + l . ([0.5]l_1 . \underline{0} \oplus [0.5]l_2 . \underline{0})$, as in the former after the execution of l the low-level agent can never observe l_2. To overcome such a limitation, the most obvious solution consists of checking explicitly the interaction between the system and every possible high-level agent F. The resulting property is the *Bisimulation-based Non-Deducibility on Composition* (BNDC), which features a universal quantification over F executing only high-level actions.

To circumvent the verification problems related to such a quantifier, several properties have been proposed that are stronger than BNDC. They all express some persistency conditions, stating that the security checks have to be extended to all the processes reachable from a secure one. Three of the most representative among such properties are: the variant of BSNNI that requires every reachable process to satisfy BSNNI itself, called *Strong* BSNNI (SBSNNI); the variant of BNDC that requires every reachable process to satisfy BNDC itself, called *Persistent* BNDC (P_BNDC); and *Strong* BNDC (SBNDC), which requires the low-level view of every reachable process to be the same before and after the execution of any high-level action, meaning that the execution of high-level actions must be completely transparent to low-level agents. In the nondeterministic case, P_BNDC and SBSNNI have been proven to be equivalent in [17], for the weak bisimilarity variants, and in [15], for the branching bisimilarity variants. In the next section we will see that this is the case also in our probabilistic setting.

4   Characteristics of Probabilistic Security Properties

In this section we investigate preservation and compositionality characteristics of the noninterference properties introduced in the previous section (Sect. 4.1) as well as the inclusion relationships between the ones based on $\approx_\mathrm{p}$ and the ones based on $\approx_\mathrm{pb}$ (Sect. 4.2). Then we relate the resulting probabilistic taxonomy with the nondeterministic one of [15] (Sect. 4.3).

4.1 Preservation and Compositionality

All the probabilistic noninterference properties turn out to be preserved by the bisimilarity employed in their definition. This means that, whenever a process E_1 is secure under any of such properties, then every other equivalent process E_2 is secure too, provided that the considered equivalence is the one in the definition of the property. This is very useful for automated property verification, as it allows one to work with the process with the smallest state space among the equivalent ones. These results immediately follow from the next lemma, which states that $\approx_p$ and $\approx_{pb}$ are congruences with respect to action prefix, parallel composition, restriction, and hiding (similar results are present in [3,35] for the non-strictly alternating model).

Lemma 1. Let $E, E_1, E_2 \in \mathbb{P}$, $\approx \in \{\approx_p, \approx_{pb}\}$, and $L \subseteq \mathcal{A}$. If $E_1 \approx E_2$, then:

- $a \,.\, E_1 \approx a \,.\, E_2$ when $E_1, E_2 \in \mathbb{P}_p$.
- $E_1 \parallel_L E \approx E_2 \parallel_L E$ when $E_1, E_2, E \in \mathbb{P}_n$ or $E_1, E_2, E \in \mathbb{P}_p$.
- $E_1 \setminus L \approx E_2 \setminus L$.
- $E_1 / L \approx E_2 / L$. ∎

Theorem 1. Let $E_1, E_2 \in \mathbb{P}$, $\approx \in \{\approx_p, \approx_{pb}\}$, and $\mathcal{P} \in \{\text{BSNNI}_\approx, \text{BNDC}_\approx, \text{SBSNNI}_\approx, \text{P\_BNDC}_\approx, \text{SBNDC}_\approx\}$. If $E_1 \approx E_2$, then $E_1 \in \mathcal{P} \iff E_2 \in \mathcal{P}$. ∎

As far as modular verification is concerned, like in the nondeterministic case [15,16] only the local properties $\text{SBSNNI}_\approx$, $\text{P\_BNDC}_\approx$, and $\text{SBNDC}_\approx$ are compositional, i.e., are preserved by some operators of the calculus in certain circumstances. Compositionality with respect to parallel composition is limited, for $\text{SBSNNI}_{\approx_{pb}}$ and $\text{P\_BNDC}_{\approx_{pb}}$, to the case in which no synchronization can take place among high-level actions. This is analogous to the nondeterministic case [15], where the same limitation holds for the branching bisimulation-based SBSNNI and P_BNDC. A similar limitation applies to hiding.

Theorem 2. Let $E, E_1, E_2 \in \mathbb{P}$, $\approx \in \{\approx_p, \approx_{pb}\}$, $\mathcal{P} \in \{\text{SBSNNI}_\approx, \text{P\_BNDC}_\approx, \text{SBNDC}_\approx\}$. Then:

1. $E \in \mathcal{P} \implies a \,.\, E \in \mathcal{P}$ for all $a \in \mathcal{A}_\mathcal{L} \cup \{\tau\}$ when $E \in \mathbb{P}_p$.
2. $E_1, E_2 \in \mathcal{P} \implies E_1 \parallel_L E_2 \in \mathcal{P}$ for all $L \subseteq \mathcal{A}_\mathcal{L}$ if $\mathcal{P} \in \{\text{SBSNNI}_{\approx_{pb}}, \text{P\_BNDC}_{\approx_{pb}}\}$ or $L \subseteq \mathcal{A}$ if $\mathcal{P} \in \{\text{SBSNNI}_{\approx_p}, \text{P\_BNDC}_{\approx_p}, \text{SBNDC}_{\approx_p}, \text{SBNDC}_{\approx_{pb}}\}$, when $E_1, E_2 \in \mathbb{P}_n$ or $E_1, E_2 \in \mathbb{P}_p$.
3. $E \in \mathcal{P} \implies E \setminus L \in \mathcal{P}$ for all $L \subseteq \mathcal{A}$.
4. $E \in \mathcal{P} \implies E / L \in \mathcal{P}$ for all $L \subseteq \mathcal{A}_\mathcal{L}$. ∎

As far as parallel composition is concerned, the compositionality of $\text{SBSNNI}_{\approx_{pb}}$ holds only for all $L \subseteq \mathcal{A}_\mathcal{L}$. For example, both $E_1 := h \,.\, [1]\underline{0} + l_1 \,.\, [1]\underline{0} + \tau \,.\, [1]\underline{0}$ and $E_2 := h \,.\, [1]\underline{0} + l_2 \,.\, [1]\underline{0} + \tau \,.\, [1]\underline{0}$ are $\text{SBSNNI}_{\approx_{pb}}$, but $E_1 \parallel_{\{h\}} E_2$ is not because the transition $(E_1 \parallel_{\{h\}} E_2) / \mathcal{A}_\mathcal{H} \xrightarrow{\tau}_a ([1]\underline{0} \parallel_{\{h\}} [1]\underline{0}) / \mathcal{A}_\mathcal{H}$ arising from the synchronization between the two h-actions cannot be matched by

$(E_1 \|_{\{h\}} E_2) \setminus \mathcal{A_H}$ in the probabilistic branching bisimulation game. As a matter of fact, the only two possibilities are $(E_1 \|_{\{h\}} E_2) \setminus \mathcal{A_H} \Longrightarrow (E_1 \|_{\{h\}} E_2) \setminus$ $\mathcal{A_H} \xrightarrow{\tau}_a ([1]\underline{0} \|_{\{h\}} [1]E_2) \setminus \mathcal{A_H} \xrightarrow{1}_p (\underline{0} \|_{\{h\}} E_2) \setminus \mathcal{A_H} \xrightarrow{\tau}_a ([1]\underline{0} \|_{\{h\}} [1]\underline{0}) \setminus \mathcal{A_H}$ as well as $(E_1 \|_{\{h\}} E_2) \setminus \mathcal{A_H} \Longrightarrow (E_1 \|_{\{h\}} E_2) \setminus \mathcal{A_H} \xrightarrow{\tau}_a ([1]E_1 \|_{\{h\}} [1]\underline{0}) \setminus$ $\mathcal{A_H} \xrightarrow{1}_p (E_1 \|_{\{h\}} \underline{0}) \setminus \mathcal{A_H} \xrightarrow{\tau}_a ([1]\underline{0} \|_{\{h\}} [1]\underline{0}) \setminus \mathcal{A_H}$ but neither $([1]\underline{0} \|_{\{h\}} [1]E_2) \setminus$ $\mathcal{A_H}$ nor $([1]E_1 \|_{\{h\}} [1]\underline{0}) \setminus \mathcal{A_H}$ is probabilistic branching bisimilar to $(E_1 \|_{\{h\}} E_2) \setminus$ $\mathcal{A_H}$ when $l_1 \neq l_2$. Note that $(E_1 \|_{\{h\}} E_2) / \mathcal{A_H} \approx (E_1 \|_{\{h\}} E_2) \setminus \mathcal{A_H}$ because $(E_1 \|_{\{h\}} E_2) / \mathcal{A_H} \xrightarrow{\tau}_a ([1]\underline{0} \|_{\{h\}} [1]\underline{0}) / \mathcal{A_H}$ is matched by $(E_1 \|_{\{h\}} E_2) \setminus$ $\mathcal{A_H} \Longrightarrow ([1]\underline{0} \|_{\{h\}} [1]\underline{0}) \setminus \mathcal{A_H}$. As noted in [15], it is not only a matter of the higher discriminating power of $\approx_{\mathrm{pb}}$ with respect to $\approx_p$. If we used the parallel composition operator of [32], which turns into τ the synchronization of two actions thus combining communication with hiding, then the parallel composition of E_1 and E_2 with restriction on $\mathcal{A_H}$ would be able to respond with a single τ-transition reaching the parallel composition of $\underline{0}$ and $\underline{0}$ with restriction on $\mathcal{A_H}$.

Like for the nondeterministic case [15,16], none of the considered noninterference properties is compositional with respect to alternative composition. As an example, let us consider the processes $E_1 := l.\underline{0}$ and $E_2 := h.\underline{0}$, where we omit [1] before $\underline{0}$. Assuming $\approx \in \{\approx_p, \approx_{\mathrm{pb}}\}$, both are BSNNI$_\approx$, as $l.\underline{0} \setminus \{h\} \approx l.\underline{0}/\{h\}$ and $h.\underline{0} \setminus \{h\} \approx h.\underline{0}/\{h\}$, but $E_1 + E_2 \notin$ BSNNI$_\approx$ because $(l.\underline{0} + h.\underline{0}) \setminus \{h\} \approx l.\underline{0} \not\approx l.\underline{0} + \tau.\underline{0} \approx (l.\underline{0} + h.\underline{0})/\{h\}$. It can be easily checked that $E_1 + E_2 \notin \mathcal{P}$ for $\mathcal{P} = \{\mathrm{BNDC}_\approx, \mathrm{SBSNNI}_\approx, \mathrm{SBNDC}_\approx\}$.

4.2 Taxonomy of Security Properties

First of all, as in the nondeterministic case the properties listed in Sect. 3 are increasingly finer. This result holds for both the $\approx_p$-based and $\approx_{\mathrm{pb}}$-based noninterference properties.

Theorem 3. Let $\approx \in \{\approx_p, \approx_{\mathrm{pb}}\}$. Then:

$$\mathrm{SBNDC}_\approx \subset \mathrm{SBSNNI}_\approx = \mathrm{P\_BNDC}_\approx \subset \mathrm{BNDC}_\approx \subset \mathrm{BSNNI}_\approx \qquad \blacksquare$$

All the inclusions are strict as we now show (we omit every occurrence of [1]):

- The process $\tau.l.\underline{0} + l.l.\underline{0} + h.l.\underline{0}$ is SBSNNI$_\approx$ (resp. P_BDNC$_\approx$) because $(\tau.l.\underline{0} + l.l.\underline{0} + h.l.\underline{0}) \setminus \{h\} \approx (\tau.l.\underline{0} + l.l.\underline{0} + h.l.\underline{0})/\{h\}$ and action h is enabled only by the initial process so every derivative is BSNNI$_\approx$ (resp. BNDC$_\approx$). It is not SBNDC$_\approx$ because the low-level view of the process reached after action h, i.e., $(l.\underline{0}) \setminus \{h\}$, is neither weak probabilistic nor probabilistic branching bisimilar to $(\tau.l.\underline{0} + l.l.\underline{0} + h.l.\underline{0}) \setminus \{h\}$.
- The process $l.\underline{0} + l.l.\underline{0} + l.h.l.\underline{0}$ is BNDC$_\approx$ because, whether there are synchronizations with high-level actions or not, the overall process can always perform either an l-action or a sequence of two l-actions. The process is not SBSNNI$_\approx$ (resp. P_BNDC$_\approx$) because the reachable process $h.l.\underline{0}$ is not BSNNI$_\approx$ (resp. BNDC$_\approx$).

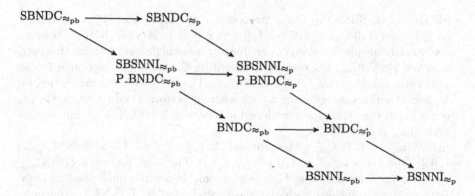

Fig. 2. Taxonomy of security properties based on probabilistic bisimilarities

– The process $l.\underline{0}+h.h.l.\underline{0}$ is $BSNNI_{\approx}$ due to $(l.\underline{0}+h.h.l.\underline{0})\setminus\{h\}\approx(l.\underline{0}+h.h.l.\underline{0})/\{h\}$, but is not $BNDC_{\approx}$ due to $(((l.\underline{0}+h.h.l.\underline{0})\parallel_{\{h\}}(h.\underline{0}))/\{h\})\setminus\{h\}\not\approx(l.\underline{0}+h.h.l.\underline{0})\setminus\{h\}$ as $(l.\underline{0}+h.h.l.\underline{0})\setminus\{h\}$ behaves as $l.\underline{0}$.

Secondly, we observe that all the $\approx_{pb}$-based noninterference properties imply the corresponding $\approx_p$-based ones, due to the fact that $\approx_{pb}$ is finer than $\approx_p$.

Theorem 4. *The following inclusions hold:*

1. $BSNNI_{\approx_{pb}}\subseteq BSNNI_{\approx_p}$.
2. $BNDC_{\approx_{pb}}\subseteq BNDC_{\approx_p}$.
3. $SBSNNI_{\approx_{pb}}\subseteq SBSNNI_{\approx_p}$.
4. $P\_BNDC_{\approx_{pb}}\subseteq P\_BNDC_{\approx_p}$.
5. $SBNDC_{\approx_{pb}}\subseteq SBNDC_{\approx_p}$. $\blacksquare$

All the inclusions above are strict due to the following result; for an example of E_1 and E_2 below, see Fig. 1.

Theorem 5. *Let $E_1, E_2 \in \mathbb{P}_n$ be such that $E_1 \approx_p E_2$ but $E_1 \not\approx_{pb} E_2$. If no high-level actions occur in E_1 and E_2, then $F \in \{E_1 + h.[1]E_2, E_2 + h.[1]E_1\}$ is such that:*

1. $F \in BSNNI_{\approx_p}$ but $F \notin BSNNI_{\approx_{pb}}$.
2. $F \in BNDC_{\approx_p}$ but $F \notin BNDC_{\approx_{pb}}$.
3. $F \in SBSNNI_{\approx_p}$ but $F \notin SBSNNI_{\approx_{pb}}$.
4. $F \in P\_BNDC_{\approx_p}$ but $F \notin P\_BNDC_{\approx_{pb}}$.
5. $F \in SBNDC_{\approx_p}$ but $F \notin SBNDC_{\approx_{pb}}$. $\blacksquare$

Based on the results in Theorems 3 and 4, the diagram in Fig. 2 summarizes the inclusions among the various noninterference properties, where $\mathcal{P} \to \mathcal{Q}$ means that $\mathcal{P}$ is strictly included in $\mathcal{Q}$. These inclusions follow the same pattern as the nondeterministic case [15]. The missing arrows in the diagram, witnessing incomparability, are justified by the following counterexamples:

– SBNDC$_{\approx_p}$ vs. SBSNNI$_{\approx_{pb}}$. The process $\tau . l . \underline{0} + l . l . \underline{0} + h . l . \underline{0}$ is BSNNI$_{\approx_{pb}}$ as $\tau . l . \underline{0} + l . l . \underline{0} \approx_{pb} \tau . l . \underline{0} + l . l . \underline{0} + \tau . l . \underline{0}$. It is also SBSNNI$_{\approx_{pb}}$ because every reachable process does not enable any more high-level actions. However, it is not SBNDC$_{\approx_p}$, because after executing the high-level action h it can perform a single action l, while the original process with the restriction on high-level actions can go along a path where it performs two l-actions. On the other hand, the process F mentioned in Theorem 5 is SBNDC$_{\approx_p}$ but neither BSNNI$_{\approx_{pb}}$ nor SBSNNI$_{\approx_{pb}}$.

– SBSNNI$_{\approx_p}$ vs. BNDC$_{\approx_{pb}}$. The process $l . h . l . \underline{0} + l . \underline{0} + l . l . \underline{0}$ is BSNNI$_{\approx_{pb}}$ as $l . \underline{0} + l . \underline{0} + l . l . \underline{0} \approx_{pb} l . \tau . l . \underline{0} + l . \underline{0} + l . l . \underline{0}$. The same process is BNDC$_{\approx_{pb}}$ too as it includes only one high-level action, hence the only possible high-level strategy coincides with the check conducted by BSNNI$_{\approx_{pb}}$. However, the process is not SBSNNI$_{\approx_p}$ because of the reachable process $h . l . \underline{0}$, which is not BSNNI$_{\approx_p}$. On the other hand, the process F mentioned in Theorem 5 is SBSNNI$_{\approx_p}$ but not BSNNI$_{\approx_{pb}}$ and, therefore, cannot be BNDC$_{\approx_{pb}}$.

– BNDC$_{\approx_p}$ vs. BSNNI$_{\approx_{pb}}$. The process $l . \underline{0} + l . ([0.5]h_1 . l_1 . \underline{0} \oplus [0.5]h_2 . l_2 . \underline{0}) + l . ([0.5]l_1 . \underline{0} \oplus [0.5]l_2 . \underline{0})$ is BSNNI$_{\approx_{pb}}$ as discussed in Sect. 3, but it is not BNDC$_{\approx_p}$. In contrast, the process F mentioned in Theorem 5 is both BSNNI$_{\approx_p}$ and BNDC$_{\approx_p}$, but not BSNNI$_{\approx_{pb}}$.

As for the nondeterministic case [15], the strongest property based on weak probabilistic bisimilarity (SBNDC$_{\approx_p}$) and the weakest property based on probabilistic branching bisimilarity (BSNNI$_{\approx_{pb}}$) are incomparable too. The former is a very restrictive property because it requires a local check every time a high-level action is performed, while the latter requires a check only on the initial state. On the other hand, as shown in Theorem 5, it is very easy to construct processes that are secure under properties based on $\approx_p$ but not on $\approx_{pb}$, due to the minimal number of high-level actions in F.

4.3 Relating Nondeterministic and Probabilistic Taxonomies

We now compare our probabilistic taxonomy to the nondeterministic one of [15]. In the following, we assume that $\approx$ denotes the weak bisimilarity of [32] and $\approx_b$ the branching bisimilarity of [21]. These can be obtained by restricting the definitions in Sect. 2.2 to nondeterministic states and by ignoring the clause involving the *prob* function. Since we are considering probabilistic choices as internal, given a process $E \in \mathbb{P}$ we can obtain its nondeterministic variant, denoted by $nd(E)$, by replacing each probability prefix by τ and each probabilistic choice operator by a nondeterministic choice operator. The next proposition states that if two processes are equivalent according to any of the weak bisimilarities in Sect. 2.2, then their nondeterministic variants are equivalent according to the corresponding nondeterministic bisimilarity.

Proposition 1. *Let $E_1, E_2 \in \mathbb{P}$. Then:*

– $E_1 \approx_p E_2 \implies nd(E_1) \approx nd(E_2)$.
– $E_1 \approx_{pb} E_2 \implies nd(E_1) \approx_b nd(E_2)$.   ∎

The inverse does not hold. Consider, e.g., the processes E_1 and E_2 defined as $[0.5]l_1 \cdot \underline{0} \oplus [0.5]l_2 \cdot \underline{0}$ and $[0.8]l_1 \cdot \underline{0} \oplus [0.2]l_2 \cdot \underline{0}$ respectively. Clearly, $E_1 \not\approx_p E_2$ (resp. $E_1 \not\approx_{pb} E_2$) but their nondeterministic counterparts are identical: $\tau \cdot l_1 \cdot \underline{0} + \tau \cdot l_2 \cdot \underline{0}$. An immediate consequence is that if a process is secure under any of the probabilistic noninterference properties in Sect. 3, then its nondeterministic variant is secure under the corresponding nondeterministic property. Therefore, the taxonomy in Fig. 2 extends to the left the one in [15], as each of the property in Sect. 3 is finer than its nondeterministic counterpart.

Corollary 1. *Let* $E \in \mathbb{P}, \approx_{pr} \in \{\approx_p, \approx_{pb}\}, \approx_{nd} \in \{\approx, \approx_b\}, \mathcal{P}_{pr} \in \{BSNNI_{\approx_{pr}}, BNDC_{\approx_{pr}}, SBSNNI_{\approx_{pr}}, P\_BNDC_{\approx_{pr}}, SBNDC_{\approx_{pr}}\},$ *and* $\mathcal{P}_{nd} \in \{BSNNI_{\approx_{nd}}, BNDC_{\approx_{nd}}, SBSNNI_{\approx_{nd}}, P\_BNDC_{\approx_{nd}}, SBNDC_{\approx_{nd}}\}.$ *Then:*

$$E \in \mathcal{P}_{pr} \implies nd(E) \in \mathcal{P}_{nd} \qquad \blacksquare$$

5 Weak Probabilistic Back-and-Forth Bisimilarity

In [14] it was shown that, for nodeterministic processes, weak back-and-forth bisimilarity coincides with branching bisimilarity. In this section we extend that result to probabilistic processes, so that probabilistic branching bisimilarity can be employed in the noninterference analysis of reversible processes.

A PLTS $(\mathcal{S}, \mathcal{A}_\tau, \longrightarrow)$ represents a reversible process if each of its transitions is seen as bidirectional. When going backward, it is of paramount importance to respect causality, i.e., the last performed transition must be the first one to be undone. Following [14] we set up an equivalence that enforces not only causality but also history preservation. This means that, when going backward, a process can only move along the path representing the history that brought the process to the current state, even in the presence of concurrency. To accomplish this, the equivalence has to be defined over computations, not over states, and the notion of transition has to be suitably revised. We start by adapting the notation of the nondeterministic setting of [14] to our strictly alternating probabilistic setting. We use ℓ for a label in $\mathcal{A}_\tau \cup \mathbb{R}_{]0,1[}$.

Definition 7. *A sequence* $\xi = (s_0, \ell_1, s_1)(s_1, \ell_2, s_2) \ldots (s_{n-1}, \ell_n, s_n) \in \longrightarrow^*$ *is a path of length* n *from state* s_0. *We let* $first(\xi) = s_0$ *and* $last(\xi) = s_n$; *the empty path is indicated with* ε. *We denote by* $path(s)$ *the set of paths from* s. $\qquad \blacksquare$

Definition 8. *A pair* $\rho = (s, \xi)$ *is called a* run *from state* s *iff* $\xi \in path(s)$, *in which case we let* $path(\rho) = \xi$, $first(\rho) = first(\xi) = s$, $last(\rho) = last(\xi)$, *with* $first(\rho) = last(\rho) = s$ *when* $\xi = \varepsilon$. *We denote by* $run(s)$ *the set of runs from state* s. *Given* $\rho = (s, \xi) \in run(s)$ *and* $\rho' = (s', \xi') \in run(s')$, *their composition* $\rho\rho' = (s, \xi\xi') \in run(s)$ *is defined iff* $last(\rho) = first(\rho') = s'$. *We write* $\rho \overset{\ell}{\longrightarrow} \rho'$ *iff there exists* $\rho'' = (\bar{s}, (\bar{s}, \ell, s'))$ *with* $\bar{s} = last(\rho)$ *such that* $\rho' = \rho\rho''$; *note that* $first(\rho) = first(\rho')$. *Moreover prob is lifted in the expected way.* $\qquad \blacksquare$

In the considered PLTS we work with the set $\mathcal{U}$ of runs in lieu of $\mathcal{S}$. Following [14], given a run ρ we distinguish between *outgoing* and *incoming* action transitions of ρ during the weak bisimulation game. Like in [8], this does not apply to probabilistic transitions, which are thus considered only in the forward direction. If the labels of incoming probabilistic transitions were taken into account, then the nondeterministic state $a \cdot \underline{0}$ and the probabilistic state $[p]a \cdot \underline{0} \oplus [1-p]a \cdot \underline{0}$ would be told apart because $a \cdot \underline{0}$ in the former state has no incoming probabilistic transitions while $a \cdot \underline{0}$ in the latter state is reached with cumulative probability 1. Even a simpler clause requiring for any two related states that they both have incoming probabilistic transitions, or neither has, would distinguish the two states exemplified before.

Definition 9. *Let* $(\mathcal{S}, \mathcal{A}_\tau, \longrightarrow)$ *be a PLTS. We say that* $s_1, s_2 \in \mathcal{S}$ *are* weakly probabilistic back-and-forth bisimilar, *written* $s_1 \approx_{\mathrm{pbf}} s_2$, *iff* $((s_1, \varepsilon), (s_2, \varepsilon)) \in \mathcal{B}$ *for some weak probabilistic back-and-forth bisimulation* $\mathcal{B}$. *An equivalence relation* $\mathcal{B}$ *over* $\mathcal{U}$ *is a* weak probabilistic back-and-forth bisimulation *iff, whenever* $(\rho_1, \rho_2) \in \mathcal{B}$, *then:*

- *For each* $\rho_1 \xrightarrow{a}_a \rho_1'$ *there exists* $\rho_2 \xRightarrow{\hat{a}} \rho_2'$ *with* $(\rho_1', \rho_2') \in \mathcal{B}$.
- *For each* $\rho_1' \xrightarrow{a}_a \rho_1$ *there exists* $\rho_2' \xRightarrow{\hat{a}} \rho_2$ *with* $(\rho_1', \rho_2') \in \mathcal{B}$.
- $prob(\rho_1, C) = prob(\rho_2, C)$ *for all equivalence classes* $C \in \mathcal{U}/\mathcal{B}$. ∎

We show that weak probabilistic back-and-forth bisimilarity over runs coincides with the forward-only probabilistic branching bisimilarity over states of [3] recalled in Sect. 2.2. We proceed by adopting the proof strategy followed in [14] to show that their weak back-and-forth bisimilarity over runs coincides with the forward-only branching bisimilarity over states of [21]. Therefore we start by proving that $\approx_{\mathrm{pbf}}$ satisfies the *cross property*. This means that, whenever two runs of two $\approx_{\mathrm{pbf}}$-equivalent states can perform a sequence of finitely many τ-transitions alternating with probabilistic transitions, such that each of the two target runs ends in a nondeterministic state and is $\approx_{\mathrm{pbf}}$-equivalent to the source run of the other sequence, then the two target runs are $\approx_{\mathrm{pbf}}$-equivalent to each other as well.

Lemma 2. *Let* $s_1, s_2 \in \mathcal{S}$ *with* $s_1 \approx_{\mathrm{pbf}} s_2$. *For all* $\rho_1', \rho_1'' \in run(s_1)$ *such that* $\rho_1' \Longrightarrow \rho_1''$ *with* $last(\rho_1'') \in \mathcal{S}_\mathrm{n}$ *and for all* $\rho_2', \rho_2'' \in run(s_2)$ *such that* $\rho_2' \Longrightarrow \rho_2''$ *with* $last(\rho_2'') \in \mathcal{S}_\mathrm{n}$, *if* $\rho_1' \approx_{\mathrm{pbf}} \rho_2''$ *and* $\rho_1'' \approx_{\mathrm{pbf}} \rho_2'$ *then* $\rho_1'' \approx_{\mathrm{pbf}} \rho_2''$. ∎

Theorem 6. *Let* $s_1, s_2 \in \mathcal{S}$. *Then* $s_1 \approx_{\mathrm{pbf}} s_2 \iff s_1 \approx_{\mathrm{pb}} s_2$. ∎

Therefore the properties $\mathrm{BSNNI}_{\approx_{\mathrm{pb}}}$, $\mathrm{BNDC}_{\approx_{\mathrm{pb}}}$, $\mathrm{SBSNNI}_{\approx_{\mathrm{pb}}}$, $\mathrm{P\_BNDC}_{\approx_{\mathrm{pb}}}$, and $\mathrm{SBNDC}_{\approx_{\mathrm{pb}}}$ do not change if $\approx_{\mathrm{pb}}$ is replaced by $\approx_{\mathrm{pbf}}$. This allows us to study noninterference properties for reversible probabilistic systems by using $\approx_{\mathrm{pb}}$ in a probabilistic process calculus like the one of Sect. 2.3, without having to resort to external memories [12] of communication keys [36].

6   Use Case: Probabilistic Smart Contracts

Consider a lottery implemented through a probabilistic smart contract [11] based on a public blockchain, like, e.g., Ethereum. Initially, anyone can buy a ticket by invoking a dedicated smart contract function that allows the user to pay a predefined amount for the ticket. When the lottery is closed, anyone can invoke another smart contract function, call it draw(), in which a random number x, between 1 and the number of sold tickets, is drawn and the entire amount of money is paid to the owner of ticket x.

In this setting, we model and verify two known vulnerabilities discussed in [11]. The former will allow us to emphasize the need for passing from the nondeterministic noninterference analysis to the probabilistic one. Indeed, the critical point is the randomization process of the function draw(), which is not natively available to smart contract programmers. A widely adopted approach consists of using the timestamp of the block including the transaction of the draw invocation as the seed for random number generation. However, this approach is vulnerable in the presence of an adversary that buys a ticket and succeeds in mining the block above by using a timestamp that allows the adversary to win the lottery.

Since both honest users and the adversary employ the same functionalities of the smart contract, we consider the invocations of the smart contract functions as publicly observable low-level actions. To distinguish the interactions of the adversary from those of honest users, such actions are guarded by a high-level action h whenever they refer to the adversary. In this way, by looking at the public behavior of the smart contract, a low-level observer can detect whether or not the functioning of the lottery can be compromised by malicious behaviors of the adversary.

For simplicity, we assume there are only two users buying one ticket each, where the adversary buys ticket 0 while the honest user buys ticket 1. This scenario can be modeled in our probabilistic framework as follows:

$$\tau . draw . ([0.5] address_0 . win_0 . \underline{0} \oplus [0.5] address_1 . win_1 . \underline{0}) +$$
$$h . draw . ([1 - \varepsilon] address_0 . win_0 . \underline{0} \oplus [\varepsilon] address_1 . win_1 . \underline{0})$$

The extraction procedure is conducted either by the honest user (action τ) or by the adversary (see the unique high-level action h). In both cases, the action $draw$, modeling the invocation of function draw(), leads to the probabilistic extraction of the ticket, the determination of the winner (actions $address_i$), and the notification to the winner (actions win_i).

By comparing the two branches, we note that in the former the probabilistic extraction is fair, while in the latter the adversary is able to pilot the extraction at will ($\varepsilon > 0$ is considered to be negligible). However, it is easy to see that this interfering behavior cannot be detected in a purely nondeterministic setting, as the two branches are identical if we abstract away from probabilities (after the initial choice, they are both mapped to the nondeterministic process $address_0 . win_0 . \underline{0} + address_1 . win_1 . \underline{0}$). As a consequence, all the nondeterministic security properties are satisfied for both bisimilarities. In the probabilistic setting, the interference is captured by the BSNNI$_{\approx_{pr}}$ property, for $\approx_{pr} \in \{\approx_p, \approx_{pb}\}$, in analogy with the counterexample discussed after Proposition 1.

While this example confirms that the detection of probabilistic covert channels requires probabilistic security properties, the second vulnerability we present emphasizes the difference between the two probabilistic bisimilarities. The critical point is the mining procedure. Even assuming that the seed governing the probabilistic extraction cannot be manipulated, if the miner invoking the function draw() is malicious and is going to lose the lottery, that miner can ignore the related block and force the mining failure. Hence, with respect to the previous example, we use additional low-level actions denoting the mining process (action *mine*) and the successful writing to the blockchain (action *success*) or its failure (action *failure*). We model the described behavior through the following process:

$$draw \,.\, ([0.5]\,address_0 \,.\, win_0 \,.\, mine \,.\, (success \,.\, \underline{0} + \tau \,.\, failure \,.\, \underline{0}) \oplus$$
$$[0.5]\,address_1 \,.\, win_1 \,.$$
$$(mine \,.\, (success \,.\, \underline{0} + \tau \,.\, failure \,.\, \underline{0}) +$$
$$h \,.\, (mine \,.\, (success \,.\, \underline{0} + \tau \,.\, failure \,.\, \underline{0}) +$$
$$mine \,.\, failure \,.\, \underline{0})))$$

As mentioned before, the adversary cannot manipulate the seed to affect the extraction. Hence, the probabilistic extraction is fair in any case. However, the adversary can try to interfere if the result of the extraction makes him lose (i.e., it is different from ticket 0). On the one hand, consider the behavior after action win_0, which models the block mining procedure. The action *mine* expresses that the mining process is initiated by a honest miner, as no high-level interaction occurred. The subsequent choice is between the successful mining (action *success*) and an event not depending on the miner (action τ) that causes the failure of the mining (action *failure*). Notice that there might be several causes for such a failure (e.g., a wrong transaction in the block or a fork in the blockchain).

On the other hand, in the behavior after action win_1, the adversary decides to compete in the mining procedure (see the choice between the action *mine*, leading to the same behavior surveyed above, and the high-level action h, modeling that the mining procedure may be governed by the adversary). If h is chosen, the race between a honest miner and the adversary is solved nondeterministically through a choice between two actions *mine*. In fact, such a nondeterministic choice models a real-world scenario in which all the potential miners try to solve the cryptographic puzzle needed to add a block to the blockchain. The former branch leads to the behavior of the honest miner, while the latter enables the malicious behavior by leading immediately to the action *failure*.

Formally, the process is SBNDC$_{\approx_p}$. In particular, it is sufficient to observe that we have only one occurrence of the high-level action h and that the subprocess $mine \,.\, (success \,.\, \underline{0} + \tau \,.\, failure \,.\, \underline{0})$ – denoting the low-level view before executing h – is weakly probabilistic bisimilar to the subprocess $mine \,.\, (success \,.\, \underline{0} + \tau \,.\, failure \,.\, \underline{0}) + mine \,.\, failure \,.\, \underline{0}$ – denoting the low-level view after executing h.

However, the process is not BSNNI$_{\approx_{pb}}$. The reason is that the subprocess $mine \,.\, (success \,.\, \underline{0} + \tau \,.\, failure \,.\, \underline{0})$ is not probabilistic branching bisimilar to the subprocess:

$$mine \,.\,(success \,.\, \underline{0} + \tau \,.\, failure \,.\, \underline{0}) +$$
$$\tau \,.\,(mine \,.\,(success \,.\, \underline{0} + \tau \,.\, failure \,.\, \underline{0}) + mine \,.\, failure \,.\, \underline{0})$$

This depends on the fact that $mine \,.\,(success \,.\, \underline{0} + \tau \,.\, failure \,.\, \underline{0})$ is not probabilistic branching bisimilar to $mine \,.\,(success \,.\, \underline{0} + \tau \,.\, failure \,.\, \underline{0}) + mine \,.\, failure \,.\, \underline{0}$, while they are equated by $\approx_p$. Indeed, the former process cannot respond whenever the latter executes the right-hand action $mine$ leading to a state where only the action $failure$ is possible.

We employ also the back-and-forth interpretation of the BSNNI$_{\approx_{pb}}$ check to show the result above in the setting of reversible systems. In the subprocess including the hidden high-level action h, notice that undoing the action $failure$ of the branch $mine \,.\, failure \,.\, \underline{0}$ reveals that the failure has been forced by the adversary. If, instead, we consider the subprocess $mine \,.\,(success \,.\, \underline{0} + \tau \,.\, failure \,.\, \underline{0})$, we observe that undoing the action $failure$ reveals that the failure has been the consequence of a choice involving also the action $success$. Hence, it was not deliberately caused by the miner. This is sufficient to expose the behavior of the adversary. In other words, in a reversible system allowing for execution flow debugging, it is possible to capture the malicious behavior of the adversary.

To conclude, the noninterference analysis based on the strongest $\approx_p$-based property of Fig. 2 fails to reveal the covert channel caused by the adversary, while the weakest $\approx_{pb}$-based property of Fig. 2 can detect it.

7   Conclusions

In this paper we have investigated a taxonomy of noninterference properties for processes featuring both nondeterminism and probabilities, along with the preservation and compositionality aspects of such properties. The two behavioral equivalences that we have considered for those noninterference properties are a weak probabilistic bisimilarity inspired by the one in [35] and the probabilistic branching bisimilarity of [3].

Since we have shown that the latter coincides with a probabilistic variant of the weak back-and-forth bisimilarity of [14], the noninterference properties based on the latter can be applied to reversible probabilistic systems, thereby extending our previous results in [15] for reversible systems that are fully nondeterministic. Our work also extends the one of [2], where generative-reactive probabilistic systems are considered, in a way that avoids additional universal quantifications over probabilistic parameters in the formalization of noninterference properties.

The nondeterministic and probabilistic model that we have employed is the strictly alternating one of [23], where states are divided into nondeterministic and probabilistic. Each of the former may have action-labeled transitions to probabilistic states, while each of the latter may have probability-labeled transitions to nondeterministic states (in the non-strictly alternating variant of [35] action transitions are admitted also between two nondeterministic states). An alternative model is the non-alternating one given by Segala simple probabilistic automata [42], where every transition is labeled with an action and goes from a state to a probability distribution over states. Regardless of the adopted model, it is worth observing that some characteristics seem to be independent from probabilities, as witnessed by almost all the counterexamples in Sect. 4.

Both the alternating model and the non-alternating one – whose relationships have been studied in [44] – encompass nondeterministic models, generative models, and reactive models as special cases. Since branching bisimulation semantics plays a fundamental role in reversible systems [7,14], in this paper we have adopted the alternating model because of the probabilistic branching bisimulation congruence developed for it in [3] along with equational and logical characterizations and a polynomial-time decision procedure. In the non-alternating model, for which branching bisimilarity has been just defined in [43], weak variants of bisimulation semantics require – to achieve transitivity – that a single transition be matched by a convex combination of several transitions – corresponding to the use of randomized schedulers – which causes such equivalences not to be decidable in polynomial time [10].

As far as future extensions are concerned, we would like to include recursion in the considered process language. This requires identifying a suitable probabilistic variant of the up-to technique for weak bisimilarity [40], to be used in the proof of certain results in place of proceeding by induction on the depth of the tree-like PLTS underlying the considered process term.

Acknowledgment. This research has been supported by the PRIN 2020 project *NiR-vAna – Noninterference and Reversibility Analysis in Private Blockchains*.

References

1. Aldini, A.: Classification of security properties in a Linda-like process algebra. Sci. Comput. Program. **63**, 16–38 (2006)
2. Aldini, A., Bravetti, M., Gorrieri, R.: A process-algebraic approach for the analysis of probabilistic noninterference. J. Comput. Secur. **12**, 191–245 (2004)
3. Andova, S., Georgievska, S., Trcka, N.: Branching bisimulation congruence for probabilistic systems. Theoret. Comput. Sci. **413**, 58–72 (2012)
4. Baier, C., Hermanns, H.: Weak bisimulation for fully probabilistic processes. In: Grumberg, O. (ed.) CAV 1997. LNCS, vol. 1254, pp. 119–130. Springer, Heidelberg (1997). https://doi.org/10.1007/3-540-63166-6_14
5. Barbuti, R., Tesei, L.: A decidable notion of timed non-interference. Fund. Inform. **54**, 137–150 (2003)
6. Bennett, C.H.: Logical reversibility of computation. IBM J. Res. Dev. **17**, 525–532 (1973)
7. Bernardo, M., Esposito, A.: Modal logic characterizations of forward, reverse, and forward-reverse bisimilarities. In: Proceedings of the 14th International Symposium on Games, Automata, Logics, and Formal Verification (GANDALF 2023). EPTCS, vol. 390, pp. 67–81 (2023)
8. Bernardo, M., Mezzina, C.A.: Bridging causal reversibility and time reversibility: a stochastic process algebraic approach. Logical Methods Comput. Sci. **19**(2:6), 1–27 (2023)

9. Brookes, S., Hoare, C., Roscoe, A.: A theory of communicating sequential processes. J. ACM **31**, 560–599 (1984)
10. Cattani, S., Segala, R.: Decision algorithms for probabilistic bisimulation[*]. In: Brim, L., Křetínský, M., Kučera, A., Jančar, P. (eds.) CONCUR 2002. LNCS, vol. 2421, pp. 371–386. Springer, Heidelberg (2002). https://doi.org/10.1007/3-540-45694-5_25
11. Chatterjee, K., Goharshady, A.K., Pourdamghani, A.: Probabilistic smart contracts: secure randomness on the blockchain. In: Proceedings of the 1st IEEE International Conference on Blockchain and Cryptocurrency (ICBC 2019), pp. 403–412. IEEE-CS Press (2019)
12. Danos, V., Krivine, J.: Reversible communicating systems. In: Gardner, P., Yoshida, N. (eds.) CONCUR 2004. LNCS, vol. 3170, pp. 292–307. Springer, Heidelberg (2004). https://doi.org/10.1007/978-3-540-28644-8_19
13. Danos, V., Krivine, J.: Transactions in RCCS. In: Abadi, M., de Alfaro, L. (eds.) CONCUR 2005. LNCS, vol. 3653, pp. 398–412. Springer, Heidelberg (2005). https://doi.org/10.1007/11539452_31
14. De Nicola, R., Montanari, U., Vaandrager, F.: Back and forth bisimulations. In: Baeten, J.C.M., Klop, J.W. (eds.) CONCUR 1990. LNCS, vol. 458, pp. 152–165. Springer, Heidelberg (1990). https://doi.org/10.1007/BFb0039058
15. Esposito, A., Aldini, A., Bernardo, M.: Branching bisimulation semantics enables noninterference analysis of reversible systems. In: Huisman, M., Ravara, A. (eds.) Formal Techniques for Distributed Objects, Components, and Systems, FORTE 2023, LNCS, vol. 13910, pp. 57–74. Springer, Cham (2023). https://doi.org/10.1007/978-3-031-35355-0_5
16. Focardi, R., Gorrieri, R.: Classification of security properties. In: Focardi, R., Gorrieri, R. (eds.) FOSAD 2000. LNCS, vol. 2171, pp. 331–396. Springer, Heidelberg (2001). https://doi.org/10.1007/3-540-45608-2_6
17. Focardi, R., Rossi, S.: Information flow security in dynamic contexts. J. Comput. Secur. **14**, 65–110 (2006)
18. Giachino, E., Lanese, I., Mezzina, C.A.: Causal-consistent reversible debugging. In: Gnesi, S., Rensink, A. (eds.) FASE 2014. LNCS, vol. 8411, pp. 370–384. Springer, Heidelberg (2014). https://doi.org/10.1007/978-3-642-54804-8_26
19. van Glabbeek, R.J.: The linear time – branching time spectrum I. In: Handbook of Process Algebra, pp. 3–99. Elsevier (2001)
20. van Glabbeek, R.J., Smolka, S.A., Steffen, B.: Reactive, generative and stratified models of probabilistic processes. Inf. Comput. **121**, 59–80 (1995)
21. van Glabbeek, R.J., Weijland, W.P.: Branching time and abstraction in bisimulation semantics. J. ACM **43**, 555–600 (1996)
22. Goguen, J.A., Meseguer, J.: Security policies and security models. In: Proceedings of the 2nd IEEE Symposium on Security and Privacy (SSP 1982), pp. 11–20. IEEE-CS Press (1982)
23. Hansson, H., Jonsson, B.: A calculus for communicating systems with time and probabilities. In: Proceedings of the 11th IEEE Real-Time Systems Symposium (RTSS 1990), pp. 278–287. IEEE-CS Press (1990)
24. Hedin, D., Sabelfeld, A.: A perspective on information-flow control. In: Software Safety and Security – Tools for Analysis and Verification, pp. 319–347. IOS Press (2012)
25. Hillston, J., Marin, A., Piazza, C., Rossi, S.: Persistent stochastic non-interference. Fund. Inform. **181**, 1–35 (2021)
26. Keller, R.M.: Formal verification of parallel programs. Commun. ACM **19**, 371–384 (1976)

27. Landauer, R.: Irreversibility and heat generation in the computing process. IBM J. Res. Dev. **5**, 183–191 (1961)
28. Lanese, I., Lienhardt, M., Mezzina, C.A., Schmitt, A., Stefani, J.-B.: Concurrent flexible reversibility. In: Felleisen, M., Gardner, P. (eds.) ESOP 2013. LNCS, vol. 7792, pp. 370–390. Springer, Heidelberg (2013). https://doi.org/10.1007/978-3-642-37036-6_21
29. Lanese, I., Nishida, N., Palacios, A., Vidal, G.: CauDEr: a causal-consistent reversible debugger for erlang. In: Gallagher, J.P., Sulzmann, M. (eds.) FLOPS 2018. LNCS, vol. 10818, pp. 247–263. Springer, Cham (2018). https://doi.org/10.1007/978-3-319-90686-7_16
30. Laursen, J., Ellekilde, L.P., Schultz, U.: Modelling reversible execution of robotic assembly. Robotica **36**, 625–654 (2018)
31. Mantel, H.: Information flow and noninterference. In: Encyclopedia of Cryptography and Security, pp. 605–607. Springer, Cham (2011)
32. Milner, R.: Communication and Concurrency. Prentice Hall, Saddle River (1989)
33. Park, D.: Concurrency and automata on infinite sequences. In: Deussen, P. (ed.) GI-TCS 1981. LNCS, vol. 104, pp. 167–183. Springer, Heidelberg (1981). https://doi.org/10.1007/BFb0017309
34. Perumalla, K., Park, A.: Reverse computation for rollback-based fault tolerance in large parallel systems - evaluating the potential gains and systems effects. Clust. Comput. **17**, 303–313 (2014)
35. Philippou, A., Lee, I., Sokolsky, O.: Weak bisimulation for probabilistic systems. In: Palamidessi, C. (ed.) CONCUR 2000. LNCS, vol. 1877, pp. 334–349. Springer, Heidelberg (2000). https://doi.org/10.1007/3-540-44618-4_25
36. Phillips, I., Ulidowski, I.: Reversing algebraic process calculi. J. Logic Algebraic Program. **73**, 70–96 (2007)
37. Phillips, I., Ulidowski, I., Yuen, S.: A reversible process calculus and the modelling of the ERK Signalling pathway. In: Glück, R., Yokoyama, T. (eds.) RC 2012. LNCS, vol. 7581, pp. 218–232. Springer, Heidelberg (2013). https://doi.org/10.1007/978-3-642-36315-3_18
38. Pinna, G.M.: Reversing steps in membrane systems computations. In: Gheorghe, M., Rozenberg, G., Salomaa, A., Zandron, C. (eds.) CMC 2017. LNCS, vol. 10725, pp. 245–261. Springer, Cham (2018). https://doi.org/10.1007/978-3-319-73359-3_16
39. Sabelfeld, A., Sands, D.: Probabilistic noninterference for multi-threaded programs. In: Proceedings of the 13th IEEE Computer Security Foundations Workshop (CSF 2000), pp. 200–214 (2000)
40. Sangiorgi, D., Milner, R.: The problem of weak bisimulation up to. In: Cleaveland, W.R. (ed.) CONCUR 1992. LNCS, vol. 630, pp. 32–46. Springer, Heidelberg (1992). https://doi.org/10.1007/BFb0084781
41. Schordan, M., Oppelstrup, T., Jefferson, D., Barnes, P., Jr.: Generation of reversible C++ code for optimistic parallel discrete event simulation. N. Gener. Comput. **36**, 257–280 (2018)
42. Segala, R.: Modeling and Verification of Randomized Distributed Real-Time Systems. PhD Thesis (1995)
43. Segala, R., Lynch, N.: Probabilistic simulations for probabilistic processes. In: Jonsson, B., Parrow, J. (eds.) CONCUR 1994. LNCS, vol. 836, pp. 481–496. Springer, Heidelberg (1994). https://doi.org/10.1007/978-3-540-48654-1_35
44. Segala, R., Turrini, A.: Comparative analysis of bisimulation relations on alternating and non-alternating probabilistic models. In: Proceedings of the 2nd Interna-

tional Conference on the Quantitative Evaluation of Systems (QEST 2005), pp. 44–53. IEEE-CS Press (2005)

45. Siljak, H., Psara, K., Philippou, A.: Distributed antenna selection for massive MIMO using reversing Petri nets. IEEE Wirel. Commun. Lett. **8**, 1427–1430 (2019)

46. Vassor, M., Stefani, J.-B.: Checkpoint/Rollback vs causally-consistent reversibility. In: Kari, J., Ulidowski, I. (eds.) RC 2018. LNCS, vol. 11106, pp. 286–303. Springer, Cham (2018). https://doi.org/10.1007/978-3-319-99498-7_20

47. Volpano, D., Smith, G.: Probabilistic noninterference in a concurrent language. In: Proceedings of the 11th IEEE Computer Security Foundations Workshop (CSF 1998), pp. 34–43. IEEE-CS Press (1998)

48. de Vries, E., Koutavas, V., Hennessy, M.: Communicating transactions. In: Gastin, P., Laroussinie, F. (eds.) CONCUR 2010. LNCS, vol. 6269, pp. 569–583. Springer, Heidelberg (2010). https://doi.org/10.1007/978-3-642-15375-4_39

JustAct: Actions Universally Justified by Partial Dynamic Policies

Christopher A. Esterhuyse$^{(\boxtimes)}$, Tim Müller ,
and L. Thomas van Binsbergen

Informatics Institute, University of Amsterdam, Amsterdam, The Netherlands
{c.a.esterhuyse,t.muller}@uva.nl, ltvanbinsbergen@acm.org

Abstract. Inter-organisational data exchange is regulated by norms originating from sources ranging from individual consent to (inter)-national laws. Verifying norm-compliance is complex because laws (e.g., GDPR) distribute responsibility and require accountability. Moreover, in some domains (e.g., healthcare), the norms themselves may be private. In contrast, standard solutions (e.g., access- and usage-control, smart contracts) reason about policies that are assumed to be public. Instead, we present a novel framework prescribing how decentralised agents decide which actions are justified, despite their partial views of the policy. Crucially, justifications are universal, e.g., accepted by future auditors. Agents establish a common notion of compliance through an (externally synchronized) agreement, which is the basis of each justification defined by policy fragments agents autonomously create, gossip, and assemble.

We demonstrate our framework with a federated medical data processing system, using Datalog with weak negation as a minimal policy language.

Keywords: Decentralised · Framework · Composition · Coordination · Multi-agent System · Policy · Program Refinement · Specification

1 Introduction

Data exchange systems are distributed systems facilitating the controlled sharing, trading, and processing of (often large) datasets and analysis results within data exchange applications, increasing the public, commercial or academic value of collected data. Following the inter-organisational nature of data exchange systems, and the (market or privacy) sensitive nature of the exchanged assets, collaborating organisations adopt (potentially complex) governance models [53] in an attempt to ensure compliance with regulations and contractual agreements. In support of such governance models, high levels of control should be given to organisations to influence the execution of data exchange applications, e.g. via access control [40,44] or usage control [25,36,59]. Furthermore, high levels of accountability are required to support dispute resolution [48] and for demonstrating legal compliance [14]. Data exchange systems exhibit a fundamental

© IFIP International Federation for Information Processing 2024
Published by Springer Nature Switzerland AG 2024
V. Castiglioni and A. Francalanza (Eds.): FORTE 2024, LNCS 14678, pp. 60–81, 2024.
https://doi.org/10.1007/978-3-031-62645-6_4

trade-off between maximising the availability of data to data users and maximising the control over data to data owners, subjects and (privacy) authorities. In this work we present a framework that enables the organisations collaborating in a data exchange system to formalise their shared and individual position with respect to this trade-off through powerful, declarative *policies*.

Our approach is to define a framework that specifies the relation between runtime system dynamics (messages and actions) and statics (policies and facts) such that they interact. In one direction: agent messages create and disseminate policies. In the other direction: policies specify which actions are permitted. Crucially, permission is decidable, despite agents having only partial knowledge of the existing policies, and despite policies being changed at runtime. Moreover, these decisions are agreed by all agents, e.g., an actor can be confident that other actors (e.g., auditors) will agree that their actions were permitted. For maximum applicability, our framework is parametric to the *policy language*, whose syntax defines the set of *policies*, and whose semantics defines their relation to *facts*. In this work, we demonstrate the framework as instantiated with the policy language *Datalog with weak negation* (Datalog⁻).

This work represents a step in an on-going investigation into generic, policy-driven data exchange systems satisfying legal requirements (e.g. accountability and auditability). The framework in this paper has a prototype implementation supported by a bespoke domain-specific policy language (not presented here). We intend to make our policy framework an integral part of the Brane workflow execution system [55], a central component in the EPI Framework [26], and demonstrate its applicability in a variety of use cases.

After some background (Sect. 2), we contribute:

1. the definition of a **framework** for agents acting on shared policies while communicating, refining, and modifying those policies (Sect. 3),
2. a **demonstrative application** of our instantiated framework to a distributed, multi-agent, medical workflow processing system (Sect. 4).

In Sect. 5, we consider implementation decisions for instantiating the framework. We discuss our contributions by their own merits (Sect. 6) and in comparison to related work (Sect. 7) before concluding with a summary (Sect. 8).

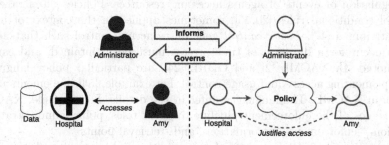

Fig. 1. Conceptual use-case of the framework. Agents autonomously choose to act, accessing data in the real world (left), as permitted by their shared policies (right).

2   Background

Distributed Systems and Algorithms. *Distributed systems* model the distribution of a stateful *configuration* over a set of *processes*; each process has its own, local *state*. *Distributed algorithms*, when implemented by each processes, give systems useful, emergent properties. Often, these algorithms assume only basic, asynchronous and unreliable message-passing, comparable to IP and UDP. Some algorithms solve distributed problems (e.g., self-stabilisation), and create useful abstractions (e.g., synchronisers).

In this work, we refer to two classes of algorithms. Firstly, *gossip* protocols disseminate information from peer (process) to peer, which results in decentralisation and robustness, by imposing minimal requirements on the network topology and process behaviour [5]. Secondly, *consensus algorithms* establish fundamental agreement on the selection of a value, consistently among processes. Consensus has been well-studied for decades [41], but has seen renewed interest in application to blockchain technologies, for example, in [29,30].

Agents and Autonomy. The field of *multi-agent systems* studies processes (called *agents*) that exhibit social phenomena as a result of their agency or *autonomy*: agents are motivated by goals to draw from their partial information to act on shared resources and interact with other agents. Literature explores a variety of (software models of) social organisations, ranging from cooperative data-sharing *consortia* (e.g., in [19]) to competitive markets (e.g., in [61]).

Agent-oriented programming studies the programming of agents, balancing the usual software- and language-engineering concerns, shared with object-oriented programming, with a unique emphasis on agent autonomy. For example, agent autonomy also tends to improve system scalability and robustness. All these ideas are present in seminal agent-oriented programming works like [51], and persist into more recent works like the survey [34].

Policy Languages. We give a very brief overview of the various forms of policy developed in various disciplines, and influencing our work.

Access control is a mainstay in cyber-physical systems that revolves around the regulation of events of agents accessing resources. Policies often take the form of conditional rules [20,45], sometimes applied in the context of meta-data attributes [47]. *Usage control* generalises access control such that access events occur for a duration of time; access must be maintained, and can be interrupted [1]. XACML [2] and ODRL [24], are particular policy languages for implementing access- and usage-control. For example, [54] implements usage control in XACML. The languages differ in the details. For example, XACML maps stages of the enforcement pipeline to agent roles: policy-administration-, -decision-, -enforcement-, -information-, and -retrieval-points.

Normative specifications specify fundamental social relations such as power, duties, rights, obligations, and permissions [3]. Legal regulations specify normative policies ("norms") in the context of executive (e.g., governmental) agencies and organisations. The EU General Data Protection Regulation [18] specifies the legal usage and access to data within the European Union. Its wide reach and impact make it influential even outside the EU. The study of norms reflects its long history in its rich nomenclature, for example, [10] clarifies the relationship between *substantive* and *procedural* norms, and [23] defines *open-texture terms*.

A wealth of other works intentionally blurs the line between these various notions of policy. For example, the eFLINT language [7] formalises norms using the Hohfeldian framework of legal proceedings [58] and has been used for access control [6]. Symboleo [49] and Fievel [57] are similar languages with similar goals, that differ in the details. For example, eFLINT particularly emphasises its logical reasoning features. These tools afford the application of various disciplines and tools to policies. For example, applying model-driven development [46], and model-checking for high-level properties in policies, e.g., expressed in Symboleo [38].

The Datalog¬ Language. *Logic programming* languages are designed to straightforwardly operationalise various logics. Here, we give an account of Datalog¬ sufficient to understand the Datalog¬ examples throughout this article.

Datalog, overviewed in [12], is a simple logic programming language: each program is a set of *Horn clauses* called *rules*. Precisely, each rule has form $(c_1 \wedge c_2 \wedge ... \wedge c_m \leftarrow a_2 \wedge a_2 \wedge ... \wedge a_n)$, where *consequents* $c_{1...m}$ and *antecedents* $a_{1...n}$ are *facts* constructed by applying a predicate symbol p to constants and (first-order) variables. The Datalog semantics gives each program a *model*, mapping *ground* facts (without variables) to Boolean values. Most literature uses the same concrete syntax: ($\leftarrow$) and ($\wedge$) are denoted (:-) and (,), respectively, and only variable identifiers begin with uppercase letters. For example, knows(amy,X) :- knows(X,amy) formalises "Amy knows everyone that knows Amy".

Various dialects of Datalog have been studied in the literature, exploring the combination of various features. Datalog¬ [50] is a useful generalisation: antecedents may be negated (with ¬, often written not), conditioning consequents on the absence of truths. This strictly improves expressiveness [28], because it affords *non-monotonic reasoning*: each reasoning step may *remove* truths [52]. Equivalently, truth is non-monotonic with respect to the addition of rules to programs. For example, fact sun is true in program sun :- not clouds, but false after rule clouds is added; we say sun is *falsified*. Unfortunately, not all Datalog¬ programs have unique logical interpretations. Accordingly, different semantics exist (e.g., stable model [22] and well-founded [56]) attributing different models to these *unstratified* (defined in [42]) programs. For example, what should be the value of p in p :- not p? Fortunately, we consider no such programs in this article.

Several tools can interpret (super-languages of) Datalog¬. For example, the Clingo answer-set solver [21][1] can interpret each Datalog¬ example in this article.

---

[1] An online Clingo interpreter is available at https://potassco.org/clingo/run.

3   Distributed Runtime Framework

This section defines the framework by supplementing Fig. 2 with requirements, explanations, motivations, and examples. We summarise the framework as follows:

Agents make statements carrying policies that model the system.
Agents gossip, assemble, and validate statements to build justifications.
Agents only take actions that are permitted by their justifications.

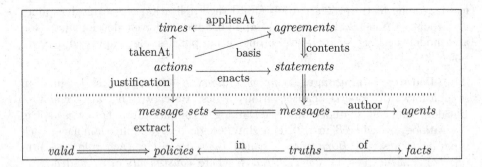

Fig. 2. Graph of sets and functions (objects) defined by users of the framework. Sets are named in italics. Functions are denoted as arrows (→) from domain to co-domain. Functions are identified by their co-domain (or by a label if given). The dotted line partitions objects into *dynamics* (above) and *statics* (below). At runtime, new elements may be added to dynamic objects, but static objects are fixed. Each (⇒) is a typed identity function, e.g., *statements* ⊆ *messages*. All functions shown are pure and total. For example, some policy is extracted from each message set.

Figure 2 defines a set of named *objects*: sets and functions over the sets. The framework is used by defining (the elements of) these objects. We partition objects into *static* and *dynamic* objects, each discussed in their own subsections. To use the framework, a user *instantiates* it by defining the objects in Fig. 2 such that the *framework requirements* are preserved. The most fundamental framework requirements are expressed in the figure; for example, each *action* has exactly one *justification*, and the *contents* of each *agreement* is a *message*. The remaining framework requirements are introduced throughout this section. The framework guarantees Properties 1 and 2, i.e., agents always agree on action *permission* and *effects*, which are both precisely defined in Sect. 3.2.

Ultimately, we explain how agents can act autonomously while enforcing the *well-behavedness* (Definition 1) of themselves and their peers in practice.

Property 1 *Agents always agree whether a given action is permitted.*

Property 2 *Agents always agree on the effects of a given action.*

Definition 1 *An agent is well-behaved iff all of its actions is permitted.*

The rest of the section discusses the framework in general, and incrementally builds an example framework instantiation, using policies built from only the Datalog⁻ rules in Table 1. We use a running example of well-behaved agents Amy and Bob. Ultimately, Bob enacts r_d, which has the effect of deleting Data1.

Henceforth, we use the following notation. We distinguish definitions ($\triangleq$) from assertions of equality ($=$). We denote disjoint set union as ($\uplus$), i.e., $a \uplus b = a \cup b$ iff sets a and b are disjoint, and otherwise, $a \uplus b$ is undefined.

3.1   Static Objects

The static objects are fixed at runtime. They concern the fundamentals of the framework: data types, and the syntax and semantics of the policy language.

The **agents**[2] of the framework author **messages** occurring dynamically as statements. We take for granted that ($\in$) relates messages to *message sets* as expected, and we treat each message m also as the singleton set $\{m\}$. Statements communicate **policies** (see **extract** below). Policies determine which subset of possible facts are *true*, defined $true(f, p) \triangleq \exists t \in truths : (of(t) = f) \wedge (in(t) = p)$. We instantiate *policies* as the subsets of the *(policy) rules* shown in Table 1. Hence, ($\cup$) is a natural policy-composition operator, unifying rules. Note that composition does not generally unify *truths*. We use the semantics of Datalog⁻ to define facts and truth: f is true in p iff $f \in [p]$, the *stable model* of policy p, for example, it holds in the case where $f = $ error and $p = \{r_m\}$.

We instantiate **valid** to characterise policies without errors. Precisely, we let $p \in valid \triangleq \neg true(\text{error}, p)$. Despite the simplicity of this definition, (in)validity emerges from complex rule interactions. For example, no valid policy is a superset of $\{r_m, r_n\}$, as these suffice to infer the truth of error. Section 4 demonstrates how (in)validity lays the groundwork for inter-agent power dynamics.

The definition of **extract** determines the policies agents can express, as agents understand policy $extract(m)$ as the subjective assertions of agent $author(m)$.

We instantiate $extract$ as a pure function of the message author and the message *payload*, which is an arbitrary policy, chosen by the author. Intuitively,

Table 1. Example *(policy) rules* expressed in Datalog⁻ and natural language. Each rule's name is suggested by the underlined keyword. A policy is any rule set.

Name	In natural language	As Datalog⁻ rules
r_m	Amy <u>must</u> confirm	`error :- not ctl-confirms(amy)`
r_n	Amy must <u>not</u> confirm	`error :- ctl-confirms(amy)`
r_c	Amy <u>confirms</u> if someone is trusted	`ctl-confirms(amy) :- ctl-trusts(amy, X)`
r_t	Amy <u>trusts</u> Bob	`ctl-trusts(amy, bob)`
r_d	Bob <u>deletes</u> Data1.	`ctl-deletes(bob, data1)`

---

[2] Unless otherwise specified, we let framework agents coincide with the agents of the underlying distributed system.

extract invalidates payloads with undesirable author-rule pairs. Precisely, we let
$extract(\{m\}) \triangleq payload(m) \cup \{\texttt{error} \mid \forall(r,a) \in owns : (r \in m \land \neg author(m,a))\}$,
where *owns* relates rule r to agent a if r has an antecedent whose predicate
is prefixed by `ctl-` and whose first parameter is constant a. For example, only
Bob owns rule `ctl-deletes(bob, data1)`, while rule `error :- confirms(amy)` has no owner
because fact `error` has neither prefix `ctrl-` nor a constant first parameter. Finally,
we let $extract(\emptyset) \triangleq \emptyset$, $extract(\{m\} \uplus M) \triangleq extract(\{m\}) \cup extract(M)$, i.e., the
policy extracted from each message set is the composition of policies extracted
from each message. This simple definition confers a property that simplifies
reasoning: *extract* commutes and associates over message set union.

The above definition of *extract* uses invalidity to constrain which subjective
assertions are available to each agent. For example, because Bob owns r_d, for
each message m, either Bob authors m, $r_d \notin payload(m)$, or $extract(m)$ is invalid.
Bob can rest assured that Amy alone cannot meaningfully assert r_d.

3.2 Dynamic Objects

Dynamic objects are defined by each system configuration at runtime. They
instantiate the statics, and must be stored and communicated by agents.

At runtime, a subset of messages are **statements**, the messages that have
been created and shared at runtime. Intuitively, statements have few restrictions, but therefore, they have little impact of their own. They are meaningful
because of their relationship with actions. In practice, we expect each statement
to be *autonomously* created by its author, i.e., as decided by the author alone.
In theory, the set of statements grows forever. In practice, agents and networks
have finite storage capacity, so we let agents forget or discard statements. For our
purposes, it suffices if the existence of a given statement is semi-decidable: agents
can decide (and prove) that it exists by observing (and showing) it. In practice,
the integrity and provenance of statements is preserved by authors cryptograph-
ically signing their statements, and agents ignoring statements without their
authors' signatures. Agents share statements with their peers (e.g., via gossip),
for their own reasons, and at their own pace. Section 4 demonstrates a case where
an agent intentionally withholds a statement from other agents.

Agreements attribute special meaning to selected statements at selected
times. We require that membership be decidable. Intuitively, this lays the
groundwork for agents agreeing which actions are permitted. In practice, agents
explicitly synchronise the set of agreements. Synchronisation may be infrequent;
e.g., one synchronisation creates agreements for times from 100 to 500. Synchronisation may be sparse; e.g., agents maintain a synchronised *current* time and
implicitly extend all current agreements until the next explicit synchronisation.
For simplicity in the examples henceforth, we assume a set of *current* agreements
which appears to change as different statements are agreed to apply at future
times.

At runtime, there is a growing set of (taken) **actions**. Each action is *takenAt*
some time, has a *basis* agreement, *enacts* a statement, and is *justified* by a message set. We call agent a the *actor* of action a' iff $a = author(enacts(a'))$. Like

statements, actions are created autonomously (by their actors) and then shared between agents by unspecified gossip. Unlike statements, actions are restricted such that they can be effectful and meaningful. Precisely, well-behaved agents only *permitted* actions, defined as preserving Properties 3 to 6. Well-behavedness has only extrinsic value: when an agent takes a non-permitted action, this violates the expectations and trust of their peers, and may have external consequences. For example, Amy is harmed if Bob deletes Data1 without permission. Well-behavedness is enforceable if Properties 3 to 6 are each decidable.

In practice, agents preserve their own well-behavedness with *ex-ante* enforcement, i.e., checking permission *before* acting. Agents enforce well-behavedness on each other using *ex-post* enforcement, i.e., checking permission of taken actions via run-time monitoring or auditing. For example, we expect real systems to require agents to remain accountable of their actions to auditors, such that they cannot preserve the appearance of well-behavedness by hiding their actions.

Property 3 (Stated) $\forall a \in actions : justification(a) \subseteq statements.$

Property 4 (Relevant) $\forall a \in actions : \{basis(a), enact(a)\} \subseteq justification(a).$

Property 5 (Valid) $\forall a \in actions : extract(justification(a)) \in valid.$

Property 6 (Based) $\forall a \in action : takenAt(a) = appliesAt(basis(a)).$

Property 3 requires that justifications consist only of statements. For example, where $author(m) =$ Bob, until Bob states m, Amy cannot take actions which necessarily include m in their justification. Property 4 ensures that each justification includes the action's basis and enacted statements. Thus, each justification is constrained by some agreement, and by the enacted statement. For example, Bob cannot enact r_d with a justification in which deletes(bob, data1) is not true. Property 5 limits justifications to those whose extracted policies are valid. For example, recall that only Bob owns r_d. Hence, Amy can make statements whose payloads include r_d, but those statements can be safely ignored, as they can never be included in valid justifications. Finally, Property 6 ensures that each action is based on an agreement that applies at the time the action is taken. Clearly, adding new agreements (e.g., to future times) does not affect past actions. However, the choice of agreements that apply in the future determines which actions are permitted in the future. For example, the selection of future agreements simulates updating the payload of the currently agreed statement m_a from $\{r_m, r_t\}$ to $\{r_t\}$, mirroring relaxations in the requirements of the GDPR. New actions are permitted to Bob in the future, as Amy's confirmation is no longer required.

Property 1 follows from agents coming to the same conclusions about the permission of each action a, as Properties 3 to 6 depend only on a's justification and the agreement when it is created (which both remain fixed). Property 2 follows from fixing the effects of each action. We propose the following definition in particular: $effects(a) \triangleq \{f \mid \forall f \in facts, true(extract(enacts(a)), f)\}$, i.e., each action's effects are the truths[3] in the enacted statement. With these properties, the framework structures the interaction between agents, and ensures that agents maintain a common understanding of actions' permission and effects.

The relaxation to agreement m_a permits Bob to take action a, which enacts m_b where $payload(m_b) = \{r_d\}$, and has agreement m_a and justification $\{m_a, m_b\}$. Amy and Bob agree that the action is permitted, because it satisfies Properties 3 to 6. Amy and Bob agree this action has one effect: Bob deletes Data1.

4   Case Study: Processing Distributed Medical Data

This section demonstrates an instantiation of the framework through an example application, using Datalog⁻ as the policy language.

We adopt the example instantiation of Sect. 3, including the definitions of *agent*, *fact*, *extract*, *valid*, and so on. However, we instead instantiate *policies* as the syntactic category of all Datalog⁻ programs. For example, Amy can author a statement with payload policy ctl-knows(bob,amy), but the extracted policy is ctl-knows(bob,amy). error, which is invalid, as it has truths $\{$ctl-knows(bob,amy), error$\}$. Furthermore, the statements of the *consortium* agent represents the consensus of the agents at large. Precisely, we instantiate *agreements* such that some agreement applies at time n with contents s if and only if s is the consortium's nth statement. Agents synchronise agreements, but only act on the most recent agreement.

Step 1 – We begin with a runtime session formalising a simple requirement: agents agree that it is an error for a data scientists to access data without the authorisation of the *administrator*. Initially, the only agreement contains s_1:

```
% Statement 's1' by 'consortium' (contents of agreement at time 1)
owns(administrator, Data) :- ctl-accesses(Accessor, Data).
error :- ctl-accesses(Accessor, Data), owns(Owner, Data),
         not ctl-authorises(Owner, Accessor, Data).
```

Via a secondary communication channel, not reflected in the framework, agent *Amy* convinces the administrator to authorise Amy's access to data x-rays.

```
% Statement 's2' by 'administrator'
ctl-authorises(administrator, amy, x-rays).
```

Amy collects the above statements, and then states s_3 (below). Amy takes action a, which enacts s_3, and has basis s_1 and has justification $j \triangleq \{s_1, s_2, s_3\}$. For clarity, just this once, we detail the reasoning of an arbitrary observer of a given action; they draw the following conclusions about a:

- a preserves Property 3, as $j \subseteq statements$ (in fact, currently, $j = statements$);
- a preserves Property 4, as $s_1 = basis(a)$; $s_3 = enacts(a)$, and $\{s_1, s_3\} \subseteq j$;

---

[3] In practice, it may be desirable to decouple truths from effects. For example, restricting effects to subset of *constant* truths $(effect(a, f) \triangleq \forall p : true(p \cup enacts(a), f))$ lets agents reason about the effects of each action via the possible justifications.

- a preserves Property 5, as where $p \triangleq extract(j)$, no p rule has the wrong author, so extraction preserves the payload-rules and adds no error, and fact error is not true in the resulting Datalog¬ model making p valid;
- a preserves Property 6, as a's basis applies at the time a is taken.

All observers agree that this action is permitted. Furthermore, they agree that a has the singleton set of effects {ctl-accesses(amy, x-rays)}, the truths of s_3. Amy mirrors this effect in the world outside, accessing the data identified by x-rays.

```
% Statement 's3' authored by 'amy'
ctl-accesses(amy, x-rays).
```

Anton "the antagonist" attempts to interfere with the normal operation of the system by making statements s_4 and s_5. However, no other agent takes any notice. Firstly, the policy extracted from s_4 is invalid, making it useless in justifying actions. Secondly, Statement s_5 is valid, but agents have no incentive to consider it, as it does not falsify owns(administrator, x-rays), instead only further restricting access. Unlike agreement s_1, agents have no need to include s_5 in justifications.

```
% Statement 's4' authored by 'anton'.
ctl-authorises(administrator, anton, x-rays).
```

```
% Statement 's5' authored by 'anton'
owns(anton, x-rays).
```

Step 2 – The administrator makes a new statement that empowers other agents to create authorisations (delegation). The administrator automatically authorises Bob's access to x-rays when authorized by both hospitals h_1 and h_2.

```
% Statement 's6' authored by 'administrator'
ctl-authorises(administrator, bob, x-rays) :- ctl-authorises(h1, bob, x-rays),
                                              ctl-authorises(h2, bob, x-rays).
```

Now, it suffices for Bob to acquire authorisation to access x-rays from the administrator or from (h_1 and h_2). Hospital h_1 further shares their power with h_2.

```
% Statement 's7' authored by 'h1'
ctl-authorises(h1, Accessor, x-rays) :- ctl-authorises(h2, Accessor, x-rays).
```

Now, it suffices for Bob to acquire authorisation to access x-rays from h_2 or from the administrator. Hospital h_2 grants this for all agents except Anton. Precisely, the authorisations of hospital h_2 are only applicable on the condition that ctl-accesses(anton, x-rays) is false. Thus, s_8 is useless to Anton.

```
% Statement 's8' authored by 'h2'
ctl-authorises(h2, Accessor, x-rays) :- ctl-accesses(Accessor, x-rays),
                                        not ctl-accesses(anton    , x-rays).
```

Bob states and enacts s_9 with justification {s_1, s_6, s_7, s_8, s_9}. Agents agree that this action is permitted and has the effect ctl-accesses(bob, x-rays).

```
% Statement 's9' authored by 'bob'
ctl-accesses(bob, x-rays).
```

An (ex-ante) access control mechanism can prevent access to Anton by observing that there is no justification for the action with the effect `ctl-accesses(anton, x-rays)`. Alternatively, a monitoring or auditing mechanism may feed any observed access violation and message history to an ex-post enforcement authority.

Step 3 – The members of the consortium re-negotiate their agreement, because the administrator currently holds too much power. For example, the administrator stating `ctl-authorises(administrator, anton, x-rays)` would have sufficed to let Anton justify accessing x-rays, circumventing the need for authorisations from the hospitals. The new agreement s_{10} gives the power of authorisation to the (virtual) consortium agent itself and distributes the power between the administrator and the hospitals: the hospitals label datasets as relevant for research into the flu (the illness) and the administrator determines which researcher can study the flu.

```
% Statement 's10' authored by 'consortium' (contents of agreement at time 2)
error :- ctl-accesses(Accessor, Data),
     not ctl-authorises(consortium, Accessor, Data).
ctl-authorises(consortium, Accessor, Data)) :-
                    ctl-labels(administrator, Accessor, flu-researcher),
                    ctl-labels(Hospital    , Data    , flu-data),
                    ctl-hospital(consortium, Hospital).
ctl-hospital(consortium, h1).
ctl-hospital(consortium, h2).
```

Dan wishes to access x-rays. Dan petitions the administrator and hospital h_1 to make the necessary statements. The two agents cooperate.

```
% Statement 's11' authored by 'administrator'
ctl-labels(administrator, dan, flu-researcher).
```

```
% Statement 's12' authored by 'h1'
ctl-labels(h1, x-rays, flu-data).
```

Dan states and enacts s_{13} with justification $\{s_{10}, s_{11}, s_{12}, s_{13}\}$. Agents agree that this action is permitted and has the effect `ctl-accesses(dan, x-rays)`.

```
% Statement 's13' authored by 'dan'
ctl-accesses(dan, x-rays).
```

Step 4 – We demonstrate how agents can act in complete confidence that their action is permitted, despite partial knowledge of the existing statements.

Hospital h_1 automates their labelling of flu data based on the consent of data subjects. However, consent is itself sensitive information; s_{14} would let an observer infer that the scans are connected to Caterina, a hospital patient. As such, hospital h_1 keeps s_{14} private; the statement is not gossiped to other agents.

```
% Statement 's14' authored by 'h1'
ctl-labels(h1, cat-scans, flu-data) :- ctl-consent(caterina, cat-scans).
```

Dan petitions hospital h_1 to label cat-scans as flu data, such that Dan can access it. The hospital does not grant Dan access immediately, but instead, acquires statement s_{15} (below) from Caterina, and then sends s_{14} and s_{15} to Dan, with the understanding that Dan will keep these statements private.

```
% Statement 's15' authored by 'caterina'
ctl-consent(caterina, cat-scans).
```

Dan states and enacts s_{16} with justification $\{s_{10}, s_{11}, s_{14}, s_{15}, s_{16}\}$. Dan publicises the statement s_{16}, but keeps the justification private. The system is established with rules for access to justifications with sensitive information. The justification is checked only by auditors with special permissions. For example, an automated auditor runs in a contained environment that leaks no information and only publicises the answer to the question: is the given action justified?

```
% Statement 's16' authored by 'dan'
ctl-accesses(dan, cat-scans).
```

Other agents negotiate and enact data accesses despite ignorance of the sensitive statements s_{14} and s_{15}. Their own actions and permissions are unaffected.

5 Implementation

This section discusses the considerations for implementing our framework in general, and describes our ongoing prototype implementation in particular.

5.1 Implementation of the Framework Statics

Sect. 3.1 specifies the requirements on policy language needed to instantiate the framework. Here, we briefly consider the practical design space in general, and describe the approach of our prototype implementation.

Deterministic Truth. To be instantiated, the framework must define *truth* as a static relation over policies and *facts*. This implies a *deterministic* semantics: the same policies always denote the same truths. This ensures that the communication of policies realises a consistent communication of understanding about the domain of discourse. For example, (complete) Prolog is unsuitable as a policy language as its inference procedure is non-terminating. Even if all agents agree on a Prolog program, generally, no agent can be certain that the conclusions drawn will be replicated consistently, e.g., by an auditor checking the validity of a key policy.

Our prototype policy language uses the operational form [39] of the well-founded semantics negation [56], assigning a unique value to each fact by isolating logical contradictions to *unknown values*. For example, p is unknown in `p :- not p.` This semantics confers the necessary property: inference of each program always terminates, and each truth is replicated by every agent every time.

Complex Facts and Reflective Extraction. Sect. 3.1 and Sect. 4 demonstrated two (similar) definitions of the *extract* function, demonstrating its role in controlling which policies authors can express.

Our prototype generalises Datalog⁻ by supporting the construction of *complex facts* like `knows(amy,owns(bob,x-rays))` from other facts. This feature affords a powerful definition of *extract* that more completely reflects the relation between true facts, statements, and authors. Precisely, *extract* injects rules into the policy that reflect the message context at a finer granularity, affording agents more context-sensitive control. For example, agent a cannot assert the truth of fact f with a rule in message m without also asserting the truth of facts `authors`(a, m) and `has-rule-asserting`(m, a). Thus, policies can reflect on the system dynamics, giving their authors more fine-grained control over actions. For example, statements can explicitly refer to particular statements, and condition validity on the author of rules resulting in the truth of particular facts.

5.2 Implementation of the Framework Dynamics

Our prototype implements a proposed policy-enforcement component [17] for the EPI framework [27]. This prescribes the agents and actions relevant to the use case, similar to our demonstration in Sect. 4. The agents include processors, administrators, and owners of sensitive data (hospitals and their patients). The agreement formalises the dependency of processors on the owners. Firstly, with the assistance of planner agents, processors make statements defining data-processing workflows. Secondly, the relevant data owners make statements authorising workflows, permitting their data access and processing actions.

Administrative agents are trusted to mediate the collection and transport of statements between data owners and processors. Agents communicate statements asynchronously, and only synchronise periodically to check for changes to the agreement. The agreement is changed only by the administrators in two circumstances: members join or leave the consortium, or to temporarily halt processing while the infrastructure underlying workflow processing is maintained.

6   Discussion

We discuss the strengths and limitations of (systems instantiating) the framework defined in Sect. 3, and demonstrated in Sect. 4.

6.1   Strengths

Highly Dynamic and Extensible. The framework is highly abstract, making it applicable to many policy languages and runtime systems.

Notably, the framework is parametric to the statically-defined policy language, admitting any formal language affording pure functions of truth and validity. This leaves significant room for systems instantiating the framework to adopt various notions of policy, with various information models, and various semantics. For example, the framework's notion of policy affords the n-ary relations and logical constraints underlying Bell-LaPadua security policies and various Rule-Based Access control policies, which are all summarised and compared in [60]. However, we leave the precise instantiation of these kinds of policy to future work.

Moreover, the relations between agents that ultimately control actions are highly dynamically configurable, by agents making statements. Different configurations confer different characteristics on the system, for example, allowing for dynamic specialisation for various use cases in reaction to runtime information. We recognise two noteworthy spectra on which particular system configurations fall. Together, these help to clarify the ways systems can change their characteristics at runtime. Firstly, systems can be centralised (where inter-agent consistency is high) or decentralised (where many agents have meaningful power to act). Secondly, systems can be highly static (where properties of interest are preserved) or dynamic (where properties can be changed by agents at runtime).

Formal Agent Power Dynamics. Agents are specified to remain well-behaved (Definition 1): agents take only permitted actions. Well-behavedness enables complex power dynamics, because action permission is influenced by statements and agreements. This lets systems model various common and useful normative concepts by delegating power. For example, Sect. 4 demonstrates the administrator sharing power with the hospitals, and also the partitioning of consortium power over the administrator and the hospitals.

Well-behavedness is robust; an agent that violates their own well-behavedness by taking a non-permitted action preserves the well-behavedness of their peers. The permission of actions is independent of (the permission) of actions; each agent must independently justify their actions from the available statements.

Autonomy and Parallelism. Agents synchronise to change agreements. All other communication can be asynchronous, delayed, and lossy. Agents are very autonomous, as they are never fundamentally compelled to act or make statements. Hence, agents are robust to unreliable peers. The framework affords realistic inter-agent enforcement of well-behavedness: agents monitor actions, and actors bear the burden of proving that their actions are permitted. Thus, agents must retain their actions' justifications. However, other statements and actions can be forgotten (e.g., to free memory) while preserving the framework guarantees.

Consistent Permission Despite Privacy. Agents always agree which actions are permitted, despite being defined by statements not known to all agents. This apparent contradiction is resolved by agents being able to decide when their known statements suffice for permission. Moreover, permission is objective; agents are certain that other agents (e.g., future auditors) agree that their actions were permitted, without involving them at all. For example, in Sect. 4, Dan observes s_{15} and Amy does not, but both agree that both are well-behaved.

6.2   Limitations

Costly Justification Search. To remain well-behaved, agents must search for justifications that permit their desired actions. In general, this problem is undecidable. In practice, the difficulty depends on which statements are available, and on the characteristics of the policy language. For example, the operational semantics of Datalog⁻ is desirably tractable. Moreover, this search problem is reducible to many problems well-studied in the literature. We are particularly interested in applying answer set solving (e.g., with Clingo [21]) or model-checking rewrite systems modulo theories (e.g., with Maude [13]) to this problem in future. The hard, general problem is made tractable by restricting policies.

No Obligation to Act (in Time). Our framework offers no fundamental mechanism for agents to compel one another to action. Thus, the framework cannot internalise normative *obligations to act*. These features can be added to systems implementing our framework, but they may have difficulty in compelling agents to act before specific deadlines, as a consequence of the aforementioned point on the search for justifications. For this reason, our framework is not a natural choice for implementations of *real-time systems*, where agents must react to stimuli within strict time limits. Future work can investigate constraints on system configurations that strike desirable compromises between system flexibility on the one hand, and predictability of actions (and their timing) on the other.

Specification of Communication. As specified in Sect. 3.2, and demonstrated in Sect. 4, agents can decide that their actions are universally permitted, despite each having only partial knowledge of the existing statements and actions. However, the framework itself does not prescribe how messages and actions are shared between agents. In future work, we want to supplement the current *(justification) agreements* with *sharing agreements*, which specify how agents share (e.g., gossip) their statements and actions with their peers.

No Privacy from the Actor. Agents are only able to act on permissions defined by *known* statements. For example, in Sect. 4, for Amy to justify access, Amy acquires the patient's consent, revealing the patient identity to Amy. This can be worked around; trusted intermediaries can forward transformed policies to hide private information. In this case, the hospital can authorise Amy's access (unconditionally) after observing the patient consent themselves. In future, we want to systematise these intermediary transformations such that the hidden policy information can always be recovered (e.g., by trusted auditors).

7   Related Work

Our framework prescribes a relation between concerns that are each independently explored in the literature: 1. blockchains can synchronise dynamic, decentralised policies, 2. trust management specifies the delegation of power between agents, and 3. Curie evaluates data access policies as a function of sensitive data.

Smart Ledgers atop Blockchains. Distributed ledgers provide a (probabilistic) means of consensus on the state between decentralised processes. Blockchains are a technology for implementing distributed ledgers. For example, Fabric emphasises scalability [4], while Ouroboros emphasises provable security [31].

Systems such as SmartAccess [37] use distributed ledgers to store policies and (meta-)data, enabling decentralised implementations of the access-control model. However, these technologies synchronise policies, making them unsuitable for private policy information (e.g., the consent rule in s_{16} in Sect. 4).

Other ledger-based systems allow a heterogeneous view on the policy state. For example, Canton [15] (whitepaper) replaces the (sequential) block*chain* with a (hierarchical) block*tree*. Agents must only synchronise the relevant sub-trees with their neighbours. This lays the groundwork for private policies.

We see ledgers and blockchains as one way for our agents to synchronise agent agreements in particular. However, they are unsuitable for distributing our agent statements in general, as their ordering and synchronisation is unnecessary.

Curie. Curie is a policy-based data exchange system [11]. Our works share a fundamentally decentralised approach to the specification and enforcement of formal policies to regulate the exchange of data, based on consortium agreements and local policies. Moreover, both works define permission to act in terms of assembled policies, for Curie, of dual policies of x sharing with y and y acquiring from x. We also see similarities between Curie and the EPI framework in their shared application to federated machine learning with sensitive medical data.

A significant feature of Curie is its specification and evaluation of data sharing policies as a function of the shared data itself. Policy decisions digest the homomorphically encrypted data [16], revealing only the evaluation result in plain text. For example, a hospital's sharing policy is conditioned on the shared data surpassing a threshold of differential privacy [35].

Our work abstracts away from the relation between policies and the effects of actions (e.g., sharing data). Instead, we focus on relating policies and agent actions and communications. Our approach affords a fundamentally multi-party approach to policy decisions. Permissions arise from the composition of statements from different agents at different times. Thus, our statements more extensively internalise the negotiation and refinement of multi-party power dynamics. For example, Sect. 4 demonstrates multiple agents participating in the incremental sharing of power to permit data access requests. By decoupling statements from their authors, statements meaningfully delegate reasoning and action to other agents. For example, also in Sect. 4, the consortium agent begins with sole power over authorisation, but after the agreement, it plays no further part.

As such, our contributions are largely orthogonal to Curie, and we are inspired to investigate the combination of the works' best features. Can (data sharing) actions be justified as a function of the shared data itself?

Trust Management. Traditional access control develops languages and tools for specifying and checking a requester's permission to access data. *Trust management* reifies the role of the accessor as a *certificate*, primarily, to enable access control in a decentralised environment, where the identities of particular requesters are not known ahead of time [9]. Much literature dates to the 1980s and 1990s, investigating policy languages suited to defining certificates and inferring them at request time from context. Many of these are specialised extensions of Datalog, adding non-monotonicity [32], constraints [33], and weights [8].

Like access control, trust management focuses agent reasoning on the access-request decision, whereas our framework emphasises the inter-relationship between agents and their actions via their synchronised agreements. However, the bulk of trust management research complements our work, because it informs the selection of particular policy languages suited to particular purposes. [43] overviews and compares (the complexity of) noteworthy trust management languages.

8   Conclusion

We define a framework for policy-driven data exchange, which minimises the requirements on the policy language itself, maximising applicability to existing work. The framework focuses on defining the relation between agent statements and the permissions on agent actions. Ultimately, we show that any definition of framework objects that satisfies our realistic requirements satisfies a useful property. Namely, agents can decide which actions are permitted, such that all other agents certainly agree. Moreover, agents are confident their decisions are universal, e.g., shared by all peers, including monitors and auditors.

Our work is motivated by its application to the exchange of sensitive (e.g., medical) data between autonomous agents, where the policies themselves are potentially private. Crucially, agents can decide, on a case-by-case basis, with whom they share their dynamic policy statements, balancing policy privacy on the one hand, with permitting peers' actions on the other hand.

Work continues to develop a policy component in the EPI framework, an existing, federated, medical workflow processing system. This entails developing our own specialised policy language, and implementing the agent reasoning and communications, by drawing from several related works.

Acknowledgments. This research is partially funded by the EPI project (NWO grant 628.011.028), the AMdEX-fieldlab project (Kansen Voor West EFRO grant KVW00309), and the AMdEX-DMI project (Dutch Metropolitan Innovations ecosystem for smart and sustainable cities, made possible by the Nationaal Groeifonds).

References

1. Akaichi, I., Kirrane, S.: Usage control specification, enforcement, and robustness: a survey. CoRR **abs/2203.04800** (2022). https://doi.org/10.48550/arXiv.2203.04800

2. Anderson, A., et al.: extensible access control markup language (xacml) version 1.0. Oasis (2003)

3. Andrighetto, G., Governatori, G., Noriega, P., van der Torre, L.W.N. (eds.): Normative Multi-Agent Systems, Dagstuhl Follow-Ups, vol. 4. Schloss Dagstuhl - Leibniz-Zentrum für Informatik (2013)

4. Androulaki, E., et al.: Hyperledger fabric: a distributed operating system for permissioned blockchains. In: Oliveira, R., Felber, P., Hu, Y.C. (eds.) Proceedings of the Thirteenth EuroSys Conference, EuroSys 2018, Porto, Portugal, 23–26 April 2018, pp. 30:1–30:15. ACM (2018). https://doi.org/10.1145/3190508.3190538

5. Bakhshi, R., Cloth, L., Fokkink, W.J., Haverkort, B.R.: Meanfield analysis for the evaluation of gossip protocols. SIGMETRICS Perform. Evaluation Rev. **36**(3), 31–39 (2008). https://doi.org/10.1145/1481506.1481513

6. van Binsbergen, L.T., Kebede, M.G., Baugh, J., van Engers, T.M., van Vuurden, D.G.: Dynamic generation of access control policies from social policies. In: Varandas, N., Yasar, A., Malik, H., Galland, S. (eds.) The 12th International Conference on Emerging Ubiquitous Systems and Pervasive Networks (EUSPN 2021) / The 11th International Conference on Current and Future Trends of Information and Communication Technologies in Healthcare (ICTH-2021), Leuven, Belgium, 1-4 November 2021. Procedia Computer Science, vol. 198, pp. 140–147. Elsevier (2021). https://doi.org/10.1016/j.procs.2021.12.221

7. van Binsbergen, L.T., Liu, L., van Doesburg, R., van Engers, T.M.: eflint: a domain-specific language for executable norm specifications. In: Erwig, M., Gray, J. (eds.) GPCE '20: Proceedings of the 19th ACM SIGPLAN International Conference on Generative Programming: Concepts and Experiences, Virtual Event, USA, November 16-17, 2020. pp. 124–136. ACM (2020). https://doi.org/10.1145/3425898.3426958

8. Bistarelli, S., Martinelli, F., Santini, F.: Weighted datalog and levels of trust. In: Proceedings of the The Third International Conference on Availability, Reliability and Security, ARES 2008, 4-7 March 2008, Technical University of Catalonia, Barcelona, Spain, pp. 1128–1134. IEEE Computer Society (2008). https://doi.org/10.1109/ARES.2008.197

9. Blaze, M., Feigenbaum, J., Lacy, J.: Decentralized trust management. In: 1996 IEEE Symposium on Security and Privacy, 6–8 May 1996, Oakland, CA, USA, pp. 164–173. IEEE Computer Society (1996). https://doi.org/10.1109/SECPRI.1996.502679

10. Boella, G., van der Torre, L.W.N.: Substantive and procedural norms in normative multiagent systems. J. Appl. Log. **6**(2), 152–171 (2008). https://doi.org/10.1016/j.jal.2007.06.006

11. Celik, Z.B., Acar, A., Aksu, H., Sheatsley, R., McDaniel, P.D., Uluagac, A.S.: Curie: Policy-based secure data exchange. In: Ahn, G., Thuraisingham, B., Kantarcioglu, M., Krishnan, R. (eds.) Proceedings of the Ninth ACM Conference on Data and Application Security and Privacy, CODASPY 2019, Richardson, TX, USA, 25–27 March 2019, pp. 121–132. ACM (2019). https://doi.org/10.1145/3292006.3300042

12. Ceri, S., Gottlob, G., Tanca, L.: What you always wanted to know about datalog (and never dared to ask). IEEE Trans. Knowl. Data Eng. **1**(1), 146–166 (1989). https://doi.org/10.1109/69.43410

13. Clavel, M., Durán, F., Eker, S., Lincoln, P., Martí-Oliet, N., Meseguer, J., Talcott, C.L.: The maude 2.0 system. In: Nieuwenhuis, R. (ed.) Rewriting Techniques and Applications, 14th International Conference, RTA 2003, Valencia, Spain, June 9-11, 2003, Proceedings. Lecture Notes in Computer Science, vol. 2706, pp. 76–87. Springer (2003). https://doi.org/10.1007/3-540-44881-0_7

14. Curry, E., Tuikka, T.: An organizational maturity model fordata spaces: a data sharing wheel approach. In: Curry, E., Scerri, S., Tuikka, T. (eds.) Data Spaces - Design, Deployment and Future Directions, pp. 21–42. Springer (2022). https://doi.org/10.1007/978-3-030-98636-0_2

15. Digital Asset: canton network: a network of networks for smart contract applications. https://www.digitalasset.com/hubfs/Canton/Canton%20Network%20-%20White%20Paper.pdf. Accessed 23 Feb 2024. (Whitepaper)

16. Doan, T.V.T., Messai, M., Gavin, G., Darmont, J.: A survey on implementations of homomorphic encryption schemes. J. Supercomput. **79**(13), 15098–15139 (2023). https://doi.org/10.1007/S11227-023-05233-Z

17. Esterhuyse, C.A., Müller, T., van Binsbergen, L.T., Belloum, A.S.Z.: Exploring the enforcement of private, dynamic policies on medical workflow execution. In: 18th IEEE International Conference on e-Science, e-Science 2022, Salt Lake City, UT, USA, 11–14 October 2022, pp. 481–486. IEEE (2022). https://doi.org/10.1109/ESCIENCE55777.2022.00086

18. European Commission: Regulation (EU) 2016/679 of the European Parliament and of the Council of 27 April 2016 on the protection of natural persons with regard to the processing of personal data and on the free movement of such data, and repealing Directive 95/46/EC (General Data Protection Regulation) (Text with EEA relevance) (2016). https://eur-lex.europa.eu/eli/reg/2016/679/oj

19. Fernandez, R.C.: Data-sharing markets: model, protocol, and algorithms to incentivize the formation of data-sharing consortia. Proc. ACM Manag. Data **1**(2), 172:1–172:25 (2023). https://doi.org/10.1145/3589317

20. Fragkos, G., Johnson, J., Tsiropoulou, E.: Dynamic role-based access control policy for smart grid applications: an offline deep reinforcement learning approach. IEEE Trans. Hum. Mach. Syst. **52**(4), 761–773 (2022). https://doi.org/10.1109/THMS.2022.3163185

21. Gebser, M., Kaufmann, B., Kaminski, R., Ostrowski, M., Schaub, T., Schneider, M.: Potassco: the potsdam answer set solving collection. AI Commun. **24**(2), 107–124 (2011). https://doi.org/10.3233/AIC-2011-0491

22. Gelfond, M., Lifschitz, V.: The stable model semantics for logic programming. In: Kowalski, R.A., Bowen, K.A. (eds.) Logic Programming, Proceedings of the Fifth International Conference and Symposium, Seattle, Washington, USA, 15–19 August 1988 (2 Volumes), pp. 1070–1080. MIT Press (1988)

23. Governatori, G., Idelberger, F., Milosevic, Z., Riveret, R., Sartor, G., Xu, X.: On legal contracts, imperative and declarative smart contracts, and blockchain systems. Artif. Intell. Law **26**(4), 377–409 (2018). https://doi.org/10.1007/s10506-018-9223-3

24. Ianella, R.: Open digital rights language (ODRL). Cultivating the Creative Commons, Open Content Licensing (2007)

25. Jung, C., Dörr, J.: Data usage control. In: Otto, B., ten Hompel, M., Wrobel, S. (eds.) Designing Data Spaces: The Ecosystem Approach to Competitive Advantage, pp. 129–146. Springer, Cham (2022). https://doi.org/10.1007/978-3-030-93975-5_8

26. Kassem, J.A., de Laat, C., Taal, A., Grosso, P.: The EPI framework: a dynamic data sharing framework for healthcare use cases. IEEE Access **8**, 179909–179920 (2020). https://doi.org/10.1109/ACCESS.2020.3028051

27. Kassem, J.A., Valkering, O., Belloum, A., Grosso, P.: EPI framework: approach for traffic redirection through containerised network functions. In: 17th IEEE International Conference on eScience, eScience 2021, Innsbruck, Austria, 20–23 September 2021, pp. 80–89. IEEE (2021). https://doi.org/10.1109/eScience51609.2021.00018

28. Ketsman, B., Koch, C.: Datalog with negation and monotonicity. In: Lutz, C., Jung, J.C. (eds.) 23rd International Conference on Database Theory, ICDT 2020, March 30-April 2, 2020, Copenhagen, Denmark. LIPIcs, vol. 155, pp. 19:1–19:18. Schloss Dagstuhl - Leibniz-Zentrum für Informatik (2020). https://doi.org/10.4230/LIPIcs.ICDT.2020.19

29. Khan, M., den Hartog, F.T.H., Hu, J.: A survey and ontology of blockchain consensus algorithms for resource-constrained IoT systems. Sensors **22**(21), 8188 (2022). https://doi.org/10.3390/S22218188

30. Khobragade, P., Turuk, A.K.: Blockchain consensus algorithms: A survey. In: Prieto, J., Martínez, F.L.B., Ferretti, S., Guardeño, D.A., Nevado-Batalla, P.T. (eds.) Blockchain and Applications, 4th International Congress, BLOCKCHAIN 2022, L'Aquila, Italy, 13–15 July 2022, LNNS, vol. 595, pp. 198–210. Springer, Cham (2022). https://doi.org/10.1007/978-3-031-21229-1_19

31. Kiayias, A., Russell, A., David, B., Oliynykov, R.: Ouroboros: a provably secure proof-of-stake blockchain protocol. In: Katz, J., Shacham, H. (eds.) Advances in Cryptology - CRYPTO 2017 - 37th Annual International Cryptology Conference, Santa Barbara, CA, USA, August 20-24, 2017, Proceedings, Part I, LNCS, vol. 10401, pp. 357–388. Springer, Cham (2017). https://doi.org/10.1007/978-3-319-63688-7_12

32. Li, N., Grosof, B.N., Feigenbaum, J.: Delegation logic: a logic-based approach to distributed authorization. ACM Trans. Inf. Syst. Secur. **6**(1), 128–171 (2003). https://doi.org/10.1145/605434.605438

33. Li, N., Mitchell, J.C.: DATALOG with constraints: a foundation for trust management languages. In: Dahl, V., Wadler, P. (eds.) Practical Aspects of Declarative Languages, 5th International Symposium, PADL 2003, New Orleans, LA, USA, 13–14 January 2003, Proceedings, LNCS, vol. 2562, pp. 58–73. Springer, Cham (2003). https://doi.org/10.1007/3-540-36388-2_6

34. Mao, X., Wang, Q., Yang, S.: A survey of agent-oriented programming from software engineering perspective. Web Intell. **15**(2), 143–163 (2017). https://doi.org/10.3233/WEB-170357

35. Mohassel, P., Zhang, Y.: Secureml: a system for scalable privacy-preserving machine learning. In: 2017 IEEE Symposium on Security and Privacy, SP 2017, San Jose, CA, USA, 22–26 May 2017, pp. 19–38. IEEE Computer Society (2017). https://doi.org/10.1109/SP.2017.12

36. Munoz-Arcentales, A., López-Pernas, S., Pozo, A., Alonso, Á., Salvachúa, J., Huecas, G.: An architecture for providing data usage and access control in data sharing ecosystems. In: Shakshuki, E.M., Yasar, A., Malik, H. (eds.) The 10th International Conference on Emerging Ubiquitous Systems and Pervasive Networks (EUSPN 2019) / The 9th International Conference on Current and Future Trends of Information and Communication Technologies in Healthcare (ICTH-2019) / Affiliated Workshops, Coimbra, Portugal, 4–7 November 2019, Procedia Computer Science, vol. 160, pp. 590–597. Elsevier (2019). https://doi.org/10.1016/J.PROCS.2019.11.042

37. de Oliveira, M.T., Reis, L.H.A., Verginadis, Y., Mattos, D.M.F., Olabarriaga, S.D.: Smartaccess: attribute-based access control system for medical records based on smart contracts. IEEE Access **10**, 117836–117854 (2022). https://doi.org/10.1109/ACCESS.2022.3217201

38. Parvizimosaed, A., Roveri, M., Rasti, A., Amyot, D., Logrippo, L., Mylopoulos, J.: Model-checking legal contracts with symboleopc. In: Syriani, E., Sahraoui, H.A., Bencomo, N., Wimmer, M. (eds.) Proceedings of the 25th International Conference on Model Driven Engineering Languages and Systems, MODELS 2022, Montreal, Quebec, Canada, 23–28 October 2022, pp. 278–288. ACM (2022). https://doi.org/10.1145/3550355.3552449

39. Przymusinski, T.C.: The well-founded semantics coincides with the three-valued stable semantics. Fundam. Inform. **13**(4), 445–463 (1990)

40. Qiu, J., Tian, Z., Du, C., Zuo, Q., Su, S., Fang, B.: A survey on access control in the age of internet of things. IEEE Internet Things J. **7**(6), 4682–4696 (2020). https://doi.org/10.1109/JIOT.2020.2969326

41. Ren, W., Beard, R.W., Atkins, E.M.: A survey of consensus problems in multi-agent coordination. In: American Control Conference, ACC 2005, Portland, OR, USA, 8-10 June 2005, pp. 1859–1864. IEEE (2005). https://doi.org/10.1109/ACC.2005.1470239

42. Ross, K.A.: Modular stratification and magic sets for DATALOG programs with negation. In: Rosenkrantz, D.J., Sagiv, Y. (eds.) Proceedings of the Ninth ACM SIGACT-SIGMOD-SIGART Symposium on Principles of Database Systems, 2–4 April 1990, Nashville, Tennessee, USA, pp. 161–171. ACM Press (1990). https://doi.org/10.1145/298514.298558

43. Sacha, K.: Trust management languages and complexity. In: Meersman, R., et al. (eds.) On the Move to Meaningful Internet Systems: OTM 2011 - Confederated International Conferences: CoopIS, DOA-SVI, and ODBASE 2011, Hersonissos, Crete, Greece, 17–21 October 2011, Proceedings, Part II, LNCS, vol. 7045, pp. 588–604. Springer, Cham (2011). https://doi.org/10.1007/978-3-642-25106-1_12

44. Samarati, P., de Vimercati, S.C.: Access control: policies, models, and mechanisms. In: Focardi, R., Gorrieri, R. (eds.) FOSAD 2000. LNCS, vol. 2171, pp. 137–196. Springer, Heidelberg (2001). https://doi.org/10.1007/3-540-45608-2_3

45. Sandhu, R.S.: Role-based access control. Adv. Comput. **46**, 237–286 (1998). https://doi.org/10.1016/S0065-2458(08)60206-5

46. Schmidt, D.C., et al.: Model-driven engineering. Computer-IEEE Comput. Soc. **39**(2), 25 (2006)

47. Servos, D., Osborn, S.L.: Current research and open problems in attribute-based access control. ACM Comput. Surv. **49**(4), 65:1–65:45 (2017). https://doi.org/10.1145/3007204

48. Shakeri, S., et al.: Modeling and matching digital data marketplace policies. In: 15th International Conference on eScience, eScience 2019, San Diego, CA, USA, 24–27 September 2019, pp. 570–577. IEEE (2019). https://doi.org/10.1109/ESCIENCE.2019.00078

49. Sharifi, S., Parvizimosaed, A., Amyot, D., Logrippo, L., Mylopoulos, J.: Symboleo: towards a specification language for legal contracts. In: Breaux, T.D., Zisman, A., Fricker, S., Glinz, M. (eds.) 28th IEEE International Requirements Engineering Conference, RE 2020, Zurich, Switzerland, August 31 - September 4, 2020, pp. 364–369. IEEE (2020). https://doi.org/10.1109/RE48521.2020.00049

50. Shi, B., Zhou, A.: Bottom-up evaluation of datalog with negation. J. Comput. Sci. Technol. **9**(3), 229–244 (1994). https://doi.org/10.1007/BF02939504

51. Shoham, Y.: Agent-oriented programming. Artif. Intell. **60**(1), 51–92 (1993). https://doi.org/10.1016/0004-3702(93)90034-9
52. Strasser, C., Antonelli, G.A.: Non-monotonic Logic. In: Zalta, E.N. (ed.) The Stanford Encyclopedia of Philosophy. Metaphysics Research Lab, Stanford University, Summer 2019 edn. (2019)
53. Torre-Bastida, A.I., Gil, G., Miñón, R., Díaz-de-Arcaya, J.: Technological perspective of data governance in data space ecosystems. In: Curry, E., Scerri, S., Tuikka, T. (eds.) Data Spaces - Design, Deployment and Future Directions, pp. 65–87. Springer, Cham (2022). https://doi.org/10.1007/978-3-030-98636-0_4
54. Um-e-Ghazia, Masood, R., Shibli, M.A., Bilal, M.: Usage control model specification in XACML policy language - XACML policy engine of UCON. In: Cortesi, A., Chaki, N., Saeed, K., Wierzchon, S.T. (eds.) Computer Information Systems and Industrial Management - 11th IFIP TC 8 International Conference, CISIM 2012, Venice, Italy, 26–28 September 2012. Proceedings. LNCS, vol. 7564, pp. 68–79. Springer, Cham (2012). https://doi.org/10.1007/978-3-642-33260-9_5
55. Valkering, O., Cushing, R., Belloum, A.: Brane: a framework for programmable orchestration of multi-site applications. In: 17th IEEE International Conference on eScience, eScience 2021, Innsbruck, Austria, 20–23 September 2021, pp. 277–282. IEEE (2021). https://doi.org/10.1109/ESCIENCE51609.2021.00056
56. Van Gelder, A., Ross, K.A., Schlipf, J.S.: The well-founded semantics for general logic programs. J. ACM **38**(3), 619–649 (1991). https://doi.org/10.1145/116825.116838
57. Viganò, F., Colombetti, M.: Symbolic model checking of institutions. In: Gini, M.L., Kauffman, R.J., Sarppo, D., Dellarocas, C., Dignum, F. (eds.) Proceedings of the 9th International Conference on Electronic Commerce: The Wireless World of Electronic Commerce, 2007, University of Minnesota, Minneapolis, MN, USA, 19–22 August 2007. ACM International Conference Proceeding Series, vol. 258, pp. 35–44. ACM (2007). https://doi.org/10.1145/1282100.1282109
58. Wesley, N.H.: Some fundamental legal conceptions as applied in judicial reasoning. Yale Law J. **23**(1), 16 (1913)
59. Zhang, X., Parisi-Presicce, F., Sandhu, R.S., Park, J.: Formal model and policy specification of usage control. ACM Trans. Inf. Syst. Secur. **8**(4), 351–387 (2005). https://doi.org/10.1145/1108906.1108908
60. Zhao, G., Chadwick, D.W.: On the modeling of bell-lapadula security policies using RBAC. In: 17th IEEE International Workshops on Enabling Technologies: Infrastructures for Collaborative Enterprises, WETICE 2008, Rome, Italy, 23–25 June 2008, Proceedings, pp. 257–262. IEEE Computer Society (2008). https://doi.org/10.1109/WETICE.2008.34
61. Zhou, X., Belloum, A., Lees, M.H., van Engers, T.M., de Laat, C.: The dynamics of corruption under an optional external supervision service. Appl. Math. Comput. **457**, 128172 (2023). https://doi.org/10.1016/J.AMC.2023.128172

Synthesis for Prefix First-Order Logic on Data Words

Julien Grange[1] and Mathieu Lehaut[2]

[1] Univ Paris Est Creteil, LACL, 94010 Creteil, France
julien.grange@lacl.fr
[2] University of Gothenburg, Gothenburg, Sweden
lehaut@chalmers.se

Abstract. We study the reactive synthesis problem for distributed systems with an unbounded number of participants interacting with an uncontrollable environment. Executions of those systems are modeled by data words, and specifications are given as first-order logic formulas from a fragment we call prefix first-order logic that implements a limited kind of order. We show that this logic has nice properties that enable us to prove decidability of the synthesis problem.

1 Introduction

Distributed algorithms have been increasingly more common in recent years, and can be found in a wide range of domains such as distributed computing, swarm robotics, multi-agent systems, and communication protocols, among others. Those algorithms are often more complex than single-process algorithms due to the interplay between the different processes involved in the computations. Another complication arises in the fact that some algorithms must be designed for distributed systems where the number of participants is not known in advance, which is often the case in applications where agents can come and leave at a moment's notice as is the case, for instance, in ad-hoc networks. Those properties make it hard for programmers to design such algorithms without any mistake, thus justifying the development of formal methods for their verification.

In this paper, we focus on the *reactive synthesis* problem. This problem involves systems that interact with an uncontrollable environment, with the system outputting some values depending on the inputs that are given by the environment. Given a specification stating what are the allowed behaviors of the whole system, the goal is to automatically build a program that would satisfy the specification. This problem dates all the way back to Church [4], whose original statement focused on sequential systems, and was solved in this context by Büchi and Landweber [3]. They reformulated this problem as a two-player synthesis game between the System and an adversarial Environment alternatively choosing actions from a finite alphabet. The goal of System is for the resulting sequence

Supported by the ERC Consolidator grant D-SynMA (No. 772459).

V. Castiglioni and A. Francalanza (Eds.): FORTE 2024, LNCS 14678, pp. 82–98, 2024.
https://doi.org/10.1007/978-3-031-62645-6_5

of actions to satisfy the specification, while Environment wants to falsify it. A winning strategy for System, if it exists, can then be seen as a program ensuring that the specification is always met.

At the cost of having one copy of the alphabet for each participant, one can adapt this setting to distributed systems where the number of participants is fixed. However, a finite alphabet is too restrictive to handle systems with an unbounded number of participants such as those we described earlier. Indeed, with a finite amount of letters in the alphabet, one cannot distinguish every possible participant when there can be any number of those, potentially more than the number of letters. At most, one can deal by grouping participants together in a finite number of classes and consider all that belong to the same class to be equivalent. This however restrict the behaviors of the system and what one could specify over the system. It is therefore worth extending this problem to infinite action alphabets. To that end, we turn to *data words*, as introduced by Bojanczyk et al. [2]. A data word is a sequence of pairs consisting of an action from a finite alphabet and a datum from an infinite alphabet. In our context the datum represents the identity of the process doing the action, meaning that a data word is seen as an execution of the system describing sequentially which actions have been taken by each process. In the corresponding synthesis game, the two players alternatively choose both an action and a process, and the resulting play is a data word.

The last ingredient needed to properly define the synthesis problem is the choice of a formalism in which specifications are written. Unfortunately, there is no strong candidate for a "standard" way of representing sets of data words, in contrast to finite automata in the case of simple words. Many formalisms have been proposed so far, but all of them lack either good closure properties (union, complementation, etc.), have bad complexity for some basic decision procedures (membership, ...), are lacking in expressivity power or do not have a good equivalent automata ⇔ logic characterization. Let us cite nonetheless register automata who were considered first by Kaminsky and Francez [11] but have seen different extensions over time, pebble automata by Neven et al. [13] and data automata [2]. On the logical side, several formalisms have been proposed, such as a variant of first-order logic [2], Freeze LTL [6] and the logic of repeating values [5]. We refer the reader to Ahmet Kara's dissertation for a more comprehensive survey [12]. Most of the previous works study the membership problem (in the case of automata) and the satisfiability problem (for logics), which are useful for model-checking applications but not enough in the synthesis context, as they lack the adversarial environment factor that is central to the problem. A few attempts have been made in this direction, notably for the logic of repeating values by Figueira and Praveen [8] and for register automata by Exibard et al. [7].

We follow previous work [1,9] and focus on synthesis for first-order logic extended to data words. In this extension, we add a predicate $\sim$ to the logic such that $x \sim y$ is true when two positions x and y of a data word share the same data value, i.e. when both actions have been made by the same process. Moreover, we partition the set of processes into System processes and Environment processes, and restrict each player to their own processes. The reason for this is two-fold:

first, when processes are shared, the synthesis problem has been shown to be undecidable even for the simplest logic possible $FO^2[\sim]$, where only two variable names are allowed. Second, inputs and outputs are usually physically located in different components of the system, such as sensors being disjoint from motors in a drone; it thus makes sense to see them as different processes.

As always, there is a trade-off between expressivity of the logic and decidability of its synthesis problem. The well-known LTL undecidability result from Pnueli and Rosner [14] occurs because the logic allows specifying properties that the system is too weak to satisfy. We must therefore find a balance between making the logic expressive enough to be useful, while limiting its power so that it cannot specify properties the system is not expected to be able to satisfy in the first place. Our previous results ([9, Theorems 3 and 4]) have shown that adding any kind of order on the positions of the data word, such as either the immediate successor predicate or the happens-before predicate, makes the synthesis problem undecidable. While those two predicates are fine from a centralized point of view that sees the whole system as a sequential machine, they are not that well suited for real-life systems. Indeed, it is ambitious to expect each process to know everything that happened on other processes in the exact order those actions happened; this would require every process to be informed instantly after every action happening in the system. What is more reasonable is simply to expect a process to know the order of occurrence of its own actions only, without knowing whether those actions happened before or after actions made by other processes.

This leads us to introduce a new operator $\lesssim$, for which $x \lesssim y$ if $x \sim y$ and x occurs before y in the data word. We call $FO[\lesssim]$ the extension of FO that includes only this new predicate. It is strictly more expressive than $FO[\sim]$, as the $\sim$ predicate can easily be simulated by $\lesssim$. Similar to $FO[\sim]$, we can study separately the class of each process. Whereas $FO[\sim]$ could only count how many times each action happened (up to some threshold), we can now express anything that $FO[<]$ can express on (simple) words. Unfortunately, the decidability of the synthesis problem for $FO[\lesssim]$ remains open. In this paper, we show a positive result for a restriction of this logic that we call *prefix first-order logic*, denoted by $FO^{PREF}[\lesssim]$. In this restriction, the first variable quantified for each process is called a bounding variable, and every subsequently defined variable belonging to the same process must occur before the bounding variable. In other words, the first variable for each class pins down a finite prefix of the class and throws away the rest of the class; the rest of the variables can only talk about positions that fall inside this prefix. This restriction allows us to obtain good properties that we leverage to show decidability of the synthesis problem.

This paper is organized as follows. We first define prefix first-order logic $FO^{PREF}[\lesssim]$ in Sect. 2, and the synthesis problem and its equivalent games in Sect. 3. We then show the synthesis problem for $FO^{PREF}[\lesssim]$ to be decidable of in Sect. 4, before concluding in Sect. 5. Omitted proofs can be found in the full version of this paper [10].

2   Prefix First-Order Logic

2.1   Data Words and Preliminaries

Fix two disjoint alphabets Σ_S and Σ_E, which are respectively the System and Environment *actions*. Let $\Sigma = \Sigma_S \uplus \Sigma_E$ denote their union. In the following, we write ε for the empty word, and $u \cdot v$ for the concatenation of the words u and v. Let $\mathbb{P}_S$ and $\mathbb{P}_E$ be two disjoint sets of System and Environment *processes*, respectively.

A *data word* is a (finite or infinite) sequence $\mathfrak{w} = (a_0, p_0)(a_1, p_1) \ldots$ of pairs $(a_i, p_i) \in (\Sigma_S \times \mathbb{P}_S) \cup (\Sigma_E \times \mathbb{P}_E)$. A pair (a, p) indicates that action a has been taken by process p. The *class* of a process p is the word $w_p = a_{k_0} a_{k_1} \cdots \in \Sigma^\star$ where $(k_i)_i$ is exactly the sequence of positions in $\mathfrak{w}$ where actions are made by p. We see data words as logical structures (and will conveniently identify a data word with its associated structure) over the vocabulary consisting of two binary predicates $\sim$, $<$, and two unary predicates $\mathbb{P}_S$, $\mathbb{P}_E$ as well as one additional unary predicate for each letter of Σ. The universe of a data word has one element for each process (called *process elements* – these are needed in order to quantify over processes that have not played any action, and will drastically increase the expressive power of $\mathrm{FO}^{\mathrm{PREF}}[\lesssim]$), and one element for each position in the data word. Predicate $\mathbb{P}_S$ (resp. $\mathbb{P}_E$) is interpreted as the set of all System (resp. Environment) process elements. For $a \in \Sigma$, the predicate a holds on every position which correspond to action a. Predicate $<$ is interpreted as the linear order on the set of positions corresponding to their order in the data word (and is thus not defined on process elements), and $\sim$ is interpreted as an equivalence relation which has one equivalence class for every process, encompassing both its process element and all positions of its class. It will be convenient to use $\mathbb{P}(x)$ as an alias for "$\mathbb{P}_S(x) \vee \mathbb{P}_E(x)$" and $x \lesssim y$ as an alias for "$x \sim y \wedge x < y$".

Let $\mathrm{DW}_\Sigma^\mathbb{P}$ denote the set of all data words over actions Σ and processes $\mathbb{P}$. We write $\mathfrak{w}[i \ldots j]$ for the factor of $\mathfrak{w}$ occurring between positions i and j (both included), and $\mathfrak{w}[i \ldots]$ for the suffix starting at position i; we extend both notations to regular words as well.

2.2   Prefix First-Order Logic on Data Words

We define *prefix first-order logic on data words* $\mathrm{FO}^{\mathrm{PREF}}[\lesssim]$ by induction on its formulas. We write $\varphi(X^{\mathrm{proc}}; X^{\mathrm{bnd}}; X^{\mathrm{pref}})$ to mean that the free variables of φ belong to the pairwise disjoint union X of the three sets X^{proc} (the *process variables*), X^{bnd} (the *bounding variables*) and X^{pref} (the *prefix variables*).

$$\varphi(X^{\text{proc}}; X^{\text{bnd}}; X^{\text{pref}}) ::=$$

$$x = y \qquad\qquad\qquad\qquad\qquad\qquad\qquad\qquad\qquad (x, y \in X)$$

$$\mid \mathbb{P}_S(x) \quad \mid \mathbb{P}_E(x) \qquad\qquad\qquad\qquad\qquad\qquad\qquad (x \in X^{\text{proc}})$$

$$\mid a(x) \qquad\qquad\qquad\qquad\qquad (x \in X^{\text{bnd}} \cup X^{\text{pref}}, a \in \Sigma)$$

$$\mid x \lesssim y \qquad\qquad\qquad\qquad\qquad\qquad\qquad\qquad (x, y \in X^{\text{pref}})$$

$$\mid x \sim y \qquad\qquad\qquad\qquad\qquad\qquad ((x, y) \in X^{\text{proc}} \times X)$$

$$\mid \varphi(X^{\text{proc}}; X^{\text{bnd}}; X^{\text{pref}}) \wedge \varphi(X^{\text{proc}}; X^{\text{bnd}}; X^{\text{pref}})$$

$$\mid \neg\varphi(X^{\text{proc}}; X^{\text{bnd}}; X^{\text{pref}})$$

$$\mid \exists x, \mathbb{P}(x) \ \wedge \ \varphi(X^{\text{proc}} \cup \{x\}; X^{\text{bnd}}; X^{\text{pref}}) \qquad\qquad (x \notin X)$$

$$\mid \exists x, \neg\mathbb{P}(x) \ \wedge \ \Big(\bigwedge_{y \in X^{\text{bnd}}} x \not\sim y \Big) \wedge \varphi(X^{\text{proc}}; X^{\text{bnd}} \cup \{x\}; X^{\text{pref}}) \qquad (x \notin X)$$

$$\mid \exists x, \ x \lesssim y \wedge \varphi(X^{\text{proc}}; X^{\text{bnd}}; X^{\text{pref}} \cup \{x\}) \qquad (x \notin X, y \in X^{\text{bnd}})$$

with $X = X^{\text{proc}} \uplus X^{\text{bnd}} \uplus X^{\text{pref}}$. The intuition is as follows.

We allow one to quantify over the process elements with process variables. Bounding and prefix variables are used to quantify over the elements of the process classes; when quantifying (existentially or universally) over an element of a process class (that is, an actual position of the data word), one must first use a bounding variable. From then on, only prefix variables can be used on this process class, which can only quantify earlier positions in the class (i.e. positions which are $\lesssim$ to the bounding position). Note that one can still quantify over other classes, using new bounding variables.

The semantics is defined as usual. As always, the *quantifier depth* of a formula is the maximal number of nested quantifiers (without regard to whether they quantify process, bounding or prefix variables).

By construction, $\text{FO}^{\text{PREF}}[\lesssim]$ is a fragment of $\text{FO}[\sim, <]$ first-order logic with $\sim$ and $<$). Example 1 below illustrates that $\text{FO}^{\text{PREF}}[\lesssim]$ encompasses $\text{FO}[\sim]$.

Example 1. Let us fix the alphabets $\Sigma_E := \{a_E\}$ and $\Sigma_S := \{a_S\}$. There exists an $\text{FO}^{\text{PREF}}[\lesssim]$ formula $\varphi_{1a_E \leftrightarrow 1a_S}$ of quantifier depth 3 stating that there exists a process with exactly one a_E if and only if there exists a process with exactly one a_S. Indeed, the existence of a process with exactly one a_E (and similarly for a_S) can be stated as

$$\exists x, \ \mathbb{P}(x) \quad \wedge \quad (\exists y, \ \neg\mathbb{P}(y) \ \wedge \ y \sim x \ \wedge \ a_E(y))$$
$$\wedge \quad \neg(\exists y, \ \neg\mathbb{P}(y) \ \wedge \ y \sim x \ \wedge \ a_E(y) \ \wedge \ \exists z, \ z \lesssim y \wedge a_E(z)).$$

Here, x is a process variable, both occurrences of y are bounding variables and z is a prefix variable.

If a (finite or infinite) word is seen as a data word with exactly one data class, then $\text{FO}^{\text{PREF}}[\lesssim]$ can in particular be seen a logic on words: it is equivalent to the restriction of first-order logic on words where

– the formula must start with a universal or existential quantification on the variable $\overline{x}$,

– after that, each new quantification must be of the form $\exists x < \bar{x}$ or $\forall x < \bar{x}$.

We will refer to this logic on words as FO^{PREF}.

Example 2. In order to get a better understanding of the expressive power of FO^{PREF} and its limitation, let us consider a finite alphabet containing, among others, the two symbols open and close.

The property stating that every occurrence of close must be preceded by an occurrence of open can be formulated as follows in FO^{PREF}:

$$\forall \bar{x}, \ \text{close}(\bar{x}) \quad \rightarrow \quad \exists y, \ y < \bar{x} \wedge \text{open}(y).$$

In contrast, one cannot state in FO^{PREF} that each occurrence of open is followed by an occurrence of close. Indeed, for a fixed quantifier depth, the two words $w = \text{open} \cdot \text{close} \cdot \text{open} \cdot \ldots \cdot \text{close}$ and $w' = w \cdot \text{open}$ cannot be distinguished if w is long enough.

For any word w, we let $\langle w \rangle^k_{\text{FOPREF}}$ denote its FO^{PREF}-type of depth k, i.e. the set of all sentences of FO^{PREF} with quantifier depth at most k satisfied in w. Having fixed an alphabet, we denote by $\text{Types}^k_{\text{FOPREF}}$ the set of FO^{PREF}-types of depth k on words.

Lemma 3. *Let $k \in \mathbb{N}$ and let $\mathfrak{w}$ and $\widehat{\mathfrak{w}}$ be two finite or infinite data-words on the same alphabet Σ, such that for every $\tau \in \text{Types}^k_{\text{FOPREF}}$, the number of classes of type τ in $\mathfrak{w}$ and $\widehat{\mathfrak{w}}$ are either the same or both at least k. Then $\mathfrak{w}$ and $\widehat{\mathfrak{w}}$ agree on all $\text{FO}^{\text{PREF}}[\lesssim]$-sentences of quantifier depth at most k.*

As a direct corollary of Lemma 3, in order to decide whether a data word $\mathfrak{w}$ satisfies an $\text{FO}^{\text{PREF}}[\lesssim]$ formula of quantifier depth k, it is enough to know, for each k-type τ for FO^{PREF}, how many (up to k) classes of $\mathfrak{w}$ have type τ. We shall use this fact later in proofs, and refer to this abstraction of a data word as its *collection* of types.

2.3 Properties of FO^{PREF} Types

Let us now try to understand the behavior of FO^{PREF} on words. In the following, we fix an alphabet Σ and an integer k.

First, note that the equivalence relation "have the same FO^{PREF}-type" is not a congruence in the monoid of finite words. Indeed, one can convince themselves (or prove formally, using the Ehrenfeucht-Fraïssé games introduced in the full version of this paper) that for any $k \in \mathbb{N}$, the two words

$$u = ababa \cdots aba$$

and

$$v = ababa \cdots abab$$

have the same FO^{PREF} k-type (as long as they are long enough with respect to k). However, $u \cdot a$ and $v \cdot a$ can be separated by the FO^{PREF}-sentence of quantifier depth 3 stating the existence of two consecutive a's.

Lemma 4. *Let u, v be words such that $\langle u \rangle^k_{FOPREF} = \langle u \cdot v \rangle^k_{FOPREF} = \tau$. Then for every prefix w of v, $\langle u \cdot w \rangle^k_{FOPREF} = \tau$.*

This lemma has a straightforward consequence in the case of infinite words: for every infinite word u, there exists some $\tau \in \text{Types}^k_{FOPREF}$ and an index $n \in \mathbb{N}$ such that for every $m \geq n$, $u[0 \ldots m]$ has type τ. Indeed, Types^k_{FOPREF} is finite, thus there must be some type appearing infinitely often in the prefixes of u. Lemma 4 ensures that such a type is unique. We refer to this type as the *stationary type* of u.

Next, we prove that the stationary type of an infinite word is none other than its own type:

Lemma 5. *Let u be an infinite word with stationary type $\tau \in \text{Types}^k_{FOPREF}$. Then $\langle u \rangle^k_{FOPREF} = \tau$.*

Combining those results we get the following:

Corollary 6. *Let $k \in \mathbb{N}$, u be an infinite word, and $\tau = \langle u \rangle^k_{FOPREF}$. Then there exists $n \in \mathbb{N}$ such that for all $m > n$, $u[0 \ldots m]$ also has type τ.*

Let us now try to understand the structure of Types^k_{FOPREF}. We consider the binary relation $\rightharpoonup_k$ defined on Types^k_{FOPREF} as follows: $\tau \rightharpoonup_k \tau'$ if and only if there exists two finite words u and v such that $\langle u \rangle^k_{FOPREF} = \tau$ and $\langle uv \rangle^k_{FOPREF} = \tau'$. We refer to $(\text{Types}^k_{FOPREF}, \rightharpoonup_k)$ as the *graph of FO^{PREF}-types of depth k*.

The following lemmas break down its properties. First, the choice of u and v above does not really matter:

Lemma 7. *Let $k \geq 1$, let τ and τ' be such that $\tau \rightharpoonup_k \tau'$ and let w be a finite word such that $\langle w \rangle^k_{FOPREF} = \tau$. There exists some finite word w' such that $\langle ww' \rangle^k_{FOPREF} = \tau'$.*

Second, $\rightharpoonup_k$ is an order:

Lemma 8. *The binary relation $\rightharpoonup_k$ is a partial order on Types^k_{FOPREF}, with minimum $\langle \varepsilon \rangle^k_{FOPREF}$.*

From those two lemmas, we conclude that $(\text{Types}^k_{FOPREF}, \rightharpoonup_k)$ can be seen as a finite directed tree rooted in $\langle \varepsilon \rangle^k_{FOPREF}$. This is illustrated in Fig. 1.

3   Synthesis and Token Games

In this section we define the standard synthesis game, and then give equivalent games that are more suitable for our purpose.

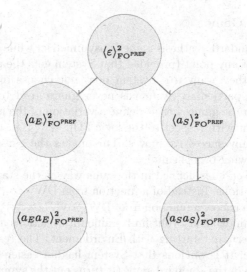

Fig. 1. A partial representation of $\text{Types}^2_{\text{FOPREF}}$ for $\Sigma_E = \{a_E\}$ and $\Sigma_S = \{a_S\}$. Types of words containing both a_E and a_S have been omitted, as data classes cannot have such a type.

3.1   Standard Synthesis Game

Given a formula φ, the *standard synthesis game* is a game played between two players, System and Environment, who collaborate to create a data word. System's goal is to make the created data word satisfy φ, while Environment wants to falsify it. Formally, a *strategy* for System is a function $\mathcal{S} : \text{DW}^{\mathbb{P}}_{\Sigma} \to (\Sigma_S \times \mathbb{P}_S) \cup \{\varepsilon\}$ which given a data word created so far (the *history*) returns either an action and process to play on, or passes its turn on output ε. A data word $\mathfrak{w} = (a_0, p_0)(a_1, p_1)\ldots$ is *compatible* with $\mathcal{S}$ if for all i, $a_i \in \Sigma_S$ implies $\mathcal{S}(\mathfrak{w}[0\ldots i-1]) = (a_i, p_i)$. Furthermore, $\mathfrak{w}$ is *fair* with $\mathcal{S}$ if either $\mathfrak{w}$ is finite and $\mathcal{S}(\mathfrak{w}) = \varepsilon$, or $\mathcal{S}(\mathfrak{w}[0\ldots i]) \neq \varepsilon$ for infinitely many $i \in \mathbb{N}$ implies $a_i \in \Sigma_S$ for infinitely many $i \in \mathbb{N}$. Intuitively, a fair data word prevents the pathological case where System wants to do some action but Environment forever prevents it by continually playing its own actions instead. Strategy $\mathcal{S}$ is said to be *winning* if all compatible and fair data words satisfy φ. System wins a synthesis game if there exists a winning strategy for System.

The *existential synthesis problem* asks, for a given alphabet Σ and formula φ, whether there exists a set of processes $\mathbb{P} = \mathbb{P}_S \uplus \mathbb{P}_E$ such that System wins the corresponding synthesis game. In the case of $\text{FO}^{\text{PREF}}[\lesssim]$, since the logic can only compare process identities with respect to equality, it is easy to see that the actual sets $\mathbb{P}_S$ and $\mathbb{P}_E$ do not matter: only their cardinality does. With that in mind, we slightly reformulate the existential synthesis problem to ask whether there exists a pair $(n_S, n_E) \in \mathbb{N}^2$ such that System wins the synthesis game for all sets of processes $\mathbb{P}_S$ and $\mathbb{P}_E$ of respective size n_S and n_E. If (n_S, n_E) is such a pair, we say that System has a (n_S, n_E)-*winning strategy* for φ.

3.2 Symmetric Game

Notice that the standard synthesis game is asymmetric: while Environment can interrupt System at any point (provided that System gets the possibility to play infinitely often if they want to), System does not choose exactly the timing of their moves. In particular, System is never guaranteed to be able to play successive moves in the game. Let us define a variation of the game, which turns out to be equivalent with respect to the logic $FO^{PREF}[\lesssim]$, in which System can play arbitrarily many successive moves. This makes the game symmetric, and will make the following proofs simpler.

The *symmetric game* is defined in the same way as the standard game, with the following exceptions. Instead of a function from $DW_\Sigma^\mathbb{P}$ to $(\Sigma_S \times \mathbb{P}_S) \cup \{\varepsilon\}$, a strategy for System is now a function from $DW_\Sigma^\mathbb{P}$ to $(\Sigma_S \times \mathbb{P}_S)^\star \cup \{\varepsilon\}$, i.e. System is allowed to play an arbitrary (but finite) amount of actions at once. Moreover, players strictly alternate, starting with Environment. The rest is defined as in the standard game. It is obvious that System has an easier time winning the symmetric game than the standard game. It turns out the symmetric game offers System no advantage when the relative positions of the classes are incomparable:

Lemma 9. *Let φ be a $FO^{PREF}[\lesssim]$-sentence, and $n_S, n_E \in \mathbb{N}$. System has an (n_S, n_E)-winning strategy for φ in the symmetric game if and only if System has an (n_S, n_E)-winning strategy for φ in the standard game.*

Note that when positions between classes can be compared, the standard and the symmetric game do not necessarily agree on who wins for a given formula: consider for instance the formula making System the winner if they manage to play twice in a row: the symmetric game is easily won by System, but is won by Environment in the standard setting.

3.3 Token Game on Words

Our goal is to give an alternative game played on a finite arena that would still be equivalent to the symmetric game. As an intermediate step, consider the (infinite) graph of all finite words over Σ: $\mathcal{A}_\Sigma = (\Sigma^\star, \varepsilon, \Delta)$ where $\Sigma^\star$ is the set of nodes, ε is the initial node and $\Delta \subseteq \Sigma^\star \times \Sigma \to \Sigma^\star$ is the transition function such that $\Delta(w, a) = w \cdot a$. We use this graph as an arena over which a number of tokens are located, each token representing one process and its location being the history of what has been played on this process. We have two sets of System and Environment tokens, numbering n_S for System tokens and n_E for Environment tokens, all of which are initially placed in the ε node. Alternatively and starting from Environment, each player picks one of their token, move it along one edge, and repeat those two operations a finite amount of times. A player can also opt not to move any of its tokens. Then the other player does the same, and this goes on forever. The winning condition is defined by the formula φ: given a play, we take the limit word reached by each token, and see if the collection of those words satisfy φ. It is easy to see that this game is simply a different view of the symmetric game: playing a word $w = (a_0, p_0) \ldots (a_n, p_n)$ is equivalent to picking the token representing p_0, moving it along the a_0-labeled edge, and so on. Thus System wins in the symmetric game if and only if System wins the token game on words, for any choice of token sets of correct sizes.

3.4   Token Game on Types

We already established as a consequence of Lemma 3 that we do not actually need to keep track of the full history of each token to know whether φ (which has depth k) is satisfied; counting how many tokens (up to threshold k) there are for each k-type of $\mathrm{FO}^{\mathrm{PREF}}$ is enough to decide. Therefore, the final step is to use the finite graph of $\mathrm{FO}^{\mathrm{PREF}}$-types as an arena instead of using the infinite graph of all words. As for the acceptance condition, the formula φ is abstracted by a set α_φ of k-counting functions of the form $\kappa : \mathrm{Types}^k_{\mathrm{FOPREF}} \to \{0, 1, \ldots, k-1, k+\}$. Each such function gives a count of how many tokens (up to k) can be found in each type, and the acceptance condition α_φ is exactly the set of those functions that satisfy φ.

Let the $\mathrm{FO}^{\mathrm{PREF}}$-arena of depth k be $\mathcal{A}_k = (\mathrm{Types}^k_{\mathrm{FOPREF}}, \langle \varepsilon \rangle^k_{\mathrm{FOPREF}}, \rightsquigarrow_k)$ where $\mathrm{Types}^k_{\mathrm{FOPREF}}$ is the set of nodes, $\langle \varepsilon \rangle^k_{\mathrm{FOPREF}}$ is the initial node, and $\rightsquigarrow_k$ is the transition function as defined in Sect. 2.3. Given a pair $(n_S, n_E) \in \mathbb{N}^2$, let us fix two arbitrary disjoint sets of System and Environment $tokens$ $\mathbb{T}_S$ and $\mathbb{T}_E$ of sizes n_S and n_E respectively, and let $\mathbb{T}$ denote their union. The $token\ game$ over $\mathbb{T}$ for a $\mathrm{FO}^{\mathrm{PREF}}[\lesssim]$ formula φ of depth k is given by the tuple $\mathfrak{G}^\mathbb{T}_\varphi = (\mathbb{T}, \mathcal{A}_k, \alpha_\varphi)$.

A $configuration$ of this game is a mapping $C : \mathbb{T} \to \mathrm{Types}^k_{\mathrm{FOPREF}}$ indicating where each token lies in the arena. The initial configuration C_0 maps every token to the initial type $\tau_0 = \langle \varepsilon \rangle^k_{\mathrm{FOPREF}}$. Starting from Environment, players alternatively pick a number of their respective tokens and move them in the arena following transitions from $\rightsquigarrow_k$. A $move$ for System (resp. Environment) is a mapping $m_S : \mathbb{T}_S \to \mathrm{Types}^k_{\mathrm{FOPREF}}$ (resp. $m_E : \mathbb{T}_E \to \mathrm{Types}^k_{\mathrm{FOPREF}}$) indicating where to move each token such that for all $t \in \mathbb{T}_S$, $C(t) \rightsquigarrow_k m_S(t)$ (and similarly for Environment). In particular, in a given configuration C, an empty System move is simply a move equal to C restricted to $\mathbb{T}_S$, indicating that all System tokens should stay where they are.

Then a $play$ π is a sequence of configuration and moves starting from an Environment move and alternating players: $\pi = C_0 \xrightarrow{m^0_E} C_1 \xrightarrow{m^1_S} C_2 \xrightarrow{m^2_E} \cdots$ such that each new configuration is the result of applying the previous move to the previous configuration. Let $\mathrm{Plays}^k_\mathbb{T}$ denote the set of plays. A play is $maximal$ if it is infinite.

For a given token $t \in \mathbb{T}$, a maximal play π generates a sequence of types $\langle \varepsilon \rangle^k_{\mathrm{FOPREF}} = \tau_0 \rightsquigarrow_k \tau_1 \rightsquigarrow_k \cdots$ such that $\tau_i = C_{2i}(t)$. Note that it is fine to skip every other configuration, as a token can only be moved during either a System or Environment move but not both. This infinite sequence eventually loops in some type τ_t forever due to the graph of types being a finite tree. The $limit$ $configuration$ for π, denoted by C^π_∞, is the configuration that returns τ_t for every token t. Note that there must exists some $i \geq 0$ such that for all $j > i$, $C_j = C^\pi_\infty$. We slightly abuse notations and denote by $\pi(t)$ the type of token t in either the last configuration of π if it is finite or its limit configuration if it is infinite. A play is *winning* if its limit configuration satisfies the acceptance condition α_φ, that is if there is a function $\kappa \in \alpha_\varphi$ such that for all $\tau \in \text{Types}^k_{\text{FO}^{\text{PREF}}}$,

$$\begin{cases} |\{t \in \mathbb{T} \mid \pi(t) = \tau\}| = \kappa(\tau) & \text{if } \kappa(\tau) < k, \text{ and} \\ |\{t \in \mathbb{T} \mid \pi(t) = \tau\}| \geq k & \text{if } \kappa(\tau) = k + . \end{cases}$$

A *strategy* for System is a function S that given a play returns a System move. A play is *compatible* with S if all System moves in that play are those given by S. A strategy for System is winning if all maximal plays compatible with it are winning. Finally, we say that a pair $(n_S, n_E) \in \mathbb{N}^2$ is winning for System if System has a winning strategy in the token game (for any choice of token sets $\mathbb{T}_S$ and $\mathbb{T}_E$ of corresponding sizes).

Lemma 10. *A pair (n_S, n_E) is winning for System in the token game for φ if and only if System has a (n_S, n_E)-winning strategy for φ in the standard synthesis game.*

For a fixed pair (n_S, n_E), the token game is a finite, albeit very large, game. Remember that our goal is to find whether there exists such a pair that is winning. We show in the next section how to reduce the search to a (large but) finite space.

4   Double Cutoff for Solving the Synthesis Problem

Recall that in terms of expressive power, $\text{FO}^{\text{PREF}}[\lesssim]$ is located somewhere between $\text{FO}[\sim]$ whose existential synthesis problem is known to be decidable [9]) and $\text{FO}[\sim, <]$ for which is it undecidable already when restricting to two variables, i.e. for $\text{FO}^2[\sim, <]$ [9]).

In this section, we make a step towards closing the gap by proving our main result:

Theorem 11. *The existential synthesis problem for $\text{FO}^{\text{PREF}}[\lesssim]$ is decidable.*

To prove Theorem 11 we follow a double cutoff strategy. We first show in Sect. 4.1 that there is no point in considering too many tokens for Environment, where the bound depends on the quantifier depth k of the formula φ but, importantly, not on the number of System tokens. As a second step, we prove in Sect. 4.2 that given a fixed number of Environment tokens (which is a reasonable assumption in view of the previous point), one can restrict one's study to a space where the number of System tokens is bounded by a function of k and the number of Environment tokens. The reasoning is detailed in Sect. 4.3.

4.1   Having More Tokens Makes Things Easier for Environment

First, we prove that beyond some threshold, if Environment can win with some number of tokens, then they can *a fortiori* win with a larger number of tokens. Let us stress that this is not true when the number of tokens is small, as witnessed by the formula φ stating the existence of at least two Environment tokens: in that case, System can benefit from Environment having more tokens.

Lemma 12. *For every $k \in \mathbb{N}$, there exists some $f_E(k)$ such that for any $n_S \in \mathbb{N}$, any $n_E \geq f_E(k)$, and any $FO^{PREF}[\lesssim]$-sentence φ of depth k, if $(n_S, n_E + 1)$ is winning for System then (n_S, n_E) is winning for System.*

Proof. Let $k \in \mathbb{N}$ and let φ be a $FO^{PREF}[\lesssim]$-sentence of depth k. Let us fix three token sets $\mathbb{T}_S^{n_S}$, $\mathbb{T}_E^{n_E}$, and $\mathbb{T}_E^{n_E+1}$ of sizes n_S, n_E, $n_E + 1$ respectively. We note $\mathbb{T} = \mathbb{T}_S^{n_S} \uplus \mathbb{T}_E^{n_E}$ and $\mathbb{T}_+ = \mathbb{T}_S^{n_S} \uplus \mathbb{T}_E^{n_E+1}$. Let $\mathfrak{G} = (\mathbb{T}, \mathcal{A}_k, \alpha_\varphi)$ be the token game over $\mathbb{T}$ for φ and $\mathfrak{G}_+ = (\mathbb{T}_+, \mathcal{A}_k, \alpha_\varphi)$ the same over $\mathbb{T}_+$. We show how to build a winning strategy for System in $\mathfrak{G}$ from a winning strategy in $\mathfrak{G}_+$. But first, let us define some useful properties.

For all types $\tau \in \mathrm{Types}^k_{FOPREF}$ we define the height of τ, denoted by $h(\tau)$, as its height in the tree of types, e.g. $h(\tau) = 0$ for any leaf in the tree. Let h_{max} denote the height of the root $\tau_0 = \langle \varepsilon \rangle^k_{FOPREF}$.

In any given configuration obtained by following a play in $\mathfrak{G}$, we say that a type τ is *large* in that configuration if there are at least k Environment tokens in τ. Intuitively, this means that the acceptance condition α_φ cannot differentiate between a configuration with a large type τ and the same configuration with even more tokens in τ. Therefore, if we can ensure that System has a strategy in $\mathfrak{G}$ that simulates the $\mathfrak{G}_+$ winning strategy while always keeping the missing Environment token in a large type, then that strategy would also be winning as α_φ (which is the same in both $\mathfrak{G}$ and $\mathfrak{G}_+$) has no way of distinguishing them.

To that end, we define what it means to have a *huge* number of Environment tokens in one type τ. This is given by a lower bound $F(\tau) = k \cdot |\mathrm{Types}^k_{FOPREF}|^{h(\tau)}$ that depends only on k and the height of τ. It guarantees the following properties:

1. A type that is huge is *a fortiori* large.
2. If τ is a huge type with $h(\tau) = 0$, it contains at least $F(\tau) = k$ Environment tokens. And since it is a leaf, all those tokens will stay in this type forever. Thus τ will remain large from this point on.
3. If τ is a huge type with height greater than 0, after any Environment move either τ still remains large, or by the pigeonhole principle there exists another type τ' whose height is strictly lower than $h(\tau)$, that can be reached from τ (i.e. such that $\tau \rightarrow_k \tau'$), and such that the number of Environment tokens in τ' is greater than $F(\tau')$, ensuring τ' is also huge.

We then define $f_E(k) = F(\tau_0) = k \cdot |\mathrm{Types}^k_{FOPREF}|^{h_{max}}$. Note that it depends only on k.

By these definitions, and since we assume that $n_E \geq f_E(k)$, τ_0 is huge in the initial configuration because all Environment tokens start in type τ_0. By the third property, this means that after any move by Environment, either τ_0 is still large, or there is (at least) one huge type τ_1 reachable from τ_0. This can be repeated until either a type of height 0 is reached, which will be large forever according to the second property, or we stay in the same large type forever. Formally, we define inductively a function $lt : \text{Plays}_\mathbb{T}^k \to \text{Types}_{\text{FOPREF}}^k$ (lt for "large type") such that $lt(C_0) = \tau_0$, $lt(\pi \xrightarrow{m_S} C) = lt(\pi)$, and $lt(\pi \xrightarrow{m_E} C) = \tau$ where τ is either a minimal (in terms of height) type such that $lt(\pi) \to_k \tau$ and τ is huge in C if such a type exists, or $\tau = lt(\pi)$ otherwise. This is well-defined due to the above-mentioned third property, and we easily obtain that $lt(\pi)$ is large in the last configuration of π for any play π.

Now assume $\mathcal{S}_+$ is a winning strategy for System in $\mathfrak{G}_+$. We define a strategy $\mathcal{S}$ for System in $\mathfrak{G}$ using lt and additionally maintaining a play π_+ of $\mathfrak{G}_+$ with the following invariant: for all plays π of $\mathfrak{G}$ that are $\mathcal{S}$-compatible, π_+ is a $\mathcal{S}_+$-compatible play such that the configuration reached after π_+ has the same number of tokens in each type as the configuration reached after π, plus one extra Environment token in $lt(\pi)$. The strategy $\mathcal{S}$ is simply defined as $\mathcal{S}(\pi) = \mathcal{S}_+(\pi_+)$, i.e. it mimics the actions of $\mathcal{S}_+$ on play π_+. Assuming that π_+ is properly defined and that the previously mentioned invariant holds, it is then easy to prove that $\mathcal{S}$ is winning. Indeed, for every configuration that can be reached from a $\mathcal{S}$-compatible play π, there is an almost similar configuration that can be reached by following π_+, which is $\mathcal{S}_+$-compatible, with the only difference being one extra Environment token in the type designated by lt. Since this type is large by definition of lt, α_φ cannot distinguish between the two configurations. Thus, for any maximal play π compatible with $\mathcal{S}$, its limit configuration is indistinguishable from the limit configuration of π_+, which satisfies α_φ by assumption of $\mathcal{S}_+$ being winning. This proves that $\mathcal{S}$ is indeed a winning strategy for System in $\mathfrak{G}$.

It only remains to explain how π_+ is defined and show it satisfies the invariant. Without loss of generality, assume that $\mathbb{T}_E^{n_E+1} = \mathbb{T}_E^{n_E} \uplus \{\gamma\}$. We strengthen the second part of the invariant so that the configuration reached after π_+ is such that every token in $\mathbb{T}_E^{n_E}$ is in the same type as in the configuration reached after π, and with γ being the extra token in type $lt(\pi)$. Initially this play π_+ is the empty play C_0 of $\mathfrak{G}_+$, which trivially satisfies both conditions. Suppose now that π is a $\mathcal{S}$-compatible play and π_+ is a $\mathcal{S}_+$-compatible play that also satisfies the (strengthened) second part of the invariant.

- On any System move m_S in $\mathfrak{G}$ leading to play $\pi \xrightarrow{m_S} C$, we simply update π_+ to $\pi_+ \xrightarrow{m_S} C_+$ where C_+ is the result of applying m_S to the last configuration of π_+. Since $\mathcal{S}$ mimics $\mathcal{S}_+$, if $\pi \xrightarrow{m_S} C$ is $\mathcal{S}$-compatible, then $\pi_+ \xrightarrow{m_S} C_+$ is $\mathcal{S}_+$-compatible. Moreover, by induction hypothesis, the last configuration of π_+ is the last configuration of π with the extra token γ in $lt(\pi)$. By applying the same System move m_S to both, we easily obtain that C_+ is the same as C plus γ in $lt(\pi \xrightarrow{m_S} C) = lt(\pi)$.

- On an Environment move m_E in $\mathfrak{G}$ resulting in play $\pi \xrightarrow{m_E} C$, let $\tau = lt(\pi)$ and $\tau' = lt(\pi \xrightarrow{m_E} C)$. Let m_E^γ be the Environment move that only affects γ by moving it from τ to τ' (the move can be empty if $\tau = \tau'$). We know such a move is possible because by definition of lt we have that $\tau \to_k \tau'$. Then with m_{E}^+ being the Environment move combining m_{E} and m_{E}^γ, we update π_+ to $\pi_+ \xrightarrow{m_{\mathrm{E}}^+} C_+$. It is trivially still $\mathcal{S}_+$-compatible since no System move has been made. The extra token γ was moved to the new large type given by lt, and all other Environment tokens made the same moves as in $\pi \xrightarrow{m_{\mathrm{E}}} C$, so the invariant still holds.

Thus π_+ is properly defined and always satisfy the required invariant, which concludes the proof. $\qquad\qquad\qquad\qquad\qquad\qquad\qquad\qquad\qquad\qquad\qquad\qquad$ $\square$

4.2   Too Many Tokens Are Useless to System

Dually, one can prove the following lemma, stating that only so many tokens can help the System win; beyond that point, no amount of additional tokens can turn the table and change a losing game into a winning one.

Lemma 13. *For every $k, n_E \in \mathbb{N}$, there exists some $f_S(k, n_E)$ such that for any $n_S \geq f_S(k, n_E)$, if System has an $(n_S + 1, n_E)$-winning strategy in a token game of depth k, then System has an (n_S, n_E)-winning strategy in that game.*

Note that contrary to Lemma 12, where the bound depends only on k, here $f_S(k, n_E)$ depends both on k and the number of tokens of Environment. This cannot be avoided, as showcased by the following example.

Example 14. Remember formula $\varphi_{1a_E \leftrightarrow 1a_S}$ from Example 1. We can show that the (n_S, n_E)-game for $\varphi_{1a_E \leftrightarrow 1a_S}$ cannot be won by System when $n_S < n_E$, as exemplified in Fig. 2. Note that we use for simplicity's sake the representation of $\mathrm{Types}^2_{\mathrm{FOPREF}}$ from Fig. 1 when we should consider $\mathrm{Types}^3_{\mathrm{FOPREF}}$, as $\varphi_{1a_E \leftrightarrow 1a_S}$ has depth 3 – this does not matter as $\varphi_{1a_E \leftrightarrow 1a_S}$ cannot distinguish $\langle a_E a_E \rangle^2_{\mathrm{FOPREF}}$ from $\langle a_E a_E a_E \rangle^2_{\mathrm{FOPREF}}$.

Starting from the initial configuration depicted in Fig. 2a, Environment can move one of their tokens from $\langle \varepsilon \rangle^2_{\mathrm{FOPREF}}$ to $\langle a_E \rangle^2_{\mathrm{FOPREF}}$ (Fig. 2b), forcing System to answer by moving on of their tokens from $\langle \varepsilon \rangle^2_{\mathrm{FOPREF}}$ to $\langle a_S \rangle^2_{\mathrm{FOPREF}}$ (Fig. 2c) in order to satisfy the win condition of $\varphi_{1a_E \leftrightarrow 1a_S}$. System could also directly move down other tokens from $\langle \varepsilon \rangle^2_{\mathrm{FOPREF}}$ to $\langle a_S a_S \rangle^2_{\mathrm{FOPREF}}$, but this would only make things worse.

Then by moving the same token to $\langle a_E a_E \rangle^2_{\mathrm{FOPREF}}$ as in Fig. 2d, Environment would force System to move as well their first token to $\langle a_S a_S \rangle^2_{\mathrm{FOPREF}}$ (cf. Figure 2e). Repeating this sequence a total of n_S times on different tokens would end up "using" all of System's tokens, which would all end up in $\langle a_S a_S \rangle^2_{\mathrm{FOPREF}}$, as illustrated in Fig. 2g. Environment then only needs to move one last token to $\langle a_E \rangle^2_{\mathrm{FOPREF}}$ to falsify the win conditions for $\varphi_{1a_E \leftrightarrow 1a_S}$.

Although the insight gained in the proof of Lemma 12 is useful when considering the proof of Lemma 13, the latter is much more involved. Let us nevertheless give the key ideas of the proof. This time, the goal is to convert an

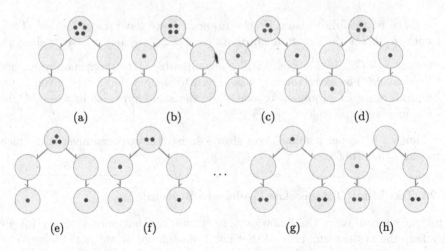

Fig. 2. System may need at least as many tokens as Environment to win.

$(n_S + 1, n_E)$-winning strategy $\mathcal{S}[+]$ for System in a token game of depth k to an (n_S, n_E)-winning strategy $\mathcal{S}[]$ for the same game.

In order to adapt $\mathcal{S}[+]$ to the situation where System has one less token, we will track a *ghost* token. The central idea of the proof is to guarantee at all time that the ghost shares its type with many other tokens, so that its presence or absence is of no import to the winning conditions of the game. Up to that point, the proof is very similar to that of Lemma 12. The main difference in this case is that the ghost is not a fixed token: its identity among the $n_S + 1$ System tokens may vary depending on the way the play unfolds. But once again, if one starts with enough System tokens and is careful in the tracking of this ghost token, it is possible to "hide it" among many others throughout the entire play.

4.3 Solving the Synthesis Problem

Remember that our goal is to decide whether there exists a pair $(n_S, n_E) \in \mathbb{N}^2$ that is winning for a given formula φ of depth k. Using Lemmas 12 and 13, we have shown that we can restrict the search space to the set $N = \{(n_S, n_E) \in \mathbb{N}^2 \mid n_E \leq f_E(k) \wedge n_S \leq f_S(k, n_E)\}$ (which is finite and computable) in the sense that if there is no winning pair in N, then there will be no winning pair in $\mathbb{N}^2$.

Recall that for a fixed pair (n_S, n_E), the corresponding token game is a finite game with finite configurations. As such, it can be solved by seeing it as a game on the graph of configurations, with a Büchi winning condition where accepting configurations are exactly those that satisfy α_φ. From there, a winning strategy can be mapped back to a winning strategy in the (n_S, n_E) token game by looking at the history of a play and constructing the configurations from it. Finally, as the proofs of equivalence in Sect. 3 are constructive, one can then go from a winning strategy in the token game back to a winning strategy in the original synthesis game. Therefore, the synthesis problem can be solved by iterating on all pairs in N and solving the token game for that pair, and then accepting the first winning pair found if there is one, and rejecting if no such pair is found (Fig. 3).

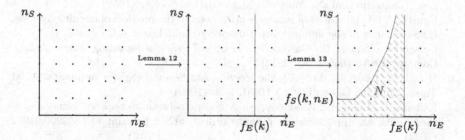

Fig. 3. Bounding the search space for winning pairs.

5   Conclusion

We have shown that the synthesis problem is decidable for $\mathrm{FO}^{\mathrm{PREF}}[\lesssim]$, the prefix first-order logic on data words. Our proof is based on successively bounding the number of Environment and System processes that are relevant for solving the problem, thus restricting the search space to a finite set.

The correctness of those bounds heavily relies on the nice properties exhibited by $\mathrm{FO}^{\mathrm{PREF}}[\lesssim]$. The most important of them is that $\mathrm{FO}^{\mathrm{PREF}}$-types on regular words form a tree, which would not be the case with the unrestricted $\mathrm{FO}[\lesssim]$. We show in the full version of this paper that $\mathrm{FO}^{\mathrm{PREF}}[\lesssim]$ is actually the finest restriction enjoying this property, in the sense that $\mathrm{FO}^{\mathrm{PREF}}$-types correspond exactly to connected components in the graph of types of $\mathrm{FO}[\lesssim]$. To the best of our knowledge, this natural restriction and the properties it enjoys have not been studied anywhere else.

On the synthesis side, our result narrows the gap between decidability and undecidability of first-order logic fragments on data words. Previous results had shown that adding unrestricted order to the allowed predicates immediately lead to undecidability, greatly reducing the kind of specifications that could be written. It turns out that the limited kind of order added by the predicate $\lesssim$ does not share the same outcome, so we obtain a fragment with more expressivity than before and for which synthesis is still decidable. The decidability for the full $\mathrm{FO}[\lesssim]$ remains open; our technique for tracking a missing ghost token cannot be easily adapted in that setting as the type structure for that logic is not as nice as in the $\mathrm{FO}^{\mathrm{PREF}}[\lesssim]$ setting. We conjecture that it remains decidable, and leave this as potential future works.

References

1. Bérard, B., Bollig, B., Lehaut, M., Sznajder, N.: Parameterized synthesis for fragments of first-order logic over data words. In: FoSSaCS 2020. LNCS, vol. 12077, pp. 97–118. Springer, Cham (2020). https://doi.org/10.1007/978-3-030-45231-5_6

2. Bojanczyk, M., Muscholl, A., Schwentick, T., Segoufin, L., David, C.: Two-variable logic on words with data. In: 21th IEEE Symposium on Logic in Computer Science LICS (2006)
3. Büchi, J.R., Landweber, L.H.: Solving sequential conditions by finite-state strategies. Transactions of the American Mathematical Society (1969)
4. Church, A.: Applications of recursive arithmetic to the problem of circuit synthesis. In: Summaries of the Summer Institute of Symbolic Logic, vol. 1 (1957)
5. Demri, S., d'Souza, D., Gascon, R.: Temporal logics of repeating values. J. Log. Comput. **22**(5), 1059–1096 (2012)
6. Demri, S., Lazić, R.: Ltl with the freeze quantifier and register automata. ACM Trans. Comput. Logic (TOCL) **10**(3), 1–30 (2009)
7. Exibard, L., Filiot, E., Khalimov, A.: A generic solution to register-bounded synthesis with an application to discrete orders. arXiv preprint arXiv:2205.01952 (2022)
8. Figueira, D., Praveen, M.: Playing with repetitions in data words using energy games. In: Proceedings of the 33rd Annual ACM/IEEE Symposium on Logic in Computer Science, LICS (2018)
9. Grange, J., Lehaut, M.: First order synthesis for data words revisited. arXiv preprint arXiv:2307.04499 (2023)
10. Grange, J., Lehaut, M.: Synthesis for prefix first-order logic on data words. arXiv preprint arXiv:2404.14517 (2024)
11. Kaminski, M., Francez, N.: Finite-memory automata. Theoret. Comput. Sci. **134**(2), 329–363 (1994)
12. Kara, A.: Logics on data words (2016)
13. Neven, F., Schwentick, T., Vianu, V.: Finite state machines for strings over infinite alphabets. ACM Trans. Comput. Logic (TOCL) **5**(3), 403–435 (2004)
14. Pnueli, A., Rosner, R.: Distributed reactive systems are hard to synthesize. In: Proceedings [1990] 31st Annual Symposium on Foundations of Computer Science, pp. 746–757. IEEE (1990)

MAGπ!: The Role of Replication in Typing Failure-Prone Communication

Matthew Alan Le Brun$^{(\boxtimes)}$ and Ornela Dardha

University of Glasgow, Glasgow, UK
{matthewalan.lebrun,ornela.dardha}@glasgow.ac.uk

Abstract. MAGπ is a Multiparty, Asynchronous and Generalised π-calculus that introduces timeouts into session types as a means of reasoning about failure-prone communication. Its type system guarantees that all possible message-loss is handled by timeout branches. In this work, we argue that the previous is unnecessarily strict. We present MAGπ!, an extension serving as the first introduction of replication into Multiparty Session Types (MPST). Replication is a standard π-calculus construct used to model infinitely available servers. We lift this construct to type-level, and show that it simplifies specification of distributed client-server interactions. We prove properties relevant to generalised MPST: subject reduction, session fidelity and process property verification.

Keywords: Multiparty Session Types · Failure · Replication

1 The Tale of the MAG(pie/π)

The magpie is a bird with deep ties to British folklore. The first known mention of their counting for fortune telling dates back to 1780, where John Brand writes what is thought to be one of the original versions of the magpie rhyme [6]:

"One for sorrow, Two for mirth, Three for a funeral, And four for a birth."

We can imagine that the natural reaction of a person who spots a solitary magpie is to scan the surrounding area for its companion. Alas, if no one is immediately visible, the person desperately waits—hoping a second magpie comes their way. But how long should one wait? The reality is that it is *impossible* to know the difference between *no magpie* and a magpie that has *not yet arrived*. To computer scientists, this is a well known *impossibility result* [2]. In the study of *distributed systems* and *fault tolerance*, mechanisms must be employed to approximate the impossibility result of determining whether a message has been *lost* or *delayed*—e.g. by using a *timeout*. Hence, the computer scientist who spots a lonely magpie knows to only wait some fixed amount of time before *assuming* that no other magpie is coming and accepting their sorrowful faith. This philosophy is the core principle of the process calculus MAGπ [17], a language designed to model communication failures (via *message loss*) with a generic type system aiming to provide configurable runtime guarantees.

© IFIP International Federation for Information Processing 2024
Published by Springer Nature Switzerland AG 2024
V. Castiglioni and A. Francalanza (Eds.): FORTE 2024, LNCS 14678, pp. 99–117, 2024.
https://doi.org/10.1007/978-3-031-62645-6_6

MAGπ is a Multiparty, Asynchronous and Generalised π-calculus, modelling distributed communication over n-participant *sessions*. Its key features include non-deterministic failure injection into the runtime of a program, asynchronous communication via *bag* buffers (allowing for total message reordering), and a generic type system capable of providing guarantees of runtime properties via *session types*. Session types [13,15,26] are *behavioural type systems* allowing for formal specification of communication protocols—their main benefit being that they provide correctness guarantees on both protocol design and implementation. *Multiparty session types* (MPST) [5,16,25] are a branch of session type theory that aims to support protocols involving *any* number of participants with interleaving communication. MAGπ builds upon a generalised form of MPST [4,25], where protocols are defined by a collection of *local types*—the communication patterns of individual participants' perspectives—which should be exhaustively checked (*e.g.* via model checking) to determine any properties they observe. Novelties of MAGπ stem from how it embraces the impossibility result of distinguishing between dropped or delayed messages; its language and type system use non-deterministic timeouts to model the *assumption* of failures. The type system guarantees that *all* failure-prone communication is handled by a timeout branch. In this work, we argue that the previous approach can, in some scenarios, be unnecessarily strict—resulting in needlessly more complex protocols. Some configurations may wish to leave the handling of failures up to senders, as opposed to recipients; these usually take the form of *client-server* interactions where servers are designed to remain infinitely available. For example, if a request to a web server were to drop, it is the client's responsibility to re-issue that request. We present an extension to MAGπ that better models infinitely available servers and simplifies failure-handling for client-server interactions.

In the π-calculus [24], a standard construct often used for representing infinite behaviour is that of *replication*. A replicated process is one which can be informally described as *infinitely available*. Naturally, the use of replicated processes lends itself well to the modelling of client-server interactions. We demonstrate how the use of replication in MAGπ can, not only better model infinitely available servers, but also simplify their protocols by relaxing the requirement of failure-handling branches from *every* receive to only *linear* receives.

Example 1 (Type-level replication). We evolve the motivating example presented in [17, Ex. 1], the *ping* protocol. Consider three participants: client c, server s, and result channel r. Communication between c and r is reliable; whereas with s is *unreliable*. The session types for a three-attempt ping in MAGπ! are:

$$S_r = \&\{c : ok.\textbf{end}, \ c : ko.\textbf{end}\}$$

$$S_c = \oplus s : ping.\& \begin{cases} s : pong. \oplus r : ok.\textbf{end}, \\ \odot. \oplus s : ping.\& \begin{cases} s : pong. \oplus r : ok.\textbf{end}, \\ \odot. \oplus s : ping.\& \begin{cases} s : pong. \oplus r : ok.\textbf{end}, \\ \odot. \oplus r : ko.\textbf{end} \end{cases} \end{cases} \end{cases}$$

$$S_s = !c : ping. \oplus c : pong.\textbf{end}$$

Client c sends a message with label ping to server s ($\oplus s : ping$) and waits for a pong response ($\&s : pong$). If successful, an ok message is sent to results role r and the session is terminated for the client (**end**). Since communication with the server is *unreliable*, receipt of the pong message is not guaranteed, and must be handled by a *timeout* branch ⊙. The client attempts to reach the server 3 times—if all attempts fail, it sends a ko message to r. The result role r waits for either of the reliable responses from c, thus no timeout is defined. Server s is defined as the replicated receive !c : ping. ⊕ c : pong. **end**, denoting its constant availability to receive a ping request and send a pong response. We highlight the absence of a failure-handling timeout branch in S_s; the server does not need to change its behaviour if a client request fails. Furthermore, if the pong reply fails, the server remains available to handle any number of retries from the client. Thus, the use of replication has offloaded the handling of failures entirely onto the client-side, has made the protocol more modular (since the type for s is now agnostic of a client's retry limit), and is simpler w.r.t. to the MAGπ specification.

Contributions. Concretely, our contributions are as follows:

1. **MAGπ! Language**: We present MAGπ! (Sect. 2), an extension of MAGπ that does away with recursion in favour of replication as a better means of modelling client-server interactions.
2. **MAGπ! Types**: We lift replication to type-level in Sect. 3. To the best of our knowledge, this work serves as the *first introduction* of replication into MPST. We improve upon the theory of MAGπ and show how three type contexts (*unrestricted, linear* and *affine*) can be used to type—and *simplify*— failure-prone communication in client-server interactions.
3. **MAGπ! Metatheory**: Sect. 4 expounds upon the metatheory of our type system. We prove *subjection reduction* and *session fidelity*, and demonstrate how they can be used for *property verification*. MAGπ! provides a *failure handling guarantee*, ensuring all failure-prone communication is handled by a timeout branch—a responsibility which servers offload to clients.

In Sect. 5 we conclude and give an account of related and future work. Details of proofs and additional examples can be found in our technical report [18].

On Delegation and Language Simplification. This work builds upon a *subset* of MAGπ [17] as our language only considers communication over a *single session*. Reasons for this are: *(i)* to simplify notation for better readability due to limited space; and *(ii)* to remove session fidelity assumptions. On the latter, generalised MPST theory assumes communication over a single session to prove *session fidelity* (a.k.a. protocol compliance) [25, Def. 5.3]. This is to remove deadlocks that can occur due to incorrect interleaving of multiple sessions. Effectively, the language subset we consider syntactically abides by the assumptions of session fidelity by assuming all communication happens over a single session and by removing delegation. We foresee no issues with extending MAGπ! to multiple sessions, although this will only improve the number of *safe* protocols that can be expressed and has *no effect* on verification of other properties. Lastly, replication in MAGπ! is a *top-level* construct only. This simplifies our type system at the cost of sacrificing expressivity of nested replication. The type system can still express meaningful examples (*e.g.* load balancers), and we intend to explore guarded and nested replication in future work.

2 Bird Songs

We present MAGπ!, an extension of MAGπ that replaces recursion with replicated processes as its preferred means of reasoning about infinite behaviour. Programs in MAGπ! represent distributed networks, consisting of concurrent and parallel processes running on machines connected over some *failure-prone* medium. We discuss how networks of various topologies are defined in Sect. 2.1. Section 2.2 details the syntax and semantics of processes.

2.1 Topology

Distributed protocols typically consist of a number of participants (or *roles*) representing physically separated devices, communicating over a *failure-prone* network. We model such a setting by associating processes to uniquely identifiable roles, which communicate asynchronously through a *bag buffer* allowing for *total message reordering*. Roles are related through a notion of *reliability*, modelling physical locations of processes—*i.e.*, reliable roles are ones that live on the same physical device and thus are not susceptible to communication errors. A formal account of networks, buffers and reliability is given below.

Networks. A program in MAGπ! models some distributed network $\mathcal{N}$. These networks consist of a parallel composition of processes, each representing specific *roles* in the network. The formal description of a network is given by Definition 1.

Definition 1 (Networks). *A network $\mathcal{N}$ is given by the following grammar:*

$$\mathcal{N} ::= \mathsf{p} \triangleleft \mathcal{P} \mid \mathcal{N} \parallel \mathcal{N} \mid \mathcal{B}$$

where $\mathcal{B}$ is a message buffer; $\mathcal{P}$ is the process instruction; and p is a role name.

A *process* $\mathsf{p} \triangleleft \mathcal{P}$ consists of a uniquely identifying role name p, and process instructions $\mathcal{P}$. It is key to note that all processes, *i.e.*, participants, of a network are syntactically defined—thus, MAGπ! assumes a finite network size where all participants are *statically* known. The $\parallel$ constructor denotes *parallel composition* of processes within a network, and $\mathcal{B}$ is its message buffer.

Buffers. MAGπ! models asynchrony through a *bag buffer* (semantics discussed in Sect. 2.2). The buffer, Definition 2, serves two purposes. Firstly, it allows for non-blocking (*fire and forget*) sends by acting as an intermediary where messages wait until recipients are ready to consume them. Second, and important to distributed communication, is that it models messages *in transit* over the network and is thus the point-of-failure in our system.

Definition 2 (Buffers). *A message $\mathcal{M}$ is defined as $\mathcal{M} ::= \langle p \to q, m \langle \tilde{v} \rangle \rangle$, i.e., a tuple identifying the source and destination of the message ($p \to q$), along with a message label and payload contents ($m \langle \tilde{v} \rangle$). A buffer $\mathcal{B}$ is a multiset of messages $\mathcal{M}$. Concatenating a message $\mathcal{M}$ with a buffer $\mathcal{B}$, written $\mathcal{B} \cdot \mathcal{M}$ corresponds to the multiset sum of $\mathcal{B} + \{\mathcal{M}\}$.*

Reliability. A network is initialised with a reliability relation $\mathcal{R}$ (Definition 3), defining roles which may communicate sans failure. All communication outwith the reliability relation is considered failure-prone; this may be used to simulate physical topologies, or to study a protocol at various degrees of reliability.

Definition 3 (Reliability). *Given a network $\mathcal{N}$, and set of roles ρ acting in $\mathcal{N}$, the reliability relation $\mathcal{R}$ is a subset of (or equal to) $\{\{p, q\} : p, q \in \rho \land p \neq q\}$. We write $\mathcal{N} :: \mathcal{R}$ to denote a network $\mathcal{N}$ governed by reliability relation $\mathcal{R}$. We use shorthand $\mathcal{N} :: \mathcal{F}$ to denote a fully reliable network, and $\mathcal{N} :: \emptyset$ to denote a fully unreliable network.*

Example 2 (Load Balancer: Network). Consider a load balancer network with server s, workers w_1, w_2, and client c. Assuming server-worker communication to be reliable, the network may be configured as below:

$$s \triangleleft \mathcal{P}_s \parallel w_1 \triangleleft \mathcal{P}_{w_1} \parallel w_2 \triangleleft \mathcal{P}_{w_2} \parallel c \triangleleft \mathcal{P}_c \parallel \mathcal{B} :: \{\{s, w_1\}, \{s, w_2\}\}$$

2.2 Processes

Definition 4 (Process syntax). *The syntax for defining process instructions $\mathcal{P}$ is given by the following grammar:*

$$\mathcal{P} ::= !_{i \in I} p_i : m_i(\tilde{x}_i) . P_i \mid \boxed{\mathcal{P} \mid \mathcal{P}} \mid P$$

$$P ::= 0 \mid \&_{i \in I} p_i : m_i(\tilde{x}_i) . P_i [, \odot . P'] \mid \oplus p : m \langle \tilde{c} \rangle . P$$

$$c ::= x \mid v \qquad v ::= \text{basic values}$$

All branching terms assume $I \neq \emptyset$ and all couples $p_i : m_i$ to be pairwise distinct. Receiving constructs act as binders on their payloads.

A process $\mathcal{P}$ can either be a replicated server or a linear process. *Replicated receive* $!_{i \in I} p_i : m_i(\tilde{x}_i) . P_i$ denotes a server constantly available to receive any of a set of messages from roles p_i with labels m_i. The received payload is bound to $\tilde{x}_i$ before pulling out a copy of P_i to run in parallel with the server. *Parallel composition* $\mid$ is a ⌈runtime⌉ only construct at the process-level. It is used to denote composition of linear continuations pulled out of a replicated receive. Linear processes $(P, Q, \ldots)$ consist of: *(i)* the *empty process* 0; *(ii)* *linear receives* $\&_{i \in I} p_i : m_i(\tilde{x}_i) . P_i [, \odot . P']$, where a role waits for one of a set of messages from some other roles p_i with labels m_i, binding the received payload to $\tilde{x}_i$ before proceeding according to P_i; *(iii)* an optional *nondeterministic*

Process semantics

P-SEND
$$p \triangleleft q \oplus m\langle \tilde{v} \rangle . P \parallel \mathcal{B} \longrightarrow_{\mathcal{R}} p \triangleleft P \parallel \mathcal{B} \cdot \langle p \rightarrow q, m\langle \tilde{v} \rangle \rangle$$

P-RECV
$$\frac{\exists k \in I \text{ s.t. } r_k = q \text{ and } m_k = n \text{ and } |\tilde{y}_k| = |\tilde{v}|}{p \triangleleft \&_{i \in I} r_i : m_i(\tilde{y}_i) . P_i \, [, \odot . P'] \parallel \mathcal{B} \cdot \langle q \rightarrow p, n\langle \tilde{v} \rangle \rangle \longrightarrow_{\mathcal{R}} p \triangleleft P_k\{\tilde{v}/\tilde{y}_k\} \parallel \mathcal{B}}$$

P-!RECV
$$\frac{\mathcal{P} = !_{i \in I} r_i : m_i(\tilde{y}_i) . P_i \qquad \exists k \in I \text{ s.t. } r_k = q \text{ and } m_k = n \text{ and } |\tilde{y}_k| = |\tilde{v}|}{p \triangleleft \mathcal{P} \parallel \mathcal{B} \cdot \langle q \rightarrow p, n\langle \tilde{v} \rangle \rangle \longrightarrow_{\mathcal{R}} p \triangleleft \mathcal{P} \mid P_k\{\tilde{v}/\tilde{y}_k\} \parallel \mathcal{B}}$$

N-$\parallel$
$$\frac{\mathcal{N} \rightarrow \mathcal{N}'}{\mathcal{N} \parallel \mathcal{N}'' \rightarrow \mathcal{N}' \parallel \mathcal{N}''}$$

P-$\mid$
$$\frac{\mathcal{N} \parallel p \triangleleft \mathcal{P} \rightarrow \mathcal{N}' \parallel p \triangleleft \mathcal{P}'}{\mathcal{N} \parallel p \triangleleft \mathcal{P} \mid \mathcal{P}'' \rightarrow \mathcal{N}' \parallel p \triangleleft \mathcal{P}' \mid \mathcal{P}''}$$

Failure semantics

F-DROP
$$\frac{\{p, q\} \notin \mathcal{R}}{\mathcal{B} \cdot \langle p \rightarrow q, m\langle \tilde{v} \rangle \rangle \longrightarrow_{\mathcal{R}} \mathcal{B}}$$

F-TIMEOUT
$$q \triangleleft \&_{i \in I} r_i : m_i(\tilde{y}_i) . P_i, \odot . P' \longrightarrow_{\mathcal{R}} q \triangleleft P'$$

Fig. 1. Network semantics.

timeout branch $[, \odot . P']$ attached to linear receives to handle possible failure of messages, instructing the process to proceed according to P'; and *(iv) linear sends* $\oplus p : m\langle \tilde{c} \rangle . P$ which sends a message towards p with label m and payload $\tilde{c}$ before continuing according to P. A payload c is either a *variable* $(x, y, \dots)$ or some assumed basic value (integers, reals, strings, ...). We omit conditional branching constructs such as if-then-else and case statements as they are routine and orthogonal to our work (we assume them in examples).

Definition 5 (Network Semantics). *Reduction on networks is parametric on a reliability relation $\mathcal{R}$. The reduction relation $\longrightarrow_{\mathcal{R}}$ is inductively defined by the rules listed in Fig. 1, up-to congruence (rules below):*

$$\mathcal{N}_1 \parallel \mathcal{N}_2 \equiv \mathcal{N}_2 \parallel \mathcal{N}_1 \qquad (\mathcal{N}_1 \parallel \mathcal{N}_2) \parallel \mathcal{N}_3 \equiv \mathcal{N}_1 \parallel (\mathcal{N}_2 \parallel \mathcal{N}_3) \qquad \mathcal{P}_1 \mid \mathcal{P}_2 \equiv \mathcal{P}_2 \mid \mathcal{P}_1$$
$$\mathcal{N} \parallel p \triangleleft 0 \equiv \mathcal{N} \text{ if } p \notin \text{roles}(\mathcal{N}) \quad (\mathcal{P}_1 \mid \mathcal{P}_2) \mid \mathcal{P}_3 \equiv \mathcal{P}_1 \mid (\mathcal{P}_2 \mid \mathcal{P}_3) \quad \mathcal{P} \mid 0 \equiv \mathcal{P}$$

Network dynamics (Fig. 1) are divided into *process* and *failure* semantics. A process sends a message via rule [P-Send] , which places the message in the network buffer and advances the sending process to its continuation. Conversely, processes receive messages (rule [P-Recv]) by consuming a message from the buffer, advancing the process to its continuation and substituting bound payloads with the received data. In a similar manner, servers may consume messages from the buffer using rule [P-!Recv] ; instead of advancing the process, a copy of its continuation is *pulled out* and placed in parallel. This allows servers to concurrently handle and receive client requests.

Message failure is modelled through rule [F-Drop] . We recall that buffers model messages *in transit*, thus this rule may—*at any time*—drop a message from the buffer if it is unreliable. It is key to note that failure in these semantics is *nondeterministic*. A client may consume a message before it is dropped, representing a successful transmission; or the message may be dropped before consumed, representing the failure case. Reduction of *timeout branches* is also nondeterministic since it is impossible to distinguish between *dropped messages* (*no magpie*) and *delayed messages* (the magpie that has *not yet arrived*). Therefore, rule [F-Timeout] can *at any time* reduce a waiting process to its timeout branch, modelling either the handling of message failure or an incorrect assumption of failure (*i.e.,* message delay).

Example 3 (Load Balancer: Processes). We present the processes of our load balancer. An output role o, which is reliable w.r.t. the client, has been added.

$$s \lhd \,!c : req(x).\,\texttt{case flip() of} \begin{cases} \texttt{heads} \to \oplus w_1 : req\langle x\rangle.\,0 \\ \texttt{tails} \to \oplus w_2 : req\langle x\rangle.\,0 \end{cases}$$

$$w_1 \lhd \,!s : req(d).\, \oplus c : ans\langle f(d)\rangle.\,0$$

$$w_2 \lhd \,!s : req(d).\, \oplus c : ans\langle f(d)\rangle.\,0$$

$$c \lhd \oplus s : req\langle 42\rangle.\, \& \begin{cases} w_1 : ans(y).\, \oplus o : output\langle y\rangle.\,0 \\ w_2 : ans(y).\, \oplus o : output\langle y\rangle.\,0 \\ \circlearrowright.\, \oplus o : err\langle\text{``Request timed out''}\rangle.\,0 \end{cases}$$

$$o \lhd \&\{c : output(out).\,0, c : err(msg).\,0\}$$

Example 4 (Interactions with Failure: Processes). Now we demonstrate interactions unique to our language which result from the use of timeouts as imperfect failure detectors. Consider the following network snippet $\mathcal{N}_f :: \emptyset$:

$$p \lhd \oplus q : m\langle 42\rangle.\, P \;\|\; q \lhd \&\{p : m(x).\,P',\ \circlearrowright.\,P''\} \;\|\; \{\langle p \to q, m\langle\text{``Life is''}\rangle\rangle\}$$

These processes denote communication between two roles (p and q), where a message labelled m with the string "Life is" has already been sent, and a second message *also* labelled m is to be sent with payload 42. There are *four* possible immediate reduction steps for this network: *(i)* role q consumes the message in the buffer via [P-Recv] (the intended behaviour); *(ii)* role p places message $\langle p \to q, m\langle 42\rangle\rangle$ in the buffer via [P-Send] , this may possibly result in message reordering due to the bag buffer semantics; *(iii)* message $\langle p \to q, m\langle\text{``Life is''}\rangle\rangle$ is dropped from the buffer via [F-Drop] , then q may either correctly assume failure through a timeout, or if the sender is quick enough the message $\langle p \to q, m\langle 42\rangle\rangle$ could still be received in its place; and *(v)* role q can incorrectly assume a failure and timeout via [F-Timeout] even though message $\langle p \to q, m\langle\text{``Life is''}\rangle\rangle$ is in the buffer. It is not difficult to see how items *(ii)* to *(iv)* may lead to errors. Our types and metatheory mitigate the occurrence of these possibly unsafe networks by enforcing a safe design of protocols.

3 Harmonisation

We now present the *multiparty, asynchronous,* and *generalised* type system for
MAGπ!. To the best of our knowledge, this is the first work to introduce *replication* and *parallel composition* for local types in MPST. We show how these
constructs lend themselves well to typing distributed client-server interactions.

3.1 Types

The syntax for MAGπ! types are given in Definition 6. Our type system does
away with tail-recursive binders (as is standard in MPST), instead opting for
a *replicated receive* type. The syntax distinguishes between different classes of
types. Namely, we present *replicated-, session-, message-* and *basic-types*—each
of which are used differently by the type contexts (Definition 7).

Definition 6 (Types). *The syntax for MAGπ! types is given by:*

$$R ::= !_{i \in I}\mathsf{p}_i : \mathsf{m}_i(\tilde{B}_i) . S_i$$

$$S ::= \oplus_{i \in I}\mathsf{p}_i : \mathsf{m}_i(\tilde{B}_i) . S_i \mid \&_{i \in I}\mathsf{p}_i : \mathsf{m}_i(\tilde{B}_i) . S_i\,[, \odot . S'] \mid \overline{\,S \mid S\,} \mid \mathbf{end}$$

$$M ::= (\mathsf{p} \rightarrow \mathsf{q}, \mathsf{m}(\tilde{B}))$$

$$B ::= \mathtt{Int, Real, String}, \ldots \text{ (basic types)}$$

Branching constructs assume $I \neq \emptyset$ *and couples* $\mathsf{p}_i : \mathsf{m}_i$ *to be pairwise distinct.
Replicated types* R *assume a pool of labels distinct from their continuations.*

A *replicated type* R defines the protocol of a server. Type $!_{i \in I}\mathsf{p}_i : \mathsf{m}_i(\tilde{B}_i) . S_i$
denotes the receipt of requests labelled m_i from p_i carrying payload types $\tilde{B}_i$
having continuation types S_i. Replicated types never appear guarded and always
have linear continuations.

Session types S describe the protocol of a *linear* process. The *selection* and
branching types ($\oplus$ and $\&$) detail possible sends and receives, indicating direction and content of payloads. Branching types may optionally include a failure-
handling *timeout branch* $\odot . S$, where S details the protocol to employ upon
assuming a failure. As in processes, types also have a notion of ⸤runtime⸥ only
parallel composition, identifying the protocols of continuations pulled out of a
replicated receive. The **end** type denotes termination of a party's protocol.

Message types M are used to type messages in a buffer. They record the
direction of communication, as well as the chosen branching label and types of
its payload. Lastly, B represents a range of assumed *basic types*.

Definition 7 (Contexts). *Context* Γ *is* **unrestricted** *and maps variables to
basic types and roles to replicated types. Context* Δ *is* **linear** *and maps roles to
session types. Context* Θ *is* **affine** *and holds a multiset of message types* M.

$$\Gamma ::= \emptyset \mid \mathsf{p} : R, \Gamma \mid x : B, \Gamma \qquad \Delta ::= \emptyset \mid \mathsf{p} : S, \Delta \qquad \Theta ::= \{M_1, \ldots, M_n\}$$

Context update

$$\frac{}{\Delta + \emptyset = \Delta} \qquad \frac{\Delta_1 + \Delta_2 = \Delta_3}{\Delta_1 + \Delta_2, \mathsf{p} : S = \Delta_3, \mathsf{p} : S} \text{ if } \mathsf{p} \notin \mathsf{dom}(\Delta_1)$$

$$\frac{\Delta_1 + \Delta_2 = \Delta_3}{\Delta_1, \mathsf{p} : S_1 + \Delta_2, \mathsf{p} : S_2 = \Delta_3, \mathsf{p} : S_1 \mid S_2}$$

Context splitting

$$\frac{}{\emptyset = \emptyset \cdot \emptyset} \qquad \frac{\Delta = \Delta_1 \cdot \Delta_2}{\Delta, \mathsf{p} : S = \Delta_1, \mathsf{p} : S \cdot \Delta_2} \qquad \frac{\Delta = \Delta_1 \cdot \Delta_2}{\Delta, \mathsf{p} : S = \Delta_1 \cdot \Delta_2, \mathsf{p} : S}$$

$$\frac{\Delta = \Delta_1 \cdot \Delta_2}{\Delta, \mathsf{p} : S_1 \mid S_2 = \Delta_1, \mathsf{p} : S_1 \cdot \Delta_2, \mathsf{p} : S_2}$$

Fig. 2. Context addition and splitting.

Updating and *splitting* operations are defined for Δ by the rules in Fig. 2. Context **composition** Γ, Γ' (resp. Δ, Δ') is defined iff $\mathsf{dom}(\Gamma) \cap \mathsf{dom}(\Gamma') = \emptyset$ (resp. $\mathsf{dom}(\Delta) \cap \mathsf{dom}(\Delta') = \emptyset$).

Figure 2 defines two relations on Δ. *Context addition* joins two contexts by performing a union on their contents (in the case that there are no conflicts in their domains). If their domains are not unique, then the types are placed in parallel, indicating a role employing multiple active session types (this is explained in more detail after introducing context reduction, *cf.* Definition 8). Context *splitting* extracts a piece of a larger context. Notably, types placed in parallel may be split using this operation; in other cases splitting functions similar to context composition.

Definition 8 (Context Reduction). *An action α is given by*

$$\alpha ::= \mathsf{p} \oplus \mathsf{q} : \mathsf{m} \mid \mathsf{p}, \mathsf{q} : \mathsf{m} \mid \circlearrowleft \mathsf{p}$$

read as (left to right) **output,** *communication, and* **timeout.** *Context* **tran-sition** $\xrightarrow{\alpha}$ *is defined by the Labelled Transition System (LTS) in Fig. 3. Context* **reduction** $\Gamma ; \Delta ; \Theta \rightarrow \Gamma ; \Delta' ; \Theta'$ *is defined iff* $\Gamma ; \Delta ; \Theta \xrightarrow{\alpha} \Gamma ; \Delta' ; \Theta'$ *for some α. We write $\Gamma ; \Delta ; \Theta \rightarrow$ iff $\exists \Delta', \Theta'$ s.t. $\Gamma ; \Delta ; \Theta \rightarrow \Gamma ; \Delta' ; \Theta'$; and $\rightarrow^*$ for its transitive and reflexive closure.*

Context reduction (Definition 8) models type-level communication by means of the LTS in Fig. 3. Transition $[\Delta\text{-}\circlearrowleft]$ allows a role p with a defined timeout to transition to the timeout continuation by firing a $\circlearrowleft \mathsf{p}$ action. Transition $[\Delta\text{-}\oplus]$ is a synchronisation action between a selection type and the type buffer Θ.

Δ-⊙

$$\Gamma \; ; \; \Delta \cdot \mathsf{p} : \&_{i \in I}\mathsf{q}_i : \mathsf{m}_i(\tilde{B}_i) . S_i, \odot . S' \; ; \; \Theta \xrightarrow{\odot_\mathsf{p}} \Gamma \; ; \; \Delta + \mathsf{p} : S' \; ; \; \Theta$$

Δ-⊕

$$S = \oplus_{i \in I}\mathsf{q}_i : \mathsf{m}_i(\tilde{B}_i) . S_i \qquad k \in I$$

$$\Gamma \; ; \; \Delta \cdot \mathsf{p} : S \; ; \; \Theta \xrightarrow{\mathsf{p} \oplus \mathsf{q}_k : \mathsf{m}_k} \Gamma \; ; \; \Delta + \mathsf{p} : S_k \; ; \; \Theta \cdot (\mathsf{p} \to \mathsf{q}_k, \mathsf{m}_k(\tilde{B}_k))$$

Δ-C

$$S = \&_{i \in I}\mathsf{q}_i : \mathsf{m}_i(\tilde{B}_i) . S_i [, \odot . S'] \qquad k \in I$$

$$\Gamma \; ; \; \Delta \cdot \mathsf{p} : S \; ; \; \Theta \cdot (\mathsf{q}_k \to \mathsf{p}, \mathsf{m}_k(\tilde{B}_k)) \xrightarrow{\mathsf{q}_k, \mathsf{p} : \mathsf{m}_k} \Gamma \; ; \; \Delta + \mathsf{p} : S_k \; ; \; \Theta$$

Γ-!C

$$R = !_{i \in I}\mathsf{q}_i : \mathsf{m}_i(\tilde{B}_i) . S_i \qquad k \in I$$

$$\Gamma, \mathsf{p} : R \; ; \; \Delta \; ; \; \Theta \cdot (\mathsf{q}_k \to \mathsf{p}, \mathsf{m}_k(\tilde{B}_k)) \xrightarrow{\mathsf{q}_k, \mathsf{p} : \mathsf{m}_k} \Gamma, \mathsf{p} : R \; ; \; \Delta + \mathsf{p} : S_k \; ; \; \Theta$$

Fig. 3. Type LTS

Effectively, a role with a send type can transition to its continuation by firing any of the paths indicated in the selection ($\mathsf{p} \oplus \mathsf{q}_k : \mathsf{m}_k$) and adding the message into the buffer context. On the receiving end, a role with a branch type can consume a message from the type buffer to model a communication action via transition [Δ-C]. Communication with replicated servers is handled seperately by transition [Γ-!C] . This rule allows a communication action to be fired when a replicated type in Γ can receive a message in the buffer. This transition has no effect on Γ (since it is an unrestricted context) and instead updates the linear context Δ with the continuation of the replicated receive. This is why types require runtime parallel composition, and context updating and splitting operations (Fig. 2), as multiple requests may be made to a replicated receive.

3.2   Typing Rules

Protocols defined in MAGπ! types are used in type judgements (Definition 9) to check whether network implementations conform to their specifications.

Definition 9 (Typing Judgement). *Type contexts are used in judgements as* $\Gamma \; ; \; \Delta \; ; \; \Theta \vdash \mathcal{N}$, *inductively defined by the rules in Fig. 4. To improve readability, empty type contexts are omitted from rules.*

Definition 10 (End Predicate). *A context* Δ *is* **end**-*typed, by:*

$$\forall i \in 1..n : S_i = \mathsf{end}$$

$$\mathsf{end}(\mathsf{p}_1 : S_1 \cdot \ldots \cdot \mathsf{p}_n : S_n)$$

Typing rules [T-S], [T-Var], [T-Val] are auxiliary judgements typing linear roles, variables and values. A role p of type S is typed by a linear context

$$\text{T-S} \quad \frac{}{\Gamma\,;\mathsf{p}:S \vdash \mathsf{p}:S}$$

$$\text{T-VAR} \quad \frac{\Gamma(x) = B}{\Gamma \vdash x : B}$$

$$\text{T-VAL} \quad \frac{v \in B}{\Gamma \vdash v : B}$$

$$\text{T-0} \quad \frac{\mathsf{end}(\Delta)}{\Gamma\,;\Delta \vdash 0}$$

$$\text{T-}\oplus \quad \frac{\Gamma\,;\Delta \vdash \mathsf{p}:\oplus_{i\in I}\mathsf{q}_i:\mathsf{m}_i(B_{i1},\ldots,B_{in}).S_i \qquad k \in I \quad \forall j \in 1..n:\Gamma \vdash c_j:B_{kj} \qquad \Gamma\,;\mathsf{p}:S_k \vdash P}{\Gamma\,;\Delta \vdash \mathsf{p} \triangleleft \mathsf{q}_k \oplus \mathsf{m}_k\langle c_1,\ldots,c_n\rangle.P}$$

$$\text{T-\&} \quad \frac{\Gamma\,;\Delta \vdash \mathsf{p}:\&_{i\in I}\mathsf{q}_i:\mathsf{m}_i(B_{i1},\ldots,B_{in}).S_i[,\circlearrowleft.S'] \qquad \forall i \in I:\Gamma,y_{i1}:B_{i1},\ldots,y_{in}:B_{in}\,;\,\mathsf{p}:S_i \vdash P_i \quad [\Gamma\,;\mathsf{p}:S' \vdash P']}{\Gamma\,;\Delta \vdash \mathsf{p} \triangleleft \&_{i\in I}\mathsf{q}_i:\mathsf{m}_i(y_{i1},\ldots,y_{in}).P_i[,\circlearrowleft.P']}$$

$$\text{T-!} \quad \frac{\Gamma(\mathsf{p}) = !_{i\in I}\mathsf{q}_i:\mathsf{m}_i(B_{i1},\ldots,B_{in}).S_i \qquad \forall i \in I:\Gamma,y_{i1}:B_{i1},\ldots,y_{in}:B_{in}\,;\,\mathsf{p}:S_i \vdash P_i}{\Gamma \vdash \mathsf{p} \triangleleft !_{i\in I}\mathsf{q}_i:\mathsf{m}_i(y_{i1},\ldots,y_{in}).P_i}$$

$$\text{T-}\|_1 \quad \frac{\Gamma\,;\Delta\,;\emptyset \vdash \mathcal{N} \qquad \Gamma\,;\emptyset\,;\Theta \vdash \mathcal{B}}{\Gamma\,;\Delta\,;\Theta \vdash \mathcal{N} \| \mathcal{B}}$$

$$\text{T-}\|_2 \quad \frac{\Gamma\,;\Delta_1 \vdash \mathcal{N}_1 \qquad \Gamma\,;\Delta_2 \vdash \mathcal{N}_2}{\Gamma\,;\Delta_1,\Delta_2 \vdash \mathcal{N}_1 \| \mathcal{N}_2}$$

$$\text{T-}| \quad \frac{\Gamma\,;\Delta_1 \vdash \mathsf{p} \triangleleft \mathcal{P}_1 \qquad \Gamma\,;\Delta_2 \vdash \mathsf{p} \triangleleft \mathcal{P}_2}{\Gamma\,;\Delta_1 \cdot \Delta_2 \vdash \mathsf{p} \triangleleft \mathcal{P}_1 \mid \mathcal{P}_2}$$

$$\text{T-EMPTY} \quad \frac{}{\Gamma\,;\emptyset\,;\Theta \vdash \emptyset}$$

$$\text{T-BUF} \quad \frac{\forall j \in 1..n:\Gamma \vdash v_j:B_j \qquad \Gamma\,;\emptyset\,;\Theta \vdash \mathcal{B}}{\Gamma\,;\emptyset\,;\Theta \cdot (\mathsf{p} \to \mathsf{q},\mathsf{m}(B_1,\ldots,B_n)) \vdash \mathcal{B} \cdot \langle \mathsf{p} \to \mathsf{q},\mathsf{m}\langle v_1,\ldots,v_n\rangle\rangle}$$

Fig. 4. Typing rules.

containing exactly a mapping of p to S; variables are typed to a basic type if that mapping is held by Γ; and values are typed to a basic type if they are constants of that type. The empty process 0 is typed by [T-0] if the linear context is **end**-typed (Definition 10), *i.e.*, Δ only contains roles mapped to **end**.

The send process $\mathsf{p} \triangleleft \mathsf{q}_k \oplus \mathsf{m}_k\langle c_1,\ldots,c_n\rangle.P$ is well typed by [T-$\oplus$] if: Δ can map p to a selection type containing the path chosen by the process; Γ verifies all payloads with their types indicated in the session type; and the continuation type can check the continuation process.

The receive process $\mathsf{p} \triangleleft \&_{i\in I}\mathsf{q}_i:\mathsf{m}_i(y_{i1},\ldots,y_{in}).P_i[,\circlearrowleft.P']$ is well typed by [T-&] if: Δ maps p to a branch with all the same paths contained in I; the payloads and continuation types of every path in the branch can type all process continuations P_i; and if a timeout process P' is defined, then it must be typed under a timeout branch in the session type.

Replicated receive $p \triangleleft !_{i \in I} q_i : m_i(y_{i_1}, \ldots, y_{i_n}).P_i$ is typed using [T-!] in a similar manner to [T-&] ; the type of p instead lives in the unrestricted context.

Network composition is typed by [T-‖₁] and [T-‖₂] . The former separates the linear context to be used on processes and the buffer context to be used on the network buffer; the latter splits context domains to type different roles in the network. Process-level composition is typed via [T-|] which utilises the context splitting operation (Fig. 2) to separate parallel session types.

Network buffers are typed by repeated applications of [T-Buf] , which removes messages from the buffer one at a time if they match a message type in the type buffer. The empty buffer is typed under [T-Empty] , allowing for possible leftover types in Θ. It is key to note that the buffer context is *affine*, as any message that gets dropped at runtime will result in an unused message type.

Example 5 (Interactions with Failure: Types). Due to the generalised nature of the type system, the type judgement alone is not enough to detect the errors that may occur in $\mathcal{N}_f$. This is because the type system does not provide *syntactic* guarantees, but rather should be used in conjunction with exhaustive verification techniques post protocol design (this is standard in generalised MPST [4,17,25]). In fact, network $\mathcal{N}_f$ can be typed under the following contexts:

$$\Gamma ; \; p : \oplus q : m(\mathbb{N}).S, q : \&\{p : m(\text{String}).S', \; \odot.S''\} ; \; \Theta \cdot (p \rightarrow q, m(\text{String}))$$

for some $\Gamma, \Theta, S, S', S''$ assuming that P, P' and P'' are well typed using S, S' and S'' respectively. Note that Γ and Θ can be non-empty since the former is unrestricted and the latter is affine. In contrast, the linear context must be exactly as stated above. We now need a way to determine this protocol as unsafe.

4   Songs About Songs

Unlike most session type theories, *generalised* MPST do not syntactically guarantee any properties on the processes they type. Rather, they provide a framework for *exhaustively checking* runtime properties on the type context, from which process-level properties may be inferred. This seemingly unconventional approach to session types was discovered to be *more expressive* than its syntactic counterpart w.r.t. the amount of well-typed programs it can capture [25]. Furthermore, its generalised nature allows for fine-tuning based on specific requirements of its applications. Informally, generalisation of the type system works by proving the metatheory parametric of a safety property; *i.e.*, all theorems proved and presented assume that the type contexts are *safe* (Sect. 4.1). With this assumption we present our main results in Sect. 4.2.

4.1   Type Safety

The technical definition of *safety* refers to the *minimal requirements* on types to guarantee *subjection reduction* (*cf.* Sect. 4.2, Theorem 1). But what does safety even mean for a distributed network with message loss, delays and reordering?

It is impossible for our type system to adopt standard notions of safety which may guarantee properties such as *no unexpected messages* or *correct ordering of messages*, since the failures experienced at runtime can mitigate such guarantees. Hence, the minimal guarantee of safety (Definition 11) in MAGπ! ensures that:

1. timeout branches are always (and only) defined for failure-prone communication between *linear* processes; and
2. if a message eventually reaches its destination, then the expected types of the payload from the recipient should match the data carried on the message.

Definition 11 (Safety Property). $\varphi_{\mathcal{R}}$ *is a safety property on contexts iff:*

φ–R_1

$$\varphi_{\mathcal{R}}(\Gamma \;;\; \Delta \cdot p : \&_{i \in I} q_i : m_i(\tilde{B}_i) . S_i \;;\; \Theta) \; implies \; \forall i \in I : \{q_i, p\} \in \mathcal{R}$$

φ–R_2

$$\varphi_{\mathcal{R}}(\Gamma \;;\; \Delta \cdot p : \&_{i \in I} q_i : m_i(\tilde{B}_i) . S_i, \odot . S' \;;\; \Theta) \; implies \; \exists k \in I : \{q_k, p\} \notin \mathcal{R}$$

φ–C

$$\varphi_{\mathcal{R}}(\Gamma \;;\; \Delta \cdot p : \&_{i \in I} q_i : m_i(\tilde{B}_i) . S_i [, \odot . S'] \;;\; \Theta \cdot (q_k \rightarrow p, m_k(\tilde{B}')))$$
$$\textit{and } k \in I \textit{ implies } |\tilde{B}_k| = |\tilde{B}'| \textit{ and } \forall j \in 1..|\tilde{B}_k| : B_{kj} = B'_j$$

φ–!C

$$\varphi_{\mathcal{R}}(\Gamma, p : !_{i \in I} q_i : m_i(\tilde{B}_i) . S_i \;;\; \Delta \;;\; \Theta \cdot (q_k \rightarrow p, m_k(\tilde{B}')))$$
$$\textit{and } k \in I \textit{ implies } |\tilde{B}_k| = |\tilde{B}'| \textit{ and } \forall j \in 1..|\tilde{B}_k| : B_{kj} = B'_j$$

φ– $\rightarrow$

$$\forall \Delta' : \varphi_{\mathcal{R}}(\Gamma \;;\; \Delta \;;\; \Theta) \; and \; \Gamma \;;\; \Delta \;;\; \Theta \rightarrow \Gamma \;;\; \Delta' \;;\; \Theta' \; implies \; \varphi_{\mathcal{R}}(\Gamma \;;\; \Delta' \;;\; \Theta')$$

Conditions [φ-r_1] and [φ-r_2] ensure that timeouts are *only* omitted (resp. defined) when communication is reliable (resp. unreliable). [φ-c] and [φ-!c] require payload types to match for any communication; note that no message is ever incorrectly delivered to a linear channel instead of a replicated (and *vice versa*) because we assume that message labels for replicated receives are not reused in their continuations. The last condition, [φ-!$\rightarrow$] , requires *all* possible reductions of safe contexts to also be safe.

Example 6 (Interactions with Failure: Safety). The type contexts presented in Example 5 do not abide by the conditions of $\varphi_\emptyset$ and thus are not safe. The types do meet conditions [φ-r_1] to [φ-!c] , but fail [φ-!$\rightarrow$] . We observe the following traces of the LTS:

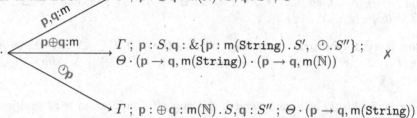

$\Gamma \;;\; p : \oplus q : m(\mathbb{N}) . S, q : S' \;;\; \Theta$

p,q:m

p$\oplus$q:m $\Gamma \;;\; p : S, q : \&\{p : m(\texttt{String}) . S', \; \odot . S''\} \;;\;$
$\Theta \cdot (p \rightarrow q, m(\texttt{String})) \cdot (p \rightarrow q, m(\mathbb{N}))$ ✗

$\odot_p$

$\Gamma \;;\; p : \oplus q : m(\mathbb{N}) . S, q : S'' \;;\; \Theta \cdot (p \rightarrow q, m(\texttt{String}))$

The transition over label p$\oplus$q:m yields contexts in violation of [φ-c]. This example highlights the impact of message labels in protocol design, as reusing labels may lead to nondeterministic receipt of messages. However, this does not mean that messages with the same label can never be reused—it is possible for this nondeterminism to still be safe w.r.t. Definition 11. *E.g.* consider the types in Example 1 reusing labels ping and pong. This is safe because the protocol has no dependency on receiving messages with the same label in a specific order.

Example 7 (Load Balancer: Types). We type our load balancer using the protocol below in a judgement as $s : R_s, w_1 : R_{w_1}, w_2 : R_{w_2} ; c : S_c, o : S_o ; \emptyset \vdash \mathcal{N} \parallel \emptyset$ where $\mathcal{N}$ contains the processes from Example 3. The protocol observes the safety property w.r.t. the reliability relation defined in Example 2, as well as with reliability $\{\{c, o\}\}$, *i.e.*, even if server-worker communication is unreliable.

$$R_s = \, !c : \text{req}(\mathbb{N}) . \oplus \left\{ \begin{array}{l} w_1 : \text{req}(\mathbb{N}) . \textbf{end} \\ w_2 : \text{req}(\mathbb{N}) . \textbf{end} \end{array} \right.$$

$$R_{w_1} = \, !s : \text{req}(\mathbb{N}) . \oplus c : \text{ans(Real)} . \textbf{end}$$

$$R_{w_2} = \, !s : \text{req}(\mathbb{N}) . \oplus c : \text{ans(Real)} . \textbf{end}$$

$$S_c = \oplus s : \text{req}(\mathbb{N}) . \& \left\{ \begin{array}{l} w_1 : \text{ans(Real)} . \oplus o : \text{output(Real)} . \textbf{end} \\ w_2 : \text{ans(Real)} . \oplus o : \text{output(Real)} . \textbf{end} \\ \circlearrowleft . \oplus o : \text{err(String)} . \textbf{end} \end{array} \right.$$

$$S_o = \& \{ c : \text{output(Real)} . \textbf{end}, c : \text{err(String)} . \textbf{end} \}$$

4.2   Type Properties

Our main results are presented below (proof details in the technical report [18]). *Subject reduction* ((Theorem 1) states that any process typed under a safe context remains well-typed and safe after reduction (even in the presence of failures). From this we obtain Corollary 1, stating that timeout branches are only omitted from linear receives if communication is reliable; hence certifying that all processes typed by safe contexts guarantee that no *linear* failure-prone communication goes unhandled. A key contribution of our work is that this corollary is relaxed to *linear* processes instead of *all* processes, since we do not wish for replicated servers to handle dropped client requests.

Theorem 1 (Subject Reduction). *If* $\Gamma ; \Delta ; \Theta \vdash \mathcal{N}$ *with* $\varphi_{\mathcal{R}}(\Gamma ; \Delta ; \Theta)$ *and* $\mathcal{N} \to_{\mathcal{R}} \mathcal{N}'$, *then* $\exists \Delta', \Theta'$ *s.t.* $\Gamma ; \Delta ; \Theta \to^* \Gamma ; \Delta' ; \Theta'$ *and* $\Gamma ; \Delta' ; \Theta' \vdash \mathcal{N}'$ *with* $\varphi_{\mathcal{R}}(\Gamma ; \Delta' ; \Theta')$.

Corollary 1 (Failure Handling Guarantee). *If* $\Gamma ; \Delta ; \Theta \vdash \mathcal{N}$ *with* $\varphi_{\mathcal{R}}(\Gamma ; \Delta ; \Theta)$ *and* $\mathcal{N} \to_{\mathcal{R}}^* p \triangleleft \&_{i \in I} q_i : m_i(\tilde{c}_i) . P_i \mid \mathcal{P} \parallel \mathcal{N}'$, *then* $\forall i \in I :$ $\{p, q_i\} \in \mathcal{R}$.

Session fidelity (Theorem 2) states the opposite implication w.r.t. subjection reduction, *i.e.*, processes typed under a safe context can always match *at least one* reduction available to the context.

Theorem 2 (Session Fidelity). *If Γ ; Δ ; $\Theta \rightarrow$ and Γ ; Δ ; $\Theta \vdash \mathcal{N}$ with $\varphi_{\mathcal{R}}(\Gamma$; Δ ; $\Theta)$, then $\exists \Delta', \Theta', \mathcal{N}'$ s.t. Γ ; Δ ; $\Theta \rightarrow \Gamma$; Δ' ; Θ' and $\mathcal{N} \rightarrow_{\mathcal{R}}^* \mathcal{N}'$ and Γ ; Δ' ; $\Theta' \vdash \mathcal{N}'$ with $\varphi_{\mathcal{R}}(\Gamma$; Δ' ; $\Theta')$.*

Using this result we can verify properties other than just safety. This is the benefit of the generalised approach to MPST, where instead of forcing protocols to abide by specific properties, types can be checked *a posteriori* to determine any properties they observe. We demonstrate for *deadlock freedom* (Definition 12).

Definition 12 (DF: Networks). *A network $\mathcal{N}$ is deadlock free, written $\mathsf{df}(\mathcal{N})$, iff $\mathcal{N} \rightarrow^* \mathcal{N}' \nrightarrow$ implies either*

1. *$\mathcal{N}' \equiv \mathbf{0} \parallel \mathcal{B}$; or*
2. *$\mathcal{N}' \equiv \mathcal{N}_1' \parallel \cdots \parallel \mathcal{N}_n' \parallel \mathcal{B}$ s.t. $\forall i \in 1..n : \mathcal{N}_i' = \mathsf{p}_i \triangleleft \, !_{j \in J} \mathsf{q}_j : \mathsf{m}_j(\tilde{x}_j) \, . \, P_j$.*

A deadlock free network is one that only gets stuck when all processes reach $\mathbf{0}$, or when the only non-$\mathbf{0}$ processes left in the network are servers. (Note, the buffer is allowed to be non-empty because of message delays.) We define deadlock freedom on types in Definition 13, stating that type contexts are deadlock free if they only get stuck when the linear context is **end**-typed.

Definition 13 (DF: Types). *Contexts Γ ; Δ ; Θ are deadlock free, written $\mathsf{df}(\Gamma$; Δ ; $\Theta)$, iff Γ ; Δ ; $\Theta \rightarrow^* \Gamma$; Δ' ; $\Theta' \nrightarrow$ implies $\mathsf{end}(\Delta')$.*

Proposition 1 (Property Verification: DF). *If Γ ; Δ ; $\Theta \vdash \mathcal{N}$ with $\varphi_{\mathcal{R}}(\Gamma$; Δ ; $\Theta)$, then $\mathsf{df}(\Gamma$; Δ ; $\Theta)$ implies $\mathsf{df}(\mathcal{N})$.*

Lastly, in Proposition 1 we state that deadlock free contexts imply deadlock freedom in the networks they type, a result which follows from Theorem 2.

Decidability. Asynchronous generalised MPST are known to be undecidable in general [17,25]. This stems from the fact that session types with asynchronous buffers can encode Turing machines [3, Theorem 2.5]. However, we note that this simulation relies on buffers with queue semantics and tail-recursion; whereas our type system uses bag buffers and replication. Comparing the expressive power of recursion and replication, previous studies show that for π-calculi with communication of free names the two are equally as expressive [22]; whereas without communication of free names (*e.g.* CCS) recursion is strictly more expressive than replication [7]. Thus, we raise the question: *"What is the expressive power of asynchronous session types with bag buffers and replication?"*, which we aim to answer in future work.

For now, we present a predicate on type contexts which can be used to determine decidable subsets of the type system. This predicate, called *trivially terminating* (Definition 14) is decidable and guarantees a finite traversable state-space, thus implying decidability of safety (and subsequently property verification).

Definition 14 (Trivially Terminating). *We say* Γ ; Δ ; Θ *are trivially terminating, written* $\text{tt}(\Gamma ; \Delta ; \Theta)$, *iff* $\forall \mathsf{p} \in \text{dom}(\Gamma) : \Gamma(\mathsf{p}) = !_{i \in I} \mathsf{q}_i : \mathsf{m}_i(\tilde{B}_i) . \tilde{S}_i$ *where* $\forall i \in I : \mathsf{q}_i \notin \text{dom}(\Gamma)$.

Proposition 2 (Decidable Subset). *For any contexts,* $\text{tt}(\Gamma ; \Delta ; \Theta)$ *is decidable and* $\text{tt}(\Gamma ; \Delta ; \Theta)$ *implies checking* $\varphi_{\mathcal{R}}(\Gamma ; \Delta ; \Theta)$ *is decidable.*

5   Encore

Modelling of failures and distributed communication is increasingly becoming a more relevant and widely researched topic within the area of programming languages. We highlight below some key related work, identifying the main differences w.r.t. MAGπ!.

Affine session types [10,14,20] use affine typing to allow sessions to be prematurely cancelled in the event of failure. They may be used in a similar fashion to try-catch blocks, where a main protocol is followed until a possible failure is met and handled gracefully. Similar in approach to MAGπ! is work by Barwell *et al.* [4], where generalised MPST theory is extended to reason about *crash-stop failures*. Where MAGπ! uses timeouts, the previous uses a "crash" message label which can be fed to a receiving process via some assumed failure detection mechanism. Viering *et al.* [27] present an *event-driven and distributed* MPST theory, where a central robust node is assumed and is capable of restarting crashed processes. Chen *et al.* [11] remove the dependency on a reliable node, instead using *synchronisation points* to handle failures as they are detected. Adameit *et al.* [1] consider session types for *link failures* where *default values* act as failure-handling mechanism to substitute lost data. MAGπ! models lower-level failures than all of these works. Most of the aforementioned assume some perfect failure-detection mechanism, whereas MAGπ! embraces timeouts as a weak failure detector to show that some degree of safety can still be achieved. Our theory is designed to operate at a lower level of abstraction, thus often providing weaker guarantees (*e.g.* consider our minimal definition of type safety) in exchange for modeling a wider set of communication failures.

The adoption of replication in MPST theory is a novel contribution of this paper. Replication in broader session types research has been utilised on numerous accounts [8,9,12,23], specifically in work pertaining to Curry-Howard interpretations of linear logic as session types, where the exponential modality from linear logic $!A$ is typically linked to replication from the π-calculus. Disregarding our modeling of failure, the largest difference between these works and ours is that we focus on a multiparty setting, whereas these theories are all based on binary communication. Furthermore, we did not opt to approach our problem from a logic-perspective, as is the main motivation behind this line of research. Instead, we build upon already-standard generalised MPST theory, adapting it towards our problem domain. We do note, however, that exploring a logical approach to replication in MPST (and, in turn, to failures in session types) is an interesting direction for future work. A more related use of replication in types is by Marshall and Orchard [19], where the authors discuss how non-linear types can be used in a controlled fashion to type behaviours such as repeatedly spawning processes. This resembles the semantics of our type system and dynamic definition of replication in our language, where replicated processes (resp. types) can be reused as necessary to pull out linear copies of their continuations. The mentioned work focuses on how to control the use of non-linear types and how this can be utilised with session types in a functional programming language. Our work, on the other hand, uses replication as a means of better modeling client-server interactions and distinguishing between failure-prone communication that should be handled by the recipient or the sender.

On session types for client-server communication, research largely takes the approach of linear-logic correspondences [8,21,23,28]. The topology these works target are of binary sessions between a pool of clients and a single server. In Qian et al. [23] a logic is developed, called CSLL (client-server linear logic), utilising the *coexponential* modality ¡A. The subtle difference between this modality and the exponential !A is that the latter represents an unlimited number of a type A, while the former serves type A as many times as required according to client requests, in a sequential yet still unordered manner. This is very similar to how our type system operates, given that replicated receives only pull out copies of continuations upon communication. Multiple requests induce non-determinism into further reductions, in our work this is seen in the extension of parallel types, which in Qian et al. [23] is observed through hyper-environments. The difference in goal between the work of [23] (followed up by [21]) and ours, is that the mentioned works focus on providing fixed static guarantees on the processes they type (the former work with a focus on deadlock freedom, the latter on weak termination) whilst we take a generalised approach. Our type system does not force programs to be deadlock-free or terminating, but rather requires a less restrictive *safety* property and allows verification of deadlock freedom and termination to be done *a posteriori*—the trade-off being our weaker form of type safety given the failure-prone nature of our setting.

To conclude, we presented MAGπ!, an extension to MAGπ made to use replication (instead of recursion) to express infinite computation—both at the language and type levels. We did so with the aim of better modelling multiparty client-server interactions, where servers are designed to remain infinitely available. Specifically, we find type-level replication to be a clean mechanism for offloading the handling of certain failures from the recipient to the sender—a practical procedure for client-server interactions. We have generalised our theory by proving our meta-theoretic results parametric of the largest safety property, allowing for more specific properties to be instantiated and used to verify runtime behaviours. As future work, we plan to investigate more specific properties for verification through our general type system. We aim to explore in detail the decidability of type-level properties and if/how they may be restricted to obtain decidable bounds in cases where they are not. Lastly, we wish to conduct a foundational study of the use of replication in MPST—we anticipate their use for modelling client-server interactions to have further benefit outwith a failure-prone setting.

Acknowledgements. We thank the anonymous reviewers for their helpful comments. A special thanks also goes to Simon Fowler for his guidance and invaluable feedback. Supported by the UK EPSRC New Investigator Award grant EP/X027309/1 "Uni-pi: safety, adaptability and resilience in distributed ecosystems, by construction".

References

1. Adameit, M., Peters, K., Nestmann, U.: Session types for link failures. In: Bouajjani, A., Silva, A. (eds.) FORTE 2017. LNCS, vol. 10321, pp. 1–16. Springer, Cham (2017). https://doi.org/10.1007/978-3-319-60225-7_1
2. Akkoyunlu, E.A., Ekanandham, K., Huber, R.V.: Some constraints and tradeoffs in the design of network communications. In: Browne, J.C., Rodriguez-Rosell, J. (eds.) Proceedings of the Fifth Symposium on Operating System Principles, SOSP 1975, The University of Texas at Austin, Austin, Texas, USA, 19-21 November 1975, pp. 67–74. ACM (1975). https://doi.org/10.1145/800213.806523
3. Bartoletti, M., Scalas, A., Tuosto, E., Zunino, R.: Honesty by typing. Log. Methods Comput. Sci. **12**(4) (2016). https://doi.org/10.2168/LMCS-12(4:7)2016
4. Barwell, A.D., Scalas, A., Yoshida, N., Zhou, F.: Generalised multiparty session types with crash-stop failures. In: Klin, B., Lasota, S., Muscholl, A. (eds.) 33rd International Conference on Concurrency Theory, CONCUR 2022, September 12-16, 2022, Warsaw, Poland. LIPIcs, vol. 243, pp. 35:1–35:25. Schloss Dagstuhl - Leibniz-Zentrum für Informatik (2022). https://doi.org/10.4230/LIPIcs.CONCUR.2022.35
5. Bettini, L., Coppo, M., D'Antoni, L., De Luca, M., Dezani-Ciancaglini, M., Yoshida, N.: Global progress in dynamically interleaved multiparty sessions. In: van Breugel, F., Chechik, M. (eds.) CONCUR 2008. LNCS, vol. 5201, pp. 418–433. Springer, Heidelberg (2008). https://doi.org/10.1007/978-3-540-85361-9_33
6. Brand, J.: Observations on popular antiquities (1780)
7. Busi, N., Gabbrielli, M., Zavattaro, G.: On the expressive power of recursion, replication and iteration in process calculi. Math. Struct. Comput. Sci. **19**(6), 1191–1222 (2009). https://doi.org/10.1017/S096012950999017X
8. Caires, L., Pérez, J.A.: Linearity, control effects, and behavioral types. In: Yang, H. (ed.) ESOP 2017. LNCS, vol. 10201, pp. 229–259. Springer, Heidelberg (2017). https://doi.org/10.1007/978-3-662-54434-1_9
9. Caires, L., Pfenning, F., Toninho, B.: Linear logic propositions as session types. Math. Struct. Comput. Sci. **26**(3), 367–423 (2016). https://doi.org/10.1017/S0960129514000218
10. Capecchi, S., Giachino, E., Yoshida, N.: Global escape in multiparty sessions. Math. Struct. Comput. Sci. **26**(2), 156–205 (2016). https://doi.org/10.1017/S0960129514000164
11. Chen, T.-C., Viering, M., Bejleri, A., Ziarek, L., Eugster, P.: A type theory for robust failure handling in distributed systems. In: Albert, E., Lanese, I. (eds.) FORTE 2016. LNCS, vol. 9688, pp. 96–113. Springer, Cham (2016). https://doi.org/10.1007/978-3-319-39570-8_7
12. Dardha, O., Gay, S.J.: A new linear logic for deadlock-free session-typed processes. In: Baier, C., Dal Lago, U. (eds.) FoSSaCS 2018. LNCS, vol. 10803, pp. 91–109. Springer, Cham (2018). https://doi.org/10.1007/978-3-319-89366-2_5

13. Dardha, O., Giachino, E., Sangiorgi, D.: Session types revisited. Inf. Comput. **256**, 253–286 (2017). https://doi.org/10.1016/j.ic.2017.06.002

14. Fowler, S., Lindley, S., Morris, J.G., Decova, S.: Exceptional asynchronous session types: session types without tiers. Proc. ACM Program. Lang. **3**(POPL), 28:1–28:29 (2019). https://doi.org/10.1145/3290341

15. Honda, K., Vasconcelos, V.T., Kubo, M.: Language primitives and type discipline for structured communication-based programming. In: Hankin, C. (ed.) ESOP 1998. LNCS, vol. 1381, pp. 122–138. Springer, Heidelberg (1998). https://doi.org/10.1007/BFb0053567

16. Honda, K., Yoshida, N., Carbone, M.: Multiparty asynchronous session types. In: Necula, G.C., Wadler, P. (eds.) Proceedings of the 35th ACM SIGPLAN-SIGACT Symposium on Principles of Programming Languages, POPL 2008, San Francisco, California, USA, 7-12 January 2008, pp. 273–284. ACM (2008). https://doi.org/10.1145/1328438.1328472

17. Le Brun, M.A., Dardha, O.: Magπ: types for failure-prone communication. In: Wies, T. (ed.) Programming Languages and Systems. ESOP 2023. LNCS, vol. 13990, pp 363–391. Springer, Cham (2023). https://doi.org/10.1007/978-3-031-30044-8_14

18. Le Brun, M.A., Dardha, O.: Magπ!: The role of replication in typing failure-prone communication (2024). https://doi.org/10.48550/arXiv.2404.16213

19. Marshall, D., Orchard, D.: Replicate, reuse, repeat: capturing non-linear communication via session types and graded modal types. In: Carbone, M., Neykova, R. (eds.) Proceedings of the 13th International Workshop on Programming Language Approaches to Concurrency and Communication-cEntric Software, PLACES@ETAPS 2022, Munich, Germany, 3rd April 2022. EPTCS, vol. 356, pp. 1–11 (2022). https://doi.org/10.4204/EPTCS.356.1

20. Mostrous, D., Vasconcelos, V.T.: Affine sessions. Log. Methods Comput. Sci. **14**(4) (2018). https://doi.org/10.23638/LMCS-14(4:14)2018

21. Padovani, L.: On the fair termination of client-server sessions. In: Kesner, D., Pédrot, P. (eds.) 28th International Conference on Types for Proofs and Programs, TYPES 2022, June 20-25, 2022, LS2N, University of Nantes, France. LIPIcs, vol. 269, pp. 5:1–5:21. Schloss Dagstuhl - Leibniz-Zentrum für Informatik (2022). https://doi.org/10.4230/LIPIcs.TYPES.2022.5

22. Palamidessi, C., Valencia, F.D.: Recursion vs replication in process calculi: expressiveness. Bull. EATCS **87**, 105–125 (2005)

23. Qian, Z., Kavvos, G.A., Birkedal, L.: Client-server sessions in linear logic. Proc. ACM Program. Lang. **5**(ICFP), 1–31 (2021). https://doi.org/10.1145/3473567

24. Sangiorgi, D., Walker, D.: The Pi-Calculus - a Theory of Mobile Processes. Cambridge University Press, Cambridge (2001)

25. Scalas, A., Yoshida, N.: Less is more: multiparty session types revisited. Proc. ACM Program. Lang. **3**(POPL), 30:1–30:29 (2019). https://doi.org/10.1145/3290343

26. Vasconcelos, V.T.: Fundamentals of session types. Inf. Comput. **217**, 52–70 (2012). https://doi.org/10.1016/j.ic.2012.05.002

27. Viering, M., Hu, R., Eugster, P., Ziarek, L.: A multiparty session typing discipline for fault-tolerant event-driven distributed programming. Proc. ACM Program. Lang. **5**(OOPSLA), 1–30 (2021). https://doi.org/10.1145/3485501

28. Wadler, P.: Propositions as sessions. J. Funct. Program. **24**(2-3), 384–418 (2014). https://doi.org/10.1017/S095679681400001X

Leaf-First Zipper Semantics

Sergueï Lenglet[1,2(✉)] and Alan Schmitt[3]

[1] Université de Lorraine, Nancy, France
lenglet@lipn.univ-paris13.fr
[2] Université Sorbonne Paris Nord, Villetaneuse, France
[3] INRIA, Rennes, France
alan.schmitt@inria.fr

Abstract. Biernacka et al. recently proposed *zipper semantics*, a semantics format from which sound and complete abstract machines for non-deterministic languages can be automatically derived. We present a new style of zipper semantics, called *leaf-first*, in which we express the semantics of two extensions of HOπ, a higher-order version of the π-calculus: one with passivation and the other with join patterns. The leaf-first style is better suited than the original one to express phenomena occurring in process calculi semantics such as scope extrusion, which is observable with passivation and complex with join patterns.

Keywords: Process calculi · Abstract machines · Scope extrusion

1 Introduction

In concurrency theory, abstract machines are used as an implementation model [9,11,19,21,27], in particular to study the distribution of computation [1,12–14,16,22]. The design of these machines is often ad-hoc, following principles which apply to the considered calculus only. Besides, some of the machines are not complete, i.e., there exist reduction paths of the language which cannot be simulated by its abstract machine [9,11,13,19,27]. To overcome these issues, Biernacka et al. [2,3] recently proposed Non-Deterministic Abstract Machines (NDAM), a generic design of abstract machines for non-deterministic languages. An NDAM explores the term in the search for a redex, making arbitrary choices when several paths are possible. The machine backtracks when it reaches a normal form, annotating it to not try it again, thus avoiding infinite loops during the search.

As writing the definition of an NDAM can be tedious, the authors also propose a sound and complete automatic derivation procedure from a *zipper semantics*, a format in between a Structural Operational Semantics (SOS) [23] and a context-based reduction semantics [7,8]. Like in a SOS, a zipper semantics explores a term with structural rules, but it remembers its position in the term using an evaluation context, a syntactic object that represents a term with a

© IFIP International Federation for Information Processing 2024
Published by Springer Nature Switzerland AG 2024
V. Castiglioni and A. Francalanza (Eds.): FORTE 2024, LNCS 14678, pp. 118–135, 2024.
https://doi.org/10.1007/978-3-031-62645-6_7

hole [8]. A zipper semantics respecting some properties can then be augmented into an NDAM by adding the annotations and backtracking mechanisms.

Biernacka et al. [2] define a zipper semantics for several calculi including HOπ [24], a process calculus where messages are executable terms. Like the π-calculus [25], HOπ features name restriction, a construct which restricts the scope of a communication channel, hiding it to the outside. When a communication happens between a sender and a receiver, it may be necessary to enlarge the scope of restricted names to include the receiver: this phenomenon is known as *scope extrusion*. Biernacka et al. consider a variant of HOπ with *eager* scope extrusion, where the scope of all name restrictions around the message output are extended to include the input. In contrast, in *lazy* scope extrusion, only the restrictions of the names occurring in the message contents are extended.

While the difference between lazy and eager scope extrusion cannot be observed in HOπ, it may lead to distinguishable behaviors in calculi with localities and *passivation* [1,18], a feature used in component models to interrupt and capture the state of running components [26]. Lazy scope extrusion is also quite intricate in presence of *join patterns* [11], where a single receiver may receive messages from different senders at once. The scope of lazily extruded names should encompass the process sending the message and the receiver, and no more. With several messages emitted at once, the scopes of names restricting two distinct messages are different and depend on the respective output processes.

In this paper, we encode lazy scope extrusion in various settings by defining a new format of zipper semantics, called *leaf-first*. Our contributions are: we express the semantics of HOπ with passivation and lazy scope extrusion in our new leaf-first format, and we show that our approach can also handle an extension of HOπ with join patterns. Our format respects the zipper semantics requirements, so we can apply Biernacka et al.'s derivation procedure to obtain an NDAM from it, and we get for free abstract machines for these calculi.

The paper is organized as follows. Section 2 presents the syntax and lazy semantics of HOπ with passivation; we recall an example illustrating how we can distinguish lazy from eager scope extrusion in that calculus. We then present a leaf-first zipper semantics for this calculus, that we prove equivalent to the usual one. Section 3 follows the same structure for HOπ with join patterns. Section 4 discusses related work and concludes. The accompanying research report [17] contains the missing proofs.

2   HOπ with Passivation

We present the lazy semantics of HOπP (HOπ with passivation) [18], that we characterize using the new zipper semantics style we propose in this paper.

2.1   Syntax and Lazy Semantics

Syntax. HOπP [18] is a higher-order calculus—where messages are executable processes—extended with hierarchical localities and passivation. We assume countable sets of channel names, ranged over by lowercase letters a, b, etc., and of process variables ranged over by X, Y, Z. The syntax of processes is as follows.

$$P, Q, R, S, M, K ::= X \mid \mathbf{0} \mid P \parallel Q \mid a(X).R \mid \overline{a}\langle M \rangle K \mid \nu a.P \mid a[P]$$

Informally, $\mathbf{0}$ is the inactive process, the parallel composition $P \parallel Q$ is executing P and Q concurrently, $\nu a.P$ restricts the scope of channel a to P, an output $\overline{a}\langle M \rangle K$ is sending M on a and continues as K, while $a(X).R$ is waiting for a message M on a to continue as R where X is replaced by M. A process may run in a locality $a[P]$, which can be *passivated* (dissolved) at any time, interrupting the execution of P and saving its current state in a message on a.

For readability, we often use S to denote a sending process, R a receiving one, M a message, and K a continuation, but these all stand for processes. In examples, we also often omit $\mathbf{0}$ in output continuations or in parallel processes, abbreviating $\overline{a}\langle P \rangle \mathbf{0}$ as $\overline{a}\langle P \rangle$ and $P \parallel \mathbf{0}$ as P. The scope of name restriction extends to the right as much as possible, writing $\nu a.(P \parallel Q)$ as $\nu a.P \parallel Q$.

Scope extrusion. The scope of a in $\nu a.P$ is restricted to P, so that a communication on a is possible inside P only. It does not prevent communication on other names, but the scope of restricted names present in a message has to be enlarged to prevent them from escaping their binder. For example, we have

$$b(X).(X \parallel \overline{c}\langle \mathbf{0} \rangle) \parallel \nu ad.\overline{b}\langle \overline{a}\langle \mathbf{0} \rangle \rangle \parallel \overline{d}\langle \mathbf{0} \rangle \xrightarrow{\tau} \nu a.\overline{a}\langle \mathbf{0} \rangle \parallel \overline{c}\langle \mathbf{0} \rangle \parallel \nu d.\overline{d}\langle \mathbf{0} \rangle$$

The scope of a is extended to include the receiver, a phenomenon known as *scope extrusion*. The scope of d, however, remains the same: we only extend the scope of names occurring in the message. The scope extrusion is thus said to be *lazy*.

In $\nu a.P$, a is bound in P, and $a(X).R$ binds X in R. We write $\mathsf{fn}(P)$ for free names of P, defined as expected. To avoid unwanted captures (in particular during scope extrusion), we henceforth assume bound names and variables to be pairwise distinct, and distinct from the free names and variables of all the processes under consideration, using α-conversion if necessary. This convention matters for instance for the rules OUTPAR, OUTLOC, and TAUCOM of Fig. 1.

Lazy semantics. Given an entity ranged over by e, we write $\overrightarrow{e}$ for a sequence $(e_1 \dots e_n)$. We write () for the empty sequence, $e' \cdot \overrightarrow{e}$ for the extension of a sequence to the left, and $\overrightarrow{e_1} \cdot \overrightarrow{e_2}$ for the concatenation of two sequences. We write $P\{Q/X\}$ for the usual capture-avoiding substitution of X by Q in P.

We define the labeled operational semantics with three judgments: $P \xrightarrow{\tau} P'$ for silent steps, $P \xrightarrow{a(M)} R$ for a process that inputs the message M on a, and $P \xrightarrow{\nu \overrightarrow{b}.\overline{a}\langle M \rangle} K$ for a process that outputs the message $\overline{a}\langle M \rangle$ while extruding the names in $\overrightarrow{b}$. We give the rules in Fig. 1, except the symmetric counterpart of the rules marked with (s), a convention we follow from now on.

A transition $P \xrightarrow{\tau} P'$ can be decomposed as follows. First, we apply the rules TAUPAR, TAULOC, and TAUNU to reach the parallel composition of the

OUTOUT
$$\overline{a}\langle M\rangle K \xrightarrow{\overline{a}\langle M\rangle} K$$

OUTPASSIV
$$a[P] \xrightarrow{\overline{a}\langle P\rangle} 0$$

OUTPAR
$$\frac{P \xrightarrow{\nu\vec{b}.\overline{a}\langle M\rangle} K}{P\parallel Q \xrightarrow{\nu\vec{b}.\overline{a}\langle M\rangle} K\parallel Q}\;(s)$$

OUTLOC
$$\frac{P \xrightarrow{\nu\vec{b}.\overline{a}\langle M\rangle} K}{c[P] \xrightarrow{\nu\vec{b}.\overline{a}\langle M\rangle} c[K]}$$

OUTEXTR
$$\frac{P \xrightarrow{\nu\vec{b}.\overline{a}\langle M\rangle} K \quad c\neq a \quad c\in \mathrm{fn}(M)}{\nu c.P \xrightarrow{\nu c\cdot\vec{b}.\overline{a}\langle M\rangle} K}$$

OUTNU
$$\frac{P \xrightarrow{\nu\vec{b}.\overline{a}\langle M\rangle} K \quad c\neq a \quad c\notin \mathrm{fn}(M)}{\nu c.P \xrightarrow{\nu\vec{b}.\overline{a}\langle M\rangle} \nu c.K}$$

INPAR
$$\frac{P \xrightarrow{a(M)} P'}{P\parallel Q \xrightarrow{a(M)} P'\parallel Q}\;(s)$$

INLOC
$$\frac{P \xrightarrow{a(M)} P'}{b[P] \xrightarrow{a(M)} b[P']}$$

INNU
$$\frac{P \xrightarrow{a(M)} R \quad c\neq a}{\nu c.P \xrightarrow{a(M)} \nu c.R}$$

ININ
$$a(X).R \xrightarrow{a(M)} R\{M/X\}$$

TAUCOM
$$\frac{P \xrightarrow{a(M)} R \quad Q \xrightarrow{\nu\vec{b}.\overline{a}\langle M\rangle} K}{P\parallel Q \xrightarrow{\tau} \nu\vec{b}.R\parallel K}\;(s)$$

TAUPAR
$$\frac{P \xrightarrow{\tau} P'}{P\parallel Q \xrightarrow{\tau} P'\parallel Q}\;(s)$$

TAULOC
$$\frac{P \xrightarrow{\tau} P'}{a[P] \xrightarrow{\tau} a[P']}$$

TAUNU
$$\frac{P \xrightarrow{\tau} P'}{\nu c.P \xrightarrow{\tau} \nu c.P'}$$

Fig. 1. Lazy Semantics of HOπP

communication. At this point, rule TAUCOM is applied, with two premises. In one premise, output rules OUTPAR, OUTLOC, OUTEXTR, and OUTNU are applied until the messaging process. The last two rules are for name restriction, the former is used when the name needs to be extruded (it is free in the message contents), while the latter is used when no extrusion is needed. The message may be the result of an output (rule OUTOUT) or a passivation (rule OUTPASSIV). In the other premise of the TAUCOM rule, the input is reached through rules INPAR, INLOC, and INNU, and the actual input is done in rule ININ. Finally, the conclusion of TAUCOM restores the name restrictions that have been extruded.

Example. We show the difference between lazy and eager scope extrusion in a calculus with passivation. We write $a(X).P$ as $a(\_).P$ if X is not free in P. Let $P = a[\nu c.\overline{b}\langle 0\rangle\overline{c}\langle 0\rangle \parallel c(\_).c(\_).\overline{d}\langle 0\rangle] \parallel b(\_).a(X).X \parallel X$. We communicate on b and then passivate the locality on a, duplicating its content. With eager scope extrusion, the scope of c is expanded outside a:

$$P \xrightarrow{\tau} \nu c.a[\overline{c}\langle 0\rangle \parallel c(\_).c(\_).\overline{d}\langle 0\rangle] \parallel a(X).(X \parallel X)$$
$$\xrightarrow{\tau} \nu c.\overline{c}\langle 0\rangle \parallel c(\_).c(\_).\overline{d}\langle 0\rangle \parallel \overline{c}\langle 0\rangle \parallel c(\_).c(\_).\overline{d}\langle 0\rangle$$

The name c is then shared between the copies of the duplicated process, and a message output on d becomes possible after two communications on c. With lazy scope extrusion, the scope of c does not change:

$$P \xrightarrow{\tau} a[\nu c.\overline{c}\langle \mathbf{0}\rangle \parallel c(\_).c(\_).\overline{d}\langle \mathbf{0}\rangle] \parallel a(X).X \parallel X$$
$$\xrightarrow{\tau} \nu c.(\overline{c}\langle \mathbf{0}\rangle \parallel c(\_).c(\_).\overline{d}\langle \mathbf{0}\rangle) \parallel \nu c.(\overline{c}\langle \mathbf{0}\rangle \parallel c(\_).c(\_).\overline{d}\langle \mathbf{0}\rangle)$$

Each duplicated process has its own copy of c, and it is no longer possible for the message output on d to trigger.

2.2 Root-First Zipper Semantics

Zipper semantics exhibits the step-by-step decomposition of a term into a context and a redex. Like a SOS [23], it traverses a term in the search for a redex using structural rules. It also makes explicit the current position in the term using an evaluation context, like in context-based reduction semantics [8]. We represent a context as a stack of elementary contexts $\mathfrak{F}$, called *frames*, of four kinds.

$$\mathbb{E}, \mathbb{F}, \mathbb{G}, \mathbb{H} ::= \bullet \mid \mathfrak{F} :: \mathbb{E} \qquad\qquad \mathfrak{F} ::= \parallel P \mid P \parallel \mid \nu a \mid a[]$$

Each frame corresponds to a set of similar structural rules in the definition of the lazy semantics. The decomposition process happening in a zipper semantics makes it more convenient to interpret a context *inside-out*: the topmost frame is the innermost one in the term. We define the operation of plugging P inside a frame $\mathfrak{F}[P]$ and inside a context $\mathbb{E}[P]$ as follows.

$$\bullet[P] \triangleq P \qquad (\mathfrak{F} :: \mathbb{E})[P] \triangleq \mathbb{E}[\mathfrak{F}[P]]$$
$$(\parallel Q)[P] \triangleq P \parallel Q \quad (Q \parallel)[P] \triangleq Q \parallel P \quad (\nu a)[P] \triangleq \nu a.P \quad (a[])[P] \triangleq a[P]$$

We use contexts to indicate where the current focus is when exploring a term: for instance, $\mathbb{E}[P \parallel Q]$ means that the current focus is on the parallel composition. To focus on P, we consider $(\parallel Q :: \mathbb{E})[P]$: going further down the term consists in pushing a frame on top of the context. In contrast, going towards the root amounts to popping the top frame from the context.

In most semantics of process calculi based on labeled transitions, an input $a(X).R$ communicates with an output $\overline{a}\langle M\rangle K$ even if they are not directly in parallel. The zipper semantics therefore aims at decomposing a term as a redex in some evaluation context $\mathbb{E}$, the redex itself being of the form $\mathbb{F}[S] \parallel \mathbb{G}[a(X).R]$ or $\mathbb{G}[a(X).R] \parallel \mathbb{F}[S]$ with $S = \overline{a}\langle M\rangle K$ or $S = a[M]$. The strategy followed by Biernacka et al. [2, Appendix C] to decompose a HOπ process P proceeds in three steps: starting from the top of P, search for the parallel composition of the communication, building $\mathbb{E}$ at the same time. At that point, P is decomposed as $\mathbb{E}[P_1 \parallel P_2]$. Then, look for the output in either P_1 or P_2, decomposing it as $\mathbb{F}[\overline{a}\langle M\rangle K]$. At the same time, $\mathbb{F}$ is split into $\mathbb{F}_\parallel$ and $\mathbb{F}_\nu$, so that $\mathbb{F}_\parallel$ contains the parallel compositions and $\mathbb{F}_\nu$ the name restrictions of $\mathbb{F}$. Finally, look for the input in the other process, decomposing it as $\mathbb{G}[a(X).R]$. Once all the ingredients have been found, the result of the communication is either $\mathbb{E}\left[\mathbb{F}_\nu\left[\mathbb{F}_\parallel[K] \parallel \mathbb{G}[R\{Q/X\}]\right]\right]$ or $\mathbb{E}\left[\mathbb{F}_\nu\left[\mathbb{G}[R\{Q/X\}] \parallel \mathbb{F}_\parallel[K]\right]\right]$. We refer to such an exploration strategy as *root-first*, because it starts the decomposition with the operator at the root of the redex (the parallel composition).

In the final result, the scope extrusion is *eager* because $\mathbb{F}_\nu$ collects all the enclosing name restrictions of $\mathbb{F}$, not only those restricting the free names of M. The problem is that the decomposition of $\mathbb{F}$ happens while going through the sending process, while the message M is not yet known: when we reach it, the decomposition of $\mathbb{F}$ is already over. Therefore, while a root-first strategy is enough to express the λ-calculus or a process calculus with eager scope extrusion, it is not fit to represent the semantics of a calculus with lazy scope extrusion.

$$\textbf{init}\quad \frac{P \xrightarrow{\bullet}_{\text{out}} P'}{P \to_{\text{zs}} P'} \qquad \textbf{outParL}\quad \frac{P \xrightarrow{\parallel Q \,::\, \mathbb{E}}_{\text{out}} P'}{P \parallel Q \xrightarrow{\mathbb{E}}_{\text{out}} P'}\,(s) \qquad \textbf{outLoc}\quad \frac{P \xrightarrow{a[] \,::\, \mathbb{E}}_{\text{out}} P'}{a[P] \xrightarrow{\mathbb{E}}_{\text{out}} P'} \qquad \textbf{outNu}\quad \frac{P \xrightarrow{\nu a \,::\, \mathbb{E}}_{\text{out}} P'}{\nu a.P \xrightarrow{\mathbb{E}}_{\text{out}} P'}$$

$$\textbf{outOut}\quad \frac{\mathbb{E} \xrightarrow{K,(),a,M}_{\text{par}} P'}{\overline{a}\langle M\rangle K \xrightarrow{\mathbb{E}}_{\text{out}} P'} \qquad \textbf{outPassiv}\quad \frac{\mathbb{E} \xrightarrow{0,(),a,P}_{\text{par}} P'}{a[P] \xrightarrow{\mathbb{E}}_{\text{out}} P'} \qquad \textbf{parL}\quad \frac{\mathbb{E} \xrightarrow{K \parallel Q,\,\overrightarrow{b},a,M}_{\text{par}} P'}{\parallel Q \,::\, \mathbb{E} \xrightarrow{K,\overrightarrow{b},a,M}_{\text{par}} P'}\,(s)$$

$$\textbf{parLoc}\quad \frac{\mathbb{E} \xrightarrow{c[K],\,\overrightarrow{b},a,M}_{\text{par}} P'}{c[] \,::\, \mathbb{E} \xrightarrow{K,\overrightarrow{b},a,M}_{\text{par}} P'} \qquad \textbf{parNu}\quad \frac{\mathbb{E} \xrightarrow{\nu c.K,\,\overrightarrow{b},a,M}_{\text{par}} P' \qquad c \neq a \qquad c \notin \text{fn}(M)}{\nu c \,::\, \mathbb{E} \xrightarrow{K,\overrightarrow{b},a,M}_{\text{par}} P'}$$

$$\textbf{parExtr}\quad \frac{\mathbb{E} \xrightarrow{K,c\cdot\,\overrightarrow{b},a,M}_{\text{par}} P' \qquad c \neq a \qquad c \in \text{fn}(M)}{\nu c \,::\, \mathbb{E} \xrightarrow{K,\overrightarrow{b},a,M}_{\text{par}} P'} \qquad \textbf{parInL}\quad \frac{R \xrightarrow{\bullet,\overrightarrow{b},a,M,\mathbb{E},K \,\parallel}_{\text{in}} P'}{\parallel R \,::\, \mathbb{E} \xrightarrow{K,\overrightarrow{b},a,M}_{\text{par}} P'}\,(s)$$

$$\textbf{inParL}\quad \frac{R \xrightarrow{\parallel Q \,::\, \mathbb{G},\,\overrightarrow{b},a,M,\mathbb{E},\mathfrak{F}}_{\text{in}} P'}{R \parallel Q \xrightarrow{\mathbb{G},\overrightarrow{b},a,M,\mathbb{E},\mathfrak{F}}_{\text{in}} P'}\,(s) \qquad \textbf{inLoc}\quad \frac{R \xrightarrow{c[] \,::\, \mathbb{G},\,\overrightarrow{b},a,M,\mathbb{E},\mathfrak{F}}_{\text{in}} P'}{c[R] \xrightarrow{\mathbb{G},\overrightarrow{b},a,M,\mathbb{E},\mathfrak{F}}_{\text{in}} P'}$$

$$\textbf{inNu}\quad \frac{R \xrightarrow{\nu c \,::\, \mathbb{G},\,\overrightarrow{b},a,M,\mathbb{E},\mathfrak{F}}_{\text{in}} P' \qquad c \neq a}{\nu c.R \xrightarrow{\mathbb{G},\overrightarrow{b},a,M,\mathbb{E},\mathfrak{F}}_{\text{in}} P'} \qquad \textbf{inCom}\quad a(X).R \xrightarrow{\mathbb{G},\overrightarrow{b},a,M,\mathbb{E},\mathfrak{F}}_{\text{in}} \mathbb{E}[\nu\,\overrightarrow{b}.\mathfrak{F}[\mathbb{G}[R\{M/X\}]]]$$

Fig. 2. Leaf-First Zipper semantics for lazy HOπP

2.3   Leaf-First Zipper Semantics

As said before, finding the extruded names in $\mathbb{F}[\![\overline{a}\langle M\rangle K]\!]$ requires us to know M when going through $\mathbb{F}$. We therefore search for the output first, then for the parallel composition and the input. Because the output is a leaf of the redex, we refer to such a strategy as a *leaf-first* zipper semantics. It is defined in Fig. 2.

A zipper transition $P \rightarrow_{zs} P'$ is defined using three auxiliary transitions (or *modes*) out, par, and in. The out mode looks for a message either from an output or a passivation. The rule init starts the search at the top of the term. The rules outParL, outParR, outLoc, and outNu change the current focus to a subterm. When we apply the rule outOut or outPassiv, the initial term is decomposed as $\mathbb{E}[\![\overline{a}\langle M\rangle K]\!]$ or $\mathbb{E}[\![a[P]]\!]$, and we switch to the par mode.

The par mode searches the parallel composition which separates the output and input processes, computing on the way the extruded names. The transition $\mathbb{E} \xrightarrow{K,\overrightarrow{b},a,M}_{\text{par}} P'$ goes through $\mathbb{E}$ looking for the parallel composition, constructing K (the continuation of the output) and $\overrightarrow{b}$ (the extruded names) while doing so, and remembering that M is sent on a. The rules outOut and outPassiv initialize the par mode with the proper continuation and with an empty sequence of extruded names. If the context is of the form $\nu c :: \mathbb{E}$, the name restriction νc surrounds the message output, so we should check that it does not prevent the communication on a, hence the premise $c \neq a$ in rules parNu and parExtr. If c occurs free in the message M, it must be extruded, and it is added to the sequence $\overrightarrow{b}$ in the rule parExtr. Otherwise, it is added to K in the rule parNu.

A locality is moved from the context to the continuation (rule parLoc). If the context is of the shape $\| Q :: \mathbb{E}$ or $Q \| :: \mathbb{E}$, we consider a process of the form $\mathbb{E}[\![K \| Q]\!]$ or $\mathbb{E}[\![Q \| K]\!]$ and we have two possibilities. If Q is not the process receiving the message, then Q has to be added to the continuation, and we continue searching for the receiver in $\mathbb{E}$ (rules parL and parR). Otherwise, we have found the parallel composition where the communication takes place, which is where the extruded names $\overrightarrow{b}$ should be restricted. We remember this position with $\mathbb{E}$, and search for the input in Q with a transition $Q \xrightarrow{\mathbb{G},\overrightarrow{b},a,M,\mathbb{E},\mathfrak{F}}_{\text{in}} P'$, where $\mathbb{G}$ is the context surrounding Q up to the parallel composition (initially $\bullet$), and $\mathfrak{F}$ records if the continuation K is to the left (then $\mathfrak{F} = K \|$) or to the right (then $\mathfrak{F} = \| K$) of Q (rules parInL and parInR).

The in mode is then going through the receiving process, pushing the constructs on the context $\mathbb{G}$ (rules inParL, inParR, parLoc, and inNu). Once the input $a(X).R$ has been found, all the pieces have been collected for the communication to happen, resulting in $\mathbb{E}\left[\!\left[\nu \overrightarrow{b}.\mathfrak{F}\left[\mathbb{G}\left[R\{M/X\}\right]\right]\right]\!\right]$. For instance, if we start from a process $\mathbb{E}[\![\mathbb{F}[\![\overline{a}\langle M\rangle K]\!] \| \mathbb{G}[\![a(X).R]\!]]\!]$, then $\mathfrak{F} = \mathbb{F}'[\![K]\!] \|$ where $\mathbb{F}'$ is what is left from $\mathbb{F}$ after removing the restricted names $\overrightarrow{b}$.

2.4 Properties of the Leaf-First Semantics

Correspondence results. We state how the leaf-first zipper semantics relates to the lazy semantics of HOπP.

Theorem 1. *If* $R \xrightarrow{G, \vec{b}, a, M, \mathbb{E}, \mathfrak{F}}_{\text{in}} P'$, *then* $R \xrightarrow{a(M)} R'$ *for some* R' *and* $P' = \mathbb{E}[\nu \vec{b}.\mathfrak{F}[G[R']]]$. *If* $\mathbb{E} \xrightarrow{K, \vec{b}, a, M}_{\text{par}} P'$, *then for all* $S \xrightarrow{\nu \vec{b}.\overline{a}\langle M \rangle} K$, *we have* $\mathbb{E}[S] \xrightarrow{\tau} P'$. *If* $P \xrightarrow{\mathbb{E}}_{\text{out}} P'$, *then* $\mathbb{E}[P] \xrightarrow{\tau} P'$.

From the last item, we deduce that $P \to_{\text{zs}} P'$ implies $P \xrightarrow{\tau} P'$. For the reverse implication, given $P \xrightarrow{\tau} P'$, we make explicit the contexts in P and P', writing them as $P = \mathbb{E}[\mathbb{H}[\overline{a}\langle M \rangle K] \parallel R]$ and $P' = \mathbb{E}[\nu \vec{b}.\mathbb{G}[K] \parallel R']$, with $R \xrightarrow{a(M)} R'$, and $\mathbb{H}$ built from $\vec{b}$ and $\mathbb{G}$. From there, we can reconstruct the zipper derivation; the proof is in the appendix.

Theorem 2. *If* $P \xrightarrow{\tau} P'$, *then* $P \to_{\text{zs}} P'$.

Derivation into a NDAM. The semantics of Fig. 2 fits the zipper semantics generic format [3]: each traversing rule (distinct from init and inCom) has exactly one premise, and is decomposing its source term one operator at a time.

A zipper semantics can be derived into an NDAM if it satisfies some properties, like being *machine constructive*: in each rule, it should be possible to construct the terms in the premise from those of the conclusion. This property holds if the meta-variables (of processes, contexts, names, etc.) of the premise are included in those of the conclusion, as one can check in Fig. 2. The semantics should also be *reversible*: conversely, we can recreate the terms in the conclusion from the premise, to allow for backtracking. It is the case because for each rule, the meta-variables of the conclusion are included in those of the premise.

Finally, the zipper semantics must be *terminating*, ensuring that the search for a redex in the NDAM does not infinitely loop. To prove it, it is enough to exhibit a strictly decreasing size on transitions such that the size of the premise is smaller than its conclusion. For each rule, the source term of the premise is a subterm of the source term of the conclusion, except when changing mode. We therefore consider a lexicographic ordering on modes first, so that out > par > in, and then on the size of the source term of the transition.

3 HOπ with Join Patterns

We consider HOπJ, an extension of HOπ with join patterns [11], where an input may receive an arbitrary number of messages simultaneously.

3.1 Syntax and Lazy Semantics

Syntax and informal semantics. We let ξ range over *message patterns*, which can be seen as multisets of elementary inputs $a_1(X_1) \mid \ldots \mid a_n(X_n)$ where the X_i are pairwise distinct. We change the input process with $\xi \triangleright R$.

$$\xi ::= a(X) \mid \xi \mid \xi \qquad P, Q, \ldots ::= X \mid \mathbf{0} \mid P \parallel Q \mid \xi \triangleright R \mid \overline{a}\langle M \rangle K \mid \nu a.P$$

A communication happens when enough message outputs are in parallel to fulfil the message pattern of an input. Like in HOπ or HOπP, name restriction delimits the scope of names, and lazy scope extrusion may be necessary during communication. However, to keep it as lazy as possible, restricted names should not be extruded further than the parallel composition enclosing the sender and receiver. Consider the following example, where $\xi = a_1(X_1) \mid a_2(X_2) \mid a_3(X_3) \mid a_4(X_4)$ and we abbreviate $\bar{b}\langle 0 \rangle 0$ as $\bar{b}$ for any b. We number the parallel compositions in the redex, which has the same parallel structure as in Fig. 4.

$$P \parallel \Big(\big(\big((\nu b.\overline{a_1}\langle \bar{b} \rangle K_1) \big) \parallel^2 \big(\nu c.\nu d.\overline{a_2}\langle 0 \rangle K_2 \parallel^3 \overline{a_3}\langle \bar{d} \rangle K_3 \big) \big) \parallel^1 \big((\nu e.\overline{a_4}\langle \bar{e} \rangle K_4) \parallel^4 \xi \rhd R \big) \Big)$$
$$\xrightarrow{\tau} P \parallel \nu b.\nu d. \Big(\big(K_1 \parallel^2 \big(\nu c.K_2 \parallel^3 K_3 \big) \big) \parallel^1 \nu e. \big(K_4 \parallel^4 R' \big) \Big)$$

The scope of c is unchanged, while b and d have been extruded to include $\parallel^1$, and e to include $\parallel^4$.

Lazy semantics. We let p range over pairs (a, M) of a message and its output channel. Given a sequence $\overrightarrow{p}$, we define the sequence of *communication names* inductively so that $\mathsf{cn}(()) \triangleq ()$ and $\mathsf{cn}((a, M) \cdot \overrightarrow{p}) \triangleq a \cdot \mathsf{cn}(\overrightarrow{p})$, and the set of *message names* as $\mathsf{mn}(()) \triangleq \emptyset$ and $\mathsf{mn}((a, M) \cdot \overrightarrow{p}) \triangleq \mathsf{fn}(M) \cup \mathsf{mn}(\overrightarrow{p})$.

We assume an operator $\xi \blacksquare \overrightarrow{p}$ which checks that there are as many messages in $\overrightarrow{p}$ as names in the pattern ξ and computes the possible matchings as substitutions. For example, $a(X) \mid a(Y) \blacksquare (a, P), (a, Q)$ generates $X \mapsto P, Y \mapsto Q$ and $X \mapsto Q, Y \mapsto P$. We let θ range over these substitutions, and write $\theta \in \xi \blacksquare \overrightarrow{p}$ when θ is a possible matching between ξ and $\overrightarrow{p}$, the latter considered as a multiset. Formally, we write $\uplus$ for the multiset union, and we define $a(X) \blacksquare (a, M) \triangleq \{x \mapsto M\}$ and $(\xi_1 \mid \xi_2) \blacksquare \overrightarrow{p} \triangleq \{\theta_1 \uplus \theta_2 \mid \theta_1 \in \xi_1 \blacksquare \overrightarrow{p_1}, \theta_2 \in \xi_2 \blacksquare \overrightarrow{p_2}, \overrightarrow{p} = \overrightarrow{p_1} \uplus \overrightarrow{p_2}\}$.[1]

We define a labeled semantics for HOπJ in Fig. 3. Pure input transitions $P \xrightarrow{\overrightarrow{p}}_{\mathsf{i}} R$ describe a process P inputting the messages $\overrightarrow{p}$ to yield R. Pure output transitions $S \xrightarrow{\nu \overrightarrow{b}.\overrightarrow{p}}_{\mathsf{o}} K$ describe a process S emitting the messages $\overrightarrow{p}$ with extruded names $\overrightarrow{b}$ to yield K. Mixed input/output transitions $P \xrightarrow{\overrightarrow{p}}_{\mathsf{io}} P'$ describe a process P that emits some messages which, combined with messages $\overrightarrow{p}$, trigger an input and result in P'. Finally, silent transitions $P \xrightarrow{\tau} P'$ describe a process that does an internal communication: we define them as a notation, standing for $P \xrightarrow{()}_{\mathsf{io}} P'$, an input/output transition with no message received.

A derivation tree of a transition is best described following a path from the root of the source process to the receiver. Upon encountering a name restriction in input/output mode (rule IONU), we check that it does not prevent communication. For a parallel composition, there are two cases: either one of the process is not involved in the communication (rule IOPAR), or it is. In that case, one process must only contain outputs, while the other either contains both an input and outputs (rule IOBOTHIO), or only an input (rule IOBOTHIN). In both cases,

---

[1] As bound variables in a join pattern are distinct, θ_1 and θ_2 have disjoint domains.

$$\text{OUTOUT}\qquad\qquad \overline{a}\langle M\rangle K \xrightarrow{(a,M)}_\circ K$$

$$\text{OUTEXTR}\qquad \frac{P \xrightarrow{\nu\vec{b}.\vec{p}}_\circ K \qquad c\notin \mathsf{cn}(\vec{p}) \qquad c\in \mathsf{mn}(\vec{p})}{\nu c.P \xrightarrow{\nu c.\vec{b}.\vec{p}}_\circ K}$$

$$\text{OUTNU}\qquad \frac{P \xrightarrow{\nu\vec{b}.\vec{p}}_\circ K \qquad c\notin \mathsf{cn}(\vec{p}) \qquad c\notin \mathsf{mn}(\vec{p})}{\nu c.P \xrightarrow{\nu\vec{b}.\vec{p}}_\circ \nu c.K}$$

$$\text{OUTPAR}\qquad \frac{P \xrightarrow{\nu\vec{b}.\vec{p}}_\circ K}{P\| Q \xrightarrow{\nu\vec{b}.\vec{p}}_\circ K\| Q}\ (s)$$

$$\text{OUTBOTH}\qquad \frac{P \xrightarrow{\nu\vec{b}.\vec{p}}_\circ K \qquad Q \xrightarrow{\nu\vec{c}.\vec{q}}_\circ K'}{P\| Q \xrightarrow{\nu\vec{b}.\vec{c}.\vec{p}.\vec{q}}_\circ K\| K'}$$

$$\text{COM}\qquad \frac{\theta\in \xi\bullet\vec{p}}{\xi\triangleright R \xrightarrow{\vec{p}}_i R\theta}$$

$$\text{INNU}\qquad \frac{P \xrightarrow{\vec{p}}_i R \qquad c\notin \mathsf{cn}(\vec{p})}{\nu c.P \xrightarrow{\vec{p}}_i \nu c.R}$$

$$\text{INPAR}\qquad \frac{P \xrightarrow{\vec{p}}_i R}{P\| Q \xrightarrow{\vec{p}}_i R\| Q}\ (s)$$

$$\text{IONU}\qquad \frac{P \xrightarrow{\vec{p}}_{io} P' \qquad c\notin \mathsf{cn}(\vec{p})}{\nu c.P \xrightarrow{\vec{p}}_{io} \nu c.P'}$$

$$\text{IOPAR}\qquad \frac{P \xrightarrow{\vec{p}}_{io} P'}{P\| Q \xrightarrow{\vec{p}}_{io} P'\| Q}\ (s)$$

$$\text{IOBOTHIN}\qquad \frac{P \xrightarrow{\nu\vec{b}.\vec{p}}_\circ K \qquad Q \xrightarrow{\vec{p}.\vec{q}}_i Q'}{P\| Q \xrightarrow{\vec{q}}_{io} \nu\vec{b}.K\| Q'}\ (s)$$

$$\text{IOBOTHIO}\qquad \frac{P \xrightarrow{\nu\vec{b}.\vec{p}}_\circ K \qquad Q \xrightarrow{\vec{p}.\vec{q}}_{io} Q'}{P\| Q \xrightarrow{\vec{q}}_{io} \nu\vec{b}.K\| Q'}\ (s)$$

Fig. 3. Lazy Semantics for $\text{HO}\pi\text{J}$

the messages and extruded names are collected in the output-only premise, and these messages $\vec{p}$ are added to the ones $\vec{q}$ received up to this point in the other premise. The name restrictions are restored at this point, as it is the parallel composition closest to both the newly collected messages and the input.

On the output-only side, messages are collected by rule OUTOUT; name restrictions are either added to the label for extrusion with rule OUTEXTR, or left in place in rule OUTNU; parallel composition either explores both processes, merging their results (rule OUTBOTH), or only one of them (rule OUTPAR). Note that output rules always collect at least one message.

On the input-only side, name restrictions are left in place (rule INNU), parallel processes only result in the exploration of one of them as there is a single input (rule INPAR), and the actual communication occurs in rule COM, where the collected messages are matched against the input pattern. Input/output rules and input-only rules are very similar and could be merged. We keep them separate as it simplifies the proof that the zipper and lazy semantics coincide.

3.2   Leaf-First Zipper Semantics

Informal description. The $\text{HO}\pi\text{J}$ zipper semantics collects all the messages by alternating between the out and par modes, before looking for the input. During the search, we record the positions where the extruded names should be restricted using contexts stored in a *global stack*. We also use a *local stack* to record checkpoints when collecting several messages in a row. We illustrate how the search proceeds using the process in Fig. 4, where we represent only the communicating outputs and input, and number the parallel compositions between them. The dotted lines show the exploration of the term within the out mode in red and the par mode in blue.

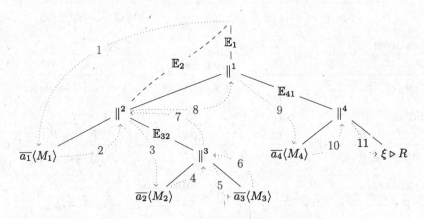

Fig. 4. Example of Process Exploration

We start by looking for an output, say M_1 (step 1), and then switch to the par mode to look for $\|^2$, computing K_1 and extruded names $\overrightarrow{b_1}$ while doing so (step 2). We create a checkpoint $(\overrightarrow{b_1}, M_1, \mathbb{E}_2, K_1)$ on the local stack, where $\mathbb{E}_2$ represents the position of $\|^2$, and then look for the next message M_2. After finding it (step 3), we go back to $\|^3$ (step 4), computing K_2 and $\overrightarrow{b_2}$. We create a checkpoint $(\overrightarrow{b_2}, M_2, \mathbb{E}_{32}, K_2)$ on the local stack, where $\mathbb{E}_{32}$ represents the position of $\|^3$ relative to $\|^2$, before searching for M_3 (step 5). We then go back to $\|^3$, computing K_3 and $\overrightarrow{b_3}$ (step 6).

To continue exploring, we pop the local stack to get back $\mathbb{E}_{32}$. We also combine the continuations $K_{23} = K_2 \| K_3$ and the names $\overrightarrow{b_{23}} = \overrightarrow{b_2} \cdot \overrightarrow{b_3}$. We go through $\mathbb{E}_{32}$ (step 7) to get back to $\|^2$. We pop the local stack again to get $\mathbb{E}_2$ and create $K_{123} = K_1 \| K_{23}$ and $\overrightarrow{b_{123}} = \overrightarrow{b_1} \cdot \overrightarrow{b_{23}}$. The search goes through $\mathbb{E}_2$ to find $\|^1$ (step 8). Because $\|^1$ separates M_1, M_2, and M_3 from the input, it is where $\overrightarrow{b_{123}}$ should be restricted: we create a checkpoint $(\overrightarrow{b_{123}}, (M_1, M_2, M_3), \mathbb{E}_1, K_{123})$ on the global stack, where $\mathbb{E}_1$ records the position of $\|^1$.

We search for M_4 (step 9), then go back to $\|^4$, building K_4 and $\overrightarrow{b_4}$ (step 10). Because $\|^4$ is where we restrict $\overrightarrow{b_4}$, we add a checkpoint $(\overrightarrow{b_4}, M_4, \mathbb{E}_{41}, K_4)$ on the global stack, where $\mathbb{E}_{41}$ records the position of $\|^4$ relative to $\|^1$. We then look for the input R and compute the result $\mathbb{E}_1 \left[\nu \overrightarrow{b_{123}}.K_{123} \|^1 \mathbb{E}_{41} \left[\nu \overrightarrow{b_4}.K_4 \|^4 R' \right] \right]$ for some R' by repeatedly popping the global stack (step 11).

This derivation collects the messages in the order M_1, M_2, M_3, M_4. It is possible to collect them in the order M_1, M_3, M_2, M_4, or M_2, M_3, M_1, M_4, or M_3, M_2, M_1, M_4. However, the design of the zipper rules forbids the remaining orders. Roughly, when considering the topmost parallel composition (here $\|^1$), the search starts on the other side of the input, so starting with M_4 is not possible. Besides, we go from one message to the nearest one, so starting from M_2, it is not possible to go to M_1 and then back to M_3.

$$\textsf{init}\;\frac{P \xrightarrow{\bullet,\epsilon,\epsilon}_{\mathsf{out}} P'}{P \to_{\mathsf{zs}} P'} \qquad \textsf{outParL}\;\frac{P_1 \xrightarrow{\| P_2 :: \mathbb{E},\pi,\rho}_{\mathsf{out}} P'}{P_1 \| P_2 \xrightarrow{\mathbb{E},\pi,\rho}_{\mathsf{out}} P'}\,(s) \qquad \textsf{outNu}\;\frac{P \xrightarrow{\nu a :: \mathbb{E},\pi,\rho}_{\mathsf{out}} P'}{\nu a.P \xrightarrow{\mathbb{E},\pi,\rho}_{\mathsf{out}} P'} \qquad \textsf{outOut}\;\frac{\mathbb{E} \xrightarrow{K,(),(a,M),\pi,\rho}_{\mathsf{par}} P'}{\overline{a}\langle M\rangle K \xrightarrow{\mathbb{E},\pi,\rho}_{\mathsf{out}} P'}$$

$$\textsf{parL}\;\frac{\mathbb{E} \xrightarrow{K_1 \| K_2,\widehat{a},\widetilde{p},\pi,\rho}_{\mathsf{par}} P'}{\| K_2 :: \mathbb{E} \xrightarrow{K_1,\widehat{a},\widetilde{p},\pi,\rho}_{\mathsf{par}} P'} \qquad \textsf{parNu}\;\frac{\mathbb{E} \xrightarrow{\nu a.K,\widehat{b},\widetilde{p},\pi,\rho}_{\mathsf{par}} P' \quad a \notin \mathsf{cn}(|\widetilde{p}|) \quad a \notin \mathsf{mn}(|\widetilde{p}|)}{\nu a :: \mathbb{E} \xrightarrow{K,\widehat{b},\widetilde{p},\pi,\rho}_{\mathsf{par}} P'}$$

$$\textsf{parExtr}\;\frac{\mathbb{E} \xrightarrow{K,a\cdot\widehat{b},\widetilde{p},\pi,\rho}_{\mathsf{par}} P' \quad a \notin \mathsf{cn}(|\widetilde{p}|) \quad a \in \mathsf{mn}(|\widetilde{p}|)}{\nu a :: \mathbb{E} \xrightarrow{K,\widehat{b},\widetilde{p},\pi,\rho}_{\mathsf{par}} P'} \qquad \textsf{parHoleL}\;\frac{\mathbb{E} \xrightarrow{K_1 \| K_2,\widehat{a_1} \| \widehat{a_2},\widetilde{p_1} \| \widetilde{p_2},\pi,\rho}_{\mathsf{par}} P'}{\bullet \xrightarrow{K_2,\widehat{a_2},\widetilde{p_2},(\widehat{a_1},\widetilde{p_1},\mathbb{E},K_1 \|) :: \pi,\rho}_{\mathsf{par}} P'}\,(s)$$

$$\textsf{parOutR}\;\frac{P \xrightarrow{\bullet,(\widehat{a},\widetilde{p},\mathbb{E},K \|) :: \pi,\rho}_{\mathsf{out}} P'}{\| P :: \mathbb{E} \xrightarrow{K,\widehat{a},\widetilde{p},\pi,\rho}_{\mathsf{par}} P'}\,(s) \qquad \textsf{parOutR}\rho\;\frac{P \xrightarrow{\bullet,\epsilon,(\widehat{a},\widetilde{p},\mathbb{E},K \|) :: \rho}_{\mathsf{out}} P'}{\| P :: \mathbb{E} \xrightarrow{K,\widehat{a},\widetilde{p},\epsilon,\rho}_{\mathsf{par}} P'}\,(s) \qquad \textsf{parInR}\;\frac{R \xrightarrow{\bullet,(\widehat{a},\widetilde{p},\mathbb{E},K \|) :: \rho}_{\mathsf{in}} P'}{\| R :: \mathbb{E} \xrightarrow{K,\widehat{a},\widetilde{p},\epsilon,\rho}_{\mathsf{par}} P'}\,(s)$$

$$\textsf{inParL}\;\frac{P_1 \xrightarrow{\| P_2 :: \mathbb{E},\rho}_{\mathsf{in}} P'}{P_1 \| P_2 \xrightarrow{\mathbb{E},\rho}_{\mathsf{in}} P'}\,(s) \qquad \textsf{inNu}\;\frac{P \xrightarrow{\nu a :: \mathbb{E},\rho}_{\mathsf{in}} P' \quad a \notin \mathsf{cn}(\mathsf{p}(\rho))}{\nu a.P \xrightarrow{\mathbb{E},\rho}_{\mathsf{in}} P'} \qquad \textsf{inCom}\;\frac{\theta \in \xi \blacksquare \mathsf{p}(\rho)}{\xi \triangleright R \xrightarrow{\mathbb{E},\rho}_{\mathsf{in}} \rho[\![\mathbb{E}[\![R\theta]\!]]\!]}$$

Fig. 5. Zipper semantics for HOπJ

Formal definitions. The zipper semantics of HOπJ is defined in Fig. 5. To make it reversible, we need more complex data structures than just sequences to collect extruded names and messages; we explain why in Sect. 3.3. We define a structure of names $\widehat{a}$ and of pairs $\widetilde{p}$ as follows:

$$\widehat{a}, \widehat{b} ::= () \mid a \cdot \widehat{b} \mid \widehat{a} \| \widehat{b} \qquad \widetilde{p}, \widetilde{q} ::= (a, P) \mid \widetilde{p} \| \widetilde{q}$$

We abbreviate a structure $a_1 \cdot \ldots a_n \cdot ()$ as $(a_1, \ldots, a_n)$ or $\overrightarrow{a}$. These structures reflect the process from which they are generated. For example, the structures corresponding to $\nu a.(\overline{a_1}\langle P_1\rangle \; \| \; \nu b.\nu c.\overline{a_2}\langle P_2\rangle)$ are $a \cdot (() \| (b, c))$ and $(a_1, P_1) \;\|$

(a_2, P_2). We define a flattening $|\cdot|$ from structures back to sequences as follows:

$$|()| \triangleq () \qquad\qquad |\widehat{a} \parallel \widehat{b}| \triangleq |\widehat{a}| \cdot |\widehat{b}| \qquad\qquad |a \cdot \widehat{b}| \triangleq a \cdot |\widehat{b}|$$

$$|(a, P)| \triangleq (a, P) \qquad\qquad |\widetilde{a} \parallel \widetilde{b}| \triangleq |\widetilde{a}| \cdot |\widetilde{b}|$$

The syntax of stacks is $\gamma ::= \epsilon \mid (\widehat{a}, \widetilde{p}, \mathbb{E}, \mathfrak{F}) :: \gamma$ where $\mathfrak{F}$ is either $\parallel K$ or $K \parallel$ for some K. We let ρ range over global stacks and π over local ones. We extend plugging to global stacks, and define $\mathsf{p}(\rho)$ as the pairs occurring in ρ.

$$\epsilon[\![P]\!] \triangleq P \qquad\qquad ((\widehat{a}, \widetilde{p}, \mathbb{E}, \mathfrak{F}) :: \rho)[\![P]\!] \triangleq \rho[\![\mathbb{E}[\![\nu|\widehat{a}|.\mathfrak{F}[\![P]\!]]\!]]\!]$$

$$\mathsf{p}(\epsilon) \triangleq () \qquad\qquad \mathsf{p}((\widehat{a}, \widetilde{p}, \mathbb{E}, \mathfrak{F}) :: \rho) \triangleq |\widetilde{p}| \cdot \mathsf{p}(\rho)$$

The rules for the output $P \xrightarrow{\mathbb{E},\pi,\rho}_{\mathsf{out}} P'$ and input modes $R \xrightarrow{G,\rho}_{\mathsf{in}} P'$ are roughly the same as in HOπP. The stacks π, ρ are passed along without being modified; ρ is used in the axiom inCom to compute the final result. The transition $\mathbb{E} \xrightarrow{K,\widehat{a},\widetilde{p},\pi,\rho}_{\mathsf{par}} P'$ is looking for the nearest parallel composition which separates the last found output to the rest of the redex, building K and $\widehat{a}$. The rules, parNu, and parExtr are the same as in HOπP, only adapted to the multiple messages $\widetilde{p}$.

When the context is $\parallel P :: \mathbb{E}$, i.e., the term is $\mathbb{E}[\![K \parallel P]\!]$, we have several possibilities. If P is not part of the communication, it is added to the continuation (rule parL). If P contains at least one output but not the input, we apply the rule parOutR to look for the next output in P and create a checkpoint on the local stack. That checkpoint popped when we apply parHoleL: after finding all the messages in P, we restore $\mathbb{E}$ to continue the search in that context.

The next possibility is that P contains at least one output and the input: we apply parOutRρ to look for the next output in P and create a checkpoint on the global stack to remember that $\mathbb{E}$ is where the names $\widehat{a}$ should be restricted. The rule parOutRρ applies only when the local stack is empty, meaning that we are done collecting messages on that side of the parallel composition. The final case is when P contains only the input: we switch to the in mode and creates the last checkpoint on the global stack. As in the previous case, the local stack must be empty. We illustrate these rules on the example of Fig. 4.

Back to the example. We start with empty local and global stacks. After reaching $\overline{a_1}\langle M_1 \rangle$, we go back to $\parallel^2$ to search for the next messages: at that point, the derivation looks like the rule on the left below. The process P_{23} contains $\overline{a_2}\langle M_2 \rangle$ and $\overline{a_3}\langle M_3 \rangle$: we use similar naming convention for processes henceforth. Let $\pi_1 \triangleq (\widehat{b_1}, (a_1, M_1), \mathbb{E}_2, K_1 \parallel^2) :: \epsilon$. We look for M_2 and then go back to $\parallel^3$, where we apply parOutR again to search for M_3 (right rule).

parOutR
$$\cfrac{P_{23} \xrightarrow{\bullet,(\widehat{b_1},(a_1,M_1),\mathbb{E}_2,K_1\parallel^2)::\epsilon,\epsilon}_{\mathsf{out}} P'}{\parallel^2 P_{23} :: \mathbb{E}_2 \xrightarrow{K_1,\widehat{b_1},(a_1,M_1),\epsilon,\epsilon}_{\mathsf{par}} P'}$$

parOutR
$$\cfrac{P_3 \xrightarrow{\bullet,(\widehat{b_2},(a_2,M_2),\mathbb{E}_{32},K_2\parallel^3)::\pi_1,\epsilon}_{\mathsf{out}} P'}{\parallel^3 P_3 :: \mathbb{E}_{32} \xrightarrow{K_2,\widehat{b_2},(a_2,M_2),\pi_1,\epsilon}_{\mathsf{par}} P'}$$

After finding M_3, we go back to $\|^3$ again and pop the local stack to restore $\mathbb{E}_{32}$ and continue the exploration of the term.

$$\frac{\text{parHoleL}}{\mathbb{E}_{32} \xrightarrow{\quad K_2\|^3 K_3,\widehat{b_2}\|\widehat{b_3},(a_2,M_2)\|(a_3,M_3),\pi_1,\epsilon \quad}_{\text{par}} P'}{\bullet \xrightarrow{\quad K_3,\widehat{b_3},(a_3,M_3),(\widehat{b_2},(a_2,M_2),\mathbb{E}_{32},K_2\|^3) \,::\, \pi_1,\epsilon \quad}_{\text{par}} P'}$$

We go through $\mathbb{E}_{32}$ to reach $\|^2$, and apply parHoleL again to restore $\mathbb{E}_2$.

$$\frac{\text{parHoleL}}{\mathbb{E}_2 \xrightarrow{\quad K_1\|^2 K_{23},\widehat{b_1}\|\widehat{b_{23}},(a_1,M_1)\|\widetilde{p_{23}},\epsilon,\epsilon \quad}_{\text{par}} P'}{\bullet \xrightarrow{\quad K_{23},\widehat{b_{23}},\widetilde{p_{23}},(\widehat{b_1},(a_1,M_1),\mathbb{E}_2,K_1\|^2) \,::\, \epsilon,\epsilon \quad}_{\text{par}} P'}$$

The next step is when we get to $\|^1$, where we create a checkpoint on the global stack (left rule below). Let $\rho_1 \triangleq (\widehat{b_{123}}, \widetilde{p_{123}}, \mathbb{E}_1, K_{123} \|^1) :: \epsilon$. We then look for M_4, and go back to $\|^4$, where we create the final checkpoint (right rule).

$$\frac{\text{parOutR}\rho}{P_{4R} \xrightarrow{\quad \bullet,\epsilon,(\widehat{b_{123}},\widetilde{p_{123}},\mathbb{E}_1,K_{123}\|^1) \,::\, \epsilon \quad}_{\text{out}} P'}{\|^1 P_{4R} :: \mathbb{E}_1 \xrightarrow{\quad K_{123},\widehat{b_{123}},\widetilde{p_{123}},\epsilon,\epsilon \quad}_{\text{par}} P'} \qquad \frac{\text{parInR}}{P_R \xrightarrow{\quad \bullet,(\widehat{b_4},(a_4,M_4),\mathbb{E}_{41},K_4\|^4) \,::\, \rho_1 \quad}_{\text{in}} P'}{\|^4 P_R :: \mathbb{E}_{41} \xrightarrow{\quad K_4,\widehat{b_4},(a_4,M_4),\epsilon,\rho_1 \quad}_{\text{par}} P'}$$

Let $\rho_2 \triangleq (\widehat{b_4}, (a_4, M_4), \mathbb{E}_{41}, K_4 \|^4) :: \rho_1$. Once we find the input, we can compute the final result $P' = \rho_2[\![R']\!]$ for some R', and one can check that $\rho_2[\![R']\!] = \mathbb{E}_1 \left[\!\left[\nu\vec{b_{123}}.K_{123} \|^1 \mathbb{E}_{41} \left[\!\left[\nu\vec{b_4}.K_4 \|^4 R' \right]\!\right] \right]\!\right]$, as wished.

3.3   Properties of the Zipper Semantics

Correspondence results. The correspondence proofs between the zipper and lazy semantics follow the same strategy as in $\text{HO}\pi\text{P}$: using the information stored in the label, we reconstruct the source and target terms of a zipper transition. For example, for each checkpoint $(\widehat{a}, \widetilde{p}, \mathbb{E}, K \|) :: \gamma$ of a local or global stack and for any $S \xrightarrow{\nu|\widehat{a}|.|\widetilde{p}|}_{\circ} K$, we know that the source process at this point is of the form $\mathbb{E}[\![S \| R]\!]$ and the target process is $\mathbb{E}[\![\nu|\widehat{a}|.K \| R']\!]$, where R and R' are computed recursively from γ.

Theorem 3. *If* $P \to_{zs} P'$, *then* $P \xrightarrow{\tau} P'$.

For the reverse implication, for any transition $P \xrightarrow{\tau} P'$, we can decompose P and P' with a global stack ρ and sending processes. We then reconstruct the zipper derivation starting with the input mode, then alternating between the par and out modes for each output, reasoning by induction on the size of ρ.

Theorem 4. *If $P \xrightarrow{\tau} P'$, then $P \to_{zs} P'$.*

Derivation into an NDAM. The rules of the zipper semantics have been designed to be machine constructive and reversible. In particular, using complex data structures for extruded names and messages ensures that the rules parHoleL and parHoleR are reversible: a structure $\widehat{a_1} \parallel \widehat{a_2}$ uniquely decomposes into $\widehat{a_1}$ and $\widehat{a_2}$, while a sequence $\overrightarrow{a}$ can be split in two in many ways.

For termination, we consider a lexicographic ordering with three sizes on transitions. The first one is the number of pairs p in the label of the transitions, including the stacks. It is constant on all rules except outOut, where it is strictly increasing between the conclusion and the premise, but bounded by the total number of outputs in the process. The second one is constantly equal to 0 for the out and in modes, and equal to the sum of the sizes of all contexts occurring in the transition (including in stacks) in par mode, where the size of a context is its number of frames plus one. It is designed to be strictly decreasing between the conclusion and the premise on all the rules defining the par mode. In particular for parHoleL and parHoleR, the size of the conclusion is equal to the size of the premise plus one. The last ordering is the subterm ordering for terms at the source of the transition, already used in HOπP. It is strictly decreasing on the rules of the out and in modes, except outOut which has already been covered. As a result we can derive a sound, complete, and terminating NDAM for HOπJ.

4   Related Work and Conclusion

Related work. Sect. 2.2 discusses the root-first zipper semantics [2] for HOπ with eager scope extrusion. As far as we know, its derived NDAM is the only machine proposed for a variant of HOπ. We discuss next the other machines for higher-order calculi and for calculi with join patterns that we are aware of.

The notion of join patterns comes from the join calculus [11], whose initial semantics takes the form of a *chemical abstract machine*, where messages can be seen as as molecules free to move around in a solution until all the messages required to trigger a join-pattern are present. The machines for the languages with passivation Kell [1] and M [13] (which also features join patterns) also rely on this chemical design, typically implemented as message queues. A major drawback of this approach is that it ignores the syntactic structure of processes, making proofs on such structure quite complex. Our approach, on the other hand, preserves the syntactic structure as much as possible, which allows us to prove an operational correspondence between the lazy and zipper semantics (and therefore the NDAM), and not only an observation-based equivalence [1]. This comes with a cost: as the syntactic structure of the term is preserved, the extruded names may enclose unrelated processes even with lazy scope extrusion. Structural congruence would be able to move these unrelated terms around, at the cost of the operational correspondence proof.

A strength and limitation of the join calculus is that it uses the same construct for restriction, reception, and replication. More precisely, definitions

$\xi_1 \triangleright R_1 \wedge \ldots \wedge \xi_n \triangleright R_n$ are replicated inputs which restrict the names $\bigcup_i \mathsf{cn}(\xi_i)$. As a result, the receivers for a given name are fixed. This reduces the expressive power of the calculus [20], but it allows for efficient implementations as long as join patterns are linear [10]. $\mathrm{HO}\pi\mathrm{J}$ is more permissive, as name restriction and input are separate constructs, and although our approach is not as efficient as the join calculus, our use of zipper semantics lets us derive an abstract machine [3].

Conclusion. Zipper semantics decomposes a term into an evaluation context and a redex. Biernacka et al. [2,3] define zipper semantics where the search for the redex starts by the operator at its root; instead, we look for an operator at its leaves. This style is well-suited to express the semantics of calculi with lazy scope extrusion, as knowing the message first lets us limit scope extrusion to the sent names. In particular, we are able to express the semantics of a calculus with join patterns, where the scope of extruded names is not the same for all the messages. As a result, we get for free a sound and complete abstract machine for this language. It shows the expressiveness of leaf-first zipper semantics.

Leaf-first zipper semantics is well-suited when the result of reduction depends on information at the leaves of the redex, like message output w.r.t. scope extrusion. Other examples are distributed calculi which restrict communication through locality boundaries [4–6,15,26]. In such cases, we need to know the message contents to determine whether it can be sent outside of a locality, so a leaf-first semantics should be more appropriate.

References

1. Bidinger, P., Schmitt, A., Stefani, J.-B.: An abstract machine for the kell calculus. In: Steffen, M., Zavattaro, G. (eds.) FMOODS 2005. LNCS, vol. 3535, pp. 31–46. Springer, Heidelberg (2005). https://doi.org/10.1007/11494881_3
2. Biernacka, M., Biernacki, D., Lenglet, S., Schmitt, A.: Non-deterministic abstract machines. Tech. Rep. 9475, Inria (2022), available at https://hal.inria.fr/hal-03545768
3. Biernacka, M., Biernacki, D., Lenglet, S., Schmitt, A.: Non-deterministic abstract machines. In: Klin, B., Lasota, S., Muscholl, A. (eds.) 33rd International Conference on Concurrency Theory, CONCUR 2022, September 12-16, 2022, Warsaw, Poland. LIPIcs, vol. 243, pp. 7:1–7:24. Schloss Dagstuhl - Leibniz-Zentrum für Informatik (2022)
4. Bugliesi, M., Crafa, S., Merro, M., Sassone, V.: Communication and mobility control in boxed ambients. Inf. Comput. **202**(1), 39–86 (2005)
5. Cardelli, L., Gordon, A.D.: Mobile ambients. In: Nivat, M. (ed.) FoSSaCS 1998. LNCS, vol. 1378, pp. 140–155. Springer, Heidelberg (1998). https://doi.org/10.1007/BFb0053547
6. Castagna, G., Vitek, J., Nardelli, F.Z.: The seal calculus. Inf. Comput. **201**(1), 1–54 (2005)
7. Danvy, O.: From reduction-based to reduction-free normalization. In: Koopman, P., Plasmeijer, R., Swierstra, D. (eds.) AFP 2008. LNCS, vol. 5832, pp. 66–164. Springer, Heidelberg (2009). https://doi.org/10.1007/978-3-642-04652-0_3
8. Felleisen, M., Hieb, R.: The revised report on the syntactic theories of sequential control and state. Theor. Comput. Sci. **103**(2), 235–271 (1992)

9. Fessant, F.L.: JoCaml: conception et implémentation d'un langage à agents mobiles. Ph.D. thesis, École polytechnique (2001)
10. Fessant, F.L., Maranget, L.: Compiling join-patterns. In: Nestmann, U., Pierce, B.C. (eds.) 3rd International Workshop on High-Level Concurrent Languages, HLCL 1998, Satellite Workshop of CONCUR 1998, Nice, France, September 12, 1998, pp. 205–224. No. 16(3) in Electronic Notes in Theoretical Computer Science, Elsevier (1998). https://doi.org/10.1016/S1571-0661(04)00143-4, https://www.sciencedirect.com/journal/electronic-notes-in-theoretical-computer-science/vol/16/issue/3
11. Fournet, C., Gonthier, G.: The reflexive CHAM and the join-calculus. In: Boehm, H., Jr., G.L.S. (eds.) Conference Record of POPL'96: The 23rd ACM SIGPLAN-SIGACT Symposium on Principles of Programming Languages, Papers Presented at the Symposium, St. Petersburg Beach, Florida, USA, January 21-24, 1996, pp. 372–385. ACM Press (1996)
12. Gardner, P., Laneve, C., Wischik, L.: The fusion machine. In: Brim, L., Křetínský, M., Kučera, A., Jančar, P. (eds.) CONCUR 2002. LNCS, vol. 2421, pp. 418–433. Springer, Heidelberg (2002). https://doi.org/10.1007/3-540-45694-5_28
13. Germain, F., Lacoste, M., Stefani, J.: An abstract machine for a higher-order distributed process calculus. Electron. Notes Theor. Comput. Sci. **66**(3), 145–169 (2002)
14. Giannini, P., Sangiorgi, D., Valente, A.: Safe ambients: abstract machine and distributed implementation. Sci. Comput. Program. **59**(3), 209–249 (2006)
15. Godskesen, J.C., Hildebrandt, T., Sassone, V.: A calculus of mobile resources*. In: Brim, L., Křetínský, M., Kučera, A., Jančar, P. (eds.) CONCUR 2002. LNCS, vol. 2421, pp. 272–287. Springer, Heidelberg (2002). https://doi.org/10.1007/3-540-45694-5_19
16. Hirschkoff, D., Pous, D., Sangiorgi, D.: An efficient abstract machine for safe ambients. J. Log. Algebraic Methods Program. **71**(2), 114–149 (2007)
17. Lenglet, S., Schmitt, A.: Leaf-first zipper semantics (2024), available at https://inria.hal.science/hal-04537440
18. Lenglet, S., Schmitt, A., Stefani, J.: Characterizing contextual equivalence in calculi with passivation. Inf. Comput. **209**(11), 1390–1433 (2011)
19. Lopes, L., Silva, F., Vasconcelos, V.T.: A virtual machine for a process calculus. In: Nadathur, G. (ed.) PPDP 1999. LNCS, vol. 1702, pp. 244–260. Springer, Heidelberg (1999). https://doi.org/10.1007/10704567_15
20. Nestmann, U.: On the expressive power of joint input. In: Castellani, I., Palamidessi, C. (eds.) Fifth International Workshop on Expressiveness in Concurrency, EXPRESS 1998, Satellite Workshop of CONCUR 1998, Nice, France, September 7, 1998, pp. 145–152. No. 16(2) in Electronic Notes in Theoretical Computer Science, Elsevier (1998). https://doi.org/10.1016/S1571-0661(04)00123-9, https://doi.org/10.1016/S1571-0661(04)00123-9
21. Phillips, A., Cardelli, L.: A correct abstract machine for the stochastic pi-calculus. In: Concurrent Models in Molecular Biology (2004)
22. Phillips, A., Yoshida, N., Eisenbach, S.: A distributed abstract machine for boxed ambient calculi. In: Schmidt, D. (ed.) ESOP 2004. LNCS, vol. 2986, pp. 155–170. Springer, Heidelberg (2004). https://doi.org/10.1007/978-3-540-24725-8_12
23. Plotkin, G.D.: A structural approach to operational semantics. Tech. Rep. FN-19, DAIMI, Department of Computer Science, Aarhus University, Aarhus, Denmark (1981)

24. Sangiorgi, D.: Bisimulation in higher-order process calculi. In: Olderog, E. (ed.) Programming Concepts, Methods and Calculi, Proceedings of the IFIP TC2/WG2.1/WG2.2/WG2.3 Working Conference on Programming Concepts, Methods and Calculi (PROCOMET '94) San Miniato, Italy, 6-10 June, 1994. IFIP Transactions, vol. A-56, pp. 207–224. North-Holland (1994)
25. Sangiorgi, D., Walker, D.: The Pi-Calculus - a theory of mobile processes. Cambridge University Press (2001)
26. Schmitt, A., Stefani, J.-B.: The kell calculus: a family of higher-order distributed process calculi. In: Priami, C., Quaglia, P. (eds.) GC 2004. LNCS, vol. 3267, pp. 146–178. Springer, Heidelberg (2005). https://doi.org/10.1007/978-3-540-31794-4_9
27. Turner, D.: The polymorphic pi-calculus:theory and implementation. Ph.D. Thesis, University of Edinburgh (1995)

Synthesizing Timed Automata with Minimal Numbers of Clocks from Optimised Timed Scenarios

Neda Saeedloei[1]([⊠]) and Feliks Kluźniak[2]

[1] Towson University, Towson, USA
nsaeedloei@towson.edu
[2] RelationalAI, Berkeley, USA

Abstract. We address the problem of synthesizing a timed automaton from a set of optimised timed scenarios, and present a simple, efficient algorithm that solves the problem. Under a simplifying assumption about the set of scenarios we show that our synthesized automaton has the minimal number of clocks in the entire class of language-equivalent automata.

1 Introduction

Using scenarios for specifying complex systems (including real time systems and distributed systems [1,2]), and synthesizing formal models of systems from scenarios have been active areas of research for several decades [3–10].

In our earlier work [11] we developed, from first principles, a formal, yet simple notation for timed scenarios. Intuitively, a scenario is a sequence of events along with a set of constraints between the times of these events, which can be used to specify the partial behaviours of a system or a component of a system (see Sec. 2.2 for more details).

We want to use such scenarios to automatically synthesize formal models in the form of timed automata. Verification of a timed automaton can be computationally expensive, and the cost depends on the number of clock regions of the automaton. The number of clock regions is exponential in the number of clocks [12][1]. We are therefore interested in the problem of synthesizing a timed automaton with a minimal number of clocks from a set of scenarios.

Previously, we studied the problem in the more limited setting of a single timed scenario [13], and proposed an algorithm for "optimising" scenarios [13]. Given a scenario, our optimisation algorithm [13] replaces the time constraints of the scenario with an equivalent set that would require the smallest number of clocks in the entire class of equivalent scenarios, when the scenarios are viewed as timed automata. *Optimality was achieved under the assumption that a timed scenario cannot be split into two* [13].

---

[1] For a timed automaton with $|K|$ clocks, the number of clock regions is at most $R = |K|!4^{|K|}\Pi_{x \in K}(\mu_x + 1)$, where μ_x is the maximum constant with which clock x is compared [12].

© IFIP International Federation for Information Processing 2024
Published by Springer Nature Switzerland AG 2024
V. Castiglioni and A. Francalanza (Eds.): FORTE 2024, LNCS 14678, pp. 136–154, 2024.
https://doi.org/10.1007/978-3-031-62645-6_8

More recently, we developed the notions of intersection, union and subsumption for scenarios [14]. We introduced appropriate operations with well-defined semantics for computing the intersection and union of two consistent scenarios, as well as for determining whether a scenario is subsumed by another one.

The contributions of the current paper are as follows:

- We use the aforementioned developments to show that even when a scenario is split into two, the number of clocks does not decrease, thereby strengthening our previous result. The consequence of this is that, if γ is the union—the reverse of splitting—of two scenarios ξ and η, then the number of clocks in the automaton corresponding to γ is not larger than that for automata corresponding to ξ and η.
- We present an efficient algorithm that, given a set of scenarios, constructs a timed automaton such that
  - the number of locations of the automaton is reasonably small (though not necessarily minimal);
  - the number of clocks of the automaton does not exceed that needed by at least one of the constituent scenarios.

It turns out that if we make a simplifying assumption about the initial set of scenarios, our synthesized automaton has the minimal number of clocks in the entire class of language-equivalent timed automata.

We then briefly discuss the consequences of relaxing our simplifying assumption, and show that such relaxation would require an additional preprocessing stage of significant computational complexity.

2 Preliminaries

2.1 Timed Automata

A *timed automaton* [15] is a tuple $\mathcal{A} = \langle \Sigma, Q, q_0, Q_f, C, T \rangle$, where Σ is a finite alphabet, Q is the (*finite*) set of locations, $q_0 \in Q$ is the initial location, $Q_f \subseteq Q$ is the set of final locations, C is a finite set of *clock* variables (clocks for short), and $T \subseteq Q \times Q \times \Sigma \times 2^C \times 2^{\Phi(C)}$ is the set of transitions. In each transition $(q, q', e, \lambda, \phi)$, λ is the set of clocks to be reset with the transition and $\phi \subset \Phi(C)$ is a set of clock constraints over C of the form $c \sim a$ (where $\sim \in \{\leq, <, \geq, >, =\}$, $c \in C$ and a is a constant in the set of rational numbers, $\mathbb{Q}$).

A *clock valuation* ν for C is a mapping from C to $\mathbb{R}^{\geq 0}$. Clock valuation ν *satisfies* $\phi \subset \Phi(C)$ iff every clock constraint in ϕ evaluates to true after each clock c is replaced with $\nu(c)$. For $\tau \in \mathbb{R}, \nu + \tau$ denotes the clock valuation which maps every clock c to the value $\nu(c) + \tau$. For $Y \subseteq C$, $[Y \mapsto \tau]\nu$ is the valuation which assigns τ to each $c \in Y$ and agrees with ν over the rest of the clocks.

A *timed word* over an alphabet Σ is a pair (σ, τ) where $\sigma = \sigma_1 \sigma_2 ...$ is a finite [16,17] or infinite [15] word over Σ and $\tau = \tau_1 \tau_2 ...$ is a finite or infinite sequence of (time) values such that (i) $\tau_i \in \mathbb{R}^{\geq 0}$, (ii) $\tau_i \leq \tau_{i+1}$ for all $i \geq 1$, and (iii) if the word is infinite, then for every $t \in \mathbb{R}^{\geq 0}$ there is some $i \geq 1$ such that $\tau_i > t$.

A run ρ of $\mathcal{A}$ over a timed word (σ, τ) is a sequence of the form $\langle q_0, \nu_0 \rangle \xrightarrow[\tau_1]{\sigma_1} \langle q_1, \nu_1 \rangle \xrightarrow[\tau_2]{\sigma_2} \langle q_2, \nu_2 \rangle \xrightarrow[\tau_3]{\sigma_3} ...$, where for all $i \geq 0$, $q_i \in Q$ and ν_i is a clock valuation such that (i) $\nu_0(c) = 0$ for all clocks $c \in C$ and (ii) for every $i > 1$ there is a transition in T of the form $(q_{i-1}, q_i, \sigma_i, \lambda_i, \phi_i)$, such that $(\nu_{i-1}+\tau_i-\tau_{i-1})$ satisfies ϕ_i, and ν_i equals $[\lambda_i \mapsto 0](\nu_{i-1} + \tau_i - \tau_{i-1})$. The set $inf(\rho)$ consists of $q \in Q$ such that $q = q_i$ for infinitely many $i \geq 0$ in the run ρ.

A run over a finite timed word is *accepting* if it ends in a final location [17]. A run ρ over an infinite timed word is *accepting* iff $inf(\rho) \cap Q_f \neq \emptyset$ [15]. The *language* of $\mathcal{A}$, $L(\mathcal{A})$, is the set $\{(\sigma, \tau) \mid \mathcal{A}$ has an accepting run over $(\sigma, \tau)\}$.

2.2 Timed Scenarios

This subsection briefly recounts our earlier work [11,18][2].

Let Σ be a finite set of symbols called *events*. A *behaviour*[3] over Σ is a sequence $(e_0, t_0)(e_1, t_1)(e_2, t_2)\ldots$, such that $e_i \in \Sigma$, $t_i \in \mathbb{R}^{\geq 0}$ and $t_{i-1} \leq t_i$ for $i \in \{1, 2 \ldots\}$. For a finite behaviour $\mathcal{B} = (e_0, t_0)(e_1, t_1) \ldots (e_{n-1}, t_{n-1})$ of length n, and for any $0 \leq i < j < n$, the *distance*, in time units, of event j from event i in $\mathcal{B}$ is denoted by $t_{ij}^{\mathcal{B}}$. That is, $t_{ij}^{\mathcal{B}} = t_j - t_i$.

A *timed scenario* (*scenario* for short) of length $n \in \mathbb{N}$ over Σ is a pair $(\mathcal{E}, \mathcal{C})$, where $\mathcal{E} = e_0 e_1 \ldots e_{n-1}$ is a sequence of events, and $\mathcal{C} \subset \Phi(n)$ is a finite set of constraints. Each constraint in $\Phi(n)$ is of the form $b \sim a$, where b is the symbol $\tau_{i,j}$ (for some integers $0 \leq i < j < n$), $\sim \in \{\leq, \geq\}$ [4] and a is a constant in the set of rational numbers, $\mathbb{Q}$. The interpretation is that $\tau_{i,j}$ is the time distance between the i-th and the j-th events in the behaviours described by a scenario. The constraints $\tau_{i,j} \geq 0$ and $\tau_{i,j} \leq \infty$ are called *default constraints*.

A behaviour $\mathcal{B} = (e_0, t_0)(e_1, t_1) \ldots (e_{n-1}, t_{n-1})$ over Σ is *allowed* by scenario $\xi = (\mathcal{E}, \mathcal{C})$ iff $\mathcal{E} = e_0 \ldots e_{n-1}$ and every $\tau_{i,j} \sim a$ in $\mathcal{C}$ evaluates to true after $\tau_{i,j}$ is replaced by $t_{ij}^{\mathcal{B}}$. If $\mathcal{B}$ is allowed by ξ, then we say $\mathcal{B}$ satisfies all constraints of ξ.

The *semantics* of scenario ξ, denoted by $[\![\xi]\!]$, is the set of behaviours that are allowed by ξ. A scenario ξ is *consistent* iff $[\![\xi]\!] \neq \emptyset$. It is *inconsistent* iff $[\![\xi]\!] = \emptyset$.

Figure 1 shows the "external representations"[5] of two scenarios. The one on the left corresponds to scenario $\gamma = (abc, \{\tau_{0,1} \leq 4, \tau_{0,2} \geq 6, \tau_{0,2} \leq 6, \tau_{1,2} \geq 3\})$. $[\![\gamma]\!] = \{(a, t_0)(b, t_1)(c, t_2) \mid t_0 \leq t_1 \leq t_2 \wedge t_1 - t_0 \leq 4 \wedge t_2 - t_0 = 6 \wedge t_2 - t_1 \geq 3\}$.

Two scenarios $\xi = (\mathcal{E}, \mathcal{C}_1)$ and $\eta = (\mathcal{E}, \mathcal{C}_2)$ are *equivalent* iff $[\![\xi]\!] = [\![\eta]\!]$. For example, γ and η of Fig. 1 are equivalent.

For a consistent scenario ξ of length n, and for $0 \leq i < j < n$, $m_{ij}^{\xi} = min\{t_{ij}^{\mathcal{B}} \mid \mathcal{B} \in [\![\xi]\!]\}$ and $M_{ij}^{\xi} = max\{t_{ij}^{\mathcal{B}} \mid \mathcal{B} \in [\![\xi]\!]\}$[6]. For any behaviour $\mathcal{B}$ in $[\![\xi]\!]$, $0 \leq m_{ij}^{\xi} \leq t_{ij}^{\mathcal{B}} \leq M_{ij}^{\xi} \leq \infty$. Moreover, the following inequations hold [11]:

$$m_{ij}^{\xi} + m_{jk}^{\xi} \leq m_{ik}^{\xi} \leq \left\{ \begin{matrix} m_{ij}^{\xi} + M_{jk}^{\xi} \\ M_{ij}^{\xi} + m_{jk}^{\xi} \end{matrix} \right\} \leq M_{ik}^{\xi} \leq M_{ij}^{\xi} + M_{jk}^{\xi} \tag{1}$$

---

[2] The comparison of our timed scenarios and other notions of scenarios can be found elsewhere [10,11].

[3] The notion of "behaviour" is equivalent to that of Alur's "timed word" [15]. We found the term "behaviour" more suitable and intuitive in the context of timed scenarios.

[4] To keep the presentation compact, sharp inequalities are not allowed [11]. Equality is expressed in terms of $\leq$ and $\geq$.

[5] Equality will be expressed directly using $=$ in the external representation.

[6] The absence of an upper bound for some i and j will be denoted by $M_{ij}^{\xi} = \infty$.

	0 : a ;	0 : a ;
	1 : b $\{\tau_{0,1} \leq 4\}$;	1 : b $\{\tau_{0,1} \leq 3\}$;
	2 : c $\{\tau_{0,2} = 6, \tau_{1,2} \geq 3\}$.	2 : c $\{\tau_{0,2} = 6\}$.
	γ	η

	1	2
0	(0, 4)	(6, 6)
1		(3, ∞)

	1	2
0	(0, 3)	(6, 6)
1		(3, 6)

Fig. 1. Two equivalent scenarios

Fig. 2. initial table of γ and stable table of γ and η (γ and η are equivalent)

Let $\xi = (\mathcal{E}, \mathcal{C})$ be a scenario of length n, such that, for any $0 \leq i < j < n$, $\mathcal{C}$ contains at most one constraint of the form $\tau_{i,j} \geq c$ and at most one of the form $\tau_{i,j} \leq c$. A *distance table* for ξ is a representation of $\mathcal{C}$ in the form of a triangular matrix $\mathcal{D}^{\xi}$: $\mathcal{D}^{\xi}[i,j] = (l_{ij}^{\xi}, h_{ij}^{\xi})$. If $\tau_{i,j} \geq c \in \mathcal{C}$ then $l_{ij}^{\xi} = c$, otherwise $l_{ij}^{\xi} = 0$; if $\tau_{i,j} \leq c \in \mathcal{C}$ then $h_{ij}^{\xi} = c$, otherwise $h_{ij}^{\xi} = \infty$. The distance table corresponding to γ of Fig. 1 is shown on the left of Fig. 2.

A distance table of size n for ξ is *valid* iff $l_{ij}^{\xi} \leq h_{ij}^{\xi}$, for all $0 \leq i < j < n$. A table that is not valid is *invalid*. If $\mathcal{D}^{\xi}$ is invalid, then ξ is obviously inconsistent.

A valid distance table of size n for ξ is *stable* iff, for all $0 \leq i < j < k < n$, the inequations in (1) hold when m_{ij}^{ξ}, m_{jk}^{ξ}, m_{ik}^{ξ} are replaced by l_{ij}^{ξ}, l_{jk}^{ξ}, l_{ik}^{ξ}, and M_{ij}^{ξ}, M_{jk}^{ξ}, M_{ik}^{ξ} are replaced by h_{ij}^{ξ}, h_{jk}^{ξ}, h_{ik}^{ξ}. If $\mathcal{D}^{\xi}$ is stable then ξ is consistent. A consistent scenario ξ can be stabilized by an algorithm whose cost is $O(n^3)$ (n is the length of ξ) [11]. The algorithm increases the values of minima and decreases the values of maxima until the inequations in (1) are satisfied.

A stable distance table[7] has two properties. First, the table includes all the constraints that are implied [18] by the initial set of constraints. Second, all the constraints represented by the table are as *tight* as possible. In other words, if ξ is a scenario of length n and $\mathcal{D}_s^{\xi}$ is its stable table, then for every $0 \leq i < j < n$, $l_{ij}^{\xi} = m_{ij}^{\xi}$ and $h_{ij}^{\xi} = M_{ij}^{\xi}$, that is, $\mathcal{D}_s^{\xi}[i,j] = (m_{ij}^{\xi}, M_{ij}^{\xi})$. $\mathcal{D}_s^{\xi}[i,j]$ specifies the set of all the possible values of t_{ij} that can appear in the behaviours allowed by ξ.

The table on the right of Fig. 2 is the stable distance table of γ in Fig. 1. $\mathcal{D}_s^{\gamma}$ represents the set of constraints $\{\tau_{0,1} \geq 0, \tau_{0,1} \leq 3, \tau_{0,2} \geq 6, \tau_{0,2} \leq 6, \tau_{1,2} \geq 3, \tau_{1,2} \leq 6\}$. Observe that $\mathcal{D}_s^{\gamma}[0,1] = (0,3)$: $m_{01}^{\gamma} = 0$, which corresponds to a default constraint, and $M_{01}^{\gamma} = 3$, which means the original constraint $\tau_{0,1} \leq 4$ was not tight.

Two scenarios ξ and η are equivalent iff $\mathcal{D}_s^{\xi} = \mathcal{D}_s^{\eta}$. For example, the stable table on the right-hand side of Fig. 2 could be obtained from the constraints of either γ or η, which shows that they are equivalent: $[\![\gamma]\!] = [\![\eta]\!]$.

Timed Scenarios and Timed Automata. If $\xi = (\mathcal{E}, \mathcal{C})$ is a scenario of length n, and $\mathcal{C}$ contains a constraint $\tau_{i,j} \sim a$ for some $0 \leq i < j < n$, and some $a \in \mathbb{Q}$, then the index i is an *anchor*. If $0 < j < n$ is the largest number such that $\tau_{i,j} \sim b$ is a constraint in $\mathcal{C}$, then $[i,j)$ is the *range* of anchor i. If i_1 and i_2 are two anchors with ranges $[i_1, j_1)$ and $[i_2, j_2)$ in ξ, then the two ranges *overlap* iff

---

[7] A detailed comparison with Dill's Difference Bounds Matrices (DBMs) [19] can be found in our earlier work [18].

Fig. 3. Equivalent timed automata corresponding to the scenarios of Fig. 1

$i_1 < i_2 < j_1$ or $i_2 < i_1 < j_2$. For example, in scenario γ of Fig. 1, the range of anchor 0 is $[0, 2)$ and the range of anchor 1 is $[1, 2)$: these are overlapping. $Anch_\xi$ is used to denote the set of anchors of ξ. If X is a set of clock variables, then a relation $alloc_\xi \subset Anch_\xi \times X$ is a clock allocation for ξ. $alloc_\xi$ is *complete* iff for every anchor $i \in Anch_\xi$ there is a clock $x \in X$ such that $(i, x) \in alloc_\xi$. $alloc_\xi$ is *incorrect* iff there exist two different anchors i and j in $Anch_\xi$ whose ranges overlap, such that $(i, x) \in alloc_\xi$ and $(j, x) \in alloc_\xi$ for some $x \in X$. $alloc_\xi$ is *correct* iff it is not incorrect. A correct and complete clock allocation is *optimal* if there is no other correct and complete allocation that uses fewer clocks. $\{(0, x), (1, y)\}$ is an optimal clock allocation for scenario γ of Fig. 1.

A scenario ξ can be trivially converted to a simple timed automaton $\mathcal{A}_\xi$, such that the language of $\mathcal{A}_\xi$ is equivalent to the set of behaviours allowed by ξ: $L(\mathcal{A}_\xi) = [\![\xi]\!]$. The conversion preserves the clock allocation. For example, Fig. 3 shows the automata obtained from scenarios γ and η of Fig. 1.

A scenario ξ can be transformed to an equivalent scenario η by *optimising* its set of constraints [13], so that (i) η has a minimal set of constraints[8], and (ii) given an optimal clock allocation for η, $\mathcal{A}_\eta$ has the *minimal* number of clocks in the entire class of automata that are language-equivalent to $\mathcal{A}_\xi$[9]. We call η the *optimised* form of ξ. For example, η of Fig. 1 is the optimised form of γ in that figure. Notice that in Fig. 3 $\mathcal{A}_\eta$ has only one clock, while $\mathcal{A}_\gamma$ requires two clocks.

For an optimised scenario $\xi = (\mathcal{E}, \mathcal{C})$ the members of $\mathcal{C}$ will be referred to as *explicit constraints*. We know that in the stable distance table, $\mathcal{D}_s^\xi$, there are also *implicit* constraints: default constraints and constraints that are implied by $\mathcal{C}$. For example, the set of explicit constraints of η of Fig. 1 is $\{\tau_{0,1} \leq 3, \tau_{0,2} \geq 6, \tau_{0,2} \leq 6\}$, while $\{\tau_{0,1} \geq 0, \tau_{1,2} \geq 3, \tau_{1,2} \leq 6\}$ is the set of implicit constraints.

2.3   Operations on Timed Scenarios

(This subsection briefly recounts our recent work [14].)

If ξ is a scenario of length n with stable distance table $\mathcal{D}_s^\xi$, then, for any $0 \leq i < j < n$, the interval I_{ij}^ξ is $\{a \in \mathbb{Q} \mid m_{ij}^\xi \leq a \leq M_{ij}^\xi\}$, where $\mathcal{D}_s^\xi[i, j] = (m_{ij}^\xi, M_{ij}^\xi)$. Intuitively, I_{ij}^ξ corresponds to a pair of constraints: for every behaviour $\mathcal{B} \in [\![\xi]\!]$, $t_{ij}^\mathcal{B}$ must be at least m_{ij}^ξ and at most M_{ij}^ξ, i.e., $t_{ij}^\mathcal{B} \in I_{ij}^\xi$.

If ξ and η are two consistent scenarios with the same sequence of events, ξ is *subsumed* by η, denoted by $\xi \sqsubseteq \eta$, when $[\![\xi]\!] \subseteq [\![\eta]\!]$. $\xi \sqsubseteq \eta$ iff $\forall_{0 \leq i < j < n} I_{ij}^\xi \subseteq I_{ij}^\eta$.

---

[8] That is, a constraint cannot be removed without changing the semantics.

[9] Optimality was achieved under the assumption that a timed scenario cannot be split into two [13].

$0 : a$;		1	2
$1 : b\ \{\tau_{0,1} \le 5\}$;	0	$(0,5)$	$(2,\infty)$
$2 : c\ \{\tau_{1,2} \ge 2\}$.	1		$(2,\infty)$

$0 : a$;		1	2
$1 : b$;	0	$(0,3)$	$(0,3)$
$2 : c\ \{\tau_{0,2} =< 3\}$.	1		$(0,3)$

Fig. 4. ξ and its stable distance table, η and its stable distance table

$\xi \uplus \eta$	$0 : a$;		1	2
	$1 : b\ \{\tau_{0,1} \le 5\}$;	0	$(0,5)$	$(0,\infty)$
	$2 : c$.	1		$(0,\infty)$

ζ	$0 : a$;		1	2
	$1 : b$;	0	$(3,3)$	$(4,4)$
	$2 : c\ \{\tau_{1,2} = 1, \tau_{0,2} = 4\}$.	1		$(1,1)$

Fig. 5. The combination of ξ and η of Fig. 4, and scenario ζ with its stabilized table

If ξ and η are two consistent scenarios of length n with the same sequence of events, $\mathcal{E}$, such that $\forall_{0 \le i < j < n}\ I_{ij}^{\xi} \cap I_{ij}^{\eta} \ne \emptyset$, then the *combination* of ξ and η, denoted by $\xi \uplus \eta$, is *defined*. In that case, $\xi \uplus \eta$ is a scenario whose sequence of events is $\mathcal{E}$ and whose constraints are given by $\mathcal{D}^{\xi \uplus \eta}$, where $\mathcal{D}^{\xi \uplus \eta}[i, j] = (\min(m_{ij}^{\xi}, m_{ij}^{\eta}), \max(M_{ij}^{\xi}, M_{ij}^{\eta}))$. The original table $\mathcal{D}^{\xi \uplus \eta}$ is stable: $\mathcal{D}^{\xi \uplus \eta} = \mathcal{D}_s^{\xi \uplus \eta}$.

If $\xi \uplus \eta$ is defined, then $[\![\xi]\!] \cup [\![\eta]\!] \subseteq [\![\xi \uplus \eta]\!]$. But, in general, $[\![\xi \uplus \eta]\!] \not\subseteq [\![\xi]\!] \cup [\![\eta]\!]$. This is because table $\mathcal{D}_s^{\xi \uplus \eta}$ allows all the behaviours in $[\![\xi]\!] \cup [\![\eta]\!]$, but there is a possibility that it may also allow some extra behaviours, namely those that satisfy all the constraints of the combination, but do not satisfy some of the constraints in ξ and some of the constraints in η. That is, $[\![\xi \uplus \eta]\!] = [\![\xi]\!] \cup [\![\eta]\!] \cup \mathcal{Z}(\xi, \eta)$, where $[\![\xi]\!] \cap \mathcal{Z}(\xi, \eta) = \emptyset$ and $[\![\eta]\!] \cap \mathcal{Z}(\xi, \eta) = \emptyset$. We call members of $\mathcal{Z}(\xi, \eta)$ *zigzagging* behaviours. As an example consider scenarios ξ and η of Fig. 4. Figure 5 shows $\xi \uplus \eta$ along with its stable table. Scenario ζ of Fig. 5 represents a set of behaviours in which the time distance between events a and b is exactly 3, and between events a and c is exactly 4 units of time. There is no behaviour in the semantics of ζ that is allowed by either ξ or η of Fig. 4, yet $[\![\zeta]\!] \subset [\![\xi \uplus \eta]\!]$. That is, all behaviours in $[\![\zeta]\!]$ belong to $\mathcal{Z}(\xi, \eta)$. *This indicates that the union of the sets of behaviours allowed by ξ and η cannot be represented by a single scenario.*

There is a sufficient condition for the non-existence of zigzagging behaviours [14]. This condition is based on the form of explicit constraints of ξ and η and provides a basis for a procedure to determine whether $\mathcal{Z}(\xi, \eta)$ is empty [14].

If $\mathcal{Z}(\xi, \eta) = \emptyset$, the combination of ξ and η becomes their *union*, denoted by $\xi \cup \eta$. Figure 6 shows two scenarios where the union of the sets of behaviours allowed by each *can be* represented by a single scenario, namely their union (see the scenario at the bottom).

In the rest of the paper when we say "the union of ξ and η exists", it means that $\xi \uplus \eta$ is defined and $\mathcal{Z}(\xi, \eta) = \emptyset$, so scenario $\xi \cup \eta$ captures the union of the sets of behaviours allowed by ξ, η or both: $[\![\xi \cup \eta]\!] = [\![\xi]\!] \cup [\![\eta]\!]$.

3   Synthesizing Automata from Sets of Optimised Scenarios

In this section we will use our previous results on optimising scenarios [13] to synthesize a timed automaton from a set Ξ of scenarios, in such a way that the automaton will have the smallest number of clocks in the entire class of equivalent automata. Optimality is obtained under the following simplifying assumption:

Assumption 1. *Each scenario in Ξ has a sequence of events that is different from that of any other scenario in Ξ.*

The assumption is not very limiting in practice. It is discussed further in Sec. 4.

We assume that each of the scenarios in Ξ describes a set of *complete* behaviours of a (sub)system, and that all such behaviours begin at the same initial state. Ξ_o is the set whose members are the optimised forms of scenarios in Ξ.

Obviously, the number of clocks in our constructed automaton should not exceed the largest number of clocks required by the optimised form of any one of the constituent scenarios, i.e., any member of Ξ_o. This is because one can always construct a trivial automaton by allowing the automata corresponding to individual optimised scenarios to share only their initial locations. So our secondary goal is to make the number of locations reasonably small, though not necessarily minimal. Next we define the problem formally.

> Let $\mathcal{TA}$ be the class of all timed automata and Ξ be a finite set of finite scenarios, such that if $\xi_1 = (\mathcal{E}_1, \mathcal{C}_1)$ and $\xi_2 = (\mathcal{E}_2, \mathcal{C}_2)$ are two different scenarios in Ξ, then $\mathcal{E}_1 \neq \mathcal{E}_2$. Let $\mathcal{TA}(\Xi) = \{\mathcal{A} \mid \mathcal{A} \in \mathcal{TA} \text{ and } L(\mathcal{A}) = \bigcup_{\xi \in \Xi} [\![\xi]\!]\}$. The goal is to synthesize an automaton $\mathcal{A} \in \mathcal{TA}(\Xi)$ in such a way that if $\mathcal{A}' \in \mathcal{TA}$ is language-equivalent to $\mathcal{A}$, then $\mathcal{A}'$ has no fewer clocks than $\mathcal{A}$.

We accomplish our objective by an algorithm that is both simple and efficient (see Sec. 3.2). The general idea is that if the sequences of events in two scenarios in Ξ have a common prefix, then *under certain circumstances* it is possible to combine the prefixes of the scenarios. We optimise each of the scenarios in Ξ and use them to build a tree, $\mathcal{T}_o^\Xi$, which can then be converted to the desired timed automaton.

As discussed in Sec. 2.3, sometimes two scenarios, ξ and η, can be combined into a single scenario, γ, that is, $\gamma = \xi \cup \eta$. Conversely, it might be possible that a scenario γ can be "split" into ξ and η. But then, if $\gamma \in \Xi_o$, it can be replaced by ξ and η in Ξ_o. In that case, for achieving optimality, we must first show that the number of clocks in $\mathcal{A}_\gamma$ will not be larger than those in $\mathcal{A}_\xi$ or $\mathcal{A}_\eta$. That is, "splitting" a scenario into two will not decrease the number of clocks.

Definition 1. *Let ξ be a scenario, and let $alloc_\xi$ be an optimal clock allocation for ξ. The* cost *of ξ is the number of clocks that is used in $alloc_\xi$.*

Definition 2. *Let Ξ be a set of scenarios. The* cost *of Ξ, denoted by $cost(\Xi)$, is the maximum of the costs of the members of Ξ.*

Observation 1. *Let* $\xi = (\mathcal{E}, \mathcal{C}_1)$ *and* $\eta = (\mathcal{E}, \mathcal{C}_2)$ *be two optimised scenarios. Let* $\gamma = \xi \cup \eta$, *and* $\mathcal{C}$ *be the set of explicit constraints of* γ. *Then* $\mathcal{C} \subseteq \mathcal{C}_1 \cup \mathcal{C}_2$.

Proof. Let $i < j$. At every interval $I_{ij}^{\xi \cup \eta}$ we have one of the following cases:

1. Both $\mathcal{D}_s^\xi[i, j] = (a_1, b_1)$ and $\mathcal{D}_s^\eta[i, j] = (a_2, b_2)$ correspond to explicit constraints. Then we must have one of the following cases:
   (a) If $a_1 > 0$, $a_2 > 0$, $b_1 < \infty$ and $b_2 < \infty$, then $\mathcal{C}$ will include two explicit constraints of the form $\tau_{i,j} \geq min(a_1, a_2)$ and $\tau_{i,j} \leq max(b_1, b_2)$.
   (b) If $a_1 = 0$ or $a_2 = 0$, and $b_1 < \infty$ and $b_2 < \infty$, then $\mathcal{C}$ will include one explicit constraint of the form $\tau_{i,j} \leq max(b_1, b_2)$.
   (c) If $a_1 > 0$ and $a_2 > 0$, and $b_1 = \infty$ or $b_2 = \infty$, then $\mathcal{C}$ will include one explicit constraint of the form $\tau_{i,j} \geq min(a_1, a_2)$.
   (d) If $a_1 = 0$ or $a_2 = 0$, and $b_1 = \infty$ or $b_2 = \infty$, then $\mathcal{C}$ will not include any explicit constraints between i and j.
2. $\mathcal{D}_s^\xi[i, j] = (a_1, b_1)$ corresponds to explicit constraint(s), but $\mathcal{D}_s^\eta[i, j] = (a_2, b_2)$ corresponds to default or implied constraints. Then $\mathcal{C}$ will have an explicit constraint of the form $\tau_{i,j} \geq a_1$ if $a_1 \leq a_2$, and an explicit constraint of the form $\tau_{i,j} \leq b_1$ if $b_2 \leq b_1$.
3. Both $\mathcal{D}_s^\xi[i, j]$ and $\mathcal{D}_s^\eta[i, j]$ correspond to default or implied constraints. Then $\mathcal{C}$ will not have any explicit constraints between i and j.

In all the cases above, an explicit constraint α between i and j will be in $\mathcal{C}$ only if at least one of $\mathcal{C}_1$ and $\mathcal{C}_2$ include α. $\qquad\square$

An important consequence of Observation 1 is that an anchor in $\gamma = \xi \cup \eta$ must be an anchor in ξ or in η.

Theorem 1. *Let* $\xi = (\mathcal{E}, \mathcal{C}_1)$ *and* $\eta = (\mathcal{E}, \mathcal{C}_2)$ *be two optimised scenarios. If there exists an optimised scenario* γ *such that* $\gamma = \xi \cup \eta$, *then* $cost(\{\gamma\}) \leq cost(\{\xi, \eta\})$.

Proof. Recall that the number of clocks in an optimal clock allocation for a scenario is determined by the number of overlapping anchors of the scenario, which, in turn, is determined by the *explicit* constraints of the scenario.

Let $\mathcal{C}$ be the set of explicit constraints of γ. By Observation 1, $\mathcal{C}$ does not include anchors that are neither in ξ nor in η. We must show that *new* overlapping ranges are not introduced in γ: existing overlapping ranges of ξ or η that are present also in γ would not require additional clocks. Therefore there are two cases to consider:

(1) i_1 and i_2 are both anchors in ξ or in η or in both. But then their ranges do not overlap, so, by Observation 1, their ranges will not overlap in γ either.

(2) i_1 is an anchor in ξ but not in η and i_2 is an anchor in η but not in ξ. We must show that γ does not have overlapping ranges of i_1 and i_2.

Let α be an explicit constraint of the form $\tau_{i_1, j_1} \sim a$ in $\mathcal{C}_1$ and β be an explicit constraint of the form $\tau_{i_2, j_2} \sim b$ in $\mathcal{C}_2$, such that the integer ranges $[i_1, j_1)$ and $[i_2, j_2)$ overlap. Moreover, assume i_1 is not an anchor in η and i_2 is not an anchor in ξ. We will show that both α and β cannot exist in $\mathcal{C}$.

Proof by contradiction. Assume both α and β are in $\mathcal{C}$.

Without loss of generality assume α is of the form $\tau_{i_1,j_1} \le a$ and β is of the form $\tau_{i_2,j_2} \le b$, where $a, b \in \mathbb{Q}$[10].

(2a) $\alpha = \tau_{i_1,j_1} \le a$ is both in $\mathcal{C}_1$ and in $\mathcal{C}$. By definition of union, $M^\eta_{i_1j_1}$ cannot be larger than a, i.e., $M^\eta_{i_1j_1} = c \le a$. Since i_1 is not an anchor in η, $M^\eta_{i_1j_1} = c$ must have been implied by some explicit constraints in η. This constraint could be implied in three cases [13]:

1. There are constraints $\tau_{i_1,j} \le u$ and $\tau_{j,j_1} \le v$ in $\mathcal{C}_2$[11] such that $i_1 < j < j_1$ and $c = u + v$. But i_1 is not an anchor in η, so this would be a contradiction.
2. There are constraints $\tau_{i_1,j} \le u$ and $\tau_{j_1,j} \ge v$ in $\mathcal{C}_2$ such that $i_1 < j_1 < j$ and $u = c + v$. But i_1 is not an anchor in η, so this would be a contradiction.
3. There are constraints $\tau_{j,j_1} \le u$ and $\tau_{j,i_1} \ge v$ in $\mathcal{C}_2$ such that $j < i_1 < j_1$ and $u = c + v$. So, for $M^\eta_{i_1j_1} = c$ to be implied, there must exist $\alpha_1 = \tau_{j,j_1} \le u$ and $\alpha_2 = \tau_{j,i_1} \ge v$.

(2b) $\beta = \tau_{i_2,j_2} \le b$ is both in $\mathcal{C}_2$ and in $\mathcal{C}$. By definition of union, $M^\xi_{i_2j_2}$ cannot be larger than b, i.e., $M^\xi_{i_2j_2} = d \le b$. Since i_2 is not an anchor in ξ, $M^\xi_{i_2j_2} = d$ must have been implied by some other constraints in ξ. By an argument similar to the one in (2a) it can be shown that there must be some constraints $\beta_1 = \tau_{j',j_2} \le u'$ and $\beta_2 = \tau_{j',i_2} \ge v'$ in $\mathcal{C}_2$ such that $j' < i_2 < j_2$ and $u' = d + v'$.

Now we consider two cases:

Case 1: $j \ne j'$, $\alpha_1 = \tau_{j,j_1} \le u \in \mathcal{C}_1$ and $\beta_1 = \tau_{j',j_2} \le u' \in \mathcal{C}_2$, where $j < i_1 < j_1$, $j' < i_2 < j_2$, and $i_1 \ne i_2$.

Case 2: $j = j'$, $\alpha_2 = \tau_{j,i_1} \ge v \in \mathcal{C}_1$ and $\beta_2 = \tau_{j',i_2} \ge v' \in \mathcal{C}_2$, where $j < i_1 < j_1$, $j' < i_2 < j_2$, and $i_1 \ne i_2$.

Both cases imply $\mathcal{Z}(\xi,\eta) \ne \emptyset$ [20], which is a contradiction: $\xi \cup \eta$ exists. $\square$

Since combining two scenarios into one does not increase the number of clocks, splitting a scenario into two will not decrease the number of clocks.

3.1 Auxiliary Definitions

Before presenting the algorithm, we will define a few concepts.

Definition 3. *Let $\xi = (e_0 e_1 \ldots e_{n-1}, \mathcal{C})$ be a scenario. The* path *for ξ, denoted by p_ξ, is defined as follows:*

- *$\{n_0, n_1, \ldots, n_n\}$ is the set of nodes of p_ξ. n_0 is the initial node.*
- *For each $0 \le j < n$ there is a transition r_j from n_j to n_{j+1}, and r_j is labeled with e_j.*
- *For every i and j such that $0 \le i < j < n$, transition r_j in p_ξ is annotated with the set of all the constraints of the form $\tau_{i,j} \sim a$ in $\mathcal{C}$.*

---

[10] If α is of the form $\tau_{i_1,j_1} \ge a$, and/or β is of the form $\tau_{i_2,j_2} \ge b$, the steps of the proof will be essentially the same.

[11] It is impossible for both $\tau_{i_1,j} \le u$ and $M^\eta_{i_1j_1} = c$ to be implied, without anchor i_1.

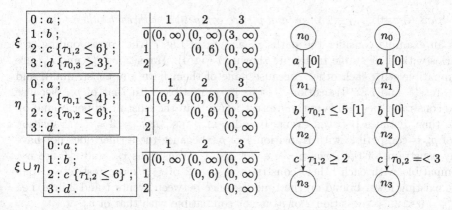

Fig. 6. Two scenarios and their union   **Fig. 7.** p_ξ and p_η for ξ and η of Fig. 4

A path is just another representation of the corresponding scenario, one that is more convenient for our current purposes. We will often denote transition r_j in a path p by r_j^p, and refer to it as the *j-th transition* or *transition j*.

Definition 4. *Let p_ξ be the path for scenario ξ. If i is an anchor in ξ whose range is $[i, k)$, then for every $i \le j < k$ transition r_j of p_ξ belongs to the range of i. We use $range(r_j)$ to denote the set of all anchors whose ranges include r_j.*

Fig. 7 shows the paths for scenarios of Fig. 4. In p_ξ, transition 0, i.e., the transition on event a is annotated with $[0]$, which signifies that the transition belongs to the range of anchor 0. Observe that transition 1 does not belong to the range of anchor 0: the range of anchor 0 ends on transition 1. Transition 2 does not belong to the range of any anchor: the range of anchor 1 ends on transition 2.

In the remainder of this section we assume that $range(r)$ is known for every transition r of a path.

Definition 5. *Let ξ be a consistent scenario. Let $\alpha = \tau_{i,j} \sim a$, for some $i < j$, $a \in \mathbb{Q}$ and $\sim \in \{\le, \ge\}$ be a constraint. We say α is too restrictive for i and j in ξ, if either $\sim$ is $\le$ and $M_{ij}^\xi > a$, or $\sim$ is $\ge$ and $m_{ij}^\xi < a$.*

Intuitively, a constraint that is not too restrictive can be added to a scenario without changing its semantics. In our synthesis algorithm (see Sec. 3.2) we will take care to ensure that such additions will not increase the number of clocks.

Definition 6. *Let ξ and η be two scenarios and p_ξ and p_η be their paths. The j-th transition of p_ξ is compatible with the j-th transition of p_η, if every constraint on $\tau_{i,j}$ on the j-th transition of p_ξ is not too restrictive for i and j in η. The j-th transitions of p_ξ and p_η are compatible with each other, if*

- *they agree on their events, and*
- *the j-th transition of p_ξ is compatible with the j-th transition of p_η, and vice versa, and*

– *transitions* $0, \ldots j - 1$ *of* p_ξ *and* p_η *are compatible with each other.*

As an example consider the paths p_ξ and p_η of Fig. 7 (the corresponding scenarios with their stable tables are shown in Fig. 4). Transitions $r_0^{p_\xi}$ and $r_0^{p_\eta}$ are compatible with each other (because none of them have any constraints), and so are $r_1^{p_\xi}$ and $r_1^{p_\eta}$. Transition 1 of p_ξ is compatible with that of p_η, because the constraint $\tau_{0,1} \leq 5$ is not more restrictive than the existing upper bound on the time distance between events 0 and 1 in η, i.e., $M_{01}^\eta = 3 < 5$. Transition 1 of p_η is compatible with transition 1 of p_ξ, because the former does not have any constraint of the form $\tau_{i,1} \sim a$, for $i < 1$. Transitions $r_2^{p_\xi}$ and $r_2^{p_\eta}$ are not compatible with each other: constraint $\tau_{1,2} \geq 2$ of ξ is more restrictive than the existing lower bound on the time distance between events 1 and 2 in η, i.e., $m_{12}^\eta = 0 < 2$, so transition 2 of p_ξ is not compatible with that of p_η.

3.2 The Synthesis Algorithm

We are now ready to present the details of the algorithm.

– Let Ξ be a set of scenarios that satisfies Assumption 1, Ξ_o be the set of optimised forms of the scenarios in Ξ, and P_{Ξ_o} be the set of paths for scenarios in Ξ_o. Let $cost(\Xi_o) = m$.
– Initialize T_o^Ξ by merging the initial nodes of the paths in P_{Ξ_o}. Let n_0 be the resulting node, which is the root of the tree.
– Let $Groups = \{(n_0, 0, P_{\Xi_o})\}$.
– While $Groups \neq \emptyset$
  1. Let (n, i, G) be a member of $Groups$.
  2. Let $Partitions$ be the set of groups of paths obtained by partitioning G in such a way that
     (a) The i-th transitions of all the paths that belong to the same group g are compatible with each other, and
     (b) $|\bigcup_{p \in g} range(r_i^p)| \leq m$.
  3. For each group $g \in Partitions$:
     (a) Merge the i-th transitions of all the paths in g to obtain a new transition r'. The source of r' is n, the target is a new node n'.
     (b) The set of constraints on r' is the union of the sets of constraints on the i-th transitions of all paths in g.
     (c) Set $range(r')$ to $\bigcup_{p \in g} range(r_i^p)$.
     (d) Remove from g those paths for which transition i is the last one.
     (e) If $g \neq \emptyset$ then $Groups := Groups \cup \{(n', i+1, g)\}$.
  4. $Groups := Groups \setminus \{(n, i, G)\}$.

The algorithm obviously terminates: each iteration removes one group in step 4, but the total number of groups added in step 3e does not exceed $N \times |P_{\Xi_o}|$, where N is the length of the longest path. The invariant is

For every $(n, k, g) \in Groups$ the following holds:
for every $p, q \in g$ and every $0 \leq j < k$, transitions r_j^p and r_j^q are compatible with each other; moreover, $|\bigcup_{p \in g} range(r_j^p)| \leq m$.

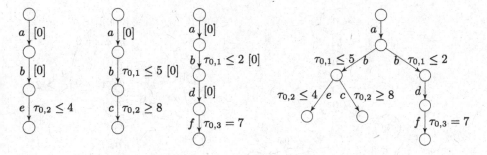

Fig. 8. Three scenarios and their synthesized tree

Notice that step 2 is under-specified. The aim, of course, is to keep the groups as large as possible, but there may be many ways to partition a group so that condition 2b can be satisfied. The choice made in one step can affect the sizes of the subtrees created in the subsequent steps, so this algorithm does not ensure that the number of locations in the resulting automaton will be minimal.

As an example consider $\xi_1 = (abe, \{\tau_{0,2} \leq 4\})$, $\xi_2 = (abc, \{\tau_{0,1} \leq 5, \tau_{0,2} \geq 8, \tau_{1,2} \geq 3\})$, and $\xi_3 = (abdf, \{\tau_{0,3} = 7, \tau_{1,3} \geq 5\})$. It is easy to see that ξ_1 requires one clock, while ξ_2 and ξ_3 require two clocks each. The optimised equivalent scenarios are $\xi_1^o = \xi_1$, $\xi_2^o = (abc, \{\tau_{0,1} \leq 5, \tau_{0,2} \geq 8\})$, and $\xi_3^o = (abdf, \{\tau_{0,1} \leq 2, \tau_{0,3} = 7\})$. Figure 8 shows the paths for the optimised forms. Observe that after optimisation the required number of clocks remained 1 in ξ_1, but it decreased from 2 to 1 in both ξ_2 and ξ_3. So $cost(\{\xi_1^o, \xi_2^o, \xi_3^o\}) = 1$. One of the synthesized trees that can be obtained by our algorithm is shown on the right of the figure.

3.3 Obtaining the Final Automaton

The tree that is produced by the algorithm can be trivially converted to a timed automaton. The root is the initial location and all the leaves are the final locations. The anchors must be replaced by clocks in such a way that two anchors with overlapping ranges are not assigned the same clock. Once clocks are allocated, the constraints must be rewritten in terms of the clocks. Our existing clock allocation algorithms [21, 22] can be used for this purpose after some trivial modifications.

In the tree of Fig. 8 there is only one anchor, so the resulting automaton will require only one clock: a clock, e.g., c_0 would be reset on the transition labeled with event a (i.e., $c_0 := 0$ would be added to the transition), and every occurrence of $\tau_{0,j}$, for $1 \leq j \leq 3$, would be replaced with c_0.

It is clear from the construction that the language accepted by the resulting automaton is the union of the behaviours allowed by the scenarios in Ξ. It is also clear that the number of clocks will not exceed $cost(\Xi_o)$.

Theorem 2. *Let Ξ be a finite set of finite scenarios that satisfies Assumption 1, and let A_Ξ be the timed automaton synthesized by the algorithm of Sec. 3.2. Then*

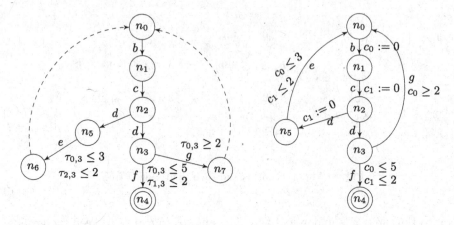

Fig. 9. A tree and its corresponding timed automaton

$\mathcal{A}_\Xi$ *has the smallest number of clocks in the entire class of language-equivalent*
automata.

Proof. The algorithm begins with optimising each scenario in Ξ and replacing
it with its optimised form, hence obtaining $\Xi_o = \{\xi_1, \dots \xi_n\}$. Let $cost(\Xi_o) = m$.

By Theorem 1, for each $\xi_i \in \Xi_o$, there are no η and γ such that $\xi_i = \eta \cup \gamma$ and
$\mathcal{A}_{\xi_i}$ requires more clocks than the automaton synthesized from η and γ. That is,
$cost(\Xi_o)$ cannot be lower than m.

Consider an automaton $\mathcal{A}$ obtained by unifying the initial locations of all $\mathcal{A}_{\xi_i}$.
Clearly, $L(\mathcal{A}) = \bigcup_{\xi_i \in \Xi_o} L(\mathcal{A}_{\xi_i}) = \bigcup_{\xi_i \in \Xi_o} [\![\xi_i]\!]$. Since each $\mathcal{A}_{\xi_i}$ has the optimal
number of clocks in the entire class of language-equivalent automata, the result
can be extended to $\mathcal{A}$.

The synthesis algorithm essentially merges the common prefixes of the paths
in $\mathcal{A}$ while making sure that the overall cost will not rise above m.   □

3.4   Handling a Limited Form of Cycles

Ξ might include scenarios that specify behaviours that all begin and end in
the same state of the system being specified. Such scenarios are used to specify
repetition of some "partial" behaviours in the system [22]. When such scenarios are used for synthesizing a timed automaton, the constructed automaton
must include cycles in order to allow an arbitrary number of repetitions of the
behaviours specified by these scenarios. But the underlying graph of the automaton generated by our algorithm takes the form of a tree, and as such cannot
support specifying repeated behaviours.

However, with some minimal effort, our trees can be extended so that certain kinds of cycles can be handled. In particular, those that specify repeated
behaviours that begin at the initial state of the system can be handled easily.

While constructing $\mathcal{T}_o^\Xi$, we can mark a leaf, say n, as a "looping leaf". Then
the root will be the "looping ancestor" of n and the path between the root and n

will be a "looping path". The looping path in $\mathcal{T}_o^{\Xi}$ represents a sequence of events that starts at the root and can be repeated in the final automaton. That is, the looping leaf and the looping ancestor will be "unified", i.e., correspond to the same location in the final automaton, and hence there will be a loop.

Figure 9 shows a tree obtained by our algorithm from the optimised set of scenarios $\{\xi_1, \xi_2, \xi_3\}$, where $\xi_1 = (bcde, \{\tau_{0,3} \le 3, \tau_{2,3} \le 2\})$, $\xi_2 = (bcdf, \{\tau_{0,3} \le 5, \tau_{1,3} \le 2\})$, and $\xi_3 = (bcdg, \{\tau_{0,3} \ge 2\})$. The tree includes two looping paths: one that begins at n_0 and ends at n_6, and one that begins at n_0 and ends at n_7. The correspondence between n_0 and n_6 and between n_0 and n_7 is shown with dashed lines. In the final automaton n_0, n_6 and n_7 will all correspond to the same location: see the automaton on the right of the figure.

Using this method we obtain automata whose initial locations are the only locations with more than one incoming transition.

It is worth mentioning that during the construction of the tree in Fig. 9 the three transitions with event d could not have been merged, as that would violate condition 2b of the algorithm: $cost(\{\xi_1, \xi_2, \xi_3\}) = 2$, but the merge would result in a transition that would belong to the ranges of all three anchors, i.e., 0, 1 and 2, and would thus increase the number of clocks in the synthesized automaton to three. So the three paths had to be partitioned into two groups: p_{ξ_1} could not have merged with p_{ξ_2}, but p_{ξ_3} could form a group either with p_{ξ_1} or with p_{ξ_2}. The automaton shown in the figure is the result of placing p_{ξ_3} and p_{ξ_2} in the same group. The other alternative (not shown here) would result in an automaton with the same number of clocks and locations.

4   Revisiting the Assumption

We will now discuss some consequences of relaxing Assumption 1 by allowing scenarios with the same sequences of events.

Let Ξ_o include two scenarios $\xi = (\mathcal{E}, \mathcal{C}^{\xi})$ and $\eta = (\mathcal{E}, \mathcal{C}^{\eta})$ that can be combined into one scenario. That is, $\mathcal{Z}(\xi, \eta) = \emptyset$ (Sec. 2.3). We investigate the question of whether it would be advantageous to replace them with $\xi \cup \eta$ in Ξ_o.

We discuss several cases using some illustrative examples.

One scenario is subsumed by the other one. Assume $\xi \subseteq \eta$, then $\xi \cup \eta = \eta$ [14]. Obviously in this case ξ can simply be removed from Ξ_o.

As an example consider the two scenarios of Fig. 10. The automaton synthesized from the two by our synthesis algorithm of Sec. 3.2 is shown on the right of Fig. 10. Observe that this automaton requires two clocks, one each for anchors 0 and 1. A simple comparison of the stable distance tables of ξ and η shows that $\xi \subseteq \eta$, therefore $\xi \cup \eta = \eta$. That is, $\mathcal{A}_\eta$, the automaton corresponding to η, would capture the semantics of both ξ and η. So $\mathcal{A}_\eta$ (shown in the middle of Fig. 10) would be equivalent to the automaton obtained by the synthesis algorithm. But $\mathcal{A}_\eta$ would require only one clock, moreover, it would have only four locations.

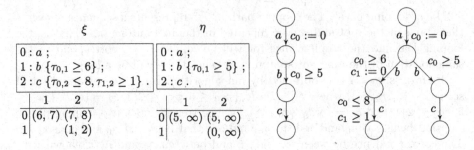

Fig. 10. $\xi \subseteq \eta$, $\mathcal{A}_{\xi \cup \eta}$ and the automaton synthesized from ξ and η

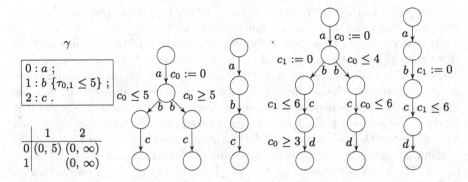

Fig. 11. η and γ with complementary constraints, the automaton synthesized from η and γ, and $\mathcal{A}_{\eta \cup \gamma}$

Fig. 12. The automaton synthesized from ξ and η of Fig. 6, and $\mathcal{A}_{\xi \cup \eta}$

Two scenarios with a pair of complementary constraints. Let ξ and η contain a pair of explicit constraints that are complementary, i.e., for some i, j and a we have $\tau_{i,j} \leq a \in \mathcal{C}^\xi$ and $\tau_{i,j} \geq a \in \mathcal{C}^\eta$. Then the only constraints on $\tau_{i,j}$ in $\xi \cup \eta$ will be implicit default constraints (i.e., $\tau_{i,j} \geq 0$ and $\tau_{i,j} \leq \infty$). If anchor i is not used in any other constraint, then it will no longer be needed, since the default constraints are not explicitly mentioned in scenarios. If anchor i is used in some other constraints, the range of i might become shorter. So in either case this may cause a reduction of $cost(\Xi)$.

For example, the scenario η of Fig. 10 and γ of Fig. 11 have a pair of complementary constraints ($\tau_{0,1} \geq 5$ and $\tau_{0,1} \leq 5$), moreover, $\mathcal{Z}(\eta, \gamma) = \emptyset$[12]. So $\eta \cup \gamma$ exists. The automaton synthesized from the two by the synthesis algorithm of Sec. 3.2, shown in the middle of Fig. 11, requires one clock. The automaton corresponding to $\eta \cup \gamma$, i.e., $\mathcal{A}_{\eta \cup \gamma}$, shown on the right of Fig. 11, would be equivalent to this. But it does not require any clock, and has fewer locations than the synthesized automaton.

---

[12] If the explicit constraints of two scenarios differ only on constraints between one pair of events, their combination cannot include zigzagging behaviours [14].

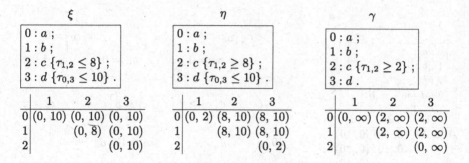

Fig. 13. Three scenarios with the same sequence of events

Two arbitrary scenarios that can be combined. ξ and η might be just some arbitrary scenarios with the same sequence of events, that can be combined into one. Figure 6 shows one such example. Neither of the scenarios ξ and η is a subset of the other one (see the stable distance tables), the two scenarios do not contain a pair of complementary constraints, yet their union exists. The automaton corresponding to their union, shown on the right of Fig. 12, requires only one clock, while the automaton synthesized from $\{\xi, \eta\}$, shown on the left of the figure, requires two clocks. Also note that $\mathcal{A}_{\xi \cup \eta}$ has fewer locations than the synthesized one.

These examples suggest that if the initial set of optimised scenarios includes some scenarios with identical sequences of events, we should try to combine them whenever possible, before applying the synthesis algorithm. This would be advantageous, as it always results in a smaller number of locations, and sometimes in a smaller number of clocks in the final synthesized automaton. But doing so is not very easy. The difficulty becomes apparent when one tries to answer the following question.

If the initial set of scenarios has more than two scenarios with the same sequence of events, some of which can be combined, would the order in which the union is applied affect the final outcome?

Let us consider the following example. Let $\varXi_o$ include four scenarios ξ, η, γ and θ such that both $\xi \cup \eta$ and $\gamma \cup \theta$ exist. Moreover, $\gamma \subseteq \xi \cup \eta$, that is, $(\xi \cup \eta) \cup \gamma = \xi \cup \eta$, but $\gamma \cup \theta \not\subseteq \xi \cup \eta$. So there are two possibilities: replacing the four scenarios with $\xi \cup \eta$ and θ in $\varXi_o$, or replacing them with $\xi \cup \eta$ and $\gamma \cup \theta$. While the first alternative may seem intuitively better, it might not be the optimal choice: as discussed above, combining γ and θ may make some of the explicit constraints in γ or θ disappear. This could result in a decrease in the overall cost, if $cost(\theta) > cost(\xi \cup \eta)$.

As a concrete example consider the three scenarios of Fig. 13, which all have the same sequences of events. Assume $\varXi_o = \{\xi, \eta, \gamma\}$ (the scenarios are already in their optimised form) and the task is to synthesize an automaton from $\varXi_o$.

Observe that ξ and η have a pair of complementary constraints ($\tau_{1,2} \leq 8$ and $\tau_{1,2} \geq 8$), and that $\eta \subseteq \gamma$. There are two options for combining the scenarios of

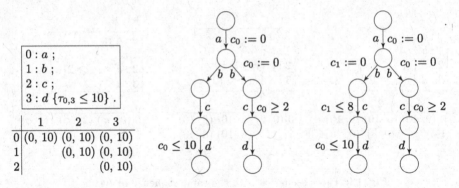

Fig. 14. $\xi \cup \eta$ **Fig. 15.** $\Xi_o = \{\xi \cup \eta, \gamma\}, \mathcal{A}_{\Xi_o}$ **Fig. 16.** $\Xi_o = \{\xi, \eta \cup \gamma\}, \mathcal{A}_{\Xi_o}$

Ξ_o before the synthesis. The first option is to combine ξ and η ($\xi \cup \eta$ is shown in Fig. 14), in which case Ξ_o will be updated to $\{\xi \cup \eta, \gamma\}$. Figure 15 shows the resulting synthesized automaton.

The second option is to combine η and γ, in which case Ξ_o will be updated to $\{\xi, \gamma\}$, because $\eta \cup \gamma = \gamma$. Figure 16 shows the automaton synthesized from Ξ_o in this case.

Observe that the first automaton requires only one clock, whereas the second one has two clocks. This example shows that if Assumption 1 is not satisfied, then obtaining the optimal result depends on the order in which scenarios are combined.

Choosing the right combination is a separate optimisation problem that may require significant computational resources to solve. Detailed discussion of this problem is outside the scope of the current paper.

5 Conclusions

We study the problem of synthesizing a timed automaton from a number of optimised timed scenarios. We present a simple and efficient algorithm[13] that, given a finite set of finite scenarios, such that each of them requires at most m clocks, constructs an automaton whose number of clocks is at most m. Moreover, the automaton has a reasonably small (though not necessarily minimal) number of locations. We show that, given a simplifying assumption about the initial set of scenarios, our synthesized automaton has the minimal number of clocks in the entire class of language-equivalent timed automata.

We then discuss the opportunities and difficulties that would arise out of relaxing our simplifying assumption, and argue that without the assumption achieving strict optimality might have a significant computational complexity.

---

[13] An implementation in C++ can be made available upon request.

References

1. Suzuki, K., Higashino, T., Yasumoto, K., El-Fakih, K. (eds.): FORTE 2008. LNCS, vol. 5048. Springer, Heidelberg (2008). https://doi.org/10.1007/978-3-540-68855-6

2. Greenyer, J.: Scenario-based modeling and programming of distributed systems, In: M. Köhler-Bussmeier, E. Kindler, H. Rölke (Eds.), In: Proceedings of the International Workshop on Petri Nets and Software Engineering 2021 co-located with the 42nd International Conference on Application and Theory of Petri Nets and Concurrency (PETRI NETS 2021), Paris, France, June 25th, 2021 (due to COVID-19: virtual conference), Vol. 2907 of CEUR Workshop Proceedings, CEUR-WS.org, pp. 241–252 (2021)

3. Somé, S., Dssouli, R., Vaucher, J.: From scenarios to timed automata: building specifications from users requirements. In: Proceedings of the Second Asia Pacific Software Engineering Conference, APSEC 1995, IEEE Computer Society, pp. 48–57

4. Chandrasekaran, P., Mukund, M.: Matching scenarios with timing constraints. In: Asarin, E., Bouyer, P. (eds.) FORMATS 2006. LNCS, vol. 4202, pp. 98–112. Springer, Heidelberg (2006). https://doi.org/10.1007/11867340_8

5. Harel, D., Kugler, H., Pnueli, A.: Synthesis revisited: generating statechart models from scenario-based requirements. In: Kreowski, H.-J., Montanari, U., Orejas, F., Rozenberg, G., Taentzer, G. (eds.) Formal Methods in Software and Systems Modeling. LNCS, vol. 3393, pp. 309–324. Springer, Heidelberg (2005). https://doi.org/10.1007/978-3-540-31847-7_18

6. Uchitel, S., Kramer, J., Magee, J.: Synthesis of behavioral models from scenarios. IEEE Trans. Softw. Eng. **29**(2), 99–115 (2003)

7. Akshay, S., Mukund, M., Kumar, K.N.: Checking coverage for infinite collections of timed scenarios. In: Caires, L., Vasconcelos, V.T. (eds.) CONCUR 2007. LNCS, vol. 4703, pp. 181–196. Springer, Heidelberg (2007). https://doi.org/10.1007/978-3-540-74407-8_13

8. Bollig, B., Katoen, J.-P., Kern, C., Leucker, M.: Replaying play in and play out: synthesis of design models from scenarios by learning. In: Grumberg, O., Huth, M. (eds.) TACAS 2007. LNCS, vol. 4424, pp. 435–450. Springer, Heidelberg (2007). https://doi.org/10.1007/978-3-540-71209-1_33

9. Alur, R., Martin, M., Raghothaman, M., Stergiou, C., Tripakis, S., Udupa, A.: Synthesizing finite-state protocols from scenarios and requirements. In: Yahav, E. (ed.) HVC 2014. LNCS, vol. 8855, pp. 75–91. Springer, Cham (2014). https://doi.org/10.1007/978-3-319-13338-6_7

10. Saeedloei, N., Kluźniak, F.: From scenarios to timed automata. In: Formal Methods: Foundations and Applications - 20th Brazilian Symposium, SBMF 2017, Proceedings, pp. 33–51

11. Saeedloei, N., Kluźniak, F.: Timed scenarios: consistency, equivalence and optimization. In: Massoni, T., Mousavi, M.R. (eds.) SBMF 2018. LNCS, vol. 11254, pp. 215–233. Springer, Cham (2018). https://doi.org/10.1007/978-3-030-03044-5_14

12. Alur, R., Madhusudan, P.: Decision problems for timed automata: a survey. In: Bernardo, M., Corradini, F. (eds.) SFM-RT 2004. LNCS, vol. 3185, pp. 1–24. Springer, Heidelberg (2004). https://doi.org/10.1007/978-3-540-30080-9_1

13. Campos, S., Minea, M. (eds.): SBMF 2021. LNCS, vol. 13130. Springer, Cham (2021). https://doi.org/10.1007/978-3-030-92137-8

14. Saeedloei, N., Kluźniak, F.: Operations on timed scenarios. In: M. Huisman, A. Ravara (Eds.), Formal Techniques for Distributed Objects, Components, and Systems - 43rd IFIP WG 6.1 International Conference, FORTE 2023, Held as Part of the 18th International Federated Conference on Distributed Computing Techniques, DisCoTec 2023, Lisbon, Portugal, June 19-23, 2023, Proceedings, Vol. 13910 of Lecture Notes in Computer Science, Springer, pp. 97–114 (2023) https://doi.org/10.1007/978-3-031-35355-0_7
15. Alur, R., Dill, D.L.: A theory of timed automata. Theor. Comput. Sci. **126**(2), 183–235 (1994)
16. Abdulla, P.A., Deneux, J., Ouaknine, J., Worrell, J.: Decidability and complexity results for timed automata via channel machines. In: Caires, L., Italiano, G.F., Monteiro, L., Palamidessi, C., Yung, M. (eds.) ICALP 2005. LNCS, vol. 3580, pp. 1089–1101. Springer, Heidelberg (2005). https://doi.org/10.1007/11523468_88
17. Baier, C., Bertrand, N., Bouyer, P., Brihaye, T.: When are timed automata determinizable? In: Albers, S., Marchetti-Spaccamela, A., Matias, Y., Nikoletseas, S., Thomas, W. (eds.) ICALP 2009. LNCS, vol. 5556, pp. 43–54. Springer, Heidelberg (2009). https://doi.org/10.1007/978-3-642-02930-1_4
18. Saeedloei, N., Kluźniak, F.: Optimization of timed scenarios. In: G. Carvalho, V. Stolz (Eds.), Formal Methods: Foundations and Applications - 23rd Brazilian Symposium, SBMF 2020, Ouro Preto, Brazil, November 25-27, 2020, Proceedings, Vol. 12475 of Lecture Notes in Computer Science, Springer, pp. 119–136 (2020) https://doi.org/10.1007/978-3-031-22476-8
19. Dill, D.L.: Timing assumptions and verification of finite-state concurrent systems. In: Sifakis, J. (ed.) CAV 1989. LNCS, vol. 407, pp. 197–212. Springer, Heidelberg (1990). https://doi.org/10.1007/3-540-52148-8_17
20. Saeedloei, N., Kluźniak, F.: Observations about timed scenarios. https://tigerweb.towson.edu/nsaeedloei/Observations.pdf
21. Saeedloei, N., Kluźniak, F.: Clock allocation in timed automata and graph colouring. In: Proceedings of the 21st International Conference on Hybrid Systems: Computation and Control (part of CPS Week), HSCC 2018, pp. 71–80. https://doi.org/10.1145/3178126.3178138
22. N. Saeedloei, F. Kluźniak, Synthesizing clock-efficient timed automata, in: B. Dongol, E. Troubitsyna (Eds.), Integrated Formal Methods - 16th International Conference, IFM 2020, Lugano, Switzerland, November 16-20, 2020, Proceedings, Vol. 12546 of Lecture Notes in Computer Science, Springer, 2020, pp. 276–294. https://doi.org/10.1007/978-3-031-07727-2

Formally Verifying a Rollback-Prevention Protocol for TEEs

Weili Wang[1], Jianyu Niu[1], Michael K. Reiter[2], and Yinqian Zhang[1]($\boxtimes$)

[1] Research Institute of Trustworthy Autonomous Systems and Department
of Computer Science and Engineering, Southern University of Science
and Technology, Shenzhen, China
12032870@mail.sustech.edu.cn, niujy@sustech.edu.cn, yinqianz@acm.org
[2] Duke University, Durham, NC, USA
michael.reiter@duke.edu

Abstract. Formal verification of distributed protocols is challenging and usually requires great human effort. Ivy, a state-of-the-art formal verification tool for modeling and verifying distributed protocols, automates this tedious process by leveraging a decidable fragment of first-order logic. Observing the successful adoption of Ivy for verifying consensus protocols, we examine its practicality in verifying rollback-prevention protocols for Trusted Execution Environments (TEEs). TEEs suffer from rollback attacks, which can revert confidential applications' states to stale ones to compromise security. Recently, designing distributed protocols to prevent rollback attacks has attracted significant attention. However, the lack of formal verification of these protocols leaves them potentially vulnerable to security breaches. In this paper, we leverage Ivy to formally verify a rollback-prevention protocol, namely the TIKS protocol in ENGRAFT (Wang *et al.*, CCS 2022). We select TIKS because it is similar to other rollback-prevention protocols and is self-contained. We detail the verification process of using Ivy to prove a rollback-prevention protocol, present lessons learned from this exploration, and release the proof code to facilitate future research (https://github.com/wwl020/TIKS-Proof-in-Ivy). To the best of our knowledge, this is the first endeavor to explain the formal verification of a rollback-prevention protocol in detail.

Keywords: Formal verification · Rollback attacks · Trusted execution environments (TEEs)

1 Introduction

The intricate nature of distributed systems makes it challenging to prove their correctness. Errors in manual proofs [2] of well-known consensus protocols have already demonstrated the difficulty of this reasoning. Given this challenge, researchers tend to leverage formal verification tools such as Coq [1], TLAPS [3], and Dafny [23], to develop more reliable machine-checked proofs. Unfortunately, applying these tools to distributed protocols usually requires tremendous human

© IFIP International Federation for Information Processing 2024
Published by Springer Nature Switzerland AG 2024
V. Castiglioni and A. Francalanza (Eds.): FORTE 2024, LNCS 14678, pp. 155–173, 2024.
https://doi.org/10.1007/978-3-031-62645-6_9

effort. For instance, the Raft proof [38] written in Coq contains approximately 50,000 lines of code (a proof-to-code ratio of 10), and the development of a state machine replication library (IronFleet [13]) in Dafny took 3.7 person-years. This daunting proof effort greatly limits the practicality of these verification tools.

Padon *et al.* [28] Ivy, a new verification tool that uses decidable logic. Protocol designers need to express their protocols in a decidable fragment and figure out inductive invariants to prove the safety of the protocols. To ease this tedious, error-prone process, Ivy will showcase counterexamples to decidability and invariance. Once the protocol is well expressed, Ivy can highly automate the verification process by generating verification conditions and leveraging the SMT solver to check their satisfiability. In this way, Ivy sacrifices the protocol description's expressiveness to reduce the verification process's complexity. Witnessing the success of Ivy in verifying distributed protocols [8,27,35] with much less human effort, we were curious whether Ivy could be used to verify rollback-prevention protocols that ensure state continuity in Trusted Execution Environments (TEEs).

TEEs such as Intel SGX [14], AMD SEV [5] and ARM CCA [7], have revolutionized the field of confidential computing, enabling the execution of sensitive operations within secure and isolated environments called enclaves. TEEs provide a hardware-based foundation for confidential computation, safeguarding the confidentiality and integrity of sensitive data. However, the presence of rollback vulnerabilities can compromise the security of TEEs and render them susceptible to unauthorized access or manipulation. In a rollback attack, an adversary rolls back the application's state to a previous one, thereby potentially bypassing security measures or gaining unauthorized control. The impact of a successful rollback attack can be severe in real-world scenarios. For example, rollback attacks can break the safety of a TEE-guarded consensus protocol [36].

To address this issue, various rollback-prevention systems have recently been proposed. Prominent examples include ROTE [25], TIKS [36], Narrator [26] TEEMS [11], and Narrator-Pro [29], which, despite their innovative approaches to rollback prevention, have not undergone rigorous formal verification for their security claims. Although the core protocol of Nimble [6], a recently proposed rollback-prevention system, has been claimed to be formally verified, there are few explanations of the verification process, which leaves a gap in understanding the verification.

In this paper, we present the formal verification of TIKS (**T**rustworthy distributed **I**n-memory **K**ey-value **S**torage), a rollback-prevention protocol by Wang *et al.* [36], using Ivy. We provide comprehensive details and insights into the specific techniques and methodologies employed in formally verifying TIKS. We study the formal verification of TIKS for several reasons. A series of rollback-prevention protocols, including ROTE [25], Narrator [26] and TIKS [36], share a common core, *i.e.*, a customized echo broadcast protocol [30]. Both TIKS and Narrator improve ROTE by directly storing states instead of monotonic counters. However, TIKS is self-contained and does not rely on external components, whereas Narrator relies on a blockchain. Therefore, TIKS is a more suitable candidate to represent these rollback-prevention protocols, and its verification can serve as a foundation for verifying other protocols. In verifying TIKS, we specifically aim to address the following research questions.

- **R1**: Is there a difference between the verification of rollback-prevention protocols and other distributed protocols?
- **R2**: What type of simplification is necessary to facilitate the verification of rollback-prevention protocols?
- **R3**: What is the user experience of using Ivy to verify rollback-prevention protocols?

We expressed TIKS in Ivy and attempted to verify it directly. There are two highly correlated challenges in this process. First, Ivy's decidability restriction limits the expressiveness of the protocol description. Second, finding proper invariants to eliminate spurious counterexamples becomes more difficult under the decidability restriction. To address these challenges, we developed reasonable simplifications to the TIKS protocol. First, we simplified the state retrieval by making the recovering node directly read other node's states. Second, we reversed the recovery steps to defer the recovering node's state reconstruction. With these simplifications, we obtained a proof that does not lie inside the decidable fragment but generates solvable verification conditions and thus we can verify it in Ivy. As TIKS shares similar core components with other rollback-prevention protocols [25, 26], we believe that our proof strategy can be generalized to other rollback-prevention protocols to facilitate their formal verification.

Contributions. Our contributions are summarized below:

- We present a step-by-step verification of the TIKS protocol in Ivy. As far as we know, this is the first endeavor to formally verify a rollback protocol in Ivy, with detailed explanation of such procedure.
- We showcase the essential protocol simplifications that make the protocol verifiable in Ivy, without affecting the core workflow of the protocol. This strategy can be generalized to other rollback-prevention protocols.
- We demonstrate the practicality of Ivy in verifying rollback-prevention protocols, paving the way for the formal verification of other similar systems.

2   Background

2.1   Rollback Attacks on TEEs

A rollback attack occurs when an adversary reverts the execution of an application by rolling back its state to a previous version. For instance, the enclave first persists state s_1 (at time t_1), followed by the state s_2 (at time t_2). At a later time t_3, the enclave needs to retrieve the newest state, possibly due to a crash. However, since the adversary controls the external storage, it can manipulate the system and provide the enclave with a stale state s_1, without being detected. As a result, the victim enclave will load s_1 and revert its execution to s_1 instead of continuing from s_2.

In reality, rollback attacks pose a significant threat to many confidential applications. Consider the case of password guessing. To prevent brute-force attacks, an application will record the number of failed login attempts and lock the account when the number exceeds a threshold. However, if the adversary can roll back the state of the application, it can bypass the protection mechanism by reverting the number of failed login attempts to a previous value, thus conducting brute-force attacks without being detected.

2.2   Formal Verification Tools

Coq [1] is an interactive theorem prover that allows users to use higher-order logic reasoning to build proofs. TLAPS [3] is a theorem prover designed for TLA+ [20], a formal specification language for modeling and validating programs. Dafny [23] is a verification-aware imperative language allowing users to write Hoare-style protocol invariants and verify the correctness with Z3 solver [4].

The aforementioned verification tools generally require great human effort. To deal with this issue, Padon *et al.* [28] leverage a decidable fragment of first-order logic to build Ivy, a verification framework that highly automates the verification process. Ivy users first express their protocols in pure first-logic and then restrict protocol descriptions to a decidable fragment. In this process, Ivy will constantly showcase counterexamples to decidability, helping users to refine protocol descriptions. After that, Ivy will generate verification conditions and leverage its SMT solver (Z3) to check the correctness. Since the generated verification conditions are in the decidable fragment, they can be discharged by the solver in finite time and thus provide timely feedback to the designers. In contrast, other tools leveraging SMT solvers (*e.g.*, Dafny) may generate undecidable verification conditions and may take an infinite amount of time to solve.

2.3   Preliminary Knowledge of Ivy

Decidable Logic. Ivy adopts Effectively Propositional Logic (EPR), a decidable fragment of first-order logic, to represent distributed protocols. A logic formula is an EPR fragment if it has a prenex normal form of $\exists X_1, X_2, ..., X_N,$ $\forall Y_1, Y_2, ..., Y_M. \ P(X_1, ..., X_N, Y_1, ..., Y_M)$, where the predicate P does not contain function symbols except the acyclic (stratified) ones. Acyclic function symbols are functions that do not have cycles in their definition. For instance, a function that maps from sort s_1 to sort s_2 and a function that maps from sort s_2 to sort s_1 are considered cyclic, and therefore not permitted in EPR.

Ivy requires users to express their protocols in EPR fragment and then Ivy will generate decidable verification conditions and leverage its SMT solver (Z3) to check their satisfiability. However, successful proofs in Ivy do not necessarily lie in the decidable fragment. Ivy supports undecidable logic fragments to express complex protocols that are not easy to represent in EPR, although undecidable verification conditions burden the SMT solver and may take an infinite amount of time to solve.

Actions. Ivy models protocol procedures as isolated actions that operate on protocol states. Similar to functions in conventional programming languages, Ivy actions also have input arguments. Actions can be invoked by other actions or the environment. Ivy uses the "export" keyword to mark an action exported, which then can be called by the environment. Although an action can be invoked inside another action, Ivy does not support recursive action calls. To simplify the concurrency reasoning, actions execute atomically without any interruption. In other words, Ivy uses the interleaving model to model concurrency—the environment can call actions in an arbitrary order and thus sequentially executed actions actually model arbitrary interleaving of protocol procedures.

Inductive Invariants. To specify the safety property of a protocol, users have the option to write assertions in the form of preconditions (using the "require" keyword) and postconditions (using the "ensure" keyword) within an action. However, in a more general sense, users should construct inductive invariants that imply the safety of the protocol being verified. These invariants must hold after the initialization phase. Moreover, Ivy checks whether the invariants hold at the beginning of an action and whether they are preserved after the execution.

3   TIKS Recap

TIKS establishes a distributed in-memory key-value (KV) storage abstraction that provides rollback protection. Each TIKS node maintains one in-memory KV store and a TIKS cluster consists of $2f + 1$ nodes, where f is the maximum number of nodes hosted on malicious hosts. Malicious nodes can drop, duplicate, and reorder network messages, as well as crash. States requiring freshness guarantees (*i.e.*, crucial states that cannot be rolled back) are stored in TIKS as key-value items. For a KV item $\langle key, value \rangle$, key uniquely identifies the state, whereas $value$ contains the state and a monotonic index indicating the version. As such, $value$ is represented as a 2-tuple: $\langle index, state \rangle$. The key of a state usually begins with the ID of the node that owns the state and ends with the state name. For example, when node A stores its states named s_1 and s_2 in TIKS, the keys of these states are A_s_1 and A_s_2, respectively.

To offer rollback protection, *i.e.*, ensuring successfully stored KV items will not be overwritten by older versions, TIKS involves a storage update sub-protocol and a storage recovery sub-protocol. We briefly introduce these two sub-protocols below and refer the readers to its original description [36] for more details.

3.1   Storage Update

TIKS use a two-round communication process to enable a node to persist states with freshness in the cluster. Whenever a node wants to update a KV item, it first updates its own KV store and then issues `Store` and `ConfirmStore` remote procedure calls (RPCs) to other nodes to update their KV stores. Figure 1 illustrates this workflow. In this three-node cluster, Node A successfully updates its KV store after collecting f `Store` responses and f `ConfirmStore` responses from other nodes.

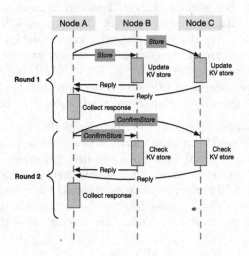

Fig. 1. Workflow of storage update in TIKS.

The First Round. The updating node first updates the KV item in its KV store, and then broadcasts `Store` RPCs. A `Store` request encapsulates the key of the to-be-updated state and its value. A benign node receiving such request will update its KV store accordingly if the index of the received state is larger than the index of the one in its own KV store, and then reply with a boolean value to indicate the update status. With at least f responses, there is a majority of nodes (including the updating node itself) that have successfully updated their KV stores, and thus the updating node passes the first round. Otherwise, the updating node continues to broadcast `Store` RPCs until it collects at least f responses from other nodes.

The Second Round. After passing the first round, the updating node then issues `ConfirmStore` requests with the same content as the `Store` requests, to the nodes having responded to the first-round requests. When receiving a `ConfirmStore` request, a benign node will reply with a success value if it meets two conditions. First, it must have responded to the corresponding `Store` request. Second, its KV store must contain an item that is identical to the one in the `ConfirmStore` request. If these conditions are not met, the benign node will simply ignore the request. If the updating node collects at least f responses in the second round, it can ensure that the state has been securely stored in TIKS. Otherwise, the updating node fails to update the state and must retry.

3.2 Storage Recovery

A TIKS node maintains an in-memory KV store, and thus it needs to recover its KV store from others after crashes, following steps below.

Inquiry. The crashed node broadcasts `RetrieveStorage` requests until it has successfully collected at least $f + 1$ responses from other nodes. A benign node receiving such a request will reply with all KV items in its KV store.

Reconstruction. By collecting $f+1$ KV stores from the alive nodes, the crashed node can recover the newest KV items. Specifically, the crashed node first reconstructs its own KV store. As TIKS uses a monotonic index to indicate the version of a state, the crashed node picks the one with the largest index among the received KV stores for each KV item. Then, the crashed node writes its own states back to the cluster using `Store` and `ConfirmStore` RPCs.

The use of a monotonic index in an alive node's aborted storage update requests may cause trouble in its later recovery as one index may be used by multiple states, which is termed as an index conflict. For instance, a node that has successfully stored $state_6$ at index 6 may crash during the process of storing the newer version (denoted as $state_7$) at index 7. In the recovery, the node may not observe $state_7$ and restore $state_6$ as $state_7$ has not been successfully stored. Later, the node may crash again when storing a different version (denoted as $state'_7$) at index 7. In this case, during recovery, the node may observe $state_7$ and $state'_7$ with the same index 7 and cannot decide which one to keep. By design, TIKS does not handle index conflicts and defers the resolution to the application layer. The application layer can randomly choose the state with the largest index or adopt other strategies to resolve conflicts. For example, ENGRAFT [36] uses the Raft leader to decide which state to keep.

4 Proof

A TIKS KV item has a structure of $\langle key, \langle index, state \rangle \rangle$. Inside the value tuple, *index* tracks the version of *state*, and the state with the largest index is the latest. As explained in Sect. 3.2, standalone TIKS protocol does not handle index conflicts and leaves it to the application layer. Consequently, the *state* field is irrelevant to rollback reasoning and we remove it in the proof. Moreover, storing nodes' multiple states (these states have different keys) in one KV store is equivalent to storing their states in multiple separate KV stores, each of which contains states with the same key. As such, we assume that each node only has one state and uses its node ID as the key. A KV item in the proof has this structure: $\langle nodeID, index \rangle$.

TIKS nodes hosted on malicious hosts cannot deviate from the protocol, but they still can drop, duplicate, and reorder network messages, as well as crash at any time. These threats are modeled in the proof.

Next, we report the attempt of using Ivy to formally prove the safety property of TIKS, *i.e.*, a TIKS node can obtain its own state ($\langle index \rangle$) maintained in the TIKS cluster when recovering from crashes.

4.1   Types and Functions

Uninterpreted Types. We do not need to represent the exact meaning of different types. For instance, we just need a type declaration of nodes when reasoning protocol participants. We use *node, quorum, index,* and *nonce* types.

The node type is used to represent a single TIKS node, while the quorum type is used to represent a majority of nodes (*i.e.*, at least $f + 1$ nodes). As Ivy does not support the mix of arithmetic reasoning and EPR, we cannot directly define the quorum type by checking the cardinality of node sets. Instead, the quorum concept in Ivy is modeled using an axiom that indicates quorum intersection [27]. First, we use a relation to reason whether a node is in a quorum: `relation member (N:node, Q:quorum)` (identifiers beginning with capital letters like "N" and "Q" are placeholders in Ivy). When member (n1, q1) is true, node n1 is in the quorum q1. Second, we define an axiom to reason quorum intersection: `axiom forall Q1:quorum, Q2:quorum. exists N:node. member (N, Q1) & member(N, Q2)`. With this reasoning, the quorum type can be used to represent a majority of nodes.

The index type is used to represent the index of a KV item $\langle nodeID, index \rangle$. In the implementation, indexes should be interpreted as integers. However, we do not need this integer interpretation and related arithmetic operations in the proof—we just need to ensure that we can compare two indexes (*i.e.*, the total order property). Ivy's built-in order library provides a module that defines unbounded sequence (0 is the minimum value), which basically establishes a total order on the type. As such, we define the index type as an instantiation of this module: `instance index: unbounded_sequence`.

Similar to the index type, the nonce type is also an instantiation of the unbounded sequence module. In our implementation, a node recovered from a crash will re-establish TLS connections with other nodes in the cluster, which enables the recovered node to distinguish its own messages sent from previous incarnations. To model this in the proof, we assign each node a nonce that is incremented after each recovery and make each sent message contain the sender's nonce.

Defined Functions. Ivy functions can be evaluated on arguments to produce deterministic results, and we use them to model partial states of a node. We define three functions to represent states that only have one value per node: n_committed_index records the largest index that a node has successfully written; n_recovered_index records the largest index that a node has successfully retrieved from the cluster in recovery; and n_nonce records the nonce of a node.

4.2   Relations

In the proof, we use relations to model KV stores, network messages, and crashes.

KV-Store Representation. To represent a node's KV store, we define: `relation n_tiks_states (N0:node, N:node, I:index)`. For example, when node n0 stores the KV item $\langle n1, i1 \rangle$ for node n1, n_tiks_states(n0,n1,i1) should be true.

Network Messages. As listed in Listing 1.1, m_store_req and m_store_resp relations denote the requests and responses of **Store** RPC. For example, when node n0 with nonce no0 wants to update its index to i1 and broadcasts **Store** requests, m_store_req(n0,no0,i1) will be set to true; when node n1 with nonce no1 receives the request and replies to node n0, m_store_resp(n1,no1,n0,no0,i1) will be set to true. Similarly, the m_confirm_store_req and m_confirm_store_resp relations represent the requests and responses of **ConfirmStore** RPC. The **RetrieveStorage** RPC is modeled using m_recover_req and m_recover_resp relations. m_recover_req(n0,no0) is set to true when the recovering node n0 with nonce no0 broadcasts **RetrieveStorage** requests. An alive node n1 with nonce no1 replying to the request will set m_recover_resp(n1,no1,n0,no0,n,i) to true if it contains an item $\langle n, i \rangle$ in its KV store (*i.e.*, n_tiks_states(n1,n,i) is true).

The above relation-based network reasoning follows the approach of the Paxos proof written in Ivy [27] and models an abstracted network layer that allows message dropping, duplication, and reordering.

Listing 1.1. Relation-based network messages representation

```
1     # Sender, sender's nonce, index
2     relation m_store_req(S:node, NO:nonce, I:index)
3     # Sender, sender's nonce, dest, dest's nonce, index
4     relation m_store_resp(S:node, SNO:nonce, D:node, DNO:nonce, I:index)
5     # Sender, sender's nonce, index
6     relation m_confirm_store_req(S:node, NO:nonce, I:index)
7     # Sender, sender's nonce, dest, dest's nonce, index
8     relation m_confirm_store_resp(S:node, SNO:nonce, D:node, DNO:nonce, I:index)
9     # Sender, sender's nonce
10    relation m_recover_req(S:node, NO:nonce)
11    # Sender, sender's nonce, dest, dest's nonce, (N, I) means n_tiks_states(S, N, I)
      ↪ holds
12    relation m_recover_resp(S:node, SNO:nonce, D:node, DNO:nonce, N:node, I:index)
```

Crash Representation. We use a relation to record node crashes: relation crash(N:node). If node n0 is crashed, crash(n0) is set to true. To ensure the presence of a majority of alive nodes, we then define an inductive invariant: invariant ~(exists Q:quorum. forall N:node. member(N, Q) -> crash(N)). Similarly, we use relation recovering(N:node) to record whether a node is recovering. A recovering node must be crashed, and thus we have: invariant forall N:node. recovering(N) -> crash(N).

4.3   Actions

Initialization. In the verification, Ivy first checks whether a program's initialization satisfies the inductive invariants. This initialization is defined using the after init keyword. The initialization action mainly sets relations to false as there are no messages and crashed nodes in the beginning.

Two-Round Communication. The first round involves the send_store action (Listing 1.2) that broadcasts `Store` requests, and the reply_store action (Listing 1.3) that processes a `Store` request. The second round involves the send_confirm_store action (Listing 1.4) broadcasting `ConfirmStore` requests, the reply_confirm_store action (Listing 1.5) handling a `ConfirmStore` request, and the store_success action (Listing 1.6) that updates a node's written index. The common precondition of these actions is that the node is not crashed.

send_store action. The preconditions require the to-be-written index is larger than the node's largest successfully written index appearing in `written_index`. The node first updates its KV store (Line 4 in Listing 1.2), broadcasts `Store` requests (Line 5) and finally replies to itself (Line 6).

Listing 1.2. The send_store action

```
1  action send_store(n:node, i:index) = {
2      require ~crash(n);
3      require i > n_committed_index(n);
4      n_tiks_states(n, n, i) := true;
5      m_store_req(n, n_nonce(n), i) := true;
6      m_store_resp(n, n_nonce(n), n, n_nonce(n), i) := true;
7  }
```

reply_store action. The preconditions require the requesting node has broadcasted `Store` requests. The responder updates its KV store per the request (Line 5 in Listing 1.3, recall that the capital letter "I" means a placeholder). In this update, the responder only updates the KV store if the index is larger than the current index (`if I <= i`); otherwise, it keeps the current state (`else n_tiks_states(n0, n, I)`). After updating the KV store, the responder sends replies to the requester (Line 6).

Listing 1.3. The reply_store action

```
1  action reply_store(n0:node, n:node, i:index) = {
2      require ~crash(n0);
3      require exists NO:nonce. m_store_req(n, NO, i);
4      require n0 ~= n;
5      n_tiks_states(n0, n, I) := true if I <= i else n_tiks_states(n0, n, I);
6      m_store_resp(n0, n_nonce(n0), n, n_nonce(n), i):= true;
7  }
```

send_confirm_store action. Before broadcasting `ConfirmStore` requests, the node in this action first ensures that it has received a majority of `Store` responses. We enforce this requirement via a precondition (Line 8 in Listing 1.4).

Listing 1.4. The send_confirm_store action

```
1   action send_confirm_store(n:node, i:index, q:quorum) = {
2       require ~crash(n);
3       require n_tiks_states(n, n, i);
4       require i > n_committed_index(n);
5       require m_store_req(n, n_nonce(n), i);
6       require m_store_resp(n, n_nonce(n), n, n_nonce(n), i);
7       # Pass the first round
8       require forall N:node. member(N, q) -> m_store_resp(N, n_nonce(N), n, n_nonce(n), i
           ↪ );
9       m_confirm_store_req(n, n_nonce(n), i) := true;
10      m_confirm_store_resp(n, n_nonce(n), n, n_nonce(n), i) := true;
11  }
```

reply_confirm_store action. The preconditions not only require the requesting node has broadcasted `ConfirmStore` requests but also ensure that the receiving node has stored the to-be-written index and responded to the `Store` RPC (Line 4 in Listing 1.5). The receiving node then replies to the requester (Line 6).

Listing 1.5. The reply_confirm_store action

```
1  action reply_confirm_store(n0:node, n:node, i:index) = {
2      require ~crash(n);
3      require exists NO:nonce. m_store_req(n, NO, i) & m_confirm_store_req(n,NO,i);
4      require m_store_resp(n0, n_nonce(n0), n, n_nonce(n),i);
5      require n0 ~= n;
6      m_confirm_store_resp(n0, n_nonce(n0), n, n_nonce(n), i) := true if n_tiks_states(n0
            ↪ , n, i) else m_confirm_store_resp(n0, n_nonce(n0), n, n_nonce(n), i);
7  }
```

store_success action. The preconditions require the node has received a majority of `ConfirmStore` responses. The node then updates its written index.

Listing 1.6. The store_success action

```
1   action store_success(n:node, i:index, q:quorum) = {
2       require ~crash(n);
3       require i > n_committed_index(n);
4       require n_tiks_states(n, n, i);
5       require m_store_req(n, n_nonce(n), i) & m_confirm_store_req(n, n_nonce(n), i);
6       # Pass the first and second round
7       require forall N:node. member(N, q) -> m_confirm_store_resp(N, n_nonce(N), n,
            ↪ n_nonce(n), i) & m_store_resp(N, n_nonce(N), n, n_nonce(n), i);
8       n_committed_index(n) := i;
9       n_recovered_index(n) := i;
10  }
```

Crash Modeling. We model the crash and recovery using eight actions. These actions include one action for crashing the node (node_crash) and seven actions for the recovery process (nonce_increase, send_recover_req, send_recover_resp, node_recover, rec_send_store, rec_send_confirm_store, and rec_store_success). The nonce_increase action and the rec_send_store action are only invoked in recovery actions and thus are not exported.

The nonce_increase action increases the recovering node's nonce. It first updates the nonce, and then clears all messages corresponding to the new nonce.

In the crash action shown in Listing 1.7, the precondition requires that only alive nodes can be crashed. A node is marked as crashed (`crash(n) := true`) if its crash does not result in a quorum with all crashed nodes. Recall that we model a set of at least $f+1$ nodes as a quorum type, and thus a quorum with all crashed nodes means there are at least $f+1$ crashed nodes, which contradicts the threat model that at most f nodes can crash.

Listing 1.7. The node_crash action

```
1  action node_crash(n:node) = {
2      require ~crash(n);
3      crash(n) := true;
4      if exists Q:quorum. forall N:node. member(N, Q) -> crash(N) {
5          crash(n) := false;
6      } else { }
7  }
```

The recovery begins with the send_recover_req action (Listing 1.8) where the recovering node increases its nonce and broadcasts `RetrieveStorage` requests. Alive nodes receiving such requests will reply with their KV stores as shown in the send_recover_resp action (Listing 1.9).

Listing 1.8. The send_recover_req action and

```
1   action send_recover_req(n:node) = {
2       require crash(n);
3       call nonce_increase(n);
4       recovering(n) := true;
5       m_recover_req(n, n_nonce(n)) := true;
6   }
```

Listing 1.9. The send_recover_resp action

```
1   action send_recover_resp(n0:node, n:node) = {
2       require ~crash(n0);
3       require m_recover_req(n, n_nonce(n));
4       require n0 ~= n;
5       m_recover_resp(n0, n_nonce(n0), n, n_nonce(n), N, I) := true if n_tiks_states(n0, N
            ↪ , I) else n_tiks_states(n0, N, I);
6   }
```

Listing 1.10 displays the node_recover action. A recovering node that has collected a majority of `RetrieveStorage` RPC responses will reconstruct its KV store and start writing back its index by invoking the rec_send_store action. The rollback-prevention is represented as a postcondition stating that a recovered node will retrieve an index not smaller than its written index right before the crash. We omit the rec_send_store, rec_send_confirm_store, and rec_store_success actions as they are similar to actions used to write an index via the two-round communication. In the rec_store_success action, the recovering node finishes the write-back operation and finally finishes the recovery.

Listing 1.10. The node_recover action

```
1    action node_recover(n:node, q:quorum, retrieved_i:index)={
2        require crash(n) & recovering(n);
3        require m_recover_req(n, n_nonce(n));
4        require forall N:node. ~member(n, q) & member(N, q) -> ~crash(N);
5        # Receive responses from the quorum
6        require forall N:node. member(N, q) -> exists I:index. m_recover_resp(N,n_nonce(N),
             ↪ n,n_nonce(n),N,I);
7        require forall S:node, I:index. m_recover_resp(S, n_nonce(S), n, n_nonce(n), n, I)
             ↪ -> I <= retrieved_i;
8        require exists N:node. member(N, q) & m_recover_resp(N, n_nonce(N), n, n_nonce(n),
             ↪ n, retrieved_i);
9        # Check rollback prevention
10       ensure n_committed_index(n) <= retrieved_i;
11       n_recovered_index(n) := retrieved_i;
12       # KV-store reconstruction
13       n_tiks_states(n, N, I) := false;
14       n_tiks_states(n, N, I) := true if (exists N0:node. member(N0, q) & m_recover_resp(
             ↪ N0, n_nonce(N0), n, n_nonce(n), N, I)) else n_tiks_states(n,N,I);
15       n_tiks_states(n, n, I) := true if I <= retrieved_i else n_tiks_states(n,n,I);
16       call rec_send_store(n);
17   }
```

4.4   Inductive Invariants

Listing 1.11 lists all used invariants in the proof. Most of them are described before or self-explanatory and thus we only explain the invariant with "safety" notation. Recall that we aim to prove that a TIKS node can obtain its own state ($\langle index \rangle$) maintained in the TIKS cluster when recovering from crashes. The safety invariant depicts this property: if an updating node N successfully writes its index I to the cluster and there is a quorum Q that does not consist of crashed nodes, then in quorum Q, there exists a node N0 storing the index I for node N. Note that a recovering node can retrieve states from a quorum containing alive nodes only, and thus the safety invariant actually states that the recovering node can obtain its own state from the quorum.

Listing 1.11. Inductive invariants

```
1   invariant ~(exists Q:quorum. forall N:node. member(N, Q) -> crash(N))
2   invariant [safety] forall N:node, Q:quorum. exists N1:node. ~(exists N0:node. member(N0
      ↪ , Q) & crash(N0)) -> member(N1, Q) & n_tiks_states(N1, N, n_committed_index(N
      ↪ ))
3   invariant m_confirm_store_resp(S, n_nonce(S), D, n_nonce(D), I) -> m_store_resp(S,
      ↪ n_nonce(S),D,n_nonce(D),I)
4   invariant m_store_resp(S, n_nonce(S), D, n_nonce(D), I) -> n_tiks_states(S, D, I)
5   invariant n_recovered_index(N) >= n_committed_index(N)
6   invariant forall I:index, N:node. I = n_committed_index(N) -> n_tiks_states(N,N,I)
7   invariant recovering(N) -> crash(N)
8   invariant recovering(N) & D ~= N -> ~m_store_resp(N, n_nonce(N), D, n_nonce(D), I)
9   invariant recovering(N) & I ~= n_recovered_index(N) -> ~m_store_resp(N, n_nonce(N), N,
      ↪ n_nonce(N), I)
10  invariant recovering(N) & D ~= N -> ~m_confirm_store_resp(N, n_nonce(N), D, n_nonce(D),
      ↪ I)
```

5   Protocol Simplifications

A successful Ivy proof mandates solvable verification conditions that can be solved by an SMT solver in finite time, and inductive invariants that imply the safety property. Without correct inductive invariants restricting the reachable states, Ivy will report spuriously unsafe states as counterexamples and fail the proof. In verification practice, finding inductive invariants for distributed protocols is a tedious and error-prone process [10,12,39]. We also encounter this challenge in the verification of the TIKS protocol, and Ivy's use of decidable logic fragment makes it even harder to represent the invariants—writing complex invariants usually leads to undecidable verification conditions.

Actually, making the proof decidable is the most challenging task throughout the verification. Protocol description and invariants easily introduce quantifier alternations [28] that result in undecidable verification conditions. Although Ivy developers propose approaches such as "derived relation" [27] and "relational abstraction" [34] to mitigate this issue, we find that their adoption in TIKS protocol is not straightforward and we cannot find a way to make the proof decidable. Fortunately, undecidable verification conditions are not necessarily unsolvable. We then turn to seek proper simplifications on the protocol to make the verification conditions solvable while preserving the core workflow of TIKS.

5.1 Simplified State Retrieval

Modeling the `RetrieveStorage` using m_recover_req and m_recover_resp relations fails the proof as the `RetrieveStorage` responses represented by m_recover_resp may not capture the KV store of the responding node at the time when it receives the `RetrieveStorage` request. We introduce the counterexample reported by Ivy below. Node 0 with the committed index 1 and nonce 1 is recovering (*i.e.*, m_recover_req(0,1) is true), and an alive node 1 with nonce 0 receives the `RetrieveStorage` request from node 0. Although node 1 has stored index 1 for node 0 (*i.e.*, n_tiks_states(1,0,1) is true), it does not reply to node 0 with this information (*i.e.*, m_recover_resp(1,0,0,1,0,1) is false). As such, in the node_recover action, node 0 cannot retrieve its latest index 1 and the proof fails. Using an invariant establishing the correspondence between m_recover_resp and n_tiks_states relations may help to eliminate this spurious counterexample. Ideally, this invariant should state that the KV store in a `RetrieveStorage` response is the same as the KV store of the responding node at the time when it receives the request. However, this reasoning involves storing KV-store histories of nodes, which makes the proof more complex and unverifiable in Ivy.

To facilitate the proof, we then simplify the recovery process by removing the `RetrieveStorage` RPC—a recovering node directly reads a majority of nodes' KV stores and then reconstructs its own KV store without broadcasting `RetrieveStorage` RPCs. As such, relations (m_recover_req and m_recover_resp) and actions (send_recover_resp and node_recover) related to the `RetrieveStorage` RPC are removed, and the node_recover_resp action is modified to directly read the KV stores of the responding nodes.

5.2 Reversed Recover Steps

In TIKS recovery, KV-store reconstruction and write-back operation are two separate steps and the finish of the latter step marks the end of recovery. A faithful modeling of this "reconstruct then write back" process yields a bogus counterexample. The counterexample shows that a recovering node having reconstructed its KV store can "forget" the reconstruction result at the time when it finishes the write-back operation, resulting a recovered node with stale KV store. Finding an invariant stating the "reconstruct then write back" order helps to eliminate this bogus counterexample but doing this in an undecidable logic fragment is more challenging, as the underlying SMT solver may be stuck for a long time. In practice, we simplify this process by reversing the order of the reconstruction and write-back steps.

As the write-back operation involves separate actions that conduct two-round communication, it is impossible to model the "reconstruct then write back" process in a single action. Instead, we reverse the order of these two steps, *i.e.*, following the "write back then reconstruct" order. When a recovering node successfully writes its retrieved index back, it then reconstructs its KV store from a majority of nodes. As such, the finish of the write-back operation and store reconstruction can occur atomically and the invariant stating the order of these two steps is no longer necessary.

This reversed order does not deviate from the original TIKS protocol much, as putting reconstruction at the end of recovery also ensures that the recovered node has the latest KV store.

5.3 Proof Result

The above simplifications eases the invariant finding task while still preserving the core workflow of the TIKS protocol. Although the resulted proof does not fit in the decidable fragment of Ivy, its verification conditions can be discharged by Z3 in a reasonable time. It is important to note that in Ivy, a proof is considered successful regardless of whether it lies within the decidable fragment. Undecidable proofs can be established as long as the SMT solver is able to solve the verification conditions within a finite amount of time.

On a machine with Intel Core i7-10700 CPU and 32 GB RAM, Ivy takes 30 s to verify the protocol. In comparison, Ivy takes 2.8 s to verify the Multi-Paxos protocol [35]. The increased verification time is expected. First, the TIKS proof involves crash and recovery modeling that is not present in the Multi-Paxos proof and thus is more complex. Second, the TIKS proof involves undecidable verification conditions that bring more workload to the SMT solver.

6 Lessons Learned

In the verification, we obtain the following answers to our research questions:

- **R1 Answer**: Verification techniques from other distributed protocols can be applied to verify TIKS, such as relation-based message modeling and quorum reasoning. However, the verification of TIKS introduces new challenges, including modeling the recovery algorithm and representing the rollback-prevention property. These complexities make the proof construction lie outside the decidable fragment of Ivy. Our proof provides insights into the differences between verifying rollback-prevention protocols and other distributed protocols in Ivy.
- **R2 Answer**: We simplify the recovery process of TIKS to facilitate the verification, by making the recovering node directly read other node's states and deferring the recovering node's state reconstruction. Our exploration demonstrates that careful simplifications will not affect the core workflow of the protocol and can facilitate the verification greatly.
- **R3 Answer**: In verifying TIKS, we find that writing a proof in Ivy is straightforward, but making the proof decidable and establishing proper invariants are challenging. Although Ivy offers an interactive way (*i.e.*, reporting counterexamples) for users to find invariants, it is not easy to use in practice. First, expressing the protocol in a decidable fragment not only results in much human effort but also makes the proof less intuitive, which is not user-friendly.

Second, a user that turns to undecidable logic to express protocol actions and invariants cannot receive timely feedback from Ivy to refine their invariants, and thus may spend a great amount of time in finding proper invariants. From our experience, using Ivy does not necessarily make the proof easier than previous approaches. Although users write much less code in Ivy, they have to spend much more time in making the proof decidable with proper invariants.

7   Related Work

Formal Verification of Distributed Systems. Numerous works leverage formal verification tools introduced in Sect. 2.2 to verify distributed systems. Verdi [37] is a Coq-based framework for implementing and verifying state machine replication algorithms like Raft [37,38]. Disel is another Coq-based framework that allows the implementation and safety verification of distributed systems in a modular way [32]. TLAPS has been widely used to prove the safety of distributed protocols including Paxos protocol [9,22], Raft reconfiguration protocol [31] and Byzantine protocols [16,21]. IronFleet [13] is a Dafny-based verification framework that divides a distributed system into three verification layers and constructs proofs in a bottom-up manner using refinement. Ivy has been used to prove multiple Paxos variants and verify their implementation [27,35].

Parameterized model checking, a technique to check a system with arbitrary system size, can also be used in distributed system verification [17,19]. For instance, ByMC [19] models threshold-guarded distributed protocols as threshold automata and verifies their correctness in a counter system [18], which depicts a set of identical protocol participants.

Despite these efforts to formally verify distributed protocols, there has been a lack of focus on rollback-prevention protocols. Our work fills this gap and provides a detailed formal verification of a rollback-prevention protocol.

Formal Methods Used in TEEs. Jangid *et al.* [15] leverage Tamarin prover [33], a symbolic verification tool, to verify the rollback-prevention property of TEE applications by approximating the application in the execution logic of Tamarin. Wang *et al.* [36] use model checking to find vulnerabilities in an in-enclave crash fault-tolerant consensus protocol. They enumerate attack vectors in the TLC model checker [40] and use it to detect error traces. Li *et al.* [24] verify the firmware of ARM CCA in Coq. They build a layered verification framework and prove that the firmware implementation refines the top-level specification. The above works do not explore the formal verification of rollback-prevention protocols for TEEs, which is the focus of our work.

8   Conclusion and Future Work

This paper presents the formal verification for a rollback-prevention protocol, TIKS. We report the step-by-step verification process and showcase the user experience of using Ivy in verifying rollback-prevention protocols, providing valuable insights for researchers and developers interested in verifying such protocols.

In future work, we plan to explore the possibility of eliminating the protocol simplifications by finding necessary invariants manually or automatically [12,39], and making the proof decidable by decomposing the proof [35]. Furthermore, it will be interesting to verify the liveness property of the TIKS protocol using Ivy.

Acknowledgments. Michael Reiter was supported in part by NIFA Award 2021-67021-34252. Yinqian Zhang was in part supported by National Key R&D Program of China (No. 2023YFB4503900). Jianyu Niu was supported in part by the NSFC under Grant 62302204.

References

1. The Coq proof assistant. https://coq.inria.fr. Accessed 03 May 2022
2. Errors found in distributed protocols. https://github.com/dranov/protocol-bugs-list. Accessed 03 May 2022
3. TLA+ proof system (TLAPS). http://tla.msr-inria.inria.fr/tlaps/content/Home.html. Accessed 03 May 2022
4. Z3 SMT solver. https://github.com/Z3Prover/z3. Accessed 03 May 2022
5. AMD secure encrypted virtualization. https://www.amd.com/en/processors/amd-secure-encrypted-virtualization
6. Angel, S., et al.: Nimble: rollback protection for confidential cloud services. In: 17th USENIX Symposium on Operating Systems Design and Implementation (OSDI 2023), pp. 193–208 (2023)
7. ARM confidential compute architecture. https://www.arm.com/architecture/security-features/arm-confidential-compute-architecture
8. Berkovits, I., Lazić, M., Losa, G., Padon, O., Shoham, S.: Verification of threshold-based distributed algorithms by decomposition to decidable logics. In: Dillig, I., Tasiran, S. (eds.) CAV 2019, Part II. LNCS, vol. 11562, pp. 245–266. Springer, Cham (2019). https://doi.org/10.1007/978-3-030-25543-5_15
9. Chand, S., Liu, Y.A., Stoller, S.D.: Formal verification of multi-paxos for distributed consensus. In: Fitzgerald, J., Heitmeyer, C., Gnesi, S., Philippou, A. (eds.) FM 2016. LNCS, vol. 9995, pp. 119–136. Springer, Cham (2016). https://doi.org/10.1007/978-3-319-48989-6_8
10. Cimatti, A., Griggio, A., Mover, S., Tonetta, S.: Infinite-state invariant checking with IC3 and predicate abstraction. Form. Methods Syst. Des. **49**, 190–218 (2016)
11. Dinis, B., Druschel, P., Rodrigues, R.: RR: a fault model for efficient tee replication. In: The Network and Distributed System Security Symposium. Internet Society (2023)
12. Hance, T., Heule, M., Martins, R., Parno, B.: Finding invariants of distributed systems: it's a small (enough) world after all. In: 18th USENIX Symposium on Networked Systems Design and Implementation (NSDI 2021), pp. 115–131 (2021)
13. Hawblitzel, C., et al.: IronFleet: proving practical distributed systems correct. In: Proceedings of the 25th Symposium on Operating Systems Principles, pp. 1–17 (2015)
14. Intel software guard extensions. https://www.intel.com/content/www/us/en/architecture-and-technology/software-guard-extensions.html

15. Jangid, M.K., Chen, G., Zhang, Y., Lin, Z.: Towards formal verification of state continuity for enclave programs. In: 30th USENIX Security Symposium (USENIX Security 2021), pp. 573–590 (2021)

16. Jehl, L.: Formal verification of HotStuff. In: Peters, K., Willemse, T.A.C. (eds.) FORTE 2021. LNCS, vol. 12719, pp. 197–204. Springer, Cham (2021). https://doi.org/10.1007/978-3-030-78089-0_13

17. John, A., Konnov, I., Schmid, U., Veith, H., Widder, J.: Parameterized model checking of fault-tolerant distributed algorithms by abstraction. In: 2013 Formal Methods in Computer-Aided Design, pp. 201–209. IEEE (2013)

18. Konnov, I., Veith, H., Widder, J.: On the completeness of bounded model checking for threshold-based distributed algorithms: reachability. Inf. Comput. **252**, 95–109 (2017)

19. Konnov, I., Widder, J.: ByMC: byzantine model checker. In: Margaria, T., Steffen, B. (eds.) ISoLA 2018. LNCS, vol. 11246, pp. 327–342. Springer, Cham (2018). https://doi.org/10.1007/978-3-030-03424-5_22

20. Lamport, L.: Specifying Systems, vol. 388. Addison-Wesley, Boston (2002)

21. Lamport, L.: Byzantizing Paxos by refinement. In: Peleg, D. (ed.) DISC 2011. LNCS, vol. 6950, pp. 211–224. Springer, Heidelberg (2011). https://doi.org/10.1007/978-3-642-24100-0_22

22. Lamport, L., Merz, S., Doligez, D.: TLAPS proof of basic PAXOS. https://github.com/tlaplus/tlapm/blob/main/examples/paxos/Paxos.tla. Accessed 03 May 2022

23. Leino, K.R.M.: Dafny: an automatic program verifier for functional correctness. In: Clarke, E.M., Voronkov, A. (eds.) LPAR 2010. LNCS (LNAI), vol. 6355, pp. 348–370. Springer, Heidelberg (2010). https://doi.org/10.1007/978-3-642-17511-4_20

24. Li, X., et al.: Design and verification of the arm confidential compute architecture. In: 16th USENIX Symposium on Operating Systems Design and Implementation (OSDI 2022), pp. 465–484 (2022)

25. Matetic, S., et al.: ROTE: rollback protection for trusted execution. In: 26th USENIX Security Symposium (USENIX Security 2017), pp. 1289–1306 (2017)

26. Niu, J., Peng, W., Zhang, X., Zhang, Y.: Narrator: secure and practical state continuity for trusted execution in the cloud. In: Proceedings of the 2022 ACM SIGSAC Conference on Computer and Communications Security, pp. 2385–2399 (2022)

27. Padon, O., Losa, G., Sagiv, M., Shoham, S.: Paxos made EPR: decidable reasoning about distributed protocols. Proc. ACM Programm. Lang. **1**(OOPSLA), 1–31 (2017)

28. Padon, O., McMillan, K.L., Panda, A., Sagiv, M., Shoham, S.: Ivy: safety verification by interactive generalization. In: Proceedings of the 37th ACM SIGPLAN Conference on Programming Language Design and Implementation, pp. 614–630 (2016)

29. Peng, W., Li, X., Niu, J., Zhang, X., Zhang, Y.: Ensuring state continuity for confidential computing: a blockchain-based approach. IEEE Trans. Depend. Secure Comput., 1–14 (2024). https://doi.org/10.1109/TDSC.2024.3381973

30. Reiter, M.K.: Secure agreement protocols: Reliable and atomic group multicast in rampart. In: Proceedings of the 2nd ACM Conference on Computer and Communications Security, CCS 1994, pp. 68–80. Association for Computing Machinery, New York (1994). https://doi.org/10.1145/191177.191194

31. Schultz, W., Dardik, I., Tripakis, S.: Formal verification of a distributed dynamic reconfiguration protocol. In: Proceedings of the 11th ACM SIGPLAN International Conference on Certified Programs and Proofs, pp. 143–152 (2022)

32. Sergey, I., Wilcox, J.R., Tatlock, Z.: Programming and proving with distributed protocols. Proc. ACM Programm. Lang. **2**(POPL), 1–30 (2017)
33. Tamarin prover. https://tamarin-prover.com/
34. Tamir, O., et al.: Counterexample driven quantifier instantiations with applications to distributed protocols. Proc. ACM Programm. Lang. **7**(OOPSLA2), 1878–1904 (2023)
35. Taube, M., et al.: Modularity for decidability of deductive verification with applications to distributed systems. In: Proceedings of the 39th ACM SIGPLAN Conference on Programming Language Design and Implementation, pp. 662–677 (2018)
36. Wang, W., Deng, S., Niu, J., Reiter, M.K., Zhang, Y.: ENGRAFT: enclave-guarded raft on byzantine faulty nodes. In: Proceedings of the 2022 ACM SIGSAC Conference on Computer and Communications Security, pp. 2841–2855 (2022)
37. Wilcox, J.R., et al.: Verdi: a framework for implementing and formally verifying distributed systems. In: Proceedings of the 36th ACM SIGPLAN Conference on Programming Language Design and Implementation, PLDI 2015, New York, NY, USA, pp. 357–368 (2015). https://doi.org/10.1145/2737924.2737958
38. Woos, D., Wilcox, J.R., Anton, S., Tatlock, Z., Ernst, M.D., Anderson, T.: Planning for change in a formal verification of the raft consensus protocol. In: Proceedings of the 5th ACM SIGPLAN Conference on Certified Programs and Proofs, pp. 154–165 (2016)
39. Yao, J., Tao, R., Gu, R., Nieh, J.: DuoAI: fast, automated inference of inductive invariants for verifying distributed protocols. In: 16th USENIX Symposium on Operating Systems Design and Implementation (OSDI 2022), pp. 485–501 (2022)
40. Yu, Y., Manolios, P., Lamport, L.: Model checking TLA$^+$ specifications. In: Pierre, L., Kropf, T. (eds.) CHARME 1999. LNCS, vol. 1703, pp. 54–66. Springer, Heidelberg (1999). https://doi.org/10.1007/3-540-48153-2_6

Full Papers with Artefact

Network Simulator-Centric
Compositional Testing

Tom Rousseaux(✉)ⓘ, Christophe Crochetⓘ, John Aogaⓘ, and Axel Legayⓘ

INGI, ICTEAM, Université catholique de Louvain, Place Sainte Barbe 2, L05.02.01,
1348 Ottignies-Louvain-la-Neuve, Belgium
{tom.rousseaux,christophe.crochet,john.aoga,axel.legay}@uclouvain.be

Abstract. This article introduces a novel methodology, Network
Simulator-centric Compositional Testing (NSCT), to enhance the verification of network protocols with a particular focus on time-varying
network properties. NSCT follows a Model-Based Testing (MBT) approach. These approaches usually struggle to test and represent time-
varying network properties. NSCT also aims to achieve more accurate
and reproducible protocol testing. It is implemented using the Ivy tool
and the Shadow network simulator. This enables online debugging of real
protocol implementations. A case study on an implementation of QUIC
(*picoquic*) is presented, revealing an error in its compliance with a time-
varying specification. This error has subsequently been rectified, highlighting NSCT's effectiveness in uncovering and addressing real-world
protocol implementation issues. The article underscores NSCT's potential in advancing protocol testing methodologies, offering a notable contribution to the field of network protocol verification.

Keywords: Model-Based Testing · Time-varying Network Properties ·
Software verification and validation · Formal Specifications · Network
Simulator · Internet protocols · QUIC · Concrete Implementation ·
Adverse Stimuli

1 Introduction

Ensuring the safety and effectiveness of systems is paramount. One way to
achieve this goal is through the use of model-checking approaches. These
approaches employ mathematical models of the system and exhaustively check
the specifications against all possible behaviors of the system. Examples of
such approaches include *SPIN* [27,42] and *NUSMV* [20,43], which use Linear-
Temporal Logic (LTL) [53] or Computation Tree Logic (CTL) [18] to describe
specifications. First, model checking results were applied to mathematical models of the system under validation. However, over the last decades, we have seen
the emergence of techniques applied directly to implementations [19]. An inherent hurdle in model-checking lies in the state-space explosion dilemma triggered
by exhaustive exploration of the entire state-space.

To tackle this challenge, researchers have proposed Statistical Model Checking (LLTYSG19, LL20). This approach entails simulating the system and using

ⓒ IFIP International Federation for Information Processing 2024
Published by Springer Nature Switzerland AG 2024
V. Castiglioni and A. Francalanza (Eds.): FORTE 2024, LNCS 14678, pp. 177–196, 2024.
https://doi.org/10.1007/978-3-031-62645-6_10

statistical algorithms to ascertain whether it meets a measurable specification within a finite execution with a certain probability and given confidence. The approach, which has been implemented in tools such as *UPPAAL-SMC* [22,34,35,37] and *PLASMA* [9,13,39], has been applied on a wide range of case studies [36]. Statistical Model Checking is primarily employed for validating properties on mathematical models. Except for specific instances like in [49], direct validation on code has been rarely proposed. Generating fair traces from the code required by the statistical algorithm is challenging. Furthermore, with few exceptions as seen in [17], specifications are typically formulated using Bounded LTL. This representation is inadequate for describing the specifications of a network protocol. In this paper, we propose an approach that leverages the principle of simulation akin to Statistical Model Checking, but within the framework of specifications described in a sophisticated language and directly validated against the implementation. This approach, known as model-based testing [50], offers a more scalable solution. Our approach also introduces specific techniques to address the challenges involved in protocol verification.

In protocol verification, traditional methodologies rely on multiple independent implementations and interoperability testing to validate protocol designs. However, comprehensive model-based verification is often lacking in well-known approaches. Ivy, a notable exception, allows working with protocol implementations and adversarial stimuli.

Ivy's mathematical model [51] serves as the language describing the system specifications, whereas model-checking approaches typically involve two mathematical models, one for the system and one for the specifications.

Network-centric Compositional Testing (NCT) [45] is an emerging methodology that was introduced within Ivy. NCT introduces a formal statement of a protocol standard, allowing effective testing of implementations for compliance, not just interoperability. NCT uses formal specifications of protocols to automatically create testing tools. These tools generate random test cases by solving constraints with the help of an SMT solver. This enables adversarial testing in real-world environments, uncovering compliance issues and ambiguities in standard protocol documents (RFCs). NCT uncovered errors and vulnerabilities in the real-world protocol QUIC [31], proving its effectiveness.

Although NCT serves as a foundation for network-centric protocol verification, it does not address time-varying network properties. Time-varying network properties describe the timed aspects of network protocols. These properties include internal timeouts to, for example, trigger a packet retransmission. These are involved in properties that are more complex to model, such as congestion control schemes in retransmission mechanisms.

Ivy deterministically generates output packets from input packets, but does not provide computation time requirements. This duration can non-deterministic-cally exceed (or not) protocol timeouts. This can impact the inputs, for example by triggering a packet retransmission. This non-determinism prevents the reproducibility of the experiments. If Ivy discovers a bug in an implementation, Ivy is not necessarily able to reproduce it.

We have developed a new approach called *Network Simulator-centric Compositional Testing* (NSCT) to address these limitations. NSCT is designed to focus on verifying time-varying network properties in network protocols and ensuring experimental reproducibility.

Our method extends Ivy to support time-related features, providing a more network-centric approach. Additionally, we have integrated the Shadow network simulator which allows online debugging of protocol implementations. This integration ensures the determinism and reproducibility of the experiments. We have successfully applied our approach to test the QUIC protocol and have demonstrated its effectiveness in verifying time-varying network properties. NSCT reveals an error on the *picoquic* implementation and the QUIC idle timeout connection termination. This approach brings advancements to the network community by enabling more detailed and accurate protocol testing and verification. It enables specifying loss detection and congestion control in QUIC defined by RFC9002 [29].

The remainder of this paper is structured as follows. Section 2 provides background information on different verification types and the emergence of Ivy. Section 3 outlines our methodology, providing details about *Network Simulator-centric Compositional Testing* (NSCT). Section 4 delves into the verification of time-varying network properties in QUIC. Then, Sect. 5 discusses our findings and proposes avenues for future work. Finally, Sect. 6 leads to the related work and the conclusion.

2   Background

There are two main ways to create adversarial tests for network protocols: with [10,52,61] or without [3,12,16,38,54] checking compliance with a standard. Approaches that do not check compliance with a standard include fuzz testing [38], white-box testing [12,54], and other methods that create a verified reference implementation [3] or prove properties of an existing implementation [16]. On the contrary, approaches that verify compliance with a standard, also known as Model-Based Testing (MBT) [50], involve constructing an abstract model with Finite State Machines (FSMs) to explore and generate test scenarios [10,52,61]. However, the incorporation of data into FSMs adds significant complexity and challenges to these formalisms [45].

Network-centric compositional (NCT) approaches avoid the use of FSMs. To grasp this and our approach, which builds upon NCT, it is crucial to understand the functioning of the *Ivy tool* that implements them.

Ivy is a verification tool implementing multiple proving techniques [44,51]. It is used to correct the design and implementation of algorithms and distributed protocols. It supports modular specifications and implementation. Ivy is used to interactively verify the safety properties of infinite-state systems. Ivy introduced a Relational Modeling Language (RML). This language allows describing the state of a program using formulas from first-order logic and uses relations (boolean predicate), functions, modules, and type objects as the main abstractions to represent the state of the system. Let us illustrate the functioning *Ivy* using a running protocol example.

MiniP (Minimalist Protocol) is a Simple Protocol. MiniP defines packets that contain frames. Any packet must contain exactly two frames. Three types of frames are defined: PING, PONG, and TIMESTAMP frames. PING frame contains a four-byte string representing the word "ping". PONG frame also contains a four-byte string expressing the word "pong". The PING frame or the PONG frame must be present in a packet. Finally, the TIMESTAMP frame contains an eight-byte unsigned integer representing the moment, in milliseconds, when the packet is sent. This frame must be present in all packets.

Figure 1 represents the finite state machines (FSM) of MiniP. The client starts by sending a packet containing the PING frame followed by the TIMESTAMP frame as payload. The server must then respond within three seconds, with a packet containing the PONG frame followed by the TIMESTAMP frame. This exchange continues until the client stops the connection. The client terminates the connection by not transmitting any packets for more than three seconds.

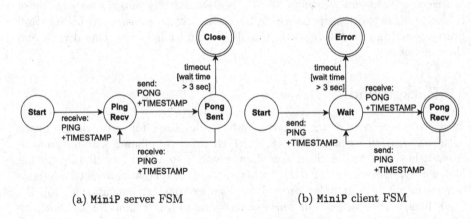

(a) MiniP server FSM   (b) MiniP client FSM

Fig. 1. MiniP Finite state machines (FSM)

Some MiniP Components Implementation with Ivy. The first and most important components to implement for this protocol are frames. In Ivy, a frame is implemented using the *type object*. Listing 1 provides an example of the frame object, which includes a subtype object representing the PING frame and a generic action handle(f:frame) that must be implemented by subtype objects. The PING frame defines a data field containing the four-byte payload as described in the specification.

1. State example

```
1   object frame = {
2     type this
3     object ping = {
4       variant this of frame = struct {
5         data : stream_data
6       }
7     }
8     action handle(f:this) = {
9       require false;
10    }
11  }
```

Ivy's "action" statement is used to manipulate the states and add requirements. An action can be considered as a procedure and cannot be stored in variables or passed as arguments. Listing 2 illustrates the handle(f:frame) action, which encompasses all the properties associated with the PING frame and adds requirements that will be checked every time a PING stream is received and generated. Lines 7 and 8 specify that the data payload must be a "ping" and have a length of four bytes. Line 9 requires that a PING frame should not be present in a packet using the relation ping_frame_pending defined on Line 1. Line 12 illustrates the invocation of the enqueue_frame(f:frame) action, which also modifies various states within the model and is used to append a frame to a packet object.

2. Object procedure example

```
1   relation ping_frame_pending
2
3   object frame = {
4     object ping = {
5       action handle(f:frame.ping)
6       around handle {
7         require f.data = ping_data;
8         require f.data.end = 4;
9         require ~ping_frame_pending;
10        ...
11        ping_frame_pending := true;
12        call enqueue_frame(f);
13      }
14    }
15  }
```

Network-Centric Compositional Testing Methodology (NCT). NCT, a specialized approach within Model-Based Testing (MBT), is specifically designed for network protocols. It provides a structured method for creating formal specifications of Internet protocols and subsequently testing them [45]. The NCT principle is demonstrated in Fig. 2 using Ivy. The process begins with converting the RFC into an Ivy formal model ⓐ. Once the Ivy code is parsed, a generator is used to create concrete and randomized testers ⓑ. Finally, the implementation of the real-life protocol is tested and verified against the testers that employ an SMT solver to satisfy the constraints of the formal protocol requirements. When a requirement fails, the resulting traces ⓒ can be analyzed to identify any potential errors or vulnerabilities.

The NCT principle is based on compositional testing, which views formal specifications as a set of interconnected components/processes with their corre-

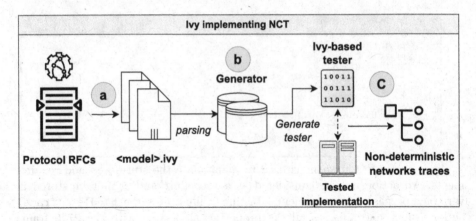

Fig. 2. Ivy implementing NCT

sponding inputs and outputs. This approach allows testing protocol behaviors as observed on the wire, rather than relying on an abstract mathematical model of the protocol. This is why this methodology is called "network-centric".

The design of MiniP is in line with the principles of the NCT methodology. In MiniP, the "Frame" process produces output that serves as input for the "Packet" process. The "assumptions" regarding the inputs of a process are treated as "guarantees" for the outputs of other processes. Figure 3 provides a visual representation of this structure. In the context of MiniP, each element represents a layer of the MiniP stack, including the frame layer ⓐ and the packet layer ⓑ. The *shim* component ⓒ is responsible for transmitting and receiving packets across the network. When a packet is received, the *shim* invokes the ping_packet_event action. This action contains all the specifications associated with the MiniP packet and will generate an error if any of the requirements are not met. For instance, it verifies that a packet always contains two frames in the correct order. The frames are similarly managed with their respective actions. In Fig. 3, the set of requirements is connected to the packet component ⓑ.

Limitations. NCT's success derives from how effectively it identifies errors and vulnerabilities in real-world protocols like QUIC [21,46]. However, NCT presents some limitations associated with its inability to test time-varying network properties.

For instance, it cannot model the congestion control mechanism specified in RFC9002. Calculating the time needed for packet generation and verification of received packets can be significant, particularly when implementations under test generate packets in bursts, leading to false congestion due to increased round-trip time.

Additionally, debugging implementations is challenging because traces have no guarantee of reproducibility. In summary, here are the current main limitations of NCT for protocol testing:

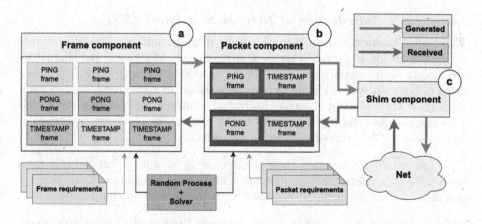

Fig. 3. MiniP Network-Centric Testing (NCT) structure

① *Lack of the Expressiveness to Handle Time-Varying Network Properties* [46]. NCT lacks the necessary capabilities to reason about precise time intervals and deadlines. It also does not provide guarantees on thread-scheduling or computation time. For example, NCT cannot verify whether a MiniP server will respond to a PING within three seconds.

② *Non-reproducible Experiments.* While NCT offers deterministic verification for formal properties, this determinism does not extend to the network (*network nondeterminism*) or the implementations being tested (*internal nondeterminism*). As a result, the experiments cannot be reproduced. For example, a MiniP server that crashes when sending an odd TIMESTAMP will not crash deterministically when tested with NCT.

③ *Computational Time Exceeding Protocol Timeout.* The computation time required to verify incoming packets and generate packets that satisfy the model can interfere with the standard behavior defined by some protocols. This also hinders the reproducibility of the experiment. For instance, a MiniP server implementation in NCT may take too long to check the integrity of a PING and exceed the response time limit of 3 s. This issue would not occur with MiniP implementation on a modern computer, but it arises with real protocols due to the inherent complexity of their RFCs, as with QUIC [46].

3   Network Simulator-Centric Compositional Testing

Network Simulator-Centric Compositional Testing (NSCT) is a specialized approach within Model-Based Testing (MBT) that aims to overcome the limitations of NCT discussed previously. NSCT, similar to NCT, adopts a network-centric perspective and employs a combination of two key ingredients.

Ingredient 1: Introduction of Network Simulators (NS)

Type of Network Simulators. NS tools permit running a model or a real executable inside a controlled network environment. Model-oriented simulators are mainly used to verify protocols during their development stage [11]. Many types of NS exist; we will focus on time-dependent NS tools that have two main properties: they proceed chronologically and maintain a simulation clock [28]. This clock is essential to verify time-related properties. There are two types of *time-dependent* NS: time-driven and event-driven.

(1) Time-driven NS advance their clocks exactly by a fixed interval of δ time units [28]. This means that the simulation has a time precision of δ. To increase precision, δ must be small, which slows down the simulation computation.

(2) Event-driven NS, by comparison, advance their clocks by variable steps. Such tools progress as events unfold; each time step jumps precisely to the next event:

Event-driven network simulator [25]

---
while *simulation is in progress* **do**
| remove smallest time-stamped event;
| set time to this timestamp;
| execute event handler;
end

Our Approach Using NS. Our solution involves integrating NCT with an event-driven, time-dependent network simulator to effectively overcome the limitations ② (*Non-reproducible experiments*) and ③ (*Computational time*), and partially limitation ① (*Time-varying network properties*).

Addressing Limitation. ②: Model-based testers and protocol implementations are real software components that must be executed rather than just modeled. When they are executed in a controlled environment, it becomes possible to stabilize and replicate desired random behaviors like encryption. This solution addresses the second limitation ②. This ensures the determinism of model-based protocol testing.

Addressing Limitation. ③: Formal specifications developed to test internet protocols with respect to NCT focus on packet events. This means that the latency of the (network) link between the model-based test and the implementation under test (IUT) determines the clock steps. Assuming a latency of l, if the IUT sends a packet at time t, the model-based tester will receive it at time $t+l$. If the model-based tester responds immediately (without waiting for a specific delay to verify a timing property), the IUT will receive the response at time $t + 2l$. This resolves ③ as the computation time does not affect the time perceived by the IUT.

Addressing (partially) Limitation. ①: To address ① (*time-varying network properties*), it is essential to employ a time-dependent NS. However, simply using a time-dependent NS is not enough. It is also necessary to have a formal verification tool that can interact with the simulation clock. We will discuss this further in the second ingredient of NSCT.

Additional Values Using NS: The use of NS provides the ability to manage and control the network. It simplifies the creation of various network-related situations, including connection migration as described in RFC9000. An NS also enables realistic simulation scenarios of advanced modern network protocols [26]. In the following sections, we will introduce the specific NS that we used for NSCT.

Specific NS. There are two modern discrete-event network simulators:

(1) The ns-3 [56] simulator is a freely available tool that has been specifically designed for research and educational purposes. It operates using models. To enable the execution of direct code within *ns-3*, the *DCE* framework [57] intercepts system calls and links them to *ns-3*. However, *DCE* does not support many of the necessary system calls required for protocol implementation, and the environment it supports has become outdated. The use of *ns-3 DCE* to simulate QUIC implementations requires significant effort and inhibits tool longevity. Researchers have recently expressed concerns about various challenges encountered while trying to simulate QUIC implementations using the *ns-3 DCE* framework [1].

(2) Shadow [32,33] is a free, open source simulator. It was primarily designed to simulate Tor networks. Shadow works by intercepting a subset of the system calls (syscalls), simulating network calls. Despite lacking support for some key system calls initially, the Shadow project remained highly active and has since added built-in implementation for several important syscalls that were originally missing. This is a positive sign for the long-term sustainability of the tool.

Shadow provides a range of network-specific functionalities that are highly beneficial for researchers and engineers. It allows users to carefully design the network topology that they want to simulate, specifying nodes, links, and their connections. Shadow allows users to adjust parameters like link latency and jitter, which are crucial for evaluating the performance of networked applications under different network conditions. Beyond its flexible design capabilities (e.g., configurable topologies), Shadow offers live debugging features to monitor and troubleshoot network behaviors in real-time during simulations.

Shadow easily supports single-threaded and multithreaded implementations. For example, if there is a multithreaded server connected to two clients, Shadow enables deterministic debugging of one client while allowing the other client and the server to operate independently within the simulation. This level of control and precision in debugging, even in complex multithreaded scenarios, provides researchers and developers with valuable insights into the behavior and interactions of various components. As a result, it improves the thoroughness of protocol analysis.

Ingredient 2: Integration of Time-Varying Network Properties Testing in Ivy

In practice, network link properties are designed in the Ivy model or directly with Shadow. Ivy then builds the simulation configuration file with those properties and references the executable used for the test. Finally, Shadow launches the IUT and the Ivy test.

Adapting Ivy for Event-Driven Network Simulation. Our approach aims to enhance the compatibility of the Ivy verifier with event-driven network simulators. To improve protocol verification in Ivy, we propose an adaptation that introduces an interface for manipulating time-related actions/relations. The interface is implemented in C++ and leverages the *'time.h'* library to facilitate the interception of system calls (syscalls) by the Shadow simulator.

This interface provides several key functionalities, including the manipulation of time in various units (seconds, milliseconds, microseconds), timer control (start and stop actions), and current-time querying. The interface supports setting time breakpoints at specific events and implements both blocking and non-blocking sleep mechanisms. Using non-blocking sleep allows the simulation to receive network events while "sleeping," resulting in simulations that more accurately mirror real-world network behavior.

Ivy's time interface is extensible, which allows for further adaptations and enhancements to meet the evolving needs of network protocol verification. The time interface is represented at Fig. 4 ⓐ.

Our progress in Ivy for simulating event-driven networks is built on an improved method for controlling event generation. We use signal handlers along with time-based signals such as SIGALRM to accurately manage event timing. This approach is illustrated in Fig. 4 ⓑ. It is especially effective in situations that require delayed responses, as it allows precise control over the timing of event generation and processing.

Finally, while Shadow's ability to modify network conditions is beneficial, it lacks flexibility, as it cannot vary the delay during the connection. To address this limitation, we developed a formal model that represents network quality, enabling us to simulate more specific scenarios of network condition. Nevertheless, we still rely on Shadow for reproducibility and intercepting time syscalls as shown in Fig. 4 ⓒ.

Monitoring Time-Varying Properties. We can now use Shadow intercepting time syscalls to define safety properties for time-varying properties in Ivy without having to modify the tools directly. Using the implemented time module and the standard Ivy key words such as "require" or "assume", we can model all the first-order logic formula with time as variable or predicate.

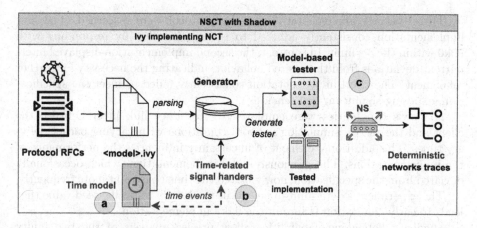

Fig. 4. Protocol Formal Verification toolchain (PFV)

Protocol Formal Verification (PFV). PFV[1] toolchain implements NSCT by leveraging Ivy and Shadow. The usability of the previous work is enhanced by implementing a multistage docker containerisation procedure [47], coupled with microservices and a basic graphical interface to initiate experiments. This architecture allows for easy testing of new protocol implementations with Ivy and Shadow. All containers implement a REST API to start Ivy.

Case Study - MiniP Protocol. In our MiniP formal specification example, we implemented the property that the PONG message should be received within 3 s after the PING message being sent, as seen in Listing 3. To achieve that, we use the concept of time breakpoint. Then we add requirement manipulating the values extracted from these breakpoints.

```
3. Testing time-varying properties
1   # Get current time from last break point
2   current_time := time_api.c_timer.now_millis_last_bp;
3   # Check that it satisfies the 3 seconds limit
4   require current_time ≤ 3000;
```

The time breakpoint is set in the PING frame event handler as presented in Listing 4:

```
4. Adding time breakpoint
1   object ping = {
2       around handle {
3           # [previous requirements]
4           ...
5           call time_api.c_timer.start; #add time break point
6           # [previous requirements]
7       }
8   }
```

This example demonstrates how simple it is to test a time-varying network property with a safety property thanks to the network-simulator assumption.

---

[1] https://github.com/ElNiak/PFV.

Three distinct implementations of the protocol were discerned. The first implementation consistently adhered to the specification by responding with PONG within the 3-s limit. In contrast, the second implementation displayed intermittent deviations from the desired behavior, indicating the necessity for further refinement. The third implementation consistently failed to meet the specification, exposing significant deficiencies.

Shadow's capabilities were employed to introduce link jitter between the client and the server, simulating network conditions with varying packet delivery times. This additional element of uncertainty influenced the performance of the implementations. The previously flaky implementation, which occasionally deviated from the specification, now violated the time constraint more frequently.

The experiment's determinism helped us to identify a specific seed value that leads to early connection failure in the flaky implementation.

Shadow's debugging capabilities allow precise analysis of the two faulty implementations. By attaching a debugger to the implementations during testing, we can precisely identify which components were responsible for the deviations from the specified behavior.

4   Threat to Validity for QUIC

This section provides an overview of how NSCT is applied to the QUIC protocol. It begins by defining the QUIC protocol and then discusses the modifications made to the formal model described in previous work [21, 46]. It also includes an analysis of the results obtained from the *picoquic* implementation, highlighting a specification violation. This issue was subsequently addressed through a pull request in the *picoquic* repository, fixing the error and aligning the implementation with the QUIC specifications.

QUIC is a modern transport protocol that combines the advantages of TCP (Transport Control Protocol) and TLS 1.3 (Transport Layer Security), while overcoming their limitations, as detailed in RFC9000 [31]. It introduces innovative secure communication methods at the transport layer. The RFC describes how data are organized into frames and packets to ensure effective data segmentation, reliability, and control.

Tested Implementation: *picoquic* is a research implementation of QUIC [15]. This implementation participated in the development of a QUIC standard by providing feedback. *picoquic* is written in C and consists of 103k lines of code. The tool incorporates various QUIC extensions and is currently under active development, making it an ideal choice for testing purposes. Moreover, QUIC has recently been chosen as the basis of HTTP/3 and is expected to handle a substantial portion of internet traffic in the coming years [46].

Table 1 summarizes the contribution to QUIC formal specification and the problems we found per RFC while testing *picoquic*:

A. Analysis of RFC9000: Our approach, integrating the time module and Shadow, has enabled enhancements to the existing QUIC model by incorporating time-related requirements as per RFC9000 specifications.

Table 1. Summary of contributions to Ivy model and problems found in *picoquic*

	A. RFC9000	B. RFC9002	C. Ack Frequency
Previous works	Partially complete	/	/
Contributions	- Ack-delay - Idle timeout	- Congestion control (rtt calculation) - Loss recovery	90% of the draft
Problems found	Max retransmission	/	Misinterpretation in a frame field

We focused on the idle timeout connection termination behavior of QUIC. QUIC outlines three primary methods for connection termination: immediate close, stateless reset, and idle timeout. We designed our tests to validate the implementation of these methods, particularly the idle timeout.

According to RFC9000 Section 10.1, an endpoint restarts its idle timer upon receiving or sending ack-eliciting packets (i.e., the packet triggering ACK mechanism), ensuring that connections remain open during active communication.

To prevent overly brief idle timeouts, QUIC mandates an idle timeout period be at least three times the current Probe Timeout (PTO). This extension allows multiple opportunities for packet transmission before a timeout.

The connection in QUIC is automatically and *silently* closed, discarding its states if it remains idle beyond the minimum duration set by the max_idle_timeout transport parameter.

Our experiments revealed some discrepancies in the implementation of the idle timeout feature not in line with the standard behavior dictated by RFC9000. We noticed deviations in the handling of retransmission thresholds and idle timeouts.

This test involved suspending packet transmission after a random period and observing if the connection closes silently, according to the specifications. However, our experiments revealed a deviation in the picoquic implementation. Rather than closing the connection after the idle timer expired, picoquic terminated it prematurely upon reaching a retransmission threshold. This behavior, probably influenced by TCP retransmission mechanism, deviates from RFC9000 standards, which require explicit notification through CONNECTION_CLOSE or APPLICATION_CLOSE frames for such terminations.

The discovered issue has been resolved through a pull request that was merged into the picoquic repository. This confirms the effectiveness of NSCT in detecting real-world anomalies in protocols.

B. Analysis of RFC9002 [58]. This RFC discusses loss detection and congestion control in QUIC, differentiating it from TCP. It includes 37 mandatory specifications and 27 recommendations as per RFC2119. Key concepts introduced include the "probe timeout" (PTO) for managing congestion windows and the round-trip time (RTT) estimation process, comprising metrics like "min_rtt", "smoothed_rtt", and "rttvar". The RFC also details a sender-side congestion control mechanism, akin to TCP/NewReno, focusing on packet losses and Explicit Congestion Notification (ECN) [5,24].

Our analysis involved implementing and testing the specified requirements and behaviors of RFC9002 in the context of congestion control and loss recovery, excluding the ECN component because it requires kernel support, which is not currently supported by Shadow. Future work could explore additional congestion control mechanisms like CUBIC [55] or BBR [14], and extensions such as QUIC-FEC [48]. Tests were conducted to evaluate the model's behavior under various network conditions, including loss, delay, and jitter, ensuring adherence to the RFC's guidelines.

While our formal specification of the RFC9002 did not identify specific problems in the *picoquic* implementation, it significantly contributed to refining the formal specification of QUIC, making it more precise and closely aligned with real-world scenarios.

C. Analysis of "QUIC Acknowledgement Frequency" [30] *Extension.* Currently in its draft-05 version, this extension enhances QUIC by allowing for delayed packet acknowledgments. It introduces the min_ack_delay transport parameter and two new frames: ACK_FREQUENCY and IMMEDIATE_ACK. The ACK_FREQUENCY frame adjusts acknowledgment rates based on the network state, while the IMMEDIATE_ACK frame assists connection liveliness.

In our examination, we analyzed the integration of this extension into the QUIC formal specification, focusing on the implications of delayed acknowledgments. During this process, an error was identified in the picoquic implementation; it incorrectly returned a FRAME_ENCODING_ERROR when processing an ACK_FREQUENCY frame. This issue, initially suspected to be a draft inconsistency, was actually due to a misinterpretation of the "ACK-Eliciting Threshold" field in *picoquic*.

5   Discussion and Future Work

It is clear that the NSCT methodology, which involves various tools, is successful in uncovering new behaviors in protocol implementations, especially in terms of their temporal dynamics. However, combining multiple tools also brings about the intrinsic limitations of each tool and difficulties from their joint use. For example, employing network simulators, such as Shadow, comes with specific constraints. The necessity for simulators to depend on system calls for interacting with implementations restricts the range of implementations that can be tested. Moreover, busy loops (an anti-pattern not very used) reduce precision in time as they do not wait through system calls. In addition, the topology part of the NSCT testing process requires scenario-based simulations, where the behavior of the network within the simulated environment is predetermined.

A natural strategy to tackle these limitations is to replace certain tools used in the existing NSCT framework. For example, employing a network simulator that accommodates dynamic topology might alleviate the restrictions of scenario-based simulations, though it would necessitate modifications to existing automation scripts. Furthermore, substituting Ivy with any tool that implements the NCT methodology could be feasible, but this would require adapting the Ivy models.

In addition to improvements related to the joint use of several tools. Other future avenues may also be investigated. For example, a further improvement of the time module can allow for a more thorough verification of different types of properties. Closer integration between Ivy's generation process and the time module could make generating events at specific time points easier. This adaptation would enhance the tool's precision and overall usefulness.

Expanding the scope of the testing to include different congestion mechanisms in various protocols would provide more detailed insight into the details related to implementation and effectiveness.

Applying the methodology and tools discussed here to a broader range and scale of QUIC implementations would better validate and improve reliability and security.

Another promising area of research lies in the examination of the synergy between formal attacks models in network and Shadow's capabilities, especially considering the ongoing development of protocols like MPQUIC [23]. Currently, MPQUIC is still in its draft phase, grappling with significant security considerations between two main solutions. Given Shadow's unique ability to create custom network topologies, our methodology stands to offer substantial assistance. It enables the modeling of both solutions under consideration for MPQUIC, providing a comprehensive framework to assess their security implications and vulnerabilities.

Furthermore, another innovative approach is to leverage AI to simplify the creation of formal models from RFCs. This integration would greatly streamline the modeling process, making it more efficient and accessible. Additionally, a Graphical User Interface (GUI) for Ivy would allow users to engage in formal modeling without needing to understand the complexities of Ivy code, thereby making the process more user-friendly and approachable.

6   Conclusion

Protocol validation methods are diverse. Notably, the *INET* suite within the *OMNeT++* simulation library offers a powerful tool for network protocol validation [60]. Previous research used *INET* to simulate a QUIC model within *OMNeT++* [62,63], but the evaluation was limited to protocol models and did not include real-world implementations. Studies like [2] used formal verification methods and simulations to validate complex protocol properties. This work measured the impact of specific attacks like Denial-of-Service on network parameters like energy consumption and computational effort, but did not use formal methods alongside simulations for verification.

Other research [7,8,40] attempted to enable the expression of time-varying network properties in the ISO standard to specify OSI protocols, known as Language Of Temporal Ordering Specification (*LOTOS*) [6]. While extensions to *LOTOS* offered varied expressiveness [8], subsequent Model-Based Testing (MBT) tools like *TorXakis* [59] only ensure guarantees about the tester's side due to its lack of a network simulator. This limits its ability to verify time-varying network properties.

In [41], the authors compose their model with a network model to control the non-determinism of the network. This approach increases determinism, but it is not as powerful as NSCT, which extends determinism to IUT. [4] proposed using a test oracle on IUT traces, which allows offline verification of time-sensitive network properties that change based on network conditions. This approach avoids the high computational cost associated with online verification. However, this approach does not allow for the expression of time-dependent scenarios. Additionally, verifying traces does not facilitate the reproducibility of errors.

In this study, we propose an extension to Network-centric Compositional Testing (NCT). NCT is a simulation-based formal verification approach previously employed to validate QUIC implementations with Ivy. However, it has certain drawbacks; Ivy and NCT cannot capture time-varying network requirements or replicate experiments due to the inherent randomness of the methodology and the network. In addition, the extensive computational time required to scrutinize actual implementations of Internet protocols may affect protocol behaviors.

This study has successfully demonstrated the efficacy of *Network Simulator-centric Compositional Testing* (NSCT) in enhancing the verification of network protocols, particularly in addressing key challenges of NCT. NSCT, through the integration of the Ivy tool and the Shadow network simulator, effectively solves several issues. These include the addition of time-varying network property verification, ensuring deterministic outcomes in protocol testing, and enhancing the reproducibility of test results. Our paper demonstrates the described method using a custom minimalist MiniP protocol. The application of NSCT in the picoquic implementation of QUIC identified a compliance error with time-varying network specifications, which was then rectified. This underscores the methodology's capability in managing complex, real-world network scenarios.

Additionally, a formal model is developed for RFC9002 that integrates congestion control and loss recovery into the existing QUIC model. The formal model of the "Acknowledgement Frequency" QUIC extension is also included.

Acknowledgement. We would like to thank Maxime Piraux for his help to validate QUIC experiment results.

Artefacts. The artefacts of this paper are available at https://zenodo.org/doi/10.5281/zenodo.10819552.

References

1. https://groups.google.com/g/ns-3-users/c/NyX71jXHgr4?pli=1. Accessed 12 Oct 2023
2. Bernardeschi, C., Dini, G., Palmieri, M., Racciatti, F.: A framework for formal analysis and simulative evaluation of security attacks in wireless sensor networks. J. Comput. Virol. Hacking Tech. **17**(3), 249–263 (2021). https://doi.org/10.1007/s11416-021-00392-0
3. Bhargavan, K., Fournet, C., Kohlweiss, M., Pironti, A., Strub, P.Y.: Implementing TLS with verified cryptographic security. In: 2013 IEEE Symposium on Security and Privacy, pp. 445–459. IEEE (2013)
4. Bishop, S., et al.: Engineering with logic: rigorous test-oracle specification and validation for TCP/IP and the sockets API. J. ACM (JACM) **66**(1), 1–77 (2018)
5. Black, D.L.: RFC 8311: relaxing restrictions on explicit congestion notification (ECN) experimentation, January 2018. https://datatracker.ietf.org/doc/html/rfc8311
6. Bolognesi, T., Brinksma, E.: Introduction to the ISO specification language LOTOS. Comput. Netw. ISDN Syst. **14**(1), 25–59 (1987)
7. Bolognesi, T., Lucidi, F.: A timed full LOTOS with time/action tree semantics. In: Theories and Experiences for Real-Time System Development, pp. 205–237. World Scientific (1994)
8. Bolognesi, T., Lucidi, F., Trigila, S.: Converging towards a timed LOTOS standard. Comput. Stand. Interfaces **16**(2), 87–118 (1994)
9. Boyer, B., Corre, K., Legay, A., Sedwards, S.: PLASMA-lab: a flexible, distributable statistical model checking library. In: Joshi, K., Siegle, M., Stoelinga, M., D'Argenio, P.R. (eds.) QEST 2013. LNCS, vol. 8054, pp. 160–164. Springer, Heidelberg (2013). https://doi.org/10.1007/978-3-642-40196-1_12
10. Bozic, J., Marsso, L., Mateescu, R., Wotawa, F.: A formal TLS handshake model in LNT. In: 3rd Workshop on Models for Formal Analysis of Real Systems and 6th International Workshop on Verification and Program Transformation, MARSVPT 2018, pp. 1–40 (2018)
11. Breslau, L., et al.: Advances in network simulation. Computer **33**(5), 59–67 (2000)
12. Cadar, C., Dunbar, D., Engler, D.R., et al.: KLEE: unassisted and automatic generation of high-coverage tests for complex systems programs. In: OSDI, vol. 8, pp. 209–224 (2008)
13. Cappart, Q., Limbrée, C., Schaus, P., Quilbeuf, J., Traonouez, L.M., Legay, A.: Verification of interlocking systems using statistical model checking. In: 2017 IEEE 18th International Symposium on High Assurance Systems Engineering (HASE), pp. 61–68 (2017). https://doi.org/10.1109/HASE.2017.10
14. Cardwell, N., Cheng, Y., Yeganeh, S.H., Swett, I., Jacobson, V.: BBR congestion control. https://datatracker.ietf.org/doc/html/draft-cardwell-iccrg-bbr-congestion-control
15. Christian Huitema: picoquic. https://github.com/private-octopus/picoquic, 4f11445
16. Chudnov, A., et al.: Continuous formal verification of Amazon S2N. In: Chockler, H., Weissenbacher, G. (eds.) CAV 2018. LNCS, vol. 10982, pp. 430–446. Springer, Cham (2018). https://doi.org/10.1007/978-3-319-96142-2_26
17. Clarke, E.M., Donzé, A., Legay, A.: On simulation-based probabilistic model checking of mixed-analog circuits. Formal Methods Syst. Des. **36**(2), 97–113 (2010). https://doi.org/10.1007/S10703-009-0076-Y

18. Clarke, E.M., Emerson, E.A.: Design and synthesis of synchronization skeletons using branching time temporal logic. In: Kozen, D. (ed.) Logic of Programs 1981. LNCS, vol. 131, pp. 52–71. Springer, Heidelberg (1982). https://doi.org/10.1007/BFb0025774

19. Clarke, E.M., Grumberg, O., Kroening, D., Peled, D.A., Veith, H.: Model Checking, 2nd edn. MIT Press (2018). https://mitpress.mit.edu/books/model-checking-second-edition

20. Classen, A., Heymans, P., Schobbens, P.Y., Legay, A.: Symbolic model checking of software product lines. In: Proceedings of the 33rd International Conference on Software Engineering, pp. 321–330 (2011)

21. Crochet, C., Rousseaux, T., Piraux, M., Sambon, J.F., Legay, A.: Verifying QUIC implementations using Ivy. In: Proceedings of the 2021 Workshop on Evolution, Performance and Interoperability of QUIC (2021). https://doi.org/10.1145/3488660.3493803

22. David, A., Larsen, K.G., Legay, A., Mikučionis, M., Poulsen, D.B.: Uppaal SMC tutorial. Int. J. Softw. Tools Technol. Transfer **17**, 397–415 (2015)

23. De Coninck, Q., Bonaventure, O.: Multipath QUIC. In: Proceedings of the 13th International Conference on Emerging Networking EXperiments and Technologies. ACM, November 2017. https://doi.org/10.1145/3143361.3143370

24. Floyd, S., Ramakrishnan, D.K.K., Black, D.L.: RFC 3168: the addition of explicit congestion notification (ECN) to IP, September 2001. https://datatracker.ietf.org/doc/html/rfc3168

25. Fujimoto, R.M.: Parallel and distributed simulation systems. In: Proceeding of the 2001 Winter Simulation Conference (Cat. No. 01CH37304), vol. 1, pp. 147–157. IEEE (2001)

26. Fujimoto, R.M., Riley, G.F., Perumalla, K.S.: Network Simulators. Springer, Cham (2007). https://doi.org/10.1007/978-3-031-79977-8

27. Holzmann, G.J.: The model checker SPIN. IEEE Trans. Software Eng. **23**(5), 279–295 (1997). https://doi.org/10.1109/32.588521

28. Issariyakul, T., Hossain, E., Issariyakul, T., Hossain, E.: Introduction to Network Simulator (NS2). Springer, New York (2009). https://doi.org/10.1007/978-0-387-71760-9

29. Iyengar, J., Swett, I.: RFC 9002. https://www.rfc-editor.org/rfc/rfc9002.html

30. Iyengar, J., Swett, I., Kühlewind, M.: QUIC acknowledgement frequency. https://datatracker.ietf.org/doc/html/draft-ietf-quic-ack-frequency-05

31. Iyengar, J., Thomson, M.: RFC 9000. https://www.rfc-editor.org/rfc/rfc9000

32. Jansen, R., Hopper, N.J.: Shadow: running tor in a box for accurate and efficient experimentation (2011)

33. Jansen, R., Newsome, J., Wails, R.: Co-opting Linux processes for high-performance network simulation. In: 2022 USENIX Annual Technical Conference (USENIX ATC 22), pp. 327–350. USENIX Association, Carlsbad, CA, July 2022. https://www.usenix.org/conference/atc22/presentation/jansen

34. Katoen, J.P.: The probabilistic model checking landscape. In: Proceedings of the 31st Annual ACM/IEEE Symposium on Logic in Computer Science, LICS 2016, pp. 31–45. Association for Computing Machinery, New York, NY, USA (2016). https://doi.org/10.1145/2933575.2934574

35. Kumar, R., Stoelinga, M.: Quantitative security and safety analysis with attack-fault trees. In: 2017 IEEE 18th International Symposium on High Assurance Systems Engineering (HASE), pp. 25–32 (2017). https://doi.org/10.1109/HASE.2017.12

36. Larsen, K.G., Legay, A.: 30 years of statistical model checking. In: Margaria, T., Steffen, B. (eds.) ISoLA 2020. LNCS, vol. 12476, pp. 325–330. Springer, Cham (2020). https://doi.org/10.1007/978-3-030-61362-4_18
37. Larsen, K.G., Mikucionis, M., Nielsen, B.: UPPAAL TRON User Manual. CISS, BRICS, Aalborg University, Aalborg, Denmark (2009)
38. Lee, H., Seibert, J., Fistrovic, D., Killian, C., Nita-Rotaru, C.: Gatling: automatic performance attack discovery in large-scale distributed systems. ACM Trans. Inf. Syst. Secur. (TISSEC) 17(4), 1–34 (2015)
39. Legay, A., Sedwards, S.: On statistical model checking with plasma. In: The 8th International Symposium on Theoretical Aspects of Software Engineering (2014)
40. Léonard, L., Leduc, G.: An introduction to ET-LOTOS for the description of time-sensitive systems. Comput. Netw. ISDN Syst. 29(3), 271–292 (1997)
41. Li, Y., Pierce, B.C., Zdancewic, S.: Model-based testing of networked applications. In: Proceedings of the 30th ACM SIGSOFT International Symposium on Software Testing and Analysis, pp. 529–539 (2021)
42. Lounas, R., Jafri, N., Legay, A., Mezghiche, M., Lanet, J.-L.: A formal verification of safe update point detection in dynamic software updating. In: Cuppens, F., Cuppens, N., Lanet, J.-L., Legay, A. (eds.) CRiSIS 2016. LNCS, vol. 10158, pp. 31–45. Springer, Cham (2017). https://doi.org/10.1007/978-3-319-54876-0_3
43. McMillan, K.L.: Symbolic Model Checking. Kluwer (1993). https://doi.org/10.1007/978-1-4615-3190-6
44. McMillan, K.L., Padon, O.: Ivy: a multi-modal verification tool for distributed algorithms. Comput. Aided Verification, 190–202 (2020). https://doi.org/10.1007/978-3-030-53291-8_12
45. McMillan, K.L., Zuck, L.D.: Compositional testing of internet protocols. In: 2019 IEEE Cybersecurity Development (SecDev) (2019). https://doi.org/10.1109/secdev.2019.00031
46. McMillan, K.L., Zuck, L.D.: Formal specification and testing of QUIC. In: Proceedings of the ACM Special Interest Group on Data Communication (2019). https://doi.org/10.1145/3341302.3342087
47. Merkel, D.: Docker: lightweight Linux containers for consistent development and deployment. Linux J. 2014(239), 2 (2014)
48. Michel, F., De Coninck, Q., Bonaventure, O.: QUIC-FEC: bringing the benefits of forward erasure correction to QUIC. In: 2019 IFIP Networking Conference (IFIP Networking), pp. 1–9 (2019). https://doi.org/10.23919/IFIPNetworking.2019.8816838
49. Ngo, V.C., Legay, A., Joloboff, V.: PSCV: a runtime verification tool for probabilistic SystemC models. In: Chaudhuri, S., Farzan, A. (eds.) CAV 2016. LNCS, vol. 9779, pp. 84–91. Springer, Cham (2016). https://doi.org/10.1007/978-3-319-41528-4_5
50. Offutt, J., Abdurazik, A.: Generating tests from UML specifications. In: France, R., Rumpe, B. (eds.) UML 1999. LNCS, vol. 1723, pp. 416–429. Springer, Heidelberg (1999). https://doi.org/10.1007/3-540-46852-8_30
51. Padon, O., McMillan, K.L., Panda, A., Sagiv, M., Shoham, S.: Ivy: safety verification by interactive generalization. ACM SIGPLAN Not. 51(6), 614–630 (2016). https://doi.org/10.1145/2980983.2908118
52. Paris, J., Arts, T.: Automatic testing of TCP/IP implementations using QuickCheck. In: Proceedings of the 8th ACM SIGPLAN Workshop on Erlang, pp. 83–92 (2009)

53. Pnueli, A.: The temporal logic of programs. In: 18th Annual Symposium on Foundations of Computer Science, Providence, Rhode Island, USA, 31 October–1 November 1977, pp. 46–57. IEEE Computer Society (1977). https://doi.org/10.1109/SFCS.1977.32

54. Rath, F., Schemmel, D., Wehrle, K.: Interoperability-guided testing of QUIC implementations using symbolic execution. In: Proceedings of the Workshop on the Evolution, Performance, and Interoperability of QUIC, pp. 15–21 (2018)

55. Rhee, I., Xu, L., Ha, S., Zimmermann, A., Eggert, L., Scheffenegger, R.: RFC 8312: cubic for fast long-distance networks, February 2018. https://datatracker.ietf.org/doc/html/rfc8312

56. Riley, G.F., Henderson, T.R.: The ns-3 network simulator. In: Wehrle, K., Güneş, M., Gross, J. (eds.) Modeling and Tools for Network Simulation, pp. 15–34. Springer, Heidelberg (2010). https://doi.org/10.1007/978-3-642-12331-3_2

57. Tazaki, H., et al.: Direct code execution: revisiting library OS architecture for reproducible network experiments. In: Proceedings of the Ninth ACM Conference on Emerging Networking Experiments and Technologies, pp. 217–228 (2013)

58. Thomson, M., Turner, S.: RFC 9001. https://www.rfc-editor.org/rfc/rfc9001.html

59. Tretmans, G., van de Laar, P.: Model-based testing with TorXakis: the mysteries of Dropbox revisited (2019)

60. Varga, A.: OMNeT++. In: Wehrle, K., Güneş, M., Gross, J. (eds.) Modeling and Tools for Network Simulation, pp. 35–59. Springer, Heidelberg (2010). https://doi.org/10.1007/978-3-642-12331-3_3

61. Veanes, M., Campbell, C., Grieskamp, W., Schulte, W., Tillmann, N., Nachmanson, L.: Model-based testing of object-oriented reactive systems with spec explorer. In: Hierons, R.M., Bowen, J.P., Harman, M. (eds.) Formal Methods and Testing. LNCS, vol. 4949, pp. 39–76. Springer, Heidelberg (2008). https://doi.org/10.1007/978-3-540-78917-8_2

62. Völker, T., Volodina, E., Tüxen, M., Rathgeb, E.P.: A QUIC simulation model for INET and its application to the acknowledgment ratio issue. In: 2020 IFIP Networking Conference (Networking), pp. 737–742. IEEE (2020)

63. Volodina, E., Rathgeb, E.P.: Impact of ack scaling policies on QUIC performance. In: 2021 IEEE 46th Conference on Local Computer Networks (LCN), pp. 41–48 (2021). https://doi.org/10.1109/LCN52139.2021.9524947

Adaptable Configuration of Decentralized Monitors

Ennio Visconti[1]([✉]) [iD], Ezio Bartocci[1] [iD], Yliès Falcone[2] [iD], and Laura Nenzi[3] [iD]

[1] TU Wien, Vienna, Austria
ennio.visconti@tuwien.ac.at
[2] Université Grenoble Alpes, Grenoble, France
[3] University of Trieste, Trieste, Italy

Abstract. Prominent challenges in runtime verification of a distributed system are the correct placement, configuration, and coordination of the monitoring nodes. This work considers state-of-the-art decentralized monitoring practices and proposes a framework to recommend efficient configurations of the monitoring system depending on the target specification. Our approach aims to optimize communication over several features (e.g., minimizing the number of messages exchanged, the number of computations happening overall, etc.) in contexts where finding an efficient communication strategy requires slow simulations. We optimize by training multiple machine learning models from simulations combining traces, formulae, and systems of different sizes. The experimental results show that the developed model can reliably suggest the best configuration strategy in a few nanoseconds, contrary to the minutes or possibly hours required by direct simulations that would be impractical at runtime.

1 Introduction

Computational systems are often spatially distributed and interconnected. To operate correctly and efficiently, they must be carefully verified and tested. The field practitioners know this very well and exploit several verification techniques to guarantee their correctness, both at design time [30] and runtime [8]. Runtime verification [2], in particular, is gaining significant momentum for several reasons: (i) it is a lightweight verification technique, and it allows checking more complex specifications or more complex systems; (ii) at runtime, some properties might be easier to express, as there is more contextual information that can help for the target analysis; (iii) runtime verification is typically more flexible, allowing to analyze system's changes *as they occur* [12,24,34], or changing requirements *on the go* [29].

However, only some techniques can exploit the system's distributed nature to provide guarantees promptly and efficiently. Among these, decentralized monitoring [5,11] is a promising approach, as it allows the distribution of the monitoring task among the components of the system by mapping requirements from the

© IFIP International Federation for Information Processing 2024
Published by Springer Nature Switzerland AG 2024
V. Castiglioni and A. Francalanza (Eds.): FORTE 2024, LNCS 14678, pp. 197–217, 2024.
https://doi.org/10.1007/978-3-031-62645-6_11

perspective of the global view of the system to the locally observable information. While this technique is promising, it still poses several challenges [5,31]: (i) It can be non-trivial to adequately express abstract/global requirements in terms of the individual components that form the system; (ii) A *distributed* monitor is a distributed system and, rep as such, can be challenging to handle by itself; (iii) Current approaches are still very rigid, as they do not encompass alternative network configurations or specification changes, and (iv) The way the monitors are deployed over the network (i.e. their configuration) can significantly impact the system's performances under scrutiny, possibly to a level where monitoring is too costly or hinders the actual observability of the requirements.

Running Example. Consider a modern WiFi setup for office space, like the one in Fig. 1a, where a different color represents every access point. In this environment, we expect two characteristics:

R1 it should guarantee no disruptions when users are moving around, and data is exchanged in real-time,

R2 it should provide an adaptive bandwidth optimized based on the usage patterns of the connected users.

In this scenario, two technologies are adequate for this task, i.e., a mesh setup (IEEE 802.11s) to avoid disconnections of moving devices (R1, represented in Fig. 1b–1d by using the same color for all the access points), and beamforming (prescribed in IEEE 802.11ac) to optimize based on the network usage patterns (R2, shown in Fig. 1c, 1d by using different shapes for the various access points to represent different traffic patterns), which can be used independently (Fig. 1b, 1c) or combined (Fig. 1d). When adopting a design like the one in Fig. 1d, the WiFi access points (APs) form a fully connected distributed network that exchanges information to assess the optimal distribution of the load coming from the requests of the devices. The requirements to ensure the mesh network is performing beamforming correctly could be easily and efficiently checked by a decentralized monitor deployed on the APs themselves. Still, the way the specific requirements are checked might change depending on the current configuration of the network, as well as the operating mode of the APs, as we will see in the following sections.

Related Work. Our work is based on the literature on decentralized monitoring of linear temporal logic [27] (LTL) with shared global clock [15,16], that resulted in the DECENTMON tool [17] also employed in our experiments. In [7], the authors address the problem of fault-tolerance in decentralized monitoring, extending the ideas presented in [18]. However, their work does not tackle the problem of optimal configuration (or placement). To the best of our knowledge, no other work addresses this problem. In the last year, runtime verification has gained increased attention in the context of artificial intelligence, both because it plays a central role in ensuring the safety and correctness of AI systems during runtime [32], and because of the benefits logic encodings can bring to word embeddings [1,26,28] (the term more commonly used to address encodings in

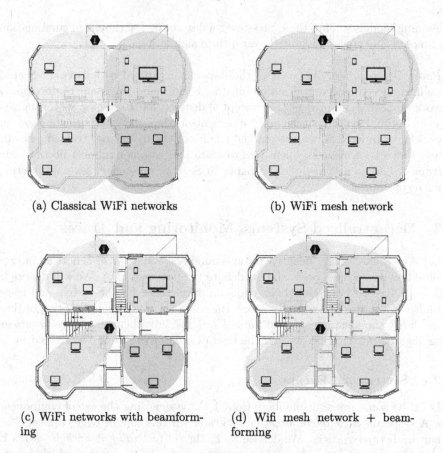

(a) Classical WiFi networks

(b) WiFi mesh network

(c) WiFi networks with beamforming

(d) Wifi mesh network + beamforming

Fig. 1. Example of four WiFi setups, from a traditional one (a) to a modern one (d). Subfigures from top to bottom show how beamforming transforms the networks' shapes, while subfigures from left to right show the impact of mesh networks in creating a unified continuous network. Original floorplans from [22].

natural language processing literature). On the other side, Machine Learning methods were exploited in several contexts related to runtime verification: for predictive monitor [9], for learning temporal logic specifications [3,6,25], and as a similarity function on formulae of temporal logic [10].

Contributions of This Paper. This paper proposes a novel approach to provide recommendations for efficiently distributing a decentralized monitor for temporal traces. We do that by (i) formalizing the decision of configurations of decentralized monitors as an optimization problem over several cost functions (ii) introducing a way to encode LTL formulae to approximate the search for the best configuration of decentralized monitors, (iii) presenting a classification and a regression task that approximate this search, together with multiple machine learning models solving these tasks over a dataset of 480 thousand combinations of monitoring traces generated over 40 h of simulation.

Paper Organization. The rest of the paper is organized as follows. In Sect. 2, we introduce the decentralized monitoring background necessary to develop our work. In Sect. 3, we present the concept of distribution strategies, we formalize it as an optimal synthesis one, and we present possible ways of finding a good one in Sect. 4. In Sect. 5, we present the results of the models we trained, showing how they can achieve excellent performance predictions in almost no time once trained. Lastly, we conclude the paper in Sect. 6, presenting several directions for future works.

2   Decentralized Systems, Monitoring and Traces

Let $\mathbb{N}$ be the set of non-negative natural numbers, and let $[a, b)$ denote an interval closed on a and open on b, and 2^A denote the powerset of A. We will denote by $\mathcal{T} = \{0, 1, \ldots, T\}$ the global time domain of reference for the system and traces (finite or infinite, i.e., when $T \to \infty$). Based on this fundamental notion of time, we clarify the meaning of *decentralized systems*, how their respective *events* are aggregated in timed *traces*, and the kind of *monitoring* we are interested in.

2.1   System and Events

Let $\mathcal{C}$ be some range of numbers from $1, \ldots, n$ denoting the set of components i. A system is a *complete graph* i.e., a graph where a unique edge connects each pair of distinct vertices. We denote by $\mathcal{E}_i$ the set of *locally observable events* by some component $i \in \mathcal{C}$. A notable element of $\mathcal{E}_i$ is the *no event* ε, which denotes the fact that no action has been observed.

Definition 1 (Local Trace). *We call local trace the sequence of events u_i that happen at all time points $t \in \mathcal{T}$ for the i-th component, i.e. $u_i : \mathcal{T} \to \mathcal{E}_i$.*

Running Example. We can consider the network of Fig. 1 as a system of four components ($\mathcal{C} = \{1, 2, 3, 4\}$), representing the WiFi Access Points (APs). Several locally observable events can be considered from a WiFi AP: an increase in the number of packets requested (e.g., a big file is being downloaded), an increase in packet priority is asked for (a video call is starting), etc. In particular, our event sets are defined as follows: all events start with a numeric id i corresponding to a unique identifier of the AP (the component) within the system; then they are optionally followed by _D_j when the event refers to a specific device communicating to the APs, where j will be used as a unique numeric id (in reality the MAC address of the device would be seen), and optionally followed by _A_k when the event is related to a specific antenna (we assume each AP has two antennas for simplicity), and completed by _n where n belongs to a finite set of specific events observable, e.g. CONNECTED, HIGH_POWER, HIGH_TRAFFIC,

IN_RANGE, etc. For example, a local trace of the component 1 is the sequences of events $(e_0, \varepsilon, e_2, \ldots)$, where e_0 is the event 1_D_1_CONNECTED, observed at time $t = 0$, no event is observed at time $t = 1$, e_2 is the event 1_D_1_WEAK_SIGNAL observed at time $t = 2$, and so on.

Definition 2 (Global Trace). *Let* $\mathcal{E} := \mathcal{E}_1 \times \ldots \times \mathcal{E}_n$ *denote the set of n-vectors of observable events* $\mathbf{e}$, *with the i-th component* e_i *of the vector* $\mathbf{e}$ *corresponding to an event observed at the component* $i \in \mathcal{C}$ *of the system. We call (global) trace a sequence of n-vectors of events* $(\mathbf{e}^0, \ldots, \mathbf{e}^T)$ *observed by all the components of the system, i.e.,* $\mathbf{u} : \mathcal{T} \to \mathcal{E}$.

Within the global trace $\mathbf{u}$, the symbol $\boldsymbol{\varepsilon} := (\varepsilon_1, \ldots, \varepsilon_n)$ will be used to denote that no event is observed in any of the components. In some cases, we will expect the system to run for an infinite amount of time, and we mark this characteristic by denoting with w and $\mathbf{w}$ respectively local and global infinite traces, and with Ω, the set of global traces.

2.2 Working Assumptions

Before addressing the problems of specifying system requirements and monitoring them, several working assumptions must be discussed, some of which are instrumental for keeping the presented work easily understandable, and some of which are oriented in keeping the scope of this work at a manageable size, but might be lifted in the future.

Fixed Number of Components. We assume the system's number of components in $\mathcal{C}$ to be known and constant.

Perfect Synchrony. By perfect synchrony, we mean that all system components share a global clock [19], i.e., they all observe the same time. This is the most prominent restriction, present in several definitions, and frequently entailed by the word *decentralized* (in contrast with *distributed,* which often also addresses the problem of time synchronization). While this assumption can seem too restrictive, it is a common strategy in the literature to abstract away the synchronization details in contexts where the system is *"fast enough"* in synchronizing without affecting the correctness of the specifications or the monitoring process. See [23] for a discussion on this topic.

Perfect Communication. By perfect communication, we mean the combination of several features of the message-exchanging interface that result in (i) messages always delivered, (ii) no transfer delays, and (iii) negligible transfer times, which combined imply that messages are always immediately delivered. These features can be significantly limiting in some cases. Still, they are perfectly reasonable for a large set of applications, e.g., in a use case like the one of Fig. 1, other layers of the networking protocols stack are responsible for guaranteeing the delivery, and the communication usually happens in the order of milliseconds, while the network optimization can typically occur within several seconds. However, future work might be directed at relaxing part of this assumption to widen the applicability to other scenarios, possibly along the lines of [4] that addressed this topic for another temporal logic.

Disjoint Events. Without loss of generality, we require that for any $i, j \in \mathcal{C}$, $\mathcal{E}_i \cap \mathcal{E}_j = \emptyset$, where $\mathcal{E}_i, \mathcal{E}_j$ are the set of events observed by i and j, respectively. In practice, this means we assume the events observed by different components are disjoint, i.e., no two components can observe the same event. This assumption is frequently made in other works on decentralized monitoring (see [5]).

Single Event per Component   As presented in Definitions 1-2, we require that each component can observe at most one event at each time point. Similarly to *Disjoint events*, this assumption does not bring any loss of generality, because for any set of shared events $\mathcal{E}$, a new set $2^{\mathcal{E}}$ can be constructed where all the possible combinations can be considered as unique events, and from it a new $\mathcal{E}' := \{(i, e) \mid i \leq n, e \in 2^{\mathcal{E}}\}$ can be derived.

2.3   Specifications

Several requirements could be needed for a system like the one in Sect. 1. For example, the designers of a mesh network might require that, within some time after a device connects, the orientation of the beam must change to a specific value. A simple yet powerful language for expressing such requirements is *linear temporal logic* (LTL) [27], although with some adaptations to support a decentralized evaluation.

Definition 3 (*LTL*Syntax [27]). *A (LTL) formula is any φ belonging to the set Φ, formed according to the following grammar:*

$$\varphi ::= p \quad | \quad \neg \varphi \quad | \quad \varphi \vee \varphi \quad | \quad \mathbf{X}\, \varphi \quad | \quad \varphi \, \mathbf{U} \, \varphi$$

where $p \in \mathcal{E}_i$ for some component $i \in \mathcal{C}$ of the system, denoting an observable local event. In addition, the following derived operators are commonly defined: $\top \equiv a \vee \neg a$, $\varphi_1 \wedge \varphi_2 \equiv \neg(\neg\varphi_1 \vee \neg\varphi_2)$, $\varphi_1 \rightarrow \varphi_2 \equiv \neg\varphi_1 \vee \varphi_2$, $\mathbf{F}\varphi \equiv \top \mathbf{U}\varphi$, $\mathbf{G}\varphi \equiv \neg\mathbf{F}(\neg\varphi)$.

Running Example. LTL formulae can be used effectively to describe the requirements of the system presented in Fig. 1, e.g., R1 can be decomposed in the following Formulae (1)-(2):

$$\text{1\_D\_1\_CONNECTED} \wedge \text{1\_D\_1\_WEAK\_SIGNAL} \wedge \text{2\_D\_1\_IN\_RANGE}$$

$$\longrightarrow$$

$$\mathbf{X}\, \text{2\_D\_1\_CONNECTED} \tag{1}$$

meaning that whenever a device is close to AP 2 and the signal of the current AP (component 1) is weak, it should connect to AP 2 as quickly as possible (in the next ($\mathbf{X}$) time unit). Or:

$$\text{1\_D\_1\_CONNECTED } \mathbf{U} \text{ (2\_D\_1\_CONNECTED} \land \neg\text{1\_D\_1\_CONNECTED)} \tag{2}$$

to denote that there is no service interruption until ($\mathbf{U}$) the device switches connection. Similarly, a possible requirement for beamforming (R2) can be the following:

$$\text{G(1\_A\_1\_HIGH\_TRAFFIC} \land \neg\text{1\_A\_2\_HIGH\_TRAFFIC)}$$
$$\rightarrow \text{(1\_A\_1\_HIGH\_POWER} \land \neg\text{1\_A\_2\_HIGH\_POWER)} \tag{3}$$

where A_k denotes the k-th antenna of the AP, meaning that as long as high traffic is experienced on one antenna and not on the other, the AP should set the power delivery of the antenna accordingly. The precise interpretation of *LTL* formulae can be described by the following relation:

Definition 4 (*LTL* semantics [27]). *By* $\models: \Omega \times \mathcal{T} \times \Phi$, *we denote traces and time instants in which a formula holds, in the following way:*

$(\mathbf{w}, t) \models p$ *iff* $\exists i \; s.t. \mathbf{w}(t)_i = p$

$(\mathbf{w}, t) \models \neg\varphi$ *iff* $(\mathbf{w}, t) \not\models \varphi$

$(\mathbf{w}, t) \models \varphi_1 \lor \varphi_2$ *iff* $(\mathbf{w}, t) \models \varphi_1 \; or \; (\mathbf{w}, t) \models \varphi_2$

$(\mathbf{w}, t) \models \mathbf{X}\varphi$ *iff* $(\mathbf{w}, t + 1) \models \varphi$

$(\mathbf{w}, t) \models \varphi_1 \mathbf{U} \varphi_2$ *iff* $\exists j \in [t, \infty) s.t. \; (\mathbf{w}, j) \models \varphi_2 \; and \; \forall k \in [t, j) : (\mathbf{w}, k) \models \varphi_1$

Note that, in the monitoring context, we typically consider infinite traces for the semantics, as this is more coherent to monitor a continuously evolving system.

2.4   Monitoring

The fundamental behavior expected by a monitoring system is to provide a verdict as soon as there is enough information to get one. In the context of the specifications we defined, such a verdict is usually a simple 'yes/no' answer to whether the trace of observed events satisfies the formula. This intuitive idea requires special care when the requirements incorporate temporal aspects, as we might not be able to provide such an answer by just considering the events observed so far, nor ever (if the trace is infinite). In the following, we consider the *definitive interpretation* of this idea: we say a trace τ of length T – (i) satisfies a formula φ when the formula would be satisfied for any trace τ' extending the current trace (i.e., such that τ' has the same events in the same order of τ and is of length $T' > T$); conversely (ii) it does not satisfy the formula φ when the formula would not be satisfied for any trace τ' extending the current trace. In other cases, we cannot provide an answer since we do not have enough information to give a definitive answer. Alternative interpretations are commonly used in the literature [14], depending on what best fits the targeted application. To clarify the previous intuitive description, we introduce the concept of *progression function P*, which is a function that maps a formula φ, a trace u and a time point t, to a three-valued logical verdict:

Definition 5 (Progression Function [5]). *We call* progression *the function* $P : \Phi \times \mathcal{E} \to \Phi_?$ *that maps formulae and events to new formulae, possibly containing the character '?' in place of some subformulae:*

$$P(\top, \mathbf{e}) = \top \qquad\qquad\qquad P(\bot, \mathbf{e}) = \bot$$

$$P(p, \mathbf{e}) = \top \ \textit{if} \ \exists \ i \ \textit{s.t.} \ e_i = p, \ \textit{otherwise} \ `?'$$

$$P(\neg\varphi, \mathbf{e}) = \neg P(\varphi, \mathbf{e})$$

$$P(\varphi_1 \vee \varphi_2, \mathbf{e}) = P(\varphi_1, \mathbf{e}) \vee P(\varphi_2, \mathbf{e})$$

$$P(X\varphi, \mathbf{e}) = P(\varphi, \mathbf{e})$$

$$P(\varphi_1 U \varphi_2, \mathbf{e}) = P(\varphi_2, \mathbf{e}) \vee P(\varphi_1, \mathbf{e}) \wedge \varphi_1 U \varphi_2$$

The character '?' is adopted in Definition 5 to denote the distinguishing aspect of decentralized monitoring against the classical centralized one. In a centralized monitor, instead of '?' we would see $\bot$ every time $\nexists i$ s.t. $\mathbf{e}_i = p$. In a decentralized context, we would continue to see $\bot$ when $\mathbf{e}_i \neq p$, for some component i where $p \in \mathcal{E}_i$. At the same time, for all the others $j \neq i$, we must wait for communication to happen in order to have a Boolean evaluation.

3   Monitors' Distribution Strategies

The specific distribution strategy of the progression function computations of Definition 5 can significantly impact the resources required to reach a verdict, and, therefore, it can be crucial to determine whether or not a given formula can conveniently be monitored at a given system node. In doing so, all the subformulae of the specification must be mapped to at least one component of the system, and possibly more than one formula is mapped to the same component. We clarify this intuition in the following definition.

Definition 6 (Distribution strategy). *Let Stfm(φ) denote the set of subformulae of φ. A monitor distribution strategy is a function $d_\varphi : \mathcal{C} \to 2^{Stfm(\varphi)}$ that maps every component $i \in \mathcal{C}$ to a set of subformulae of φ that must be monitored at that component. Moreover, every subformula must be mapped to at least one component, i.e., $\forall \psi \in Stfm(\varphi), \exists i \ s.t. \ \psi \in d_\varphi(i)$.*

In principle, any use case might have an ideal d_φ of Definition 6 (e.g. a notable case is when a given sub-formula is mapped to multiple components – like it is often the case when developing resilient or traffic-efficient systems). For that reason, the efficiency of the actual run can be significantly impacted by a poor choice of a distribution strategy, for some chosen cost function γ. That said, most of the times practitioners consider a restricted set of cost functions [5]; in the rest of our work, we focus on the following ones:

Definition 7 (Monitoring cost). *We call monitoring cost any of the following:*

- *N. of progressions: Computational iterations of the P function required to reach a final verdict.*
- *N. of messages: Number of messages exchanged to complete the monitoring task.*
- *Avg. message size: Average size of the messages exchanged.*
- *Trace length: Evaluation delay between the observed events and the actual result.*

Running Example. In the network we are considering, we might want to minimize the number of progressions to reduce the computational load on the APs (e.g. when several devices often do real-time calls), or maybe we want to minimize the average message size (e.g., when most of the traffic is for intensive downloads and uploads, like in a video-making setting).

In the experiments of Sect. 5, we consider a specific monitoring cost function for any evaluation. In the following, we denote by γ the chosen monitoring cost function. For a fixed formula φ and a system $\mathcal{C}$, it is not trivial in general to decide which monitoring distribution strategy d_φ to pursue since the variability of the input traces can significantly affect any monitoring cost one is willing to optimize. For example, consider the case of Fig. 2 where alternative strategies are compared for a system similar to the one described in Sect. 1: when observing a trace having $\neg c$ at time 1, orchestration and choreography will lead to a result immediately, while migration will require some extra messages and processing steps, as it has to go through the node $\{e\}$ first. Generally, the *best* distribution strategy can be defined as follows.

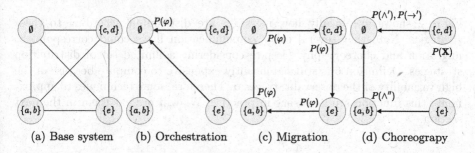

(a) Base system   (b) Orchestration   (c) Migration   (d) Choreograpy

Fig. 2. Example of the different distribution strategies for the system of Fig. 1 and Formula 1, i.e. $\varphi = (a \wedge b \wedge c) \rightarrow \mathbf{X}d$, where, for brevity, a replaces 1_D_1_CONNECTED, b replaces 1_D_1_WEAK_SIGNAL, c replaces 2_D_1_IN_RANGE, d replaces 2_D_1_CONNECTED, and e some other generic event not affected by the current formula. The sets denote the events locally observable by each node; P represents the progression function evaluation, while $'$ and $''$ are used to distinguish the two occurrences (in order of occurrence) of the symbol $\wedge$ in the formula. Arrows denote the communication flow.

Definition 8 (Best distribution strategy). *The best distribution strategy of formula φ, if it exists, is the distribution strategy d_φ that minimizes the accumulated monitoring cost function γ, over all the components i of the system $\mathcal{C}$, for any trace $\mathbf{u}$.*

$$\hat{d}_\varphi := \arg\min_{d_\varphi} \sum_{i \leq n} \gamma(d_\varphi(i), \mathbf{u})$$

Unfortunately, the variability of formulae and observable traces can be so high that the exact computation of Definition 8 becomes prohibitive for any realistic use cases. Therefore, some approximations must be developed to answer this question promptly so that the monitoring task can start without significant penalties. To face this problem, focusing on specific monitoring strategies frequently adopted in practice is convenient (see [11, 15]).

- $\mathcal{D}_1$ (*Orchestration*): the class of traditional centralized monitors that assumes (or waits for) global observability. It corresponds to the mapping $0 \mapsto Stfm(\varphi)$.
- $\mathcal{D}_2$ (*Migration*): the class of monitors where the state of a monitor is progressed by a node when some relevant local event is observed or otherwise transferred to the *next* node. It maps the whole specification to all components, i.e., $i \mapsto \varphi, \forall i$.
- $\mathcal{D}_3$ (*Choreography*): the class of monitoring functions where the formula is broken down in a directed acyclic graph over several nodes of the system, and only results are communicated, such that $i \mapsto \{\psi \in Stfm(\varphi) \mid i \in \arg\max_{j \leq n} s_\psi(j)\}$, where $s_\psi(j)$ denotes some scoring rule for ψ at node j (e.g. the number of atomic propositions in the formula that are locally observable).

Figure 2 shows graphically how messages are distributed according to these strategies. Note that several other communication flows could correspond to migration and choreography. Despite considering a limited set of distribution strategies, Definition 6 is still significantly expensive to compute because of the high variability of the observable traces $\mathbf{u}$. Therefore, some techniques to approximate this function are necessary in practice. We will present them in the next section.

4   Choosing Good Distribution Strategies

We know that the optimal distribution strategy $\hat{d}_\varphi$ depends on the specific number of components of the system n, on the cost function of interest γ, and the formula φ being monitored. In use cases like the one described in our running example, the number of components of the system is fixed for the lifespan of the system, therefore we drop the dependency on the constant n to simplify the presentation. Still, the exact computation of the optimal distribution strategy is costly and too slow to take the timely decisions that are needed to accommodate the system and the requirements of Formulae 1–3. In the following, we consider an alternative approach to approximate the best distribution strategy, where we extract some ahead-of-time knowledge of our system to select the distribution strategy $\mathcal{D}_k$ with the highest probability of being the best for the current system $\mathcal{C}$ and specification φ, more precisely:

$$\text{If } \hat{d}_\varphi = d' \text{ then } d' = \arg\max_{d_j} Pr(\hat{d}_\varphi = d_j | \varphi) \tag{4}$$

The part of (4) after *then* introduces the probability space over distribution functions for a given formula φ on a system of n components. While an exact computation of this probability does not save us from having to consider all the possible traces $\mathbf{u}$, a statistical estimation when d_j is restricted to the strategies $\mathcal{D}_1, \mathcal{D}_2, \mathcal{D}_3$ is more easily achievable, and it might also get us very close to the optimal distribution strategy. To pursue this approach, some aspects must be clarified:

- what information we can extract from the formula φ to approximate the best distribution strategy $\hat{d}_\varphi$
- whether we can recommend a good/better strategy for some cost function γ when some information about the current system is available (e.g., we know the cost for some previous trace and distribution strategy of the system);
- whether we can predict the cost function γ for different distribution strategies, given some observations.

We explore these aspects respectively in Sect. 4.1–4.3, while we postpone the actual implementation details to Sect. 5.

4.1 Formula Encoding

To properly compare the possible distribution strategies, it is crucial to encode the target formula φ so that some characteristics are kept. (i) It must communicate the primary aspects that could affect the performance of the distribution strategies. (ii) It must provide a compact representation that allows treating in a similar way formulae that are expected to behave similarly in terms of time required to complete the evaluation. (iii) It must be easily exploitable for the recommendation and prediction tasks we are interested in.

Definition 9 (Encoding). *We call encoding $E : \Phi \to \mathbb{R}^k$ a function that maps a specification φ to a vector of k real numbers.*

In [5], the authors define an *urgency level* to support the definition of an evaluation priority among the subformulae to monitor, with the idea that some temporal operators might affect more significantly the time required to complete the evaluation of a formula. That intuition inspires the structural delay encoding presented in Definition 10.

Definition 10 (Structural Delay). *Let T_φ be the syntax tree of the formula φ, and let $T_\varphi[i]$ denote the i-th node of T_φ given a left-to-right top-to-bottom ordering of its nodes. We will call $\overline{E}$:*

$$\overline{E}(\varphi)[i] = \begin{cases} 0 & if \quad T_\varphi[i] = \top \mid \bot \mid \neg \mid \wedge \\ 1 & if \quad T_\varphi[i] = p \ s.t. \ \exists j, p \in \mathcal{E}_j \\ 1 & if \quad T_\varphi[i] = \mathbf{X} \\ 2 & if \quad T_\varphi[i] = \mathbf{U} \end{cases} \tag{5}$$

The structural delay encoding of φ.

For a formula $\varphi = (a \vee b)\mathbf{U}\neg c$, the encoding steps are the following (summarized in Fig. 3):

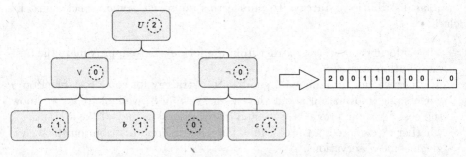

Fig. 3. Encoding steps for a formula $\varphi = (a \vee b)\mathbf{U}\neg c$. First, the tree is built (left), then numbers are extracted (rounded numbers on left), and lastly, the numbers are linearized (right).

1. The formula is first rewritten so only to contain the symbols in Definition 3.
2. A binary tree is generated from φ, where all atomic propositions are leaves, and all logical operators are internal nodes of the tree. Unary operators are represented as binary operators with a dummy leaf.
3. The encoding of Definition 10 is applied, with the respective numeric encoding associated with every symbol of the formula. Dummy leaves are encoded as zeros.
4. The binary tree is linearized as a sequence of dataset features in a classical left-to-right breadth-first traversal. In this process, all the formulae are normalized as if they were of the maximum length by padding the shorter ones with zeros.

4.2   Recommending a Better Distribution Strategy

In scenarios where the monitoring cost $\overline{\gamma}$ of some distribution strategy was observed ahead of time (e.g. when a similar trace was monitored in the past), one might want to check whether a better distribution strategy could be chosen. In this case, the goal is to improve the monitoring cost, thanks to the recent experience. We can formalize the following classification problem:

Definition 11 (Classification problem). *Given the encoding* $\overline{E}(\varphi)$ *of the formula* φ, *and a set of distribution strategies (or* classes*) like* $\{\mathcal{D}_1, \mathcal{D}_2, \mathcal{D}_3\}$, *we want to select* $\hat{\mathcal{D}}_k$ *in the following way:*

$$\hat{\mathcal{D}}_k = \underset{\mathcal{D}_k \ k=1,2,3}{\arg\max} \ Pr(\gamma(\mathcal{D}_k, \mathbf{u}) \leq \overline{\gamma} \mid \overline{E}(\varphi), \overline{\gamma})$$

$\hat{\mathcal{D}}_k$ denotes the "best" distribution strategy as the one that maximizes the probability of yielding a lower cost γ for some trace $\mathbf{u}$ that will be observed in future monitoring instances. Note that these traces are unknown, so a training stage is needed to estimate the costs correctly.

4.3 Predicting the Monitoring Cost

A more challenging problem is predicting the cost of a distribution strategy for a given system without having any information about previous traces. In this case, the only information for the input would be the specification φ, and the goal is to have some prediction of the monitoring cost, which can be used to decide directly which of the options provides the best-predicted cost, and therefore, which strategy to adopt. We can cast this as a regression problem:

Definition 12 (Regression problem). *We want to predict the monitoring cost for a given distribution strategy* $\mathcal{D}_k$.

$$\gamma(\mathcal{D}_k, \mathbf{u}) \approx f_k(\overline{E}(\varphi))$$

The f_k function approximates the γ function that predicts the cost of a given distribution strategy $\mathcal{D}_k$ without simulating it. To correctly approximate it, a proper training stage is required.

Running Example. Consider our network where R1 and R2 are being monitored as the Formulae (2) and (3) respectively. Which strategy should they follow when the system starts? A good guess could come from substituting Definition 12 in Definition 11, where, in the absence of information on the trace, an estimation of the monitoring cost γ informs the strategy to follow (say, e.g. an orchestration choreography where the monitoring is happening only on the AP with id = 3). At some point, a sequence of events 1_A_1_HIGH_TRAFFIC is recorded (e.g. $\overline{\mathbf{u}} = \{..., 1\_A\_1\_HIGH\_TRAFFIC, 1\_A\_1\_HIGH\_TRAFFIC\}$). Should the APs change the monitoring strategy to accommodate the new traffic? To decide, one could use Definition 11 to assess whether the orchestration is the best strategy for the currently observed traffic (they now can directly observe $\gamma(\mathcal{D}_1, \overline{\mathbf{u}})$). A simulation-based approach, on the contrary, could require several seconds to evaluate the cost for the three distribution strategies we selected, for a single trace, a result that should be replicated with some variation of the trace to make the choice more robust. In the following, we will show how our approach can significantly outperform a direct simulation.

5 Experimental Evaluation

We have seen in Sect. 4 that the problem of deciding a decentralized distribution strategy over a system can be interpreted in several ways, and it might be constrained over several dimensions (e.g., number of messages or message size). In a use case like the one described in Sect. 1, a change to the decentralization strategy of the monitor has to happen in very little time, not more than a few seconds, and should not impact the computational power of the components, that could be already under-stress for satisfying the bandwidth demand of the connected devices.

5.1 Studied Dataset

To generate a suitable dataset for our models, we used DecentMon [17], a tool for benchmarking decentralized monitors. The data was collected by running DecentMon over randomly generated formulae containing between 2 and 50 logical operators, over systems of 3, 5, 7, and 9 components, and traces of 100-time steps. The traces were generated by independently sampling each event from a uniform distribution for any component of the system, and the monitor was run over them until an overall simulation memory bound was reached. If the bound is reached without a verdict, the combination of formula-trace is discarded. Our formulae have been randomly generated following the nine popular formula patterns from [13], which were selected for covering 92% of a dataset of 555 real-world LTL specifications and that are frequently adopted as a reference in the literature (see [5,21]). Common examples of patterns from [13], are $G(q \rightarrow G(\neg p))$ to denote the "absence" of p (i.e. it is false), or $G((\neg q) \vee F(q \wedge Fp))$ to denote the "existence" of p (i.e. at some point it becomes true). The monitoring of each generated formula is then simulated for the three analyzed strategies (orchestration, migration, choreography) over a randomly extracted trace. The final dataset contains approximately 480 thousand entries (i.e., each entry being a combination of *strategy*, *formula*, and *trace*), over a feature space of 709 numerical dimensions, that we used to train and test our models. The dataset has been generated over approximately 40 h of multi-thread simulations on 12 cores of a 2.1 GHz Intel Xeon (Cascade Lake), L1 cache 384 KB, L2 cache 48 MB, L3 cache 192 MB, and 16 GB of RAM. For our experiments, an independent model was trained for any combination of the system size and the cost function, using 70% of the dataset for training and the rest for testing the models. For the classification problem, after some preprocessing, the final training dataset contains, on average, 10250 rows per model, while for the regression problem, the final training dataset contains, on average, 76000 rows per model. Check the accompanying artifact for a replication package[1].

---

[1] Live repository at https://github.com/ennioVisco/predicting-decentmon, paper snapshot at [33].

5.2   Classification Problem

For the classification problem of Sect. 4.2, all *monitoring cost* functions from previous evaluations can be observed, and, therefore, a more informed decision can be made. We used a K-Nearest Neighbors classifier implemented in Python's `scikit-learn` over the three distribution strategies presented on our target dataset. We collected the accuracy and $F1$ scores for the different system sizes. The results are shown in Table 1.

Table 1. Classification model *accuracy* and $F1$ scores for each system size in terms of the number of components (denoted as |**System**|), and for each class. The columns show the prediction accuracy and the $F1$ metric for each class (we chose not to take the average because of how unbalanced the classes are). Both accuracy and $F1$ can range from 0 (very bad) to 1 (perfect). A '$-$' sign denotes insufficient data points in that class to compute a reliable $F1$ score.

|System| # comp.	Cost function	Accuracy score	F1 score		
			Orchestration	Migration	Choreography
3	N. of progressions	0.956	0.166	–	0.978
	N. of messages	0.873	0.574	0.926	–
	Avg. message size	0.951	0.760	0.235	0.975
	Trace length	0.976	0.043	–	0.924
5	N. of progressions	0.976	0.043	–	0.988
	N. of messages	0.880	0.647	0.928	–
	Avg. message size	0.955	0.757	0.471	0.976
	Trace length	0.895	0.155	–	0.944
7	N. of progressions	0.983	0.172	–	0.991
	N. of messages	0.881	0.680	0.927	–
	Avg. message size	0.955	0.765	0.489	0.977
	Trace length	0.906	0.115	–	0.950
9	N. of progressions	0.980	0.084	–	0.990
	N. of messages	0.878	0.746	0.920	–
	Avg. message size	0.948	0.717	0.575	0.973
	Trace length	0.905	0.180	–	0.950

The results of Table 1 clearly show that the classification problem is somehow straightforward (contrary to the regression one that we will see later), as is apparent from the very high accuracy scores. This is unsurprising, as it can exploit the information from an actual evaluation for subsequent computations. Nevertheless, the combination with the $F1$ score uncovers certain aspects: (i) Some classes have very low $F1$ scores despite the high accuracy, showing that the dataset was very unbalanced. Note that unbalanced classes mean that the number of entries (e.g., the number of combinations of *formula-trace*) where the best number of progressions is observed with choreography is $>>$ than the one of migration. This is even more apparent by looking at the $-$ signs (particularly when pursuing migration), which report that the difference in the cardinality of that class versus the others was so big that no reasonable $F1$ score could be extracted. This means the optimal strategy consistently leaned towards one distribution strategy for most cost functions (except for the average message size). (ii) We do not observe a significant change in the scores as the number of the components in the system increases; this means that, from the data we have and the hypotheses we made, we can conclude that the size of the system does not play a significant role in moving the convenience from one strategy to another.

5.3 Regression Problem

Only the formula's encoding is available for the regression problem of Sect. 4.3. On our target dataset, we tested two alternative approximation techniques, a simple linear regression, also regularized via Ridge and Lasso, and a multi-layer perceptron of 1 hidden layer, 100-neurons with a ReLU [20] activation function and no activation function for the output – the default settings from the implementation we used from Python's scikit-learn, over the *monitoring cost* functions previously presented. We collected the R^2 scores for the different sizes of the system and for the adopted regression techniques, which denote the proportion of the variation in the monitoring cost that can be predicted from the input data. The results are shown in Table 2.

Table 2. Regression model R^2 scores for the system's different sizes and regression techniques. The R^2 score denotes the proportion of the variation in the monitoring cost that can be predicted from the input data. It ranges from $-\infty$ (very bad) to 1 (perfect).

|System| # comp.	Technique	# Progressions	# Messages	Avg. |Message|	|Trace|
3	Linear Regressor	0.697	0.478	0.322	0.738
	L.R. + Ridge Regularization	0.443	0.345	0.608	0.584
	L.R. + Lasso Regularization	0.650	0.284	0.558	0.383
	Multi-Layer Perceptron	0.501	0.564	0.828	0.785
5	Linear Regressor	-1.318	$-4.097*10^2$	-9.056	0.607
	L.R. + Ridge Regularization	0.395	0.275	0.666	0.620
	L.R. + Lasso Regularization	0.682	0.209	0.651	0.381
	Multi-Layer Perceptron	0.656	0.679	0.903	0.868
7	Linear Regressor	0.062	0.113	0.130	-1.452
	L.R. + Ridge Regularization	0.628	0.232	0.494	0.638
	L.R. + Lasso Regularization	0.844	0.163	0.479	0.386
	Multi-Layer Perceptron	0.477	0.762	0.910	0.900
9	Linear Regressor	$-5.479*10^3$	$-6.064*10$	$-1.526*10^2$	$-9.567*10^2$
	L.R. + Ridge Regularization	0.664	0.204	0.521	0.637
	L.R. + Lasso Regularization	0.797	0.134	0.500	0.388
	Multi-Layer Perceptron	0.397	0.761	0.901	0.906

The results of the regression problem in Table 2, instead, give some insights into the challenges in predicting the actual cost: (i) The R^2 scores of the linear regressors become quickly worse as the system size increases; this fact provides a clear benchmark of the nonlinearity of the problem, as it becomes significantly more challenging to predict it by linear approximation (e.g. for the n. of messages R^2 goes from 0.478 to 0.134 selecting the best performing linear models). (ii) A Multi-Layer Perceptron (MLP) without any specific structuring of the layers performs already very well in several dimensions (e.g., the Avg. Message Size is always above 0.900, the Trace Size is always above 0.780, and the # Messages is above 0.670 except for a system of 3 nodes). The previous points are more clearly depicted in Fig. 4, which compares the predictions for the number of messages for a system of 5 components: the linear models, even the one regularized via Lasso, are not able to define a good prediction model. In contrast, the Multi-Layer Perceptron captures the metric more precisely (they are more spread along the identity diagonal, representing $R^2 = 1$). (iii) The number of progressions needed to complete the monitoring is inherently harder to predict for non-regularized models, (e.g. for a system of 9 components $R^2 = 0.397$, is significantly lower than the next worse predicted measure, i.e. $R^2 = 0.761$ for # Messages). (iv) While the number of progression gets harder to predict as the system grows, the results seem to get better with Lasso regularization, suggesting that the growth in size helps the model in selecting some dominant features over the others. Lastly, (v) in line with the scores from the classification problem, the size of the system seems not to significantly affect the prediction score (all values are in a range never larger than ±0.200 as the system grows).

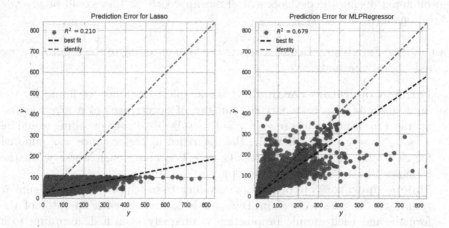

Fig. 4. Comparison of Lasso (left) vs Multi-Layer Perceptron (right) regressors scores for predicting the number of messages exchanged in a system of 5 nodes. y denotes the real value while $\hat{y}$ is the predicted one. In a perfect predictor, the values would be all along the identity line.

5.4   Computational Performances

The memory allocation of the trained K-Nearest Neighbors model is approximately 30 MB, while for the Multi-layer Perceptron model, it is 0.9 MB. The simulation time is harder to estimate accurately because of the high variation from the specific parameters in a particular scenario. In our experiments, for a system of 5 components, the simulation time for extracting 5276 combinations of formulae and traces for a single formula pattern from [21] is 134 min (1.52 s on average for a single formula/trace combination), while our regressor models can evaluate 35 thousands combinations in 200 ms.

5.5   Discussion

The principal argument in support of the proposed learning-based approach, in contrast to a direct simulation-based approach, comes from the runtime benefit of the recommendations, and this is very clear when addressing the classification problem, as well as the regression one via MLP, except perhaps for the # of Progressions that proved to be the most challenging metric for both problems. The memory required and testing time from the trained models are negligible (among all the models we tested, the testing time was very small for large sets of values, i.e. 200 ms for 35k entries). In contrast, a simulation of the system would require much larger amounts of memory and several seconds in the optimal case where a few traces are sufficient. We now briefly mention some of the pitfalls we encountered during the development of our approach, as they could be guiding directions for future work.

Alternative Encodings.   Before reaching the final encoding of the input data, we tested several alternatives:

- **Formula operators cardinality**: the simplest encoding we found for the input formula φ is to report the number of occurrences of a given logical operator for that formula (e.g. in $\varphi = F(a \wedge b) \vee (c \wedge d)$, the encoding would be F = 1, $\wedge$ = 2, $\vee$ = 1). While the difference in performance was minimal for elementary formulae, the results were becoming much worse when the formulae had several levels of nesting.
- **Unique operators encoding**: an encoding we tested providing very similar results to the ones showed in Table 1-2 is one where each operator of the formula and each atomic proposition is uniquely identified according to a shared dictionary (e.g., in $\varphi = F(a \wedge b) \vee (c \wedge d)$, the encoding would be F = 1, $\wedge$ = 2, $\vee$ = 3, a = -1, b = -2, c = -3). The numbers were generally slightly worse, although in that case, the increase in the model's size showed even more minor negative effects. Perhaps this information can be exploited in future, using more clever encodings.
- **Trace events**: To incorporate the information about the evaluated trace (particularly relevant for the Classification problem), we included the exact sequence of events that occurred in every component at every time step.

While this encoding was quite costly (we observed an average 30% increase in the preprocessing time of the dataset), it made the classifiers perform worse overall. We explain this by noting that the trace space is much larger than the formula space (and grows faster as the system gets larger), and the classifier cannot generalize well enough to the unseen traces. That said, we do not exclude that some information from the traces could be helpful, perhaps in the form of general statistics (e.g., average number of events per component, average number of events per time step, events frequency, etc.).

6 Conclusions

We proposed a new formalization for optimally distributing decentralized monitors in the context of unknown ideal network configurations framed on the use case of a WiFi mesh network with beamforming. We developed two models based on state-of-the-art simulators and machine-learning techniques to approximate this problem and provide reliable answers instantly at runtime. Several directions could be followed in future work: firstly, some of the initial scenario assumptions could be lifted, most notably considering a weighted network would allow to account for *imperfect communication* and to extend the methodology to several other scenarios. A clear direction of study could come from an end-to-end test of our solution, where a real system is systematically stressed to test how beneficial our approach can be when compared to simulation. Another interesting direction would be to allow for dynamic distribution strategies. These strategies could exploit contextual information (e.g., deviations from the expected costs or extra not-predicted information) to guide a reconfiguration, effectively reacting to environmental changes. Lastly, in the direction of perfecting the predictions, alternative layouts of the Multi-Layer Perceptron (e.g. more hidden layers), or alternative learning techniques (e.g. Support Vector Machine-based ones) could provide substantial improvements.

Acknowledgments. The authors acknowledge funding from the Austrian Science Fund (FWF) for the project "High-dimensional statistical learning: New methods to advance economic and sustainability policies" (ZK 35), jointly carried out by the University of Klagenfurt, the University of Salzburg, TU Wien, and the Austrian Institute of Economic Research (WIFO). The work was also partially supported by the WWTF project ICT22-023. The work was also partially supported by SEVERITAS ANR-20-CE39-0009 of the French national research agency.

References

1. Asudani, D.S., Nagwani, N.K., Singh, P.: Impact of word embedding models on text analytics in deep learning environment: a review. Artif. Intell. Rev., 1–81 (2023). https://api.semanticscholar.org/CorpusID:257098478
2. Bartocci, E., Falcone, Y., Francalanza, A., Reger, G.: Introduction to runtime verification. In: Bartocci, E., Falcone, Y. (eds.) Lectures on Runtime Verification. LNCS, vol. 10457, pp. 1–33. Springer, Cham (2018). https://doi.org/10.1007/978-3-319-75632-5_1

3. Bartocci, E., Mateis, C., Nesterini, E., Nickovic, D.: Survey on mining signal temporal logic specifications. Inf. Comput. **289**(Part), 104957 (2022)
4. Basin, D., Klaedtke, F., Zalinescu, E.: Failure-aware Runtime Verification of Distributed Systems. In: Harsha, P., Ramalingam, G. (eds.) 35th IARCS Conference on Foundations of Software Technology and Theoretical Computer Science (FSTTCS 2015), Dagstuhl, Germany (2015)
5. Bauer, A., Falcone, Y.: Decentralised LTL monitoring. In: Giannakopoulou, D., Méry, D. (eds.) FM 2012. LNCS, vol. 7436, pp. 85–100. Springer, Heidelberg (2012). https://doi.org/10.1007/978-3-642-32759-9_10
6. Bombara, G., Belta, C.: Offline and online learning of signal temporal logic formulae using decision trees. ACM Trans. Cyber Phys. Syst. **5**(3), 22:1–22:23 (2021)
7. Bonakdarpour, B., Fraigniaud, P., Rajsbaum, S., Rosenblueth, D., Travers, C.: Decentralized asynchronous crash-resilient runtime verification. J. ACM **69**(5), 1–31 (2022)
8. Bornholt, J., et al.: Using lightweight formal methods to validate a key-value storage node in amazon S3. In: SOSP 2021 (2021)
9. Bortolussi, L., Cairoli, F., Paoletti, N., Smolka, S.A., Stoller, S.D.: Neural predictive monitoring and a comparison of frequentist and Bayesian approaches. Int. J. Softw. Tools Technol. Transf. **23**(4), 615–640 (2021)
10. Bortolussi, L., Gallo, G.M., Kretínský, J., Nenzi, L.: Learning model checking and the kernel trick for signal temporal logic on stochastic processes. In: Fisman, D., Rosu, G. (eds.) TACAS 2022. LNCS, vol. 13243, pp. 281–300. Springer, Cham (2022). https://doi.org/10.1007/978-3-030-99524-9_15
11. Colombo, C., Falcone, Y.: Organising LTL monitors over distributed systems with a global clock. In: Bonakdarpour, B., Smolka, S.A. (eds.) RV 2014. LNCS, vol. 8734, pp. 140–155. Springer, Cham (2014). https://doi.org/10.1007/978-3-319-11164-3_12
12. Deshmukh, J.V., Donzé, A., Ghosh, S., Jin, X., Juniwal, G., Seshia, S.A.: Robust online monitoring of signal temporal logic. Formal Methods Syst. Des. **51**, 5–30 (2015)
13. Dwyer, M.B., Avrunin, G.S., Corbett, J.C.: Patterns in property specifications for finite-state verification. In: Proceedings of the 21st International Conference on Software Engineering, ICSE 1999. Association for Computing Machinery (1999)
14. Eisner, C., Fisman, D., Havlicek, J., Lustig, Y., McIsaac, A., Van Campenhout, D.: Reasoning with temporal logic on truncated paths. In: Hunt, W.A., Somenzi, F. (eds.) CAV 2003. LNCS, vol. 2725, pp. 27–39. Springer, Heidelberg (2003). https://doi.org/10.1007/978-3-540-45069-6_3
15. El-Hokayem, A., Falcone, Y.: On the monitoring of decentralized specifications: semantics, properties, analysis, and simulation. ACM Trans. Softw. Eng. Methodol. **29**, 1–57 (2020)
16. Falcone, Y.: On decentralized monitoring. In: Nouri, A., Wu, W., Barkaoui, K., Li, Z.W. (eds.) VECoS 2021. LNCS, vol. 13187, pp. 1–16. Springer, Cham (2022). https://doi.org/10.1007/978-3-030-98850-0_1
17. Falcone, Y.: DecentMon: an OCaml benchmark for decentralised monitoring of LTL (2023). https://gricad-gitlab.univ-grenoble-alpes.fr/falconey/decentmon
18. Fraigniaud, P., Rajsbaum, S., Travers, C.: On the number of opinions needed for fault-tolerant run-time monitoring in distributed systems. In: Bonakdarpour, B., Smolka, S.A. (eds.) RV 2014. LNCS, vol. 8734, pp. 92–107. Springer, Cham (2014). https://doi.org/10.1007/978-3-319-11164-3_9

19. Francalanza, A., Pérez, J.A., Sánchez, C.: Runtime verification for decentralised and distributed systems. In: Bartocci, E., Falcone, Y. (eds.) Lectures on Runtime Verification. LNCS, vol. 10457, pp. 176–210. Springer, Cham (2018). https://doi.org/10.1007/978-3-319-75632-5_6

20. Fukushima, K.: Cognitron: a self-organizing multilayered neural network. Biol. Cybern. **20**(3), 121–136 (1975)

21. Gruhn, V., Laue, R.: Patterns for timed property specifications. Electron. Notes Theoret. Comput. Sci. **153**(2), 117–133 (2006). Proc. of QAPL 2005

22. HABS VA,2-ALB,1- (sheet 2 of 8): Company House, State Route 719, Alberene, Albemarle County, VA, HABS VA,2-ALB,1- (Sheet 2 of 8)

23. Jantsch, A.: Chapter four - the synchronous model of computation. In: Modeling Embedded Systems and SoC's. Systems on Silicon. Morgan Kaufmann (2003)

24. Mamouras, K., Chattopadhyay, A., Wang, Z.: A compositional framework for quantitative online monitoring over continuous-time signals. In: Feng, L., Fisman, D. (eds.) RV 2021. LNCS, vol. 12974, pp. 142–163. Springer, Cham (2021). https://doi.org/10.1007/978-3-030-88494-9_8

25. Nenzi, L., Silvetti, S., Bartocci, E., Bortolussi, L.: A robust genetic algorithm for learning temporal specifications from data. In: McIver, A., Horvath, A. (eds.) QEST 2018. LNCS, vol. 11024, pp. 323–338. Springer, Cham (2018). https://doi.org/10.1007/978-3-319-99154-2_20

26. Neto, W.L., Moreira, M.T., Amarù, L.G., Yu, C., Gaillardon, P.E.: Read your circuit: leveraging word embedding to guide logic optimization. In: 2021 26th Asia and South Pacific Design Automation Conference (ASP-DAC), pp. 530–535 (2021). https://api.semanticscholar.org/CorpusID:231730639

27. Pnueli, A.: The temporal logic of programs. In: 18th Annual Symposium on Foundations of Computer Science (SFCS 1977), pp. 46–57 (1977)

28. Racharak, T.: On approximation of concept similarity measure in description logic ELH with pre-trained word embedding. IEEE Access **9**, 61429–61443 (2021). https://api.semanticscholar.org/CorpusID:233433689

29. Rufino, J.: Towards integration of adaptability and non-intrusive runtime verification in avionic systems. SIGBED Rev. **13**(1), 60–65 (2016)

30. Rungta, N.: A billion SMT queries a day (invited paper). In: Shoham, S., Vizel, Y. (eds.) CAV 2022. LNCS, Springer, Cham (2022). https://doi.org/10.1007/978-3-031-13185-1_1

31. Sánchez, C., et al.: A survey of challenges for runtime verification from advanced application domains (beyond software). Formal Methods Syst. Des. **54**(3), 279–335 (2019)

32. Seshia, S.A., Sadigh, D., Sastry, S.S.: Toward verified artificial intelligence. Commun. ACM **65**(7), 46–55 (2022)

33. Visconti, E., Bartocci, E., Falcone, Y., Nenzi, L.: Predicting Decentmon (Source code + Docker Image), March 2024. https://doi.org/10.6084/m9.figshare.25465243.v2

34. Visconti, E., Bartocci, E., Loreti, M., Nenzi, L.: Online monitoring of spatio-temporal properties for imprecise signals. In: Proceedings of MEMOCODE 2021. ACM (2021)

Short Papers

AuDaLa is Turing Complete

Tom T. P. Franken$^{(\boxtimes)}$ and Thomas Neele

Eindhoven University of Technology, Eindhoven, The Netherlands
{t.t.p.franken,t.s.neele}@tue.nl

Abstract. AuDaLa is a recently introduced programming language that follows the new data autonomous paradigm. In this paradigm, small pieces of data execute functions autonomously. Considering the paradigm and the design choices of AuDaLa, it is interesting to determine the expressiveness of the language and to create verification methods for it. In this paper, we take our first steps to such a verification method by implementing Turing machines in AuDaLa and proving that implementation correct. This also proves that AuDaLa is Turing complete.

Keywords: AuDaLa · Verification · Turing Complete

1 Introduction

Nowadays, performance gains are increasingly obtained through parallelism. The focus is often on how to get the hardware to process the program efficiently and languages are often designed around that, focusing on threads and processes. Recently, AuDaLa [10] was introduced, which completely abstracts away from threads. In AuDaLa, data is *autonomous*, meaning that the data executes its own functions. It follows the new data autonomous paradigm [10], which abstracts away from active processor and memory management for parallel programming and instead focuses on the innate parallelism of data. This paradigm encourages parallelism by making running code in parallel the default setting, instead of requiring functions to be explicitly called in parallel. The paradigm also promotes separation of concerns and a bottom-up design process. A compiler for AuDaLa [16] enables execution of AuDaLa on GPUs.

AuDaLa is built to be simple and focusses fully on parallel data elements. This design principle relates AuDaLa to domain specific languages, which are often less expressive than general purpose languages. It is therefore relevant to establish the expressiveness of AuDaLa, as AuDaLa is built as a general purpose language. Additionally, establishing the expressiveness of AuDaLa also indicates how expressive the data-autonomous paradigm is. AuDaLa has a fully defined semantics, unlike many other languages, which we can use to answer this question.

Turing Completeness is a well known property in computer science, which applies to a language or system that can simulate Turing machines. As a Turing machine can compute all effectively computable functions following the Church-Turing thesis [5], a Turing complete language or system can do the same. Two

© IFIP International Federation for Information Processing 2024
Published by Springer Nature Switzerland AG 2024
V. Castiglioni and A. Francalanza (Eds.): FORTE 2024, LNCS 14678, pp. 221–229, 2024.
https://doi.org/10.1007/978-3-031-62645-6_12

approaches to showing Turing completeness are implementing a Turing machine in the target language [4,17] and implementing μ-recursive functions [6,13].

To prove AuDaLa's expressiveness, we prove AuDaLa Turing complete. We do this by implementing a Turing machine in AuDaLa (Sect. 2.2). We then give the intuition of the proof that this implementation is correct (Sect. 3). Constructing this implementation to exhibit correct behaviour is intricate due to AuDaLa's view on the behaviour of data elements and proofs involve detailed reasoning about the semantics and the inference rules defined in it and lay the foundation for proving AuDaLa programs correct. Due to the heavy use of AuDaLa semantics for proving Lemma 3 and 6 correct, we have not included the full proofs for these lemmas in the paper; the full proof can be found in the Appendix of the preprint on arXiv [9].

Related Work. AuDaLa is a *data-autonomous* language and related to other data-focused languages, like standard data-parallel languages (CUDA [11] and OpenCL [3]), languages which apply local parallel operations on data structures (Halide [19], RELACS [20]) and actor-based languages (Ly [21], A-NETL [1]).

Though the expressivity of actor languages has been studied before [2] and there is research into suitable Turing machine-like models for concurrency [15,18,22], there does not seem to be a large focus on proving Turing completeness of parallel languages. We estimate that this is because many of these languages extend other languages, e.g., CUDA and OpenCL are built upon C++. For these languages, Turing completeness is inherited from their base language. Furthermore, parallel domain specific languages such as Halide [19] are simple by design, only focusing on their domain. Languages may also not be Turing complete on purpose [8,12], for example to make automated verification decidable.

The proof for the Turing completeness of Circal [7] follows the same line of our proof. Other parallel systems that have been proven Turing complete include water systems [13] and asynchronous non-camouflage cellular automata [23].

2   The Turing Machine Implementation

2.1   Basic Concepts

We define a Turing machine following the definition of Hopcroft *et al.* [14]. Let $\mathbb{D} = \{L, R\}$ be the set of the two directions *left* and *right*. A Turing machine T is a 7-tuple $T = (Q, q_0, F, \Gamma, \Sigma, B, \delta)$, with a finite set of control states Q, an initial state $q_0 \in Q$, a set of accepting states $F \subseteq Q$, a set of tape symbols Γ, a finite set of input symbols $\Sigma \subseteq \Gamma$, a blank symbol $B \in \Gamma \setminus \Sigma$ (the initial symbol of all cells not initialized) and a partial transition function $\delta : (Q \setminus F) \times \Gamma \nrightarrow Q \times \Gamma \times \mathbb{D}$.

Every Turing machine T operates on an infinite *tape* divided into *cells*. Initially, this tape contains an input string $S = s_0 \ldots s_n$ with symbols from Σ, but is otherwise blank. The cell the Turing machine operates on is called the *head*. We represent the tape as a function $t : \mathbb{Z} \to \Gamma$, where cell i contains symbol $t(i) \in \Gamma$. In this function, cell 0 is the head, cells i s.t. $i < 0$ are the cells left from the head and cells i s.t. $i > 0$ are the cells right from the head. We restrict ourselves to deterministic Turing machines. We also assume the input string is not empty, without loss of generality.

We define a *configuration* to be a tuple (q, t), with q the current state of the Turing machine and t the current tape function. Given input string $S = s_0 \ldots s_n$, the *initial configuration* of a Turing machine T is (q_0, t_S), with q_0 as defined for T, and $t_S(i) = s_i$ for $0 \le i \le n$ and $t_S(i) = B$ otherwise.

During the execution, a Turing machine T performs *transitions*, defined as:

Definition 1 (Turing machine transition). *Let* $T = (Q, q_0, F, \Gamma, \Sigma, B, \delta)$ *be a Turing machine and let* (q, t) *be a configuration such that* $\delta(q, t(0)) = (q', s', D)$, *with* $D \in \mathbb{D}$. *Then* $(q, t) \to (q', t')$, *where* t' *is defined as*

$$t'(i) = \begin{cases} s' & \text{if } i = 1 \\ t(i-1) & \text{otherwise} \end{cases} \text{ if } D{=}L \text{ and } t'(i) = \begin{cases} s' & \text{if } i = -1 \\ t(i+1) & \text{otherwise} \end{cases} \text{ if } D{=}R.$$

We say a Turing machine T *accepts* a string S iff, starting from (q_0, t_S) and taking transitions while possible, T halts in a configuration (q, t) s.t. $q \in F$.

2.2   The Implementation of a Turing Machine in AuDaLa

In this section, we describe the implementation of a Turing machine in AuDaLa. Let $T = (Q, \Sigma, \Gamma, \delta, q_0, B, F)$ be a Turing machine and S an input string. We implement T and initialize the tape to S in AuDaLa. W.l.o.g., we assume that $Q \subseteq \mathbb{Z}$ with $q_0 = 0$ and that $\Gamma \subseteq \mathbb{Z}$ with $B = 0$.

An AuDaLa program contains three parts: the definitions of the data types and their parameters are expressed as *structs*, functions to be executed in parallel are given to these data types as *steps*, and these steps are ordered into the execution of a method by a *schedule* separate from the data system. *Steps* cannot include loops, which are instead managed by the schedule.

We model a cell of T's tape by a struct *TapeCell*, with a left cell (parameter *left*), a right cell (*right*) and a cell symbol (*symbol*). The control of T is modeled by a struct *Control*, which saves a tape head (variable *head*), a state $q \in Q$ (*state*) and whether $q \in F$ (*accepting*). See Listing 1.1.

```
1  struct TapeCell (left: TapeCell, right: TapeCell, symbol: Int){} //def. of TapeCell
2  struct Control (head: TapeCell, state: Int, accepting: Bool) {
3      transition {see Listing 1.2 and 1.3}      //definition of the step "transition"
4      init {see Listing 1.4}                     //definition of the step "init"
5  }
6  init < Fix(transition)      //schedule: run "init" once and then iterate "transition"
```

Listing 1.1. The AuDaLa program structure

The step *transition* in the *Control* struct models the transition function δ. For every pair $(q, s) \in Q \times \Gamma$ s.t. $\delta(q, s) = (q', s', D)$ with $D \in \mathbb{D}$, *transition* contains a clause as shown in Listing 1.2 (assuming $D = R$). This clause updates the state and symbol, and saves whether the new state is accepting. It also moves the head

```
1  if (state == q && head.symbol == s) then {
2     head.symbol := s'; //update the head symbol
3     state := q'; //update the state
4     accepting := (q' ∈ F); //the new state is accepting or rejecting
5     if (head != null && head.right == null) then {
6        head.right := TapeCell(head, null, 0); //call constructor to create a new
          TapeCell
7     }
8     head := head.right; //move right
9  }
```

Listing 1.2. A clause for $\delta(q, s) = (q', s', R)$.

```
1  transition {
2     if (state == q_1 && head.symbol == s_1) then{ /*clause 1*/ }
3     else if (state == q_2 && head.symbol == s_2) then { /*clause 2*/ }
4     else if (state == q_3 && head.symbol == s_3) then { /*clause 3*/ }
5     // etc.
6  }
```

Listing 1.3. The *transition* step. The shown pairs all have an output in δ.

and creates a new *TapeCell* if there is no next element, which we check in line 5. For this, as s can be *null*, we need to explicitly check whether *head* is a *null*-element. Note that $B = 0$, and that if $D = L$ the code only minimally changes.

The clauses for the transitions are combined using an if-else if structure (syntactic sugar for a combination of ifs and variables), so only one clause is executed each time *transition* is executed. See Listing 1.3. In the step *init* in the *Control* struct, we create a *TapeCell* for every symbol $s \in S$ from left to right, which are linked together to create the tape. We also create a *Control*-instance. Listing 1.4 shows this for an example tape $S = s_0, s_1, s_2$.

In the semantics of AuDaLa [10], the initial state of any program contains only the special *null*-element of each struct. All parameters of the *null*-element are fixed to a *null*-value. They can create other elements but cannot write to their own parameters. Therefore, the call of *init* in the schedule causes the *null*-element of *Control* to initialize the tape. It also initializes a single non-*null* element of *Control*. The schedule will then have that element of *Control* run the *transition* step until the program stabilizes. Listing 1.1 shows the final structure of the program.

3   Turing Completeness

In this section, we show why AuDaLa is Turing Complete. We establish an equivalence between the configurations of a Turing machine and the configurations that can be extracted from the semantics of the corresponding AuDaLa program.

```
1  init {
2      TapeCell cell0 := TapeCell(null, null, s₀); // initialize the tape
3      TapeCell cell1 := TapeCell(null, null, s₁);
4      TapeCell cell2 := TapeCell(null, null, s₂);
5      cell1.left := cell0; // connect the tape
6      cell0.right := cell1;
7      cell2.left := cell1;
8      cell1.right := cell2;
9      Control(cell0, 0, (q₀ ∈ F)); //initialize the control
10 }
```

Listing 1.4. Initializing input string S.

We use the fact that the steps executed by the implementation are deterministic, as there is at most one non-*null* *Control* structure that executes the steps. We omit the full proof of Lemmas 3 and 6, which can be found in the Appendix in the preprint [9].

Henceforth, let P_{TS} be the implementation of a Turing machine T and an input string $S = s_0 \ldots s_n$ as specified in Sect. 2.2. In AuDaLa's semantics, a *struct instance* is a data element instantiated from a struct during runtime. For the proof we consider a specific kind of AuDaLa state, the *idle state*, which has the property that none of its the struct instances are in the process of executing a step. In AuDaLa, the next step to be executed from an idle state is determined by the schedule. With this we define *implementation configurations*:

Definition 2 (Implementation Configuration). *Let P be an idle state of P_{TS} containing a single non-null instance c of Control. Then we define the implementation configuration of P as a tuple (q_P, t_P) s.t. q_P is the value of the state parameter of c and $t_P : \mathbb{Z} \to \mathbb{Z}$ defined as:*

$$
t_P(i) = \begin{cases} c.head.symbol & \text{if } i = 0 \\ c.head.left^{-i}.symbol & \text{if } i < 0 \,, \\ c.head.right^i.symbol & \text{if } i > 0 \end{cases}
$$

where the dot notation $x.p$ indicates the value of parameter p in x and, for $i \geq 1$, $x.p^i$ is inductively defined as $x.p.p^{i-1}$ (with $x.p^0 = x$).

Note that an implementation configuration is also a Turing machine configuration. Next we define determinism for AuDaLa, as well as *data races*.

Definition 3 (Determinism). *Let s be a step in an AuDaLa program. Then s is deterministic iff for all states that can execute s, there exists exactly one state that is reached by executing s.*

Definition 4 (Data Race). *Let s be a step of P_{TS}. Let P be an idle state. Then s contains a data race starting in P iff P can execute s (according to its schedule) and during this execution, there exist a parameter v which is accessed* by two distinct struct instances a and b, with one of these accesses writing to v. We call a data race between writes a write-write data race, and a data race between a read a read-write data race.

We use*this to prove the following lemma:

Lemma 1 (AuDaLa Determinism). *An AuDaLa step s is deterministic if it cannot be executed by an idle state P in the execution of P_{TS} s.t. s contains a data race starting in P.*

Proof. If s contains no data races but is not deterministic, then some parameter v can have multiple possible values after executing s from some idle state P. As the operational semantics of AuDaLa do not allow interleaving by a single struct instance (as defined in the semantics of AuDaLa [10]), v must have been accessed by multiple struct instances during execution. The semantics also do not allow randomness, which means that all non-determinism in AuDaLa results from data races. These struct instances must then be in a data race. This is a contradiction.   □

In practice, when a step is deterministic we can ignore interleaving of struct instances during the execution of the step.

Lemma 2. *The execution of init in P_{TS} is deterministic.*

Proof. To prove this we need to prove that the execution of *init* contains no data races (Lemma 1). The step *init* is only executed once, at the start of the program, by the *null*-instance of *Control* (as no other instances exist). As only one instance exists, there cannot be a data race between two struct instances.□

Lemma 3 (Executing *init* in the initial state). *Let P_0 be the idle state at the start of executing P_{TS} and let the input string $S = s_0 \ldots s_n$. Executing the step init on P_0 results in a state P_1 with a single non-null Control instance such that (q_0, t_S) is the implementation configuration of P_1.*

Proof. The proof consists of sequentially walking through the statements of *init* when executed from the initial state (which is idle) of P_{TS} as defined in the semantics of AuDaLa, processing the statements using those semantics.   □

Lemma 4. *Let P be an idle state reachable in P_{TS} with a single non-null Control instance. Any execution of transition executed from P is deterministic.*

Proof. As per Lemma 1, we prove that the execution contains no data races. Let c be an arbitrary clause in the *transition* step (Listing 1.2). If *transition* has a data race during the execution of c, this data race must occur between the one non-*null* instance and the *null*-instance of *Control*. Let the non-*null* instance be x_0 and let x_1 be the *null*-instance of *Control*. Then the parameter which is accessed must be shared by both. This can only be *head.symbol*, as x_0 will not get through the if-statement and the other parameters are relative to x_0 and x_1. However, as $x_0.head = null$, this means *head.symbol* cannot be written to, as parameters of *null*-instances cannot be written to in AuDaLa. This contradicts that it can be in a data race.   □

Lemma 5. *Every transition step executed in P_{TS} is deterministic.*

Proof. By induction. As a base case, the first execution of *transition* happens from P_1 as defined in Lemma 3, which has only one non-*null* *Control* instance.

Then consider the execution of *transition* from an idle state P' with one non-*null* *Control* instance, resulting in idle state P. Due to Lemma 4, we know that the execution of *transition* is deterministic, so we can consider the sequential execution of *transition*. As *transition* is made up of multiple mutually exclusive clauses, considering only a single clause suffices. As in none of the statements a *Control* instance is created, as seen in Listing 1.2, it follows that P will also have only a single non-*null* *Control* instance. □

Lemma 6 (Effect of a *transition*execution). *Let P be an idle state of P_{TS} from which transition can be executed and let (q, t) be the implementation configuration of P. Assume that (q, t) is also a configuration of T. Then the result of a transition in T is a configuration (q', t') iff the result of executing the transition step from P in P_{TS} is an idle state P' such that (q', t') is its implementation configuration.*

Proof. We know from Lemma 5 that p has one non-*null* *Control* instance. The proof consists of walking through the statements of *transition* starting at p. □

By induction, using Lemma 3 as base case and Lemma 6 as step, any idle state of P_{TS} after executing *init* corresponds directly to a state (q, t) of T, including terminating and accepting states. We conclude:

Theorem 1. *AuDaLa is Turing complete.*

4   Conclusion

In this paper, we have proven AuDaLa Turing complete by implementing a sequential Turing machine. In future work, we hope to extend the principles here to a full system to prove AuDaLa programs correct. We may also extend the proofs to the weak memory model variant of the AuDaLa semantics [16].

References

1. Baba, T., Yoshinaga, T.: A-NETL: a language for massively parallel object-oriented computing. In: PMMPC Proceedings, pp. 98–105. IEEE (1995). https://doi.org/10.1109/PMMPC.1995.504346
2. de Boer, F.S., Jaghoori, M.M., Laneve, C., Zavattaro, G.: Decidability problems for actor systems. In: Koutny, M., Ulidowski, I. (eds.) CONCUR 2012. LNCS, vol. 7454, pp. 562–577. Springer, Heidelberg (2012). https://doi.org/10.1007/978-3-642-32940-1_39
3. Chong, N., Donaldson, A.F., Ketema, J.: A sound and complete abstraction for reasoning about parallel prefix sums. SIGPLAN Not. **49**(1), 397–409 (2014). https://doi.org/10.1145/2578855.2535882

4. Churchill, A., Biderman, S., Herrick, A.: Magic: The Gathering Is Turing Complete. In: 10th International Conference on Fun with Algorithms (FUN 2021). Leibniz International Proceedings in Informatics (LIPIcs), vol. 157, pp. 9:1–9:19. Schloss Dagstuhl-Leibniz-Zentrum für Informatik, Dagstuhl, Germany (2020). https://doi.org/10.4230/LIPIcs.FUN.2021.9

5. Copeland, B.J.: The Church-Turing Thesis (1997). https://plato.stanford.edu/ENTRIES/church-turing/. Modified 10 Nov 2017

6. Date, P., Potok, T., Schuman, C., Kay, B.: Neuromorphic Computing is Turing-Complete. In: Proceedings of the International Conference on Neuromorphic Systems 2022, pp. 1–10. ICONS '22, Association for Computing Machinery (2022). https://doi.org/10.1145/3546790.3546806

7. Detrey, J., Diessel, O.: A Constructive Proof of the Turing Completeness of Circal. University of New South Wales, Australia, School of Computer Science and Engineering (2002)

8. Deursen, A.V., Klint, P.: Little languages: little maintenance? J. Softw. Maint. Res. Pract. **10**, 75–92 (1998). https://doi.org/10.1002/(SICI)1096-908X(199803/04)10:2<75::AID-SMR168>3.0.CO;2-5

9. Franken, T.T.P., Neele, T.: Audala is turing complete (preprint with appendix) (2024). https://arxiv.org/abs/2404.12934

10. Franken, T.T.P., Neele, T., Groote, J.F.: An autonomous data language. In: Ábrahám, E., Dubslaff, C., Tarifa, S.L.T. (eds.) Theoretical Aspects of Computing – ICTAC 2023: 20th International Colloquium, Lima, Peru, December 4–8, 2023, Proceedings, pp. 158–177. Springer Nature Switzerland, Cham (2023). https://doi.org/10.1007/978-3-031-47963-2_11

11. Garland, M., et al.: Parallel computing experiences with CUDA. IEEE Micro **28**(4), 13–27 (2008). https://doi.org/10.1109/MM.2008.57

12. Gibbons, J.: Functional programming for domain-specific languages. In: Zsók, V., Horváth, Z., Csató, L. (eds.) CEFP 2013. LNCS, vol. 8606, pp. 1–28. Springer, Cham (2015). https://doi.org/10.1007/978-3-319-15940-9_1

13. Henderson, A., Nicolescu, R., Dinneen, M.J., Chan, T.N., Happe, H., Hinze, T.: Turing completeness of water computing. J. Membr. Comput. **3**(3), 182–193 (2021). https://doi.org/10.1007/s41965-021-00081-3

14. Hopcroft, J.E., Motwani, R., Ullman, J.D.: Introduction to automata theory, languages, and computation. Addison-Wesley, Boston, 2nd ed edn. (2001)

15. Kozen, D.: On parallelism in turing machines. In: 17th Annual Symposium on Foundations of Computer Science (sfcs 1976), pp. 89–97 (1976). https://doi.org/10.1109/SFCS.1976.20

16. Leemrijse, G.: Towards relaxed memory semantics for the Autonomous Data Language (2023). MSc. thesis, Eindhoven University of Technology

17. Pitt, L.: Turing tumble is turing-complete. Theoret. Comput. Sci. **948**, 113734 (2023). https://doi.org/10.1016/j.tcs.2023.113734

18. Qu, P., Yan, J., Zhang, Y.H., Gao, G.R.: Parallel turing machine, a proposal. J. Comput. Sci. Technol. **32**, 269–285 (2017). https://doi.org/10.1007/s11390-017-1721-3

19. Ragan-Kelley, J., et al.: Halide: decoupling algorithms from schedules for high-performance image processing. Commun. ACM **61**, 106–115 (2017). https://doi.org/10.1145/3150211

20. Raimbault, F., Lavenier, D.: RELACS for systolic programming. In: ASAP Proceedings, pp. 132–135. IEEE (1993). https://doi.org/10.1109/ASAP.1993.397128

21. Ungar, D., Adams, S.S.: Harnessing emergence for manycore programming: early experience integrating ensembles, adverbs, and object-based inheritance. In: OOPSLA Proceedings, pp. 19–26. ACM (2010). https://doi.org/10.1145/1869542.1869546
22. Wiedermann, J.: Parallel Turing Machines. University of Utrecht The Netherlands, Department of Computer Science (1984)
23. Yamashita, T., Isokawa, T., Peper, F., Kawamata, I., Hagiya, M.: Turing-completeness of asynchronous non-camouflage cellular automata. In: Dennunzio, A., Formenti, E., Manzoni, L., Porreca, A.E. (eds.) AUTOMATA 2017. LNCS, vol. 10248, pp. 187–199. Springer, Cham (2017). https://doi.org/10.1007/978-3-319-58631-1_15

Guess and Then Check: Controller Synthesis for Safe and Secure Cyber-Physical Systems

Rong Gu[✉][iD], Zahra Moezkarimi[iD], and Marjan Sirjani[iD]

Mälardalen University, Västerås, Sweden
{rong.gu,zahra.moezkarimi,marjan.sirjani}@mdu.se

Abstract. In this paper, we report our ongoing work on safe and secure controller synthesis for cyber-physical systems (CPS). Our approach separates the synthesis process into three phases, in which we alternatively perform exhaustive and selective exploration of the system's state space. In this way, we combine the strengths of exhaustive search and learning to mitigate the state-space-explosion problem in controller synthesis while preserving the guarantee of safety and security. We implement the synthesis algorithms in the Rebeca (Reactive Objects Language) platform, which provides modelling, verification, and state-space visualization. We evaluate the new approach in an experiment, demonstrating the reduced number of explored states, which shows the potential of our approach for synthesizing safe and secure controllers for complex CPS.

1 Introduction

Correctness by Construction was introduced by Church [7], who first brought up the famous synthesis problem. Since then, a great amount of effort has been made to address this problem [4,11,16]. Controller synthesis for *cyber-physical systems* (CPS) is different from that of pure software or hardware systems due to the close interaction of the cyber components and the physical components. Hence, the correctness of CPS depends on not only what and when actions are performed but also the reactions of the environment, which can be nondeterministic or stochastic. Besides, safety and security are also crucial for CPS. Safety means the system must not cause damage to itself and the environment, whereas security is concerned with external intrusion into the system [5]. In this paper, we aim to synthesize CPS controllers that are functionally correct, safe, and secure.

Exhaustive-Search-Based Synthesis. As synthesis is about finding a combination of the desired behaviour of CPS, a natural method is to exhaustively explore the state space of the system while collecting the desired execution traces, i.e., sequences of state-action pairs [1,6]. The exhaustive-search-based synthesis has a correctness guarantee by the nature of exhaustive search. However, the state space for searching can easily grow to a scale that is unsolvable by the exhaustive-search-based methods [16]. Although many heuristics have been proposed to improve the performance of such methods in practical problems,

© IFIP International Federation for Information Processing 2024
Published by Springer Nature Switzerland AG 2024
V. Castiglioni and A. Francalanza (Eds.): FORTE 2024, LNCS 14678, pp. 230–238, 2024.
https://doi.org/10.1007/978-3-031-62645-6_13

bounded scalability is still the dominant factor limiting the application of the exhaustive-search-based synthesis.

Learning-Based Synthesis. Learning bears the hope of overcoming the challenge of scalability in synthesis, as it has the potential to exploit the experience of other systems [11] or its own experience in the previous episodes of learning [10]. The key advantage of learning is that exhaustive exploration is not needed anymore. Instead, learning uses traces sampled from random simulations, and thus the state-space-explosion problem is alleviated. However, the sacrifice of using random simulation is the correctness guarantee. As a safety-critical system, an error in CPS may cause casualties, whereas accidents and attacks on CPS are becoming pervasive in our society, such as crashes involving Tesla's driver-assistance system [17], Jeep hacking on a highway [19], and a fatal crash caused by a self-driving car of Uber [3]. Therefore, learning needs complementary methods for safety and security guarantees.

Fig. 1. Synthesis process

Our Aim. In this paper, we aim to combine the strengths of exhaustive exploration and learning in controller synthesis of CPS to tackle the state-space-explosion problem and preserve the guarantee of safety and security for the synthesized controllers. We model the CPS and its external environment as a Markov Decision Process where the actions of the CPS (resp., environment) are modelled as controllable (resp., uncontrollable) actions. Now controller synthesis is about finding the combination of controllable actions that satisfy the requirements regardless of how the uncontrollable actions take place. Our method is called *Guess and Check* as the synthesis starts with guessing a controller that *may* be correct and then thoroughly checks the *guessed* controller in the following phases (see Fig. 1). Briefly, we alternatively adopt exhaustive search and learning (or random search) in different phases, which enable us to deal with large state spaces that are not solvable by pure exhaustive methods and still guarantee the safety and security of the synthesized controllers.

The remainder of the paper is organized as follows. Section 2 defines the problem and illustrates it in an example. Section 3 describes the algorithms, the platform, and a preliminary evaluation. In Sect. 4, we compare our method to other studies and envision future work.

2 Problem Description

2.1 Problem Definition

Functional correctness, safety, and security may refer to different meanings in different areas. To avoid confusion, we adapt the definitions of system models in the literature [14] and define CPS and its requirements as follows.

Definition 1 (CPS). *A CPS denoted by $\mathcal{C}$ is a quadruple $\mathcal{C}=(X, X_0, A, T)$, where X is a (possibly infinite) set of states, $X_0 \subseteq X$ is a (possibly infinite) set* *of initial states, A is a (possibly infinite) set of actions, and $T \subseteq X \times A \times X$ is a transition relation.*

If a CPS has finite sets of states and actions, it is a finite or symbolic system. A transition $t \in T$ is denoted as $t = (x, a, x')$, or $t(x, a) = x'$, where x' is the successor of state x when the system's action is a. If a CPS is deterministic, given any state $x \in X$ and any action $a \in A$, $t(x, a)$ returns either an empty set or a set with only one state; otherwise, the CPS is either non-deterministic (i.e., $t(x, a)$ can return multiple states) or stochastic (i.e., $t(x, a)$ returns a probabilistic distribution over X). Given a CPS and an action sequence $a_1 a_2 \dots \in A^*$, one can induce a state sequence $x_1 x_2 \dots \in X^*$, where $x_n = t(x_{n-1}, a_{n-1})$. We also call a state sequence a trace and denote it by π. One can obtain a finite trace by cutting a trace at any of its states. A finite part of a trace is denoted by π_f. A CPS's states can be partially observable, so we call $O(\pi)$ the observable part of trace π and $H(\pi)$ the hidden part.

Definition 2 (Controller). *Given a CPS C, a controller of C is a partial function $\sigma : \pi_f \to A$. If C is Markovian, the controller can be memoryless, that is, $\sigma : last(\pi_f) \to A$, where $last(\pi_f)$ is the last state of trace π_f.*

Given a CPS C controlled by a controller σ (denoted by $C|\sigma$), one can induce a set of traces Π_σ s.t. $\forall \pi \in \Pi_\sigma$, $\exists a \in \sigma(\pi_f)$. Let $G \subseteq X$ be the goal states that CPS aims to reach and $U \subseteq X$ be the unsafe states that CPS must avoid, this paper is about synthesizing $C|\sigma$ for a nondeterministic and Markovian CPS such that its Π_σ satisfies the following three properties.

– **Functional correctness**: $\forall \pi \in \Pi_\sigma$, $\exists x \in \pi$ s.t. $x \in G$.
– **Safety**: $\forall \pi \in \Pi_\sigma$, $\forall x \in \pi$ s.t. $x \cap U = \emptyset$.
– **Security**: $\forall \pi \in \Pi_\sigma$, $\exists \pi' \in \Pi_\sigma$ s.t. $H(\pi) \neq H(\pi')$ and $O(\pi) = O(\pi')$.

Assuming a CPS is non-deterministic due to the uncertain reaction from the environment, intuitively, functional correctness means the CPS must always eventually reach the goal state regardless of the environment's reaction. Similarly, safety means the system must always avoid unsafe states. We can express the safety and functional correctness as invariance and reachability properties of temporal logic [2], respectively. Assuming confidential information is contained in the hidden part of a CPS's states, security here means this information must not be revealed to unauthorized ones, like intruders. Therefore, the definition of security above means that intruders must not be able to deduce confidential information from the observable states. Formally, security is also formulated as hyperproperties [8] as it involves multiple traces. We elaborate CPS and the three types of requirements in the following example.

2.2   Illustrative Example

In this section, we illustrate the problem in an example abstracted from an industrial use case, where robots are employed in a factory for goods delivery (Fig. 2). For simplicity, we discretize the environment as a 7×4 grid, in which robot R1 (resp., R2) must finish tasks T1 and T2 (resp., J1 and J2) at the right cells, and then they meet at an M cell as the destination of the mission. The robots can go through the cells without performing the tasks. The grey (resp., blue) cells are obstacles (resp., wet floors), where the robots must not enter (resp., may slip). When robots slip on a wet floor, they may end in the wrong position, i.e., one cell below the target. The robots' trajectories are planned at the edge-computing server (ECS) whereas the high-level tasks are scheduled at the cloud-computing server (CCS). An intruder is trying to attack the ECS and change the task order but he cannot access the CCS.

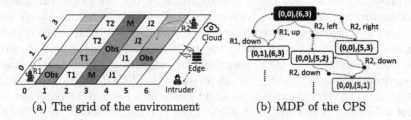

(a) The grid of the environment   (b) MDP of the CPS

Fig. 2. An example of CPS: two robots collaborating in a confined environment.

When modelling this example, we employ a *Markov Decision Process* (MDP) for a *2-player* game [12], where actions of the CPS and the environment are assigned to different transitions of the model (see Fig. 2(b)), that is, controllable ones (blue arrows) and uncontrollable ones (dotted violet arrows). At each state, a robot gets to choose a controllable action, e.g., moving up/down, after which the environment's actions take place, which decides the robot's ending positions. A correct and safe controller must guarantee the robot reaches the specific cells for task execution and never enters the unsafe cells despite the environment's actions. For security, we mean confidential information, e.g., task order, must not be revealed to the intruder. Although the intruder does not have access to the CCS, he can deduce the task order by using the robots' trajectories. For instance, $trace_1$ is insecure because the only chance for R1 to execute T1 is at cell $(2,1)$, and it is before the T2 cells being visited (e.g., $(2,2)$). In contrast, $trace_2$ is secure as R1 visits the T1 and T2 cells alternatively more than once, so the intruder cannot deduce R1's task execution order from its moving trajectory.

$trace_1$: $(0,0)$->$(0,1)$->$(1,1)$->$(2,1)$->$(2,2)$->$(2,3)$->$(3,3)$

$trace_2$: $(0,0)$->$(0,1)$->$(1,1)$->$(2,1)$->$(2,2)$->$(2,1)$->$(2,2)$->$(2,3)$->$(3,3)$

Functional correctness means the robots must finish all tasks within a time frame. To synthesize a functional correct, safe and secure controller is not trivial, especially when considering the uncertain actions of the environment. Next, we introduce our solution.

3   Solution and Preliminary Evaluation

In this section, we introduce the algorithms of our method *Guess and Check* and explain the thoughts behind the algorithms.

Phase 1: Guess for a Controller. Our goal of the first phase is to guess a controller that *may* satisfy the requirements. Generally, we explore the state space of the model by following two rules: i) exhaustive exploration of controllable actions, and ii) selective exploration of uncontrollable actions. Algorithm 1 presents how guessing is conducted. For simplicity, we assume that the state-space exploration is depth-first. However, using other orders of exploration does not affect the correctness of the algorithm. As a recursive function, the termination conditions of Algorithm 1 are defined in lines 3–8. Specifically, when the state-space exploration reaches a state where the reachability property is satisfied (line 3), the trace is added to the *controller*, which is a global variable used in all algorithms. Alternatively, when the exploration reaches an *unsafe* state, or a loop, or a deadlock where no action is available (line 6), the trace is pruned from the controller. In both cases, the trace is fed into a learning algorithm (line 4 and line 7), e.g., Q-learning [18], for calculating a policy that enables the environment to *win* the game faster (i.e., the *BEST* function in line 10), that is, leading the exploration to an unsafe state. Lines 9–14 implement the exploration rules i) and ii). After phase 1, we find an *optimistic* controller that may be correct as we only explore the environment's actions partially.

Algorithm 1: Guess for an optimistic controller

```
1  Set<Pair<State, Action>> σ                                    // controller
2  Function GUESS(State x, Trace π, Set<State> 𝒢, Set<State> 𝒰)
3      if x ∈ 𝒢 then
4          LEARN&ADD(σ, π)
5          return
6      if x ∈ 𝒰 ∨ (∃pair ∈ π ∧ x ∈ pair) ∨ x.actions = ∅ then
7          LEARN&PRUNE(σ, π)
8          return
9      if ∃a ∈ x.actions ∧ a.type = ENVIRONMENT then
10         Action best := BEST(x.actions)
11         GUESS(best.target, π.push(x, best), 𝒢, 𝒰)
12     if ∀a ∈ x.actions ∧ a.type = SYSTEM then
13         while (Action next := NEXT(x.actions) ≠ LAST(x.actions)) do
14             GUESS(next.target, π.push(x, next), 𝒢, 𝒰)
15     return
```

Algorithm 2: Check for the safety requirement

```
1  Function C4SA(State x, Trace π, Set<State> 𝒢, Set<State> 𝒰)
2      Boolean pass := false
3      if x ∈ 𝒢 then
4          return (true)
5      if x ∈ 𝒰 ∨ (∃pair ∈ π ∧ x ∈ pair) ∨ x.actions = ∅ then
6          LEARN&PRUNE(σ, π)
7          return (false)
8      if ∃a ∈ x.actions ∧ a.type = ENVIRONMENT then
9          pass := true
10         for a ∈ x.actions ∧ a.type = ENVIRONMENT ∧ pass do
11             pass := pass ∧ C4SA(a.target, π.push(x, a), 𝒢, 𝒰)
12     if ∀a ∈ x.actions ∧ a.type = SYSTEM then
13         if x ∉ σ.getAllStates() then
14             for a ∈ x.actions do
15                 GUESS(a.target, π.push(x, a), 𝒢, 𝒰)
16         for a ∈ x.actions ∧ Pair(x, a) ∈ σ do
17             pass := pass ∨ C4SA(a.target, π.push(x, a), 𝒢, 𝒰)
18     return (pass)
```

Phase 2: Check for Safety. In Algorithm 2, we start to check the optimistic controller for the safety property. Generally, we replace the rules of state-space exploration with two new rules: i) selectively exploring controllable actions that are contained in the optimistic controller, and ii) exhaustive exploration of uncontrollable actions. Similarly to Algorithm 1, lines 3–7 in Algorithm 2 show the termination conditions of the recursive algorithm, that is, when the check passes or fails. Lines 8–11 depict the exhaustive exploration of the environment's actions until one trace fails to pass the check. If we see a state that only has the system's actions to choose but is not contained in the controller (line 13), we go back to guess a new controller starting from that state (line 15). We use ∨ in line 17 because one of the system's actions passing the check is enough for the state to be included in the controller. However, we use ∧ in line 11 because all the environment's actions need to pass the check. After phase 2, we have obtained a safe and functionally correct controller. Next, we check for security.

Phase 3: Check for Security. By following the generated controller, we explore the state space again to check for the security properties (Algorithm 3). We formulate the confidential and public information as properties P_s and P_c, respectively. As lines 3 - 4 show, if a trace π_1 satisfies P_s, there must be a trace π_2 that satisfies P_c, and π_1 and π_2 are similar enough to prevent the intruders from distinguishing them (i.e., $D(\pi_1, \pi_2) \leq \tau$), where D is a function for computing the distance of two traces. The function can be replaced by an equation $O(\pi_1) = O(\pi_2)$ for discrete state spaces, where O returns the observable part of a trace. The definition of the distance function is not the focus of this paper. Interested readers are referred to the literature [14].

Algorithm 3: Check for the security requirement

---

1 **Function** C4CE(*State* x, *Property* P_s, *Property* P_c)
2   Set<Trace> Π_σ := EXPLORE(x, σ)
3   **for** $\pi_1 \in \Pi \wedge \pi_1 \models P_s$ **do**
4   **if** $\neg((\exists \pi_2 \in \Pi_\sigma \wedge \pi_2 \models P_c) \wedge D(\pi_1,\pi_2) \leq \tau)$ **then**
5   LEARN&PRUNE(σ, π_1)
6   **return**

Fig. 3. Platform

Platform and Evaluation. We aim to realize the algorithms in a platform including a GUI for modelling CPS in various branches of Rebeca, a back-end state-space explorer, and external libraries for learning. Figure 3 shows the architecture of our platform, where the GUI supports modelling the CPS in two languages, which are all based on Rebeca and extended to support games [12], that is, the modelling of controllable actions of CPS and uncontrollable actions of the environments. The back-end explorer includes a simulator that can randomly explore the state space via Monte-Carlo Simulation, a set of model checkers that are suitable for different kinds of models, and a synthesizer that calls the simulator and model checkers for controller synthesis. The learning module is an external library such that the platform is extendable and adaptive.

Now, we present our experiment for a preliminary evaluation of the platform[1] We show how the *Guess and Check* method reduces the number of states explored in phase 1 and phase 2[2]. We build several models based on the example in Fig. 2.

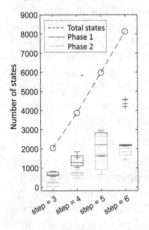

Fig. 4. Result

In these models, we set the maximum number of steps that robots can move and adjust their goals accordingly. Then we generate the state space of the models and synthesize a controller for each of the models using our algorithms. Note that we use random simulation instead of learning in phase 1, and we repeat the experiment 10 times and use a box plot to show the numbers of explored states in the experiments (Fig. 4). The experimental results show that in both phases 1 and 2, the number of explored states is much less than the total number of states. The encouraging results demonstrate that our approach has the potential to solve problems that are too complex to be solved by the exhaustive-search-based methods and preserve the guarantee of safety and security that is impossible for pure reinforcement learning.

4   Discussion and Future Work

Related Work. Due to the page limit, we only compare our method with the latest studies in this section. The most recent work in learning-based synthesis [11] introduces a method for winning strategy synthesis in parity games derived from LTL synthesis. Parker et al. [13,15] propose binary decision diagrams and synthesis algorithms based on probabilistic model checking. Our primary distinction from prior methods is that we integrate exhaustive search and learning, leveraging the unique advantages of each in a synergistic manner.

Future Work. We will finish implementing our platform in an open-source toolset of *Rebeca* [9], in which we integrate the features of Rebeca, Timed Rebeca, and Probabilistic Timed Rebeca to facilitate the synthesis algorithms. As Rebeca has been applied in many CPS applications, we will experiment with our new algorithms on these real-world problems. We implement the learning module as an external library, which enables us to explore various learning models, such as neural networks (NN), in our synthesis algorithms. In this line of research, we will try to see how model checking and machine learning can benefit each other in controller synthesis. As safety-critical CPS are often working alongside humans,

---

[1] Code of the experiment is published: https://github.com/rgu01/RebecaLearning.

[2] The number of states in phase 3 depends on the controller size, not on the approach.

we would like to consider the human factors in the controller synthesis of CPS, such as investigating best-effort strategies when the environmental constraints are too restrictive for the CPS to achieve all of their goals. We aim to make our approach adaptive for multiple objectives aligned with human preferences.

References

1. Asarin, E., Maler, O., Pnueli, A., Sifakis, J.: Controller synthesis for timed automata. IFAC Proc. Volumes **31**(18), 447–452 (1998)
2. Baier, C., Katoen, J.P.: Principles of model checking. MIT press (2008)
3. BBC: Uber's self-driving operator charged over fatal crash. https://www.bbc.com/news/technology-54175359 (September 16th, 2020)
4. Bloem, R., Jobstmann, B., Piterman, N., Pnueli, A., Saár, Y.: Synthesis of reactive (1) designs. J. Comput. Syst. Sci. **78**(3), 911–938 (2012)
5. Burns, A., McDermid, J., Dobson, J.: On the meaning of safety and security. Comput. J. **35**(1), 3–15 (1992). https://doi.org/10.1093/comjnl/35.1.3
6. Cassez, F., David, A., Fleury, E., Larsen, K.G., Lime, D.: Efficient on-the-fly algorithms for the analysis of timed games. In: Abadi, M., de Alfaro, L. (eds.) CONCUR 2005 – Concurrency Theory, pp. 66–80. Springer Berlin Heidelberg, Berlin, Heidelberg (2005). https://doi.org/10.1007/11539452_9
7. Church, A.: Application of recursive arithmetic to the problem of circuit synthesis. J. Symbolic Logic **28**(4) (1963)
8. Clarkson, M.R., Schneider, F.B.: Hyperproperties. J. Comput. Secur. **18**(6), 1157–1210 (2010)
9. Group, R.R.: Rebeca (2017). https://rebeca-lang.org/
10. Gu, R., Jensen, P.G., Seceleanu, C., Enoiu, E., Lundqvist, K.: Correctness-guaranteed strategy synthesis and compression for multi-agent autonomous systems. Sci. Comput. Program. **224**, 102894 (2022)
11. Křetínský, J., Meggendorfer, T., Prokop, M., Rieder, S.: Guessing winning policies in LTL synthesis by semantic learning. In: Enea, C., Lal, A. (eds.) Computer Aided Verification: 35th International Conference, CAV 2023, Paris, France, July 17–22, 2023, Proceedings, Part I, pp. 390–414. Springer Nature Switzerland, Cham (2023). https://doi.org/10.1007/978-3-031-37706-8_20
12. Kumar, P.R., Shiau, T.H.: Existence of value and randomized strategies in zero-sum discrete-time stochastic dynamic games. SIAM J. Control. Optim. **19**(5), 617–634 (1981)
13. Kwiatkowska, M., Norman, G., Parker, D., Santos, G.: Symbolic verification and strategy synthesis for turn-based stochastic games. In: Raskin, J.-F., Chatterjee, K., Doyen, L., Majumdar, R. (eds.) Principles of Systems Design: Essays Dedicated to Thomas A. Henzinger on the Occasion of His 60th Birthday, pp. 388–406. Springer Nature Switzerland, Cham (2022). https://doi.org/10.1007/978-3-031-22337-2_19
14. Liu, S., Trivedi, A., Yin, X., Zamani, M.: Secure-by-construction synthesis of cyber-physical systems. Annu. Rev. Control. **53**, 30–50 (2022)
15. Parker, D.: Multi-agent verification and control with probabilistic model checking. In: Jansen, N., Tribastone, M. (eds.) Quantitative Evaluation of Systems: 20th International Conference, QEST 2023, Antwerp, Belgium, September 20–22, 2023, Proceedings, pp. 1–9. Springer Nature Switzerland, Cham (2023). https://doi.org/10.1007/978-3-031-43835-6_1

16. Pnueli, A., Rosner, R.: On the synthesis of an asynchronous reactive module. In: Ausiello, G., Dezani-Ciancaglini, M., Della Rocca, S.R. (eds.) Automata, Languages and Programming, pp. 652–671. Springer Berlin Heidelberg, Berlin, Heidelberg (1989). https://doi.org/10.1007/BFb0035790

17. Post, T.W.: 17 fatalities, 736 crashes: The shocking toll of tesla's autopilot (2023). https://www.washingtonpost.com/technology/2023/06/10/tesla-autopilot-crashes-elon-musk/

18. Sutton, R.S., Barto, A.G.: Reinforcement learning: An introduction. MIT press (2018)

19. Wired: Hackers remotely kill a jeep on the highway-with me in it (2015). https://www.wired.com/2015/07/hackers-remotely-kill-jeep-highway/

Author Index

© IFIP International Federation for Information Processing 2024
Published by Springer Nature Switzerland AG 2024
V. Castiglioni and A. Francalanza (Eds.): FORTE 2024, LNCS 14678, p. 239, 2024.
https://doi.org/10.1007/978-3-031-62645-6

Printed in the United States
by Baker & Taylor Publisher Services